Contact Information

Mrs. Jane H. Walker is available for programs and speaking engagements in homes, churches, organizations, and book signings.

Other books
by
Jane H. Walker

Widow of Sighing Pines
Recipient of the President's Award for Best Adult Fiction in 2003
Florida Publishers Association, Inc.

The Dodge Land Troubles, 1868-1923
Coauthored with Chris Trowell, Professor Emeritus of South Georgia College

In the Lion's Paw

Telfair County Images of America
Coauthored with Robert Herndon

Mrs. Walker can be reached through her website or by phone.

website: widowofsighingpines.biz
Telephone number: 229-868-2243
P.O. Box #55357
McRae-Helena, Georgia 31055

janewriter51@yahoo.com

Can We Fathom the Nature of God?
(And America's Exceptionalism)
By
Jane H. Walker

CAN WE FATHOM THE NATURE OF GOD?
(AND AMERICA'S EXCEPTIONALISM)

Copyright Jane H. Walker
October, 2018

Published By Parables
October, 2018

All Rights Reserved. No part of this book may be reproduced or utilized in any form or by any means, electronic or mechanical, including photocopying, recording, or by any information storage and retrieval system, without permission in writing from the author.

    ISBN 978-1-945698-55-2
    Printed in the United States of America

Readers should be aware that Internet Web sites offered as citations and/or sources for further information may have been changed or disappeared between the time this was written and the time it is read.

Can We Fathom the Nature of God?
(and America's Exceptionalism)
By
Jane H. Walker

Earthly Stories with a Heavenly Meaning

JANE H. WALKER

Dedicated

to

my children,

Laura Lei and Billy Ware

and to

Robbie

Chapter One

Can we fathom the nature of God? I think we can. Since the Bible offers clues to God's nature, we have to read the Bible to find these clues. I am not a theologian, but I am a student of the Bible, which I believe is the inspired and inerrant word of God. Having taught Sunday School in the Methodist Church for over forty years, using the Bible as my text, and having read the Bible from cover to cover many times, I have found answers to many of my questions. In addition, I did take courses in the Old Testament and the New Testament in my college studies.

I hasten to add, however, that though I have found many answers, other questions remain unresolved, but that is the mystique of the Bible. If we understood everything, we would be like God. In fact, Adam and Eve were driven from the Garden of Eden because God did not want them to eat from the tree of life, which would have opened their eyes to God himself. He was not ready for that yet.

At the outset, I want to impart to you, my Reader, that the nature of God is closely intertwined and revealed through the Church, since its birth after the death and resurrection of Jesus, on up to the present day. Christianity and Judaism are so closely associated that this study will reveal God's nature through the ongoing continuum of these great religions. The entire Bible is the legacy of Jesus Christ. Also, we must remember that Jesus was a Jew.

In Genesis, around 4,004 B.C., according to my Bible, God created the heaven and the earth, also light and darkness or day and night. (More is included about the date which marks the beginning of recorded history, and how it was determined, later in this book.) Then, the Lord concentrated on the earth, establishing the boundaries of the land and seas and creating the sun, the moon and stars. He also created time, as we know it, using the sun and moon to set the measurements of days and years and seasons.

In the deep waters he made sea creatures and, in the air, fowl that flew above the earth. He filled the land with animals. Lastly, he created two humans to have dominion over the earth.

This is but one aspect of the nature of God - his creativity involving man and his surroundings. Man is still discovering what God created, from the tiniest parts of atoms to new galaxies in the universe. Parts of the oceans of the earth (some over six miles deep) and their inhabitants are still being discovered ("Mariana Trench–Wikipedia.")

Not long ago, we heard of the discovery of a hidden tribe of people, living in the deep jungle of a South American country here on planet earth ("Lost Amazon tribe in Peru emerging from jungle–NY Daily News"). Another even more recent newspaper article told of yet another tribe of people in Peru, who are appearing on the bank of a jungle river. Are there others who have not yet made their existence known?

The same article stated that some "15 uncontacted tribes" live in the jungles of the Peruvian Amazon, with some 12,000 – 15,000 people living in the jungles east of the Andes. The photo of a man and woman of the latest contacted tribe, sitting on a log, looked like something from the Stone Age. Brazil has some 100 indigenous tribes living in its vast Amazon region, making it the most populous country of uncontacted tribes in the world ("Uncontacted Indians of Brazil–Survival International").

Man is preparing to travel farther into the seemingly endless universe. Have aliens from other places in the vast cosmos ever visited our planet? We have all heard and read of people who claim to have had contact with aliens here on earth. Scientists are constantly studying other planets to determine whether life as we know it could exist there. It is intriguing that we who inhabit the earth may not be alone in space.

The Bible, however, was written for those of us who inhabit

the earth. It plainly says so in its first book, Genesis, as the first sentence attests: **"In the beginning God created the heaven and the earth."** For this reason, I am using the Bible to try to understand more of the nature of God. Also, I realize that I am only using the King James Version of the Bible and *Halley's Bible Handbook* for biblical and related references, not because other translations and concordances are not worthwhile but simply because these are my favorites. Different translations appeal to different people and that's the reason for them. Whatever brings you nearer to God is what you should use.

Human life is likely the greatest experiment in the history of the universe. Each life is allotted a certain amount of time to live, and virtually each minute of our existence is filled with the counter forces of good and evil. Constantly, we are called upon to battle these forces not only within our own selves but also outside ourselves.

Of course, this experiment determines where our existence will continue after our physical death. The Bible clearly describes the two options we have, as we live our daily lives. After we die, heaven and hell are the only places that exist for us. This is the end result of the great experiment that God is performing, and it gives us insight into his divine nature.

According to the Bible, man was created in the image of God with the ability to think and to process thoughts. David says in Psalm 139:14 that he was "...**fearfully and wonderfully made**..." This applies to all of us. Probably every normal person who ever lived has wondered about his existence on this planet that hurtles through space in an established orbit in the universe. What is the meaning of it all? This is something we struggle with each day of our lives. Surely, knowing more about the nature of God will give more meaning to our existence.

For hundreds of years after his creation, mankind did not live as God meant for them to live, and God regretted that he had created man. Here we have another unusual and mysterious attribute of God: regret. Don't we as people have regrets? We are reminded again of our likeness to the image of God.

Because of his regret, God decided to destroy all of mankind by a great Flood. We read this in Genesis 6:5-7:

" And God saw that the wickedness of man was great in the earth, and that every imagination of the thoughts of his heart was only evil continually. And it repented the Lord that he had made man on the earth, and it grieved him at his heart. And the Lord said, I will destroy man whom I have created from the face of the earth; both man, and beast, and the creeping thing, and the fowls of the air; for it repenteth me that I have made them."

The world population before the Flood had grown rapidly as the progeny of Adam and Eve spread over the earth and lived out their lengthy lifetimes, some living nearly a thousand years. Noah himself lived 950 years (Genesis 9:28). One source I read stated that ten trillion people, an entire ancient civilization, were completely destroyed in the great Flood ("4. Population Growth–How Many Died in Noah's Flood?/Bible").

However, *Halley's Bible Handbook* (24th edition, 1965) states, on page 74:

"Accepting the Bible account as it is, there had been only TEN generations from Adam, the first man. How could ONE family, in TEN generations, with primitive modes of travel, populate the whole earth? Most likely the race had not spread far outside the Euphrates basin."

Noah, however, his wife, his three sons and their wives were spared because of the goodness of Noah, alone, in the world. In Genesis 6:9, we read: **"...Noah was a just man and perfect in his generations, and Noah walked with God."** Therefore, eight people were saved to populate the earth once more, and all of us derive from this family.

To survive the flood according to God's instructions, Noah built an ark to accommodate his family and the animals that populated the earth – seven pairs of clean animals and one pair of each of the others. The ark was 450 feet long, seventy-five feet wide, and forty-five feet high (Genesis 6:15 in cubits; *Halley's*; p. 73, in feet). It was a huge task to build such a water vessel, especially under the certain scrutiny of nonbelievers who undoubtedly were scornful of Noah's efforts (Hebrews 11:7).

Were dinosaurs on the ark? Dorothy Sayers (1893-1957), good friend of *Narnia* author C. S. Lewis, believed so. She wrote, "Yes, to be sure there were dragons in the Ark, or there wouldn't have been one for St. George to fight with; but they are all dead now." ("Dinosaurs on the Ark?/Bible-Science guy") Dinosaur pictographs and carvings on cave walls promote extra-Biblical evidence that man knew dinosaurs ("Controversial Opinion: Dinosaurs and Early Man Coexisted"). The Book of Job mentions battles between ancient mariners and terrifying sea monsters such as Behemoth and Leviathan (Job 40:15-24; Job 41).

After raining nonstop for forty days, the ark finally came to rest on Mt. Ararat, which is 17,000 feet high (*Halley's,* p. 74). This highlights two facets of the nature of God: his extraordinary power and his control over the affairs of mankind. Jesus spoke of the flood as an historical fact, likening the time of his reappearance on earth to the days of Noah (Matthew 24:37-39). The rain came for forty days and prevailed on the earth for around five months. According to *Halley's*, p. 74, the time Noah and his family spent in the ark was one year and seventeen days: five months floating and seven months on the mountain.

After the flood, God made a covenant with Noah that never again would he destroy the earth with water. In Genesis 9:8-17, we read:

"And God spake unto Noah, and to his sons with him, saying, And I, behold, I establish my covenant with you, and with your seed after you; And with every living creature that is with you, of the fowl, of the cattle, and of every beast of the earth with you; from all that go out of the ark, to every beast of the earth. And I will establish my covenant with you; neither shall all flesh be cut off any more by the waters of a flood to destroy the earth. And God said, This is the token of the covenant which I make between me and you and every living creature that is with you, for perpetual generations:

"I do set my bow in the cloud, and it shall be for a token of a covenant between me and the earth. And it shall come to pass, when I bring a cloud over the earth, that the bow shall be seen in the cloud: And I will remember my covenant, which is between me and you and every living creature of all flesh; and the waters shall no more become a flood to destroy all flesh.

"And the bow shall be in the cloud; and I will look upon it, that I may remember the everlasting covenant between God and every living creature of all flesh that is upon the earth. And God said unto Noah, This is the token of the covenant, which I have established between me and all flesh that is upon the earth."

* * * * * * * * * * * * *

In Genesis 11:1, we read, **"And the whole earth was of one language, and of one speech."** Noah's family had multiplied with the passage of time, until around a hundred years had passed since the great flood. This was around the fourth generation after Noah, according to *Halley's,* p.83.

It was during this time that Noah's descendants conceived the idea of building a city and a tower whose top might **"reach unto heaven."** (Genesis 11:4) God did not approve of this, as he said in Genesis 11:7-9:

"Go to, let us go down, and there confound their language, that they may not understand one another's speech. So the Lord scattered them abroad from thence upon the face of all the earth: and they left off to build the city. Therefore is the name of it called Babel; because the Lord did there confound the language of all the earth: and from thence did the Lord scatter them abroad upon the face of all the earth."

* * * * * * * * * * * * *

To discover the nature of God, we follow in the Old Testament the way that God created the nation of Israel. God called Abraham who lived in Ur in Babylonia, present-day Iraq, to move with his family to a place called Canaan (Genesis 12:5) by the Mediterranean Sea. Salem was the capital city of Canaan which later became the land of Israel. Hundreds of years later, Salem became Jeru...salem, or Jerusalem.

CAN WE FATHOM THE NATURE OF GOD?

In Genesis 14:12-24, we read that Abraham's nephew, Lot, was taken prisoner by neighboring tribes. Abraham rescued Lot and returned to Salem, where he met Melchizedek, king of Salem and priest of God. Melchizedek refreshed Abraham with bread and wine, then blessed him.

An interesting and important aside here is that Melchizedek has long been considered by Jewish and other scholars to be Shem, Noah's son who survived the Great Flood (*Halley's*, p. 97). Shem was 98 years old when the Flood occurred. He was 450 years of age when Abraham was born and 550 years old when Isaac was born. In all, Shem lived to be 600 years old, being the most renowned and revered person on earth at that time. He is considered the most important of Noah's three sons, because Jesus Christ descended from him.

Shem's life spanned the years of Pre-Flood history with those of Post-Flood history, enabling him to give his blessing to Abraham who would begin the family lineage of Christ. ("Disk: Melchizedek–1– Godward .org"). Abraham, in turn, honored Shem, or Melchizedek, with tithes from all he had acquired during his recent battle (Genesis 14:18-20). Melchizedek is also mentioned in Psalm 110:4 and in Hebrews 5, 6, and 7.

Psalm 110:4 states: **"The Lord hath sworn, and will not repent, Thou art a priest for ever after the order of Melchizedek."**

Hebrews 5:6 is recorded, as follows: **"As he saith also in another place, Thou art a priest for ever after the order of Melchisedek."**

Hebrews 6:20 reads, as follows: **"Whither the forerunner is for us entered, even Jesus, made an high priest for ever after the order of Melchisedek."**

Hebrews 7:1-3 bears record, as follows: **"For this Melchisedek, king of Salem, priest of the most high God, who met Abraham returning from the slaughter of the kings, and blessed him; To whom also Abraham gave a tenth part of all; first being by interpretation King of righteousness, and after that also King of Salem, which is, King of peace; Without father,** without mother, without descent, having neither beginning of days, nor end of life; but made like unto the Son of God; abideth a priest continually."**

Oh, Reader, when I read the last two lines, I realized that they describe God, for God is **"without father, without mother, without descent, having neither beginning of days, nor end of life..."** In other words, Melchizedek was a prototype of Jesus Christ who said, **"I and my father are one."** (John 10:30) Melchizedek was known for his righteousness, as was Christ. God used Melchizedek as a foregleam of his own Son.

* * * * * * * * * * * * *

God most certainly secured the historical record of his purposes on planet earth through the creation of writing. According to H. H. Halley, writing began when God put a mark on Cain who killed his brother, Abel (*Halley's*, p. 70). This mark was a symbol for an idea. Marks, or signs, or pictures, were used to record ideas, words, and combinations of words. These marks were in ancient times painted or engraved on pottery or clay tablets.

Though it once was commonly believed that some of the Old Testament books were written long after the events they described, and only handed down by oral tradition, the spade of the archaeologist has refuted this claim. We now know that written records of important events were made from the dawn of history. God preserved the foundation of the Bible and guarded its transmission and growth throughout the ages.

Though some modern scholars may claim otherwise, Halley believed that the Tigris-Euphrates valley is where the earth's earliest people lived and where the Bible narrative began. Serious archaeological interest in this area began in the nineteenth century and continues today. Archaeologists continue to uncover artifacts that substantiate Bible history.

From 1845-51, Sir Austin Henry Layard, an Englishman called "the father of Assyriology," discovered at Ninevah and Calah the ruins of palaces of five Assyrian kings who are named in the Bible. He also discovered the large library of Assurbanipal, in Ninevah, which is estimated to have contained 100,000 volumes (*Halley's*, p. 42).

The oldest known Outline of World History, called the Weld Prism, was found in 1922 at Larsa by the Weld-Blundell Expedition. Written in 2170 B.C. by a scribe named Nur-Ninsubur, it recorded a list of kings, which included ten long-lived Pre-Flood kings. It is a prism of baked clay. These kings lived and reigned for thousands of years, one reigning for 64,000 years! (*Halley's*, p. 71).

In our Bible, Methuselah is named as being the person of greatest longevity, having lived for 969 years (Genesis 5:27). Others lived to be over 900 years old, including Adam (930 years); Seth (912 years); Enoch (905 years); Kenan (910 years); Jared (962 years), and Noah (950 years) (Genesis 5). For some reason, not understood by modern man, some Pre-Flood humans lived for thousands of years. Could the years of that time period have been measured differently from ours?

Hammurabi, king of Babylon around 2000 B.C., was a contemporary of Abraham (*Halley's*, p. 50). Assyriologists have identified Hammurabi as Amraphel of Genesis 14, who was one of the kings Abraham pursued to rescue his nephew, Lot. Hammurabi induced his scribes to engrave the laws of his kingdom on stones which men set up in his principal cities. This Code of Hammurabi is one of the most important archaeological discoveries ever made.

A French expedition led by M. J. de Morgan found one of these stone codes in 1902. It is an oval block of black diorite stone, eight feet high, two feet wide and one and a half feet thick. Written in Semitic Babylonian language, it bears testimony to the fact that as early as Abraham's time writing had reached an advanced stage (*Halley's*, pp.50-51).

From Abraham's family came the patriarchs of the Old Testament, who were the ancestors of Jesus Christ. One of these ancestors, a man named Jacob, had his name changed from Jacob to Israel by God, as recorded in Genesis 32:28. This happened when Jacob wrestled with an angel and prevailed. Jacob then asked God to bless him. God said:

"...Thy name shall be called no more Jacob, but Israel:

for as a prince hast thou power with God and with men, and hast prevailed."

Also in Genesis 35:10-12, God said unto Jacob: **"Thy name is Jacob: thy name shall not be called any more Jacob, but Israel shall be thy name: and he called his name Israel. And God said unto him, I am God Almighty: be fruitful and multiply; a nation and a company of nations shall be of thee, and kings shall come out of thy loins; And the land which I gave Abraham and Isaac, to thee will I give it, and to thy seed after thee will I give the land."**

From this name and this ancestor of Jesus, we have the beginning of the nation of Israel. Jacob's son, Judah, is the ancestor of Jesus. No one's ancestry has ever been as carefully documented as that of Jesus Christ. This, too, is a measure of the nature of God.

Jacob, or Israel as he was later called, had twelve sons who were the heads of the twelve tribes of Israel. This is recorded in Genesis 29-30. Joseph was perceived by the other sons to be their father's favorite, and they were jealous of him to the extent that they sold him to a caravan of Ishmaelites who carried him to Egypt. Jacob grieved for his son and thought that an **"evil beast"** had killed Joseph (Genesis 37:33). Joseph, however, prospered in Egypt and became the Pharaoh's governor, second only to the Pharaoh himself (Genesis 41:39-46).

When famine came to all of the countries in the area, Jacob heard there was corn in Egypt, so he sent his sons to bring some food back to his family. The sons became reunited with Joseph who forgave his brothers and urged them to bring all of their family, including Jacob, to live in Egypt (Genesis 42-47). His family at that time numbered seventy persons (Deuteronomy 10:22). Jacob rejoiced upon hearing that Joseph was still alive and was governor of Egypt. Jacob and his family lived in Egypt for many generations for a period of 430 years (about 1800-1400 B.C.), according to *Halley's Bible Handbook*), pages 109-111, until an unfriendly ruler made the Israelites a nation of slaves (Exodus 1).

This is when God chose Moses to lead his people out of Egypt (Exodus 3). God performed many miracles to do this, including the parting of the Red Sea so that the Israelites could walk across dry land. He provided food and water for some 3,000,000 people in an inhospitable wilderness for a period of forty years (*Halley's*, p. 146). Their clothes and shoes did not wear out, nor did their feet swell (Deuteronomy 8:24). They had to fight their way back to the promised land, and God always helped them win their battles. During their lengthy journey through the forbidding land, many people died and many were born.

One can look at a map and see how geographically near to the promised land of Canaan the Israelites were, yet they wandered through the wilderness for forty years! Though they were in close proximity to the promised land, only God knew why his people traveled in a circuitous route through a vast desert to arrive there, and we have Scriptures that answer this for us.

In Exodus 13:17-18, we are given one reason why God did not lead his people in the nearest way to the promised land:

"And it came to pass when Pharaoh had let the people go, that God led them not through the way of the land of the Philistines, although that was near; for God said, Lest peradventure the people repent when they see war, and they return to Egypt: But God led the people about, through the way of the wilderness of the Red sea: and the children of Israel went up harnessed out of the land of Egypt."

In Deuteronomy 8:2-4, we read of another reason of God for making his people travel forty years in the wilderness: **"And thou shalt remember all the way which the Lord thy God led thee these forty years in the wilderness, to humble thee, and to prove thee, to know what was in thine heart, whether thou wouldest keep his commandments, or no. And he humbled thee, and suffered thee to hunger, and fed thee with manna, which thou knewest not, neither did thy fathers know; that man doth not live by bread only, but by every word that proceedeth out of the mouth of the Lord doth man live. Thy raiment waxed not old upon thee, neither did thy foot swell, these forty years."**

Before Joseph died, he requested that his kinsmen should carry his bones with them, if they should leave Egypt, as recorded in

Genesis 50:25-26. This desire was obviously passed on to generation after generation, for a period of over 400 years, until the time of the exodus of the Israelites from Egypt, for Moses honored Joseph's request and carried his bones back to the promised land of Canaan, as recorded in Exodus 13:19. Can we imagine such a request over a period of 400 years, involving any of our families? Obviously, the Hebrews kept good records of their family lineage and honored the wishes of their ancestors of hundreds of years before.

* * * * * * * * * * * * *

To understand the nature of a person, we immediately want to see that person. Has anyone ever seen God? The words **"No man hath seen God at any time."** are recorded in I John 4:12, but other Scriptures state that certain men saw at least a part of God. Exodus 33:11 states: **"And the Lord spake unto Moses face to face, as a man speaketh unto his friend."** Chapter 33:20 reads: **"...Thou canst not see my face: for there shall no man see me and live."** In the same chapter, verse 23 says, **"...I will take away mine hand, and thou shalt see my back parts: but my face shall not be seen."**

In Exodus 24:10, we read what Moses, Aaron, Nadab, Abihu and seventy of the elders of Israel saw when they went up the mountainous Sinai: **"And they saw the God of Israel: and there was under his feet as it were a paved work of a sapphire stone, and as it were the body of heaven in his clearness. And upon the nobles of the children of Israel he laid not his hand: also they saw God, and did eat and drink."**

Obviously, God allowed them to see a part but not all of his being. Verse 17 of the 24th chapter reads: **"And the sight of the glory of the Lord was like devouring fire on the top of the mount in the eyes of the children of Israel."**

When Moses was on Mt. Sinai, talking to God, he asked the Lord: **"...Behold, when I come unto the children of Israel and shall say unto them, the God of your fathers hath sent me unto you; and they say to me, what is his name? What shall I say unto them? And God said unto Moses, I AM that I AM: and he said thus shalt thou say unto the children of Israel, I AM hath sent me unto you."** (Exodus 3:13-14)

This is an instance when we have to suspend the earthly reality that everything ages, for God obviously does not age. Malachi 3:6 states: **"For I am the Lord, I change not..."**

Moses is one of the grand figures of the Bible. I found Winston Churchill's opinion of Moses quoted on page 156 of *Halley's Bible Handbook*. It reads as follows:

"We reject with scorn all those learned and labored myths that Moses was but a legendary figure upon whom the priesthood and the people hung their essential social, moral and religious ordinances. We believe that the most scientific view, the most up-to-date and rational conception, will find its fullest satisfaction in taking the Bible story literally. We may be sure that all these things happened just as they are set out according to Holy Writ. We may believe that they happened to people not so very different from ourselves, and that the impressions those people received were faithfully recorded, and have been transmitted across the centuries with far more accuracy than many of the telegraphed accounts we read of goings on of today. In the words of a forgotten work of Mr. Gladstone, we rest with assurance upon 'The Impregnable Rock of Holy Scripture.' Let men of science and learning expand their knowledge, and probe with their researches, every detail of the records which have been preserved to us from those dim ages. All they will do is to fortify the grand simplicity and essential accuracy of these recorded truths which have so far lighted the pilgrimage of man."

* * * * * * * * * * * * * *

According to I John 4:8, **"...God is love,"** but other manifestations of God's nature also occur in the Scriptures. Though many people may not realize it, God also created evil. Isaiah 45:5-8 records, as follows:

"I am the Lord, and there is none else, there is no God beside me: I girded thee, though thou hast not known me: That they may know from the rising of the sun, and from the west, that there is none beside me. I am the Lord, and there is none else. I form the light, and create darkness: I make peace, and create evil: I the Lord do all these things."

Another Scripture which tells of God's control of evil is Jeremiah 6:19, wherein God is speaking to Jeremiah about his anger and disappointment in regard to his people. It reads, as follows:

"Hear, O earth: behold, I will bring evil upon this people, even the fruit of their thoughts, because they have not hearkened unto my words, nor to my law, but rejected it."

Lest anyone should be surprised or question the merits of the Lord creating the good and the evil, it stands to reason (according to our earthly limitations) that we could not know good without knowing its antithesis. How can we distinguish between the beautiful and the ugly or the good and the bad, unless we have seen and experienced both? We can't truly know certain things without knowing their opposites.

God wanted man to observe specific rules as he lived his life, so: **"... he gave unto Moses, when he had made an end of communing with him upon mount Sinai, two tables of testimony, tables of stone, written with the finger of God."** (Exodus 31:18)

These Ten Commandments are descriptive of the nature of God. They are as follows:

> **"Thou shalt have no other gods before me.**
> **"Thou shalt not make unto thee any graven image...**
> **"Thou shalt not take the name of the Lord thy God in vain...**
> **"Remember the sabbath day, to keep it holy...**
> **"Honour thy father and thy mother...**
> **"Thou shalt not kill.**
> **"Thou shalt not commit adultery.**
> **"Thou shalt not steal.**
> **"Thou shalt not bear false witness against thy neighbor.**
> **"Thou shalt not covet..."** (Exodus 20:3-17).

In addition to the Ten Commandments, God gave his chosen people, the Israelites, many other laws and rules to govern their lives. Surrounded by heathen nations, the newly formed country of Israel was like the proverbial sheep in the midst of ravening wolves. This analogy still holds today, as Israel is yet encompassed by nations who would do her harm.

Conquered in 70 A.D. by the Roman army, Israel is the only nation in the history of the world to achieve nationhood once again in 1948. In other words, no nation has fallen and then risen again, over a period of 1878 years, except Israel. The age of miracles is not past, for this in itself is a modern-day miracle ("Prediction: Israel Would Become A Nation Again –Fresh Light Source").

* * * * * * * * * * * * * *

Of the twelve sons of Jacob, God chose one son, Levi, to head the tribe of priests. Moses and Aaron were of the tribe of Levi, also. The Book of Leviticus which derives from the root word "Levi" describes the duties of the priests. God went to great lengths to describe to Moses the clothes that the priests should wear. These holy garments consisted of an ephod or apron, a girdle, a breastplate and a holy crown or mitre of pure gold. Beautiful colors of blue, purple and scarlet, along with precious stones adorned the priestly vestments. The description of the Levitical garments in Exodus 39 is filled with great beauty. Fine linen fabric and exquisite lace were to be used in the construction of the clothing. This is another insight into the nature of God – his desire for that which is perfect and beautiful.

One might inquire where the Israelites derived the beautiful stones and fabrics to create these vestments, as they traveled through the vast wilderness. The answer is that God instructed Moses, before he led the Jewish people out of Egypt, to tell his people to borrow the following: **"...of the Egyptians jewels of silver, and jewels of gold, and raiment: And the Lord gave the people favour in the sight of the Egyptians, so that they lent unto them such things as they required."** (Exodus 12:35-36)

The people brought these precious possessions to Moses for the construction of the ark, the tabernacle and its furnishings, and the priestly garments. According to *Halley's Bible Handbook*, p. 129, the gold and silver used in the construction of the portable tabernacle and its furniture is estimated to have cost around $1,250,000. Today, the cost would be from two to five billions of dollars (*Halley's*, p. 218)

When God ordered his people to make a Tabernacle and an Ark of the Covenant, he gave details for these creations of worship, which helped the Israelites to keep their focus on the Lord while wandering in the wilderness for forty years. This tabernacle was a likeness of the temple that would be built, once the Jewish people reached the land which their ancestors had left some four hundred years before. The ark was a chest which held the two stone tables of the Ten Commandments, a pot of manna which was food for the wandering Israelites, and Aaron's rod. Aaron was Moses' brother. All of these preparations give us an insight into the nature of God.

Since Aaron, and Aaron's sons, were of the priestly tribe of Levi, they were "anointed," so as to be hallowed in the work of the Lord, which involved ministering intimately to the Lord in the holy tabernacle. No one else could assume the role of the priests. The Israelites built the tabernacle during their trek through the wilderness, fashioning it according to the command and the "pattern" that God gave Moses in Exodus 25:8, which reads as follows: **"And let them make me a sanctuary; that I may dwell among them. According to all that I shew thee, after the pattern of the tabernacle, and the pattern of all the instruments thereof, even so shall ye make it."**

The early tabernacle, and later the temple, was the center of Jewish life. The tabernacle was built so that it could be dismantled and transported through the wilderness. When the Israelites reached their next stopping place, they would reassemble it and it would be their place of worship. It measured forty-five feet long, fifteen feet wide and fifteen feet high *(Halley's,* p. 129). Remember, it was measured in cubits, and a cubit is about eighteen to twenty inches in length. It was a prototype of the temple that would be built by King Solomon some four hundred years later (*Halley*'s, p. 218).

As ordered by God, the portable tabernacle had a long curtain or veil, measuring over forty feet in height. The Scripture for this commandment is found in Exodus 26:1-2. Following are the instructions which God gave to Moses:

"Moreover thou shalt make the tabernacle with ten curtains of fine twined linen, and blue, and purple, and scarlet: with cherubims of cunning work shalt thou make them. The length of one curtain shall be eight and twenty cubits, and the breadth of one curtain four cubits: and every one of the curtains shall have one measure."

The Scripture goes on to record that ten of these curtains were to be coupled together. Most likely, when the first stationary temple was built, the curtain would have been even larger. Later in this writing, I describe the temple that was being built by King Herod when Jesus walked the earth. At Jesus's death, the veil of that temple was **"rent in twain from the top to the bottom,"** according to Matthew 27:51. This was a miracle of God, since the veil would have been tremendous, possibly sixty feet tall in Herod's temple, and required 300 priests to move it ("Tearing of the Temple Curtain: Why Was This Significant?").

Inside the tabernacle was a place called the Holy of Holies. According to God's instructions, the Ark of the Covenant was the only structure in the room. The ark was designed by God, also, and it featured a cherub at each end, facing each other, their wings spread outward, and looking downward to the Mercy-Seat. God chose this place for his earthly presence, speaking to his people from the Mercy-Seat between the wings of the cherubim. No one was allowed in the Holy of Holies, except the priest who entered only once a year (*Halley's*, p. 130).

God made it plain that he wanted the Israelites to put him first in all things. He wanted the first fruits of everything in their lives – the first-born sons of their families, the first-born of all flocks and herds, and the first fruits of the land. We are still supposed to put him first, to put him at the center of our lives.

Our God is strict, never deviating from his course, unless it is one he regrets and then he brings about momentous changes to accomplish his purposes. The nature of God unfolds as we study the way that God began to mold his people, the Israelites, into the template that he envisioned for them. To isolate his people from the idolatrous nations around them, God gave the Jews explicit and detailed rules in regard to every aspect of their lives but especially their worship of him.

In the Book of Leviticus, the various types of offerings are impressed upon the Jewish people. I had read the Bible through a number of times before I really began to notice and wonder about the many different types of offerings. The first nine chapters of Leviticus are filled with these offerings. The following is a list of some of the offerings which the Israelites made to God: burnt offerings, meal offerings, meat offerings, peace offerings, voluntary offerings (meaning a vow), sin offerings, trespass offerings, freewill offerings, drink offerings, jealousy offerings, guilt offerings, wave offerings, and heave offerings. In regard to the unusual final two offerings named above, the people would hold a certain part of the sacrificial animal and "wave" or "heave" it before the Lord. In Leviticus 2:13, we read one of many verses about the value of salt: **"...with all thine offerings thou shalt offer salt."**

Repeatedly, God told Moses to have his people offer burnt sacrifices as **"...a sweet savour unto the Lord."** (Leviticus 3:5) These words indicate that God could smell the meat cooking, just as his people could smell it. We are truly made in the image of God. In the first three chapters of Leviticus, the **"sweet savour"** is mentioned often.

I only recently read about four-legged fowl in Leviticus 11:20, which the Israelites were forbidden to eat. I cannot think of any four-legged fowl that "**creep, going upon all four**." Can you? I wonder whether this harks back to the age of dinosaurs, when four-legged fowl flew above the earth, such as the pterodactyls. The pterodactyls also walked on all fours. This sheds light on the possibility that man lived during the time of the dinosaurs, regardless of what some in the scientific community espouse. Missionaries and people in the countries of Kenya, Papua New Guinea, most of Africa, the Philippines, and Brazil have reported sightings of Pterodactyl type animals in this modern time ("Pterodactyls in Torah?/New 2 Torah–Torah Observant Followers of...")

Throughout the entire Book of Leviticus, God impresses upon the Jewish people that he is their God. The words, **"I am the Lord,"** occur more than forty times in the entire book and fifteen times in Chapter 19, alone. God did not want his chosen people to worship any other god.

* * * * * * * * * * * * * * *

Probably the first hint of blood sacrifice in the Jewish nation occurred when God commanded Abraham to offer his son, Isaac, as a sacrifice to him (Genesis 22:1-18). In doing this, God tested Abraham's obedience and his faith. Trusting God completely, Abraham prepared to kill his son, until God intervened and stayed his hand, providing instead a ram caught in a thicket for the sacrifice. This is another aspect of God's nature - the intimacy of his relationships with people. It is also a symbolic prophecy of the sacrifice of Christ some 2000 years later. In both scenarios, the father was to sacrifice the son, only God actually followed through with it when he allowed his only Son to die on the cross.

In Leviticus 6:13, we read that the fire on the altar was never to go out. The altar, of course, must have been a bloody place, as the blood from the offerings was constantly, even daily, being shed. The Israelites were admonished not to ingest the blood (Leviticus 7:26). This bloodletting of the sacrificial animals was symbolic of the blood that Jesus would one day shed on the cross. He would be the final sacrifice.

The Jewish people were also instructed not to eat the fat of the sacrificial animals in Leviticus 7:25:

"For whosoever eateth the fat of the beast, of which men offer an offering made by fire unto the Lord, even the soul that eateth it shall be cut off from his people."

This is in line with modern-day medical advice that we should not eat the fat. In Leviticus 3:16, we read that "**...all the fat is the Lord's.**" Anyone who cooks will tell you that the fat sizzling is what whets the appetite for the meat.

Jane H. Walker

Chapter Two

During the Israelites' journey back to Israel, God ordered a census to be taken at the beginning of the trip and another at the end of the sojourn in the wilderness (Numbers 1:2 and 26). The Book of Numbers is named for these censuses. Perhaps God wanted his people to feel a cohesiveness with each census, a feeling of being set apart from other peoples. They had a special calling as a nation. Even today, tiny Israel is at the center of world interest and global politics. God's nature is evident in the creation and maintenance of the country of Israel.

After the many trials and tribulations experienced by Moses during the long journey back to Canaan, God forbade him to enter the promised land. This is first recorded in Deuteronomy 1:37.

In Deuteronomy 3:25, Moses begs God to allow him to enter the promised land with these words: **"I pray thee, let me go over, and see the good land that is beyond Jordan, that goodly mountain, and Lebanon."**

However, because God was **"wroth"** or angry with Moses, he refused to let Moses cross over the Jordan River and enter the promised land, as the following words attest from Deuteronomy 3:26-27: **"...Let it suffice thee; speak no more to me of this matter. Get thee up into the top of Pisgah, and lift up thine eyes westward, and northward, and southward, and eastward, and behold it with thine eyes: for thou shalt not go over this Jordan."**

In Deuteronomy 32:48-52, we read what must have been heart-wrenching words that God spoke to Moses, who had faithfully led his people during forty years of trials and tribulations through a barren wilderness: **"And the Lord spake unto Moses that selfsame day, saying, Get thee up into this mountain Abarim, unto mount Nebo, which is in the land of Moab, that is over against Jericho; and behold the land of Canaan, which I give unto the children of Israel for a possession. And die in the mount whither thou goest up, and be gathered unto thy people; as Aaron thy brother died in mount Hor, and was gathered unto his people: Because ye trespassed against me among the children of Israel at the waters of Meribah-Kadesh, in the wilderness of Zin; because ye sanctified me not in the midst of the children of Israel. Yet thou shalt see the land before thee; but thou shalt not go thither unto the land which I give the children of Israel."**

In Deuteronomy 34:7, we read that Moses was 120 years old at his death but **"....his eye was not dim, nor his natural force abated."**

In our humanness, this is difficult to comprehend, but it brings out another dimension of the nature of God – his retribution for disobedience. I tremble when I consider my own disobedience and am reminded that God expects much from his people. **"The fear of the Lord,"** according to Proverbs 9:10, **"is the beginning of wisdom...."**

The above is an instance of God's resoluteness in not changing his mind to accommodate Moses' request. Yet, we have other instances in the Bible where God did change his mind. One involved the prophet Jonah who was called by God to deliver a message of woe to the great but wicked city of Nineveh. I'm almost certain you remember the story of how Jonah fled from God and boarded a ship bound for Tarshish. When a violent storm arose, Jonah knew it was because of his attempting to thwart the will of God, and he asked the ship's crew to cast him into the sea. A big fish swallowed him, but eventually deposited him upon dry land.

After a journey of three days, Jonah reached Nineveh, where he cried out that Nineveh would be overthrown by God. Upon hearing this, the king and people of Nineveh turned from their evil ways. Every man put on sackcloth and fasted and prayed that God would spare Nineveh. God indeed changed his mind and spared the destruction of Nineveh. All of this is recorded in the little Book of Jonah.

Another example of God's changing his mind involved King Hezekiah of the southern kingdom of Judah, as recorded in Isaiah 38, the entire chapter. When the prophet Isaiah told the king to **"...Set thine house in order: for thou shalt die, and not live,"** Hezekiah wept and prayed to God to make him well again. Hezekiah knew that the siege of Jerusalem was imminent, and he wanted to be well in order to lead his country during its threat from Assyria.

God once again changed his mind and added fifteen years (Isaiah 38:5) to the life of Hezekiah. Isaiah prescribed the cure for Hezekiah, surely by God's instructions, for he ordered that a lump of figs be laid as a plaster upon Hezekiah's boil (Isaiah 38:21). Hezekiah recovered and lived another fifteen years. These are examples which illustrate the nature of God in being willing to change his mind.

* * * * * * * * * * * * * *

We often hear news reports about Israel's perilous existence in the midst of hostile countries who either want to annihilate the small nation or confiscate more and more of its land. This is in dire contradiction to God's specific boundaries of the land as set forth in the thirty-fourth chapter of Numbers. Woe to those who would do harm to God's chosen country, Israel, and his chosen people. Lest we Christians forget, our Lord Jesus was himself a Jew.

The boundaries of Israel, as established by God in Numbers 34:3-12, are as follows: **"Then your south quarter shall be from the wilderness of Zin along by the coast of Zin along by the coast of Edom, and your south border shall be the outmost coast of the salt sea eastward:**

"And your border shall turn from the south to the ascent of Akrabbim, forth thereof shall be from the south to Kadesh-barnea, and shall go on to Hazar-addar, and pass on to Azmon: And the border shall fetch a compass from Azmon unto the river of Egypt, and the goings out of it shall be at the sea.

"And as for the western border, ye shall even have the great sea for a border: this shall be your west border. And this

shall be your north border: from the great sea ye shall point out for you mount Hor: From mount Hor ye shall point out your border unto the entrance of Hamath; and the goings forth of the border shall be to Zedad:

"And the border shall go on to Ziphron, and the goings out of it shall be at Hazar-enan: this shall be your north border. And ye shall point out your east border from Hazar-enan to Shepham:

'And the coast shall go down from Shepham to Riblah, on the east side of Ain; and the border shall descend, and shall reach unto the side of the sea of Chinnereth eastward:

"And the border shall go down to Jordan, and the goings out of it shall be at the salt sea: this shall be your land with the coasts thereof round about."

After Moses' death, Joshua led the Israelites on to the land which God had given them. This trip was accomplished only by God performing many miracles, as the way led through many hostile places and many warlike people. Upon reaching the walled city of Jericho, God called upon his people to march around the city and to blow upon their rams' horns, finally shouting a great shout and the walls came tumbling down, allowing the Israelites to go in and capture the city (Joshua 6).

The Israelites had to fight every inch of the way back to their land, but God led them by day in a pillar of a cloud and by night in a pillar of fire (Exodus 13:21), so that they could travel by day or by night, if need be. In fighting their enemies along the way, the Jewish people looked to God to deliver them, for many times, they were sorely outnumbered.

On one occasion, God ordered the sun and the moon to stand still, so his chosen people would have enough light to see to win their battle at Gibeon, a great city about ten miles northwest of Jerusalem. This is recorded in the Book of Joshua 10:13-14:

"And the sun stood still, and the moon stayed, until the people had avenged themselves upon their enemies. Is not this written in the book of Jasher? So the sun stood still in the midst of heaven, and hasted not to go down about a whole day. And there was no day like that before it or after it, that the Lord hearkened unto the voice of a man: for the Lord fought for Israel."

Dear Reader, you may wonder, as I did, about the "book of Jasher" mentioned in the Scripture above. I looked for it on the internet and found a book which is a translation of Jasher from Hebrew into English in 1840. It was published by Parry and Company in 1887. Though it was not included in the canon of our Bible, it may cast another light of history upon our understanding of all that went on during the ancient of days.

In the preface of this book about Jasher, the translator says the following:

"The printed Hebrew copy, in the hands of the translator, is without points. During his first perusal of it, some perplexities and doubts rose up in his mind respecting its authenticity, but the more closely he studied it, the more its irresistible evidence satisfied him, that it contained a treasure of information concerning those earlier times, upon which the history of other nations are either silent, or cast not a single ray of real light, and he was more especially delighted to find that the evidence of the whole of its contents went to illustrate and confirm the great and inestimable truths which are recorded in divine history, down to a few years later than the death of Joshua, at which period the book closes."

According to the translator, "the most important value of this book (of Jasher) is the large quantity of additional detail it gives to various accounts in the Old Testament than our current translations. For instance, the translator states in his preface: 'This book contains a more detailed account of the awful circumstances attending the commencement of the flood, and the conduct of Noah toward the terrified multitude who had assembled about the ark, when the fatal moment had arrived, and their doom was irrevocably fixed.

'Connected with this period of the history is given an account of Nimrod, in which is strikingly depicted the arbitrary and violent character and conduct of his government...

'From this book we learn that Noah and Abraham were contemporaries. How beautiful the contemplation of the meeting between these two Patriarchs, the one being a monument of God's mercy, the other having the promise of the favor and grace of God, not only to himself, but to his seed after him.

'The history of Joseph has always been considered one of the most admirable and interesting on record...This history, in Jasher, enters more into detail concerning the affairs of Potiphar's wife Zelicah, Joseph's magnificent procession through the cities of Egypt, on coming into power, the pomp with which he was attended by Pharaoh's chariots, officers and people, when he went up to meet his father, the affecting scene which then took place, together with other remarkable incidents.'

"Following the preface of the book are certificates of endorsement from four noted religious scholars of the day, their statements all dated in April 1840, the year it was first published, each one giving his endorsement to the correctness and reliability of the translation."

In regard to the verses about Joshua are the following words from the book of Jasher 10:13:

"And when they were smiting, the day was declining toward evening, and Joshua said in the sight of all the people, Sun, stand thou still upon Gibeon, and thou moon in the valley of Ajalon, until the nation shall have revenged itself upon its enemies.

"And the Lord hearkened to the voice of Joshua, and the sun stood still in the midst of the heavens, and it stood still six and thirty moments, and the moon also stood still and hastened not to go down a whole day.

"And there was no day like that, before it or after it, that the Lord hearkened to the voice of a man, for the Lord fought for Israel."

These are just a few examples of the awesome power of God and his devotion to Israel. The devastating earthquakes in Haiti and Chile and the horrifying tsunami and powerful earthquakes in Japan remind us that God is all-powerful. Though we are made in his image, we lack his consummate power. He is God and we worship him, for he created us. All power is a major component of his nature. He alone is Lord of everything.

The land which God promised to his people is further described in Deuteronomy 11:11-12: **"But the land whither ye go to possess it, is a land of hills and valleys and drinketh water of the rain of heaven: A land which the Lord thy God careth for: the eyes of the Lord thy God are always upon it, from the beginning of the year even unto the end of the year."**

When the Israelites were about to enter the promised land, they were subjected to a blessing and a curse, as determined by God in Deuteronomy 11:26-28:

"Behold, I set before you this day a blessing and a curse; A blessing if ye obey the commandments of the Lord your God, which I command you this day: And a curse, if ye will not obey the commandments of the Lord your God, but turn aside out of the way which I command you this day, to go after other gods, which ye have not known."

Again, we are reminded that God is a **jealous** God. This is repeated over and over in the Bible. In Exodus 34:14, we read, **"For thou shalt worship no other god: for the Lord, whose name is Jealous, is a jealous God."** God even ascribes the name **"Jealous,"** spelled with a capital "J" to himself.

We have all likely heard people comment that the same God is worshiped by people of different faiths, whether they be Christian, Jewish, Hindu, Islamic, Buddhist or any other faith. I do not subscribe to this ecumenical and all-inclusive belief. Having studied the Bible in depth for many years, I know that it speaks of many gods, but only one true God. The true God is the God of Abraham, Isaac, and Jacob; and his Son, Jesus, is the Savior of those who accept and acknowledge him as their Savior. No one, according to the Bible, can gain entrance into heaven, except through Jesus Christ (John 14:6).

JANE H. WALKER

Chapter Three

Jesus and his saving power are the dual purposes of all Scripture, so let us return in this writing to the time when the Israelites settled once again in the land which God gave them and Joshua died. The Lord then raised up judges who delivered the Jews from those who would harm them, though his people repeatedly went **"... whoring after other gods, and bowed themselves unto them.**" (Judges 2:17) God would always help them when they admitted their sins and turned back to him. This shows God's willingness to forgive, a facet of his nature which draws us to him during our times of sinfulness and true repentance.

* * * * * * * * * * * * * *

The turbulent period of the Book of Judges, which lasted around three hundred years (*Halley's*, p.168), is followed by the short but lovely Book of Ruth. This poignant Scripture portrays the messianic family whose progeny would one day produce the Savior of the world. This family represents the fusion of the idolatrous Moabitess, Ruth, with a son of the Bethlehem family of Elimelech and Naomi. This outside blood becomes an integral part of the family of Jesus Christ. This is a foregleam of Jesus being the Messiah for all nations. Ruth is the grandmother of David who becomes the second king of Israel.

A thousand years earlier, Abraham had founded the nation that had been chosen by God to produce the Messiah. Around 1100 years after Ruth and Boaz's marriage, Jesus was born of the Davidic (of David) line (*Halley*'s, p. 175-176). God had his own time frame in molding the nation that would nurture his Son.

* * * * * * * * * * * * * *

In I Samuel 5-6, we read that the Ark of God was taken by the Philistines who were constantly at war with Israel. The Philistines took the ark to Ashdod and placed it in the house of Dagon, their god. When they entered the house of Dagon the next morning, their god was face down on the earth before the ark. The Philistines took their man-made god and set it back in its place. However, the next morning, they found only a stump of Dagon left. The head and palms of its hands were cut off.

God used his great power to destroy some of the people of Ashdod and to afflict others with painful emerods (hemorrhoids) because of their capture and mistreatment of the ark. The people of Ashdod were terribly afraid of the God of the Israelites, and they longed to rid themselves of the Ark of God. They called their priests and diviners and asked them to advise them about the ark.

They were told to send it back to Israel, along with a trespass offering of **five golden emerods** and **five golden mice.** They were to make a new cart and tie two "**milch kine**" or milk cows to it. After putting the ark and the coffer, which held the trespass offering, on the cart, they sent the cart away. Lowing as they went, and without a driver, the cows pulled the cart with its unusual but precious cargo back to the Israelites.

During the thousand years between the Book of Ruth and the birth of Jesus, many influences came to bear on the small nation of Israel. With no strong central government, the Hebrew nation was a confederacy of twelve independent tribes with no cohesive force except their God. This was the way that God wanted it to be, as he himself wanted to be their ruler and king. However, his people had other ideas. They wanted an earthly king (I Samuel 8:5).

Samuel was known as a judge and oral prophet of Israel. When he was an old man, the Jewish people cried out for a king. In 1 Samuel 8:5-7, the elders spoke to Samuel:

"And said unto him, Behold, thou art old, and thy sons

walk not in thy ways; now make us a king to judge us like all the nations. But the thing displeased Samuel, when they said, Give us a king to judge us. And Samuel prayed unto the Lord.

"**And the Lord said unto Samuel, Hearken unto the voice of the people in all that they say unto thee: for they have not rejected thee, but they have rejected me, that I should not reign over them.**"

The Lord appeared to Samuel and told him to anoint Saul of the tribe of Benjamin as the first king of Israel (I Samuel 9:17). Over six hundred years had lapsed from the time that God changed Jacob's name to Israel to the anointing of Saul as the country's first king [note dates from Jacob's name change to Israel (Genesis 32:28) to Saul anointed king (I Samuel 9-10) in margins of the Bible]. At first humble, Saul's humility gave way to pride and self-importance. After three terrible mistakes involving Saul's disobedience to God, Samuel told him: "**...Because thou hast rejected the word of the Lord, he hath also rejected thee from being king.**" (I Samuel 15:23)

This is a different element in the nature of God. He was willing for the people to have their way, knowing that a king to rule over them was not in their best interest. He wanted his people to look to him of their own accord, rather than forcing himself on anyone.

Again, we read that God had regret, as stipulated in I Samuel 15:11: "**It repenteth me that I have set up Saul to be king: for he is turned back from following me, and hath not performed my commandments. And it grieved Samuel; and he cried unto the Lord all night.**"

Immediately after denying Saul the kingship of Israel, God told Samuel to go to Bethlehem, for he had chosen a young boy of the family of Jesse to be the next king of Israel. Seven of Jesse's sons appeared before Samuel, but God rejected each one as the future king of his people (I Samuel 16). When Samuel wondered that God kept rejecting the sons of Jesse, the nature of God shone forth when he told Samuel: "**...Look not on his countenance, or on the height of his stature; because I have refused him: for the Lord seeth not** as man seeth; for man looketh on the outward appearance, but the Lord looketh on the heart."** (I Samuel 16:7)

When Samuel took his horn of oil and anointed David, the youngest son of Jesse, to be the future king of Israel, **"...the Spirit of the Lord came upon David from that day forward."** (I Samuel 16:13) However, the Spirit of the Lord left King Saul and **"an evil spirit from the Lord troubled him."** (I Samuel 16:14) This is another instance of God's being in control of evil. In our own lives, we are reminded that we must choose between good and evil. In this way, we differ from God, because he can use his great power to wield evil as retribution for a person's evil ways. We are always supposed to choose the good, never the evil. In other words, **"...Vengeance is mine; I will repay, saith the Lord."** (Romans 12:19) We are instructed never to be vengeful.

When the evil spirit kept troubling Saul, and David played his harp to soothe him, the king didn't know that his young musician had already been anointed to succeed him as king. The relationship between King Saul and David was a fractious one of love and hatred. As Saul fell more and more out of favor with God, he became more jealous of David (I Samuel 18:6-15).

A great show of God's power in regard to the young David occurred when David challenged Goliath in the seventeenth chapter of I Samuel. The Philistines, arch enemies of the Israelites, were encamped on a mountain on one side of the valley of Elah, around fifteen miles west of the town of Bethlehem. The Israelis were on the side of another mountain, with the valley between them ("17:1-58 David and Goliath–Calvary Chapel Fullerton"). The giant Goliath was around nine feet tall and wore armor which weighed 150 pounds. Carrying a twenty-pound spear-head (*Halley*'s, p. 182), the Philistine challenged Israel to choose a man to fight him (I Samuel 17:23-51).

David finally persuaded King Saul to let him fight the giant. Choosing five smooth stones from the nearby brook, David put them in his shepherd's bag. With his sling in his hand, he drew near to the huge warrior.

When the Philistine cursed David by his gods, David said: **"...Thou comest to me with a sword, and with a spear, and with a shield: but I come to thee in the name of the Lord of hosts, the God of the armies of Israel, whom thou hast defied."** (I Samuel 17:45) David withdrew a stone and smote the Philistine who died instantly, falling face down to the ground.

From the time that David was anointed by Samuel, God favored him as the one whose family kingdom would reign forever in Israel. In II Samuel 7:16, we read, **"...thy throne shall be established forever."** God meant for his only begotten Son to be born at a later time to the family of David.

Though David is described as **"...of a beautiful countenance, and goodly to look to,"** (I Samuel 16:12) we also know by reading about him in the Bible that he had great musical and writing abilities. He was also a renowned man of war. However, with all of his good qualities, he yet was prone to great sinfulness, especially in regard to his adultery with Bathsheba and his having her husband, Uriah, killed in the thick of battle (II Samuel 11:1-27).

God forgave David for his terrible sins but he told him, **"...the sword shall never depart from thine house."** (II Samuel 12:10) The words were truly prophetic. David suffered many heartaches within his own family, which included the rape of his daughter, Tamar, by her brother, Amnon (II Samuel 13), who in turn was killed in retribution by their brother, Absalom (II Samuel 13:22-39).

Absalom himself was tragically killed, also (II Samuel 18:9-33). Out of the deeply held beliefs and sorrows of his life, David created most of the beautiful Psalms which have comforted people throughout the ages. W. E. Gladstone, English statesman and lay leader of the Church of England, said of the Psalms, "All the wonders of Greek Civilization heaped together are less Wonderful than is this simple Book of the Psalms." (*Halley's*, p. 248)

Yet, through all of the tragedies of his life, David remained true to God. As recorded in I Samuel 13:14, the Lord sought a man who was a **"...man after his own heart..."** God used an imperfect man - as we all are imperfect - to form his eternal dynasty. In fact, Jesus descended from the marital union of David and Bathsheba.

In I Chronicles 28-29 (written by Ezra, according to *Halley's Bible Handbook* p. 213), David wanted to build a house of God, but God told him that he must not build the temple, as David was a man of war and had shed much blood. Rather, David's son, Solomon, would be the builder of the temple. In Chapter 28:3, God spoke to David, as follows: **"But God said unto me, Thou shalt not build an house for my name, because thou hast been a man of war, and hast shed blood."**

In Chapter 28:6, God continued to speak to David: **"And he said unto me, Solomon thy son, he shall build my house and my courts: for I have chosen him to be my son, and I will be his father."**

God gave to David the pattern for the building of the temple, which included every detail of the house. This brings to mind the pattern that God gave to Moses for the building of the movable tent tabernacle in Exodus 26. In Chapter 28:19 of I Chronicles, we read:

"All this, said David, the Lord made me understand in writing by his hand upon me, even all the works of this pattern."

Here, again, we read that God used writing to convey his ideas in regard to the pattern for the temple. Remember that the Ten Commandments were written by God on stone tablets in the language that David and his people knew, probably ancient Hebrew ("God Gave Humanity the Alphabet–Jesus Center").

* * * * * * * * * * * * *

Solomon, the son of David and Bathsheba, became the third king of Israel (I Kings 1:43). Though known for his wisdom, he was also known for his foolishness. He had 700 wives and 300 concubines (I Kings 11:3). Many of these women were idolatrous (I Kings 11:1-10). Under Solomon's reign, Israel became the most powerful kingdom in all of the world. Jerusalem was the most magnificent city and the temple was the most glorious building on earth (*Halley's,* p. 191).

Though Solomon built the first temple at Jerusalem, he also built heathen altars alongside it for his idolatrous wives. Whereas

David had tried to suppress idolatry, it was reestablished during Solomon's reign (I Kings 11:4-10). The undivided kingdom lasted 120 years, with each king - Saul, David, and Solomon - reigning forty years (*Halley's*, p. 193). These were the golden yet increasingly decadent years of the kingdom of Israel.

Yet, in spite of Solomon's treachery to God, he managed to convey words of wisdom in the almost flippant yet profound Book of Ecclesiastes, when he wrote the cherished words below, which are also descriptive of the nature of God (Ecclesiastes 3:1-11). Reader, please remember the discussion earlier in this work about good and evil, then note the word play of opposites in King Solomon's words. This is one of my favorite passages in the Bible:

"To everything there is a season, and a time to every purpose under the heaven:

"A time to be born, and a time to die; a time to plant, and a time to pluck up that which is planted;

"A time to kill, and a time to heal; a time to break down, and a time to build up;

"A time to weep, and a time to laugh; a time to mourn, and a time to dance;

"A time to cast away stones, and a time to gather stones together; a time to embrace, and a time to refrain from embracing;

"A time to get, and a time to lose; a time to keep, and a time to cast away;

"A time to rend, and a time to sew; a time to keep silence, and a time to speak;

"A time to love, and a time to hate; a time of war, and a time of peace.

"What profit hath he that worketh in that wherein he laboureth? I have seen the travail, which God hath given to the sons of men to be exercised in it. He hath made every thing beautiful in his time: also he hath set the world in their heart, so that no man can find out the work that God maketh from the beginning to the end."

In Proverbs 6:17-19, Solomon mentions seven things that the Lord hates, which are an abomination to him. They are:

"A proud look, a lying tongue, and hands that shed innocent blood,

"An heart that deviseth wicked imaginations, feet that be swift in running to mischief,

"A false witness that speaketh lies, and he that soweth discord among brethren."

These definitely describe certain aspects of the nature of God.

Solomon encourages gaiety or mirth in the Book of Ecclesiastes (Ecclesiastes 2). A distinct part of our human makeup is the desire for joy. We love to laugh. What does the Bible say about God and laughter? Actually, it says very little. In Psalm 2:4, in response to kings and rulers who discredit God, the psalmist states in verse four that **"He that sitteth in the heavens shall laugh: the Lord shall have them in derision."** In other words, God's laugh is one of derision.

Since there are so few references to this part of God's nature, we naturally infer that God wants us to live our lives with a seriousness of purpose, with dignity and sincerity, and with adherence to his plans for us. Indeed, much more is said about God's wrath and his vengeance, especially in regard to man's disobedience to him. Our God is not fun-loving or fickle but obviously consumed with a serious purpose in regard to his creation.

Chapter Four

After the corruption of the united kingdom of Israel during Solomon's reign, the kingdom divided into the northern kingdom of Israel and the southern kingdom of Judah (I Kings 11:31-12). The northern kingdom adopted calf worship, the religion of Egypt, as its state religion (I Kings 12:28). The southern kingdom sporadically continued its worship of the true God. Though most of its kings degenerated into worshiping idols, several kings of strong faith managed to bring the southern kingdom of Judah back to worshiping the one and only God, who had brought them out of Egypt and planted them once again in the promised land of Israel (I and II Kings).

Attempting to guide both kingdoms into becoming the holy nation worthy of producing his beloved Son, God turned not to the priests, who were often the wickedest men in the nation (*Halley's*, p. 281) but to the prophets. Each prophet was directly called by God (*Halley's*, p. 281). Their mission was to try to save Israel from its idolatry and sinfulness and its invasion by other countries (*Halley's*, p. 281).

The period of the sixteen prophets covered around four hundred years (800 B.C. - 400 B.C.) (*Halley's*, p. 281). When the divided kingdom did not turn back to God, the prophets announced that it would be destroyed, but a remnant would be saved (Isaiah 10:20-24). From this remnant would come the one person in all of history who would bring all nations to God (*Halley's*, p. 281). God persevered through the centuries to prepare the nation of Israel for his birth. Obviously, the welfare of Israel being uppermost in his mind for thousands of years is a testament to the nature of God.

Thirteen of the prophets, whose books are named in the Old Testament, were active during the destruction of the Hebrew nation and three during its restoration (*Halley's*, p. 280). When the Israelites refused to abandon their idolatry, God allowed the countries of Assyria and Babylonia to take them away from the Promised Land and make them their servants.

The northern kingdom of Israel fell in 721 B.C. to the conquering Assyrians, and the terrible prophecy of the prophet, Hosea, rang true (Hosea 11:1-12). Assyria was known for its cruelty in dealing with its prisoners. To inspire terror, it was known to skin its captives alive and to cut off their hands, ears, noses, and feet and, also, to put out their eyes and pull out their tongues (*Halley's*, p. 209). Captives were led away from their homelands with hooks through their lips ("King Put Hooks in Their Lips [Bible History Online"]).

God used this depraved kingdom to fan the tiny flame of truth and righteousness that would grow stronger in comparison to the lack of it and the resulting depravity of its captors. Israel would truly suffer for its disobedience to God. Another prediction of Hosea in regard to the Israelites was the following: **"My God will cast them away, because they did not hearken unto him: and they shall be wanderers among the nations."** (Hosea 9:17)

This prophecy has been fulfilled throughout the ages.

From the Book of Isaiah to the Book of Malachi, the prophets were godly and courageous men who endured great hardships and literally gave their lives to accomplish their missions on earth. In Isaiah 1:4, the Lord speaks to Isaiah in a vision about the idolatry of his people: **"Ah sinful nation, a people laden with iniquity, a seed of evildoers, children that are corrupters: they have forsaken the Lord, they have provoked the Holy One of Israel unto anger, they are gone away backward."**

At the command of God, Isaiah walked naked and barefoot for three years, trying to deliver Israel from the approaching Assyrians

(Isaiah20:1-4). In this, he was successful. What would we think if, today, someone acted in such a strange way?

Isaiah is quoted in the New Testament more than any other prophet (*Halley's*, p. 285). He prophesied events which occurred during his lifetime and after his lifetime and some which are yet to occur. He speaks of the coming Messiah with intimate knowledge of his birth, his life, and his death. According to Isaiah's prophecy, death will be destroyed, along with the earth itself. A New Heaven and a New Earth will be created and the saints of God and the wicked will be eternally separated (*Halley's,* pp. 302-306). Tradition survives that Isaiah was fastened between two planks and **"...sawn asunder,"** thus suffering a horrible death. (Hebrews 11:37 refers to this.)

In Isaiah 40:12, the prophet gives his own description of the nature of God: '**Who hath measured the waters in the hollow of his hand, and meted out heaven with the span, and comprehended the dust of the earth in a measure, and weighed the mountains in scales, and the hills in a balance?"**

Another verse, Isaiah 40:28-31 also gives us insight into God's nature: **"Hast thou not known? hast thou not heard, that the everlasting God, the Lord, the Creator of the ends of the earth fainteth not, neither is weary? There is no searching of his understanding. He giveth power to the faint; and to them that have no might he increaseth strength. Even the youths shall faint and be weary, and the young men shall utterly fall: But they that wait upon the Lord shall renew their strength; they shall mount up with wings as eagles; they shall run, and not be weary; and they shall walk, and not faint."**

* * * * * * * * * * * * * *

Jeremiah is known as the weeping prophet because he constantly wept about the certain destruction of his sinful nation. He lived about one hundred years after Isaiah (*Halley's,* p. 307). In Jeremiah I:5, God said to Jeremiah: **"Before I formed thee in the belly I knew thee; and before thou camest forth out of the womb I sanctified thee, and I ordained thee a prophet unto the nations."**

When the Babylonian army under Nebuchadnezzar approached Jerusalem in 606 B.C (*Halley's*, p. 309), God told the Israelites through Jeremiah that he himself would fight against his chosen people, because of their idolatry. God said in Jeremiah 21:10:

"For I have set my face against this city for evil, and not for good, saith the Lord; it shall be given into the hand of the king of Babylon, and he shall burn it with fire."

The stark nature of God in this respect is such that he would let his chosen people be conquered by a heathen nation, because of their disobedience to him in making and worshiping other gods. Here again, God uses evil to destroy Jerusalem because of his people's disobedience.

This reminds us again that we are to fear God. How many times in the Bible has he shown his wrath, from the Great Flood to the destruction of Sodom and Gomorrah to the destruction of the nation of Israel for nearly two thousand years? God used famines and pestilence and even **"evil beasts"** to punish unbelievers and to bring about his desires, especially insofar as the nation of Israel was concerned (Ezekiel 5:17). Does he still bring about death and destruction on our planet, when we disregard and disobey him?

In Jeremiah 19:5-9, God speaks to Jeremiah about the terrible sins of his people and also what will happen to the Israelites because of their idolatry: **"They have built also the high places of Baal, to burn their sons with fire for burnt offerings unto Baal, which I commanded not, nor spake it, neither came it into my mind:**

"Therefore, behold, the days come, saith the Lord, that this place shall no more be called Tophet, nor The valley of the son of Hinnom, but The valley of slaughter. And I will make void the counsel of Judah and Jerusalem in this place; and I will cause them to fall by the sword before their enemies, and by the hands of them that seek their lives: and their carcases will I give to be meat for the fowls of the heaven, and for the beasts of the earth.

"And I will make this city desolate, and an hissing; every one that passeth thereby shall be astonished and hiss because of all the plagues thereof. And I will cause them to eat the flesh

of their sons and the flesh of their daughters, and they shall eat every one the flesh of his friend in the siege and straitness, wherewith their enemies, and they that seek their lives, shall straiten them."

It is somewhat surprising to read that Israel's idolatry never entered the mind of God, as denoted in the first sentence of the quotation above. This underscores the fact that God created man with a free will. It also substantiates that life as we know it is experimental and that God doesn't take it upon himself to know what the outcome of everything will be. When something occurs, however, that is contrary to what he wants, he can quickly remedy the situation. How often have we had terrible things happen to us, things that never came into our minds? Isn't this another attribute of God's nature?

Another very human attribute of God is mentioned in Jeremiah 35:14, when God is described as **"...rising early and speaking."** This begs the question of whether God ever sleeps. Jeremiah 31:26 appears to answer that question, for in this verse God says, "...**my sleep was sweet unto me.**" Some readers of this Scripture would say that these words are Jeremiah's words, speaking of himself rather than of God. In Psalm 121:4, we read, **"Behold, he that keepeth Israel shall neither slumber nor sleep."** Perhaps the psalmist was merely stressing the importance of Israel to God, or it may be true that God doesn't sleep.

Jeremiah was imprisoned, placed in stocks, thrown into a dungeon of mire with no food and water, and constantly threatened with death (Jeremiah 38). He even went about the city with an ox yoke around his neck to draw attention to his message from God that Israel would suffer defeat by the Babylonian army (Jeremiah 28:10-14). The Israelites did not believe Jeremiah, and they hated him (Jeremiah 26:7-11) because of his prophecy, which nonetheless became true.

God chose another good man, Ezekiel, as a prophet during the captivity of Israel by Babylon. He was carried to Babylon in 597 B.C., eleven years before Jerusalem was destroyed (*Halley's*, p. 323). His message to the displaced Israelites was that they were being punished by living in a heathen nation, so that they would return to the worship of the true God. The dominant theme of the Book of Ezekiel is, **"...they shall know that I am the Lord."** (Ezekiel 6:14)

These words occur some sixty-two times in the Book of Ezekiel (*Halley's,* p.324). Ezekiel endured many hardships and much suffering as a prophet of God. He was dumb, unable to speak for a long period of time (Ezekiel 3:26). God asked him to lie on his left side for 390 days (well over a year) as penitence for the sins of the Northern Kingdom of Israel and forty days on his right side as penance for the sins of the Southern Kingdom of Judah (Ezekiel 4:5-6). He had to eat loathsome food, and his beloved wife was taken from him in death (Ezekiel 24:15-18).

In the Book of Ezekiel, we read about the idolatry of the Israelites who were left back in Judaea. This greatly aroused God's wrath to the extent that, in Chapter 8:3, we read about Ezekiel's being lifted up by a lock of his hair (or head) and being transported to the door of the temple, where God met him in a vision. God told him that terrible abominations were going on. God told Ezekiel to go through the door of the temple to observe the **"wicked abominations"** that were happening. Ezekiel 8:9-18 describes what the prophet saw, which included creeping things, abominable beasts and idols which the Israelites were worshiping. Seventy of the ancients of Israel said that God did not see what they were doing in secret, for God had forsaken the earth. Another twenty-five of the men had turned their backs to the temple of the Lord, and with their faces toward the East, they worshiped the sun.

"Then he said unto me, Hast thou seen this, O son of man: Is it a light thing to the house of Judah that they commit the abominations which they commit here: For they have filled the land with violence, and have returned to provoke me to anger; and, lo, they put the branch to their nose.

"Therefore will I also deal in fury: mine eye shall not spare, neither will I have pity: and though they cry in mine ears with a loud voice, yet will I not hear them."

(Note: Though I didn't include part of the above Scripture which mentions "**Tammuz,**" this refers to a Babylonian god, whose worship included wild orgies of immorality (*Halley's,* p. 327. Also, the Scripture records "**there sat women weeping for Tammuz.**")

While he was a captive in Babylon, Ezekiel had a vision of being in a valley with dry bones all around him (Ezekiel 37:1-12). God asked him whether the bones could live again. Ezekiel answered, "**...O Lord God, thou knowest.**" God breathed life into the dry bones which began shaking until the bones came together, covered by flesh, and they stood up as an exceedingly great army. God said the bones were the whole house of Israel which would once again return to the land that God gave them (Ezekiel 4:1-14).

In Ezekiel 20:12, I read something interesting about Jews (and later Christians) assembling themselves. The Scripture reads as follows: "**Morever also I gave them my sabbaths, to be a sign between me and them, that they might know that I am the Lord that sanctify them.**" The sabbaths, or in our case "Sundays" come once a week. I believe, as Ezekiel says, that this day of the week is a sign from God that we are to meet with other Christians. In the New Testament, we have similar instructions in Hebrews 10:23-25. This reads: "**Let us hold fast the profession of our faith without wavering; (for he is faithful that promised;) And let us consider one another to provoke unto love and to good works: Not forsaking the assembling of ourselves together, as the manner of some is; but exhorting one another: and so much the more, as ye see the day approaching.**"

The prophet Daniel had been captive in Babylon some nine years before Ezekiel arrived *(Halley's,* p. 323). Babylon was the wonder city of the ancient world. It was known as a "**...golden city...,**" as recorded in Isaiah 14:4. According to ancient historians, its walls were sixty miles in circumference, three hundred feet high, eighty feet thick, and extending thirty-five feet below the ground, so its enemies could not tunnel under to the city. Its Hanging Gardens were one of the wonders of the ancient world (*Halley's,* p. 336-337). This heathen city held the Israelites captive for seventy years *(Halley's,* p. 349).

Daniel was taken captive as a young boy to Babylon, along with three friends. All were handsome, brilliant Jewish boys whom God used to bear witness to the idol-worshiping Babylonians (Daniel 1:1-7). As a test of the Israelites' faith, the Babylonian king, Nebuchadnezzar, ordered that Daniel's three friends be bound and placed in a fiery furnace. In the midst of the fire, a fourth person, Jesus, appeared who loosed the boys' bonds, and the four of them walked about in the fire. Though the men who bound the young boys were killed by the heat of the fire, Daniel's three friends suffered no harm. The astonished Nebuchadnezzar bowed before the true God of the Israelites and promoted the three young Jewish boys in his kingdom (Daniel 3:12-30).

God used the prideful Babylonian King Nebuchadnezzar to demonstrate how quickly a powerful ruler could be brought low. Nebuchadnezzar not only lost his kingdom, but he also lost his mind. In Daniel 4:33, we read that the king: **"...was driven from men, and did eat grass as oxen, and his body was wet with the dew of heaven, till his hairs were grown like eagles' feathers, and his nails like birds' claws."**

Whereas Nebuchadnezzar had taken credit for his own greatness and the majesty of his kingdom, God swiftly showed him who was actually the power behind the throne. After God had stripped the king of everything, including his sanity, the king acknowledged that God was truly the one who was powerful, not himself. In Daniel 4:37, he said with rightful humility after recovering his mind:

"Now I Nebuchadnezzar praise and extol and honour the King of heaven, all whose works are truth, and his ways judgment: and those that walk in pride he is able to abase."

This is but one example among many in the Bible which demonstrate God's powerful intervention in the affairs of mankind, especially when a person takes credit for his or her own success. Much is said about pride in the Bible and God's disdain of it.

In Daniel 9:21-24, when the Babylonian captivity of the Jews was nearing its end, the angel Gabriel tells Daniel that the coming of the Messiah would occur within "**seventy weeks**." Scholars have interpreted this to mean seventy weeks of seventy years, or 490 years. In other words, the period between the captivity of the Jews for seventy years and the arrival of the Messiah would be seven times that long, or 490 years. The date from which the seventy weeks began was the main decree from one of the Persian kings to rebuild Jerusalem (Daniel 9:25), which was in 457 B.C.

The seventy weeks are divided into increments of **seven weeks**, **sixty-two weeks**, and **one week** in verses 25 and 27 of the same Chapter 9 of the Book of Daniel. Though the "**seven weeks**" is difficult to construe, the "**sixty-nine weeks**" (which includes the "**seven weeks**") equals 483 days, according to the year-day theory mentioned in Ezekiel 4:6, which states: **"I have appointed thee each day for a year."**

Between the decree to rebuild Jerusalem in 457 B.C. and the coming of the Messiah was a period of 483 years. This brings us to A.D. 26, the year that Jesus was baptized and began his ministry. Some Bible scholars believe that Daniel suspended God's chronology at the death of Christ and that the "**one week**" is reserved for the end of time. Dear Reader, I do not pretend to understand this reasoning, but I included it because it is accepted as biblical fact by many Bible scholars. Again, I relied on *Halley's Bible Handbook,* p. 349, for his interpretation of this chronology.

On the eve of the destruction of Babylon, Daniel had been captive in the city seventy years and was an old man (*Halley's*, p. 344). Belshazzar, the king of Babylon and son of former King Nabonidus, held a great feast for a thousand of his lords. They drank wine from the golden vessels that were taken out of the Jewish temple at Jerusalem some seventy years before. As they drank, they praised the gods of gold, silver, brass, iron, wood, and stone (Daniel 5:1-4).

Suddenly, as a candle burned before the plastered wall of the king's palace, the fingers of a man's hand appeared, writing a message on the wall. No one could interpret the message, not even the king's soothsayers and astrologers. The queen suggested that Daniel be brought in to decipher the writing recorded in Daniel 5:25:

"...Mene, Mene, Tekel, Upharsin."

When Daniel arrived at the great feast, he first chastised Belshazzar for his lack of humility, especially in regard to the true God of Israel. He reminded the king and those in attendance that they were drinking wine from the vessels of the Jewish temple. They were praising the false gods of silver, gold, brass, iron, wood and stone, which could neither see nor hear nor know (Daniel 5:13-23).

Daniel interpreted the dire prophecy for the king as recorded in Daniel 5:26-28: **"This is the interpretation of the thing: Mene; God hath numbered thy kingdom, and finished it. Tekel; Thou art weighed in the balances, and art found wanting. Peres; Thy kingdom is divided, and given to the Medes and Persians."**

I looked up "**Peres**" and "**Upharsin**" on the internet and found several different resources, which all corroborated that "**Peres**" was the singular of "**Upharsin**." "**Peres**" can mean either "divided" or "Persia." Some sites on the internet stated that "**Peres**" meant "the kingdom divided." ("What Is the Difference Between Upharsin and Peres? [Dan. 5:25-28]")

That very night, Daniel's prophecy came true, for Belshazzar was slain and his kingdom seized by Darius the Median (Daniel 5:30-31). Media became a part of Persia in 550 B.C., when Cyrus became ruler of Persia ("Cyrus the Great–Wikipedia").

Daniel's faith was tested when a decree went out from the new king, Darius, that anyone caught asking a petition of any god or man, except King Darius himself, would be thrown into a den of lions (Daniel 6:7). When Daniel was caught praying to God, he was cast into a den of lions, but was found unhurt the next morning. God had sent an angel to shut the lions' mouths (Daniel 6:22). Not only does this reveal God's nature in being able to control the lions but also he wanted Daniel to finish his book, so that mankind would be blessed by it in years to come.

The Book of Daniel prophesies about the end of the world, when there will be terrible trouble like never before. This will be followed by the resurrection of the dead and the everlasting glory of the saved. As the end of the world nears, it will be as follows: **"many shall run to and fro, and knowledge shall be increased."**

(Daniel 12:4)

God used other prophets in attempting to bring Israel back to him. The Lord told the prophet Hosea to do the following: **"...Go, take unto thee a wife of whoredoms and children of whoredoms: for the land hath committed great whoredom, departing from the Lord."** (Hosea I:2)

This was obviously in reference to Israel's being the **"whore"** who had broken God's commandments. Now, Israel would pay the great price for its disobedience by being held captive for many years in successive heathen nations. Hosea predicted this in the Book of Hosea 8:7: **"For they have sown the wind, and they shall reap the whirlwind..."**

* * * * * * * * * * * * * *

With the destruction of the Babylonian kingdom by the Medes, the Israelites were once again the conquered subjects of a heathen nation. The Book of Esther relates the Jews' deliverance from total extermination by a beautiful Hebrew girl named Esther who became the queen of the Persian King Xerxes (also known as Ahasuerus). This is recorded in Esther 2:1-17. Using her influence as queen, Esther thwarted the annihilation of her people by those who hated the Jewish people and wanted them gone from the empire. If not for Esther, the Jewish nation would have been totally destroyed and its role of producing the Savior of the world sabotaged. All of this is recorded in the Book of Esther.

The Jews were allowed to return to their homeland under the Persian King Cyrus, whom Isaiah had called by name some 200 years before. In Isaiah 44:26-28 and 45:1-13, the prophet predicted that **"Cyrus"** would allow the Hebrews to return and to rebuild Jerusalem. Isn't this amazing that Isaiah would even call by name the king that would allow this? God certainly gave him the name of this Persian king.

According to articles I read on the internet, Cyrus was likely a Zoroastrian. Zoroastrianism was an Iranian religion founded by Zoroaster (1400-1000 B.C.). It is based on belief in a supreme deity, Ahura Mazda, and a cosmic struggle between good and evil. God's nature is such that he instructed a heathen king to allow the Jews to return to their homeland ("About Cyrus the Great and Zoroastrian–Their Relations?").

Unlike the Assyrian and Babylonian empires, which took captive people out of their own lands and scattered them in other lands, the Persian empire believed in sending their captives back to their former homes (*Halley's*, p. 230). Again, the powerful yet succinct nature of God was at work. The first return of the Jews to their homeland began in 536 B.C. when Zerubbabel the Governor and Joshua the Priest returned with 42,360 Jews, 7,337 servants, 200 singers, 736 horses, 245 mules, 435 camels, 6,720 asses, and 5,400 gold and silver vessels (Ezra 1-2; also *Halley's*, p. 229-230). During this time period, from 536-516 B.C., the temple was rebuilt (*Halley*'s, p. 230). The older men who had seen the first temple built by King Solomon wept aloud, because the second temple was so insignificant in comparison (Ezra 3:11-13).

* * * * * * * * * * * * * *

In trying to understand the nature of God, one must know more about the importance of the Jewish temples, i.e. the first one built by Solomon which stood for 400 years; the second one built by Zerubbabel which stood for 500 years; and the third one built by Herod that lasted 90 years (*Halley's,* p. 220). The temple that was in existence during Jesus' life was the one built by Herod the Great. According to *Halley's Bible Handbook,* p. 220-222, it was built of marble and gold and was "magnificent beyond description" (*Halley's,* p. 535). Herod's temple was destroyed in 70 A.D. *(Halley's,* p. 221) by the Roman army of Titus, and it has never been rebuilt. All that is left of it is the western wall, called the "wailing wall" by some ("WAILING WALL–Jerusalem's Western Wall"/Wailing Wall").

Since Herod's temple was the one that existed when Christ walked the earth, I believe it is incumbent upon us to know more about it. According to John 2:20, the building of Herod's temple continued for forty-six years. It was built by Herod the Great. It required 10,000 men to spend ten years in building just the retaining walls around the Temple Mount, on top of which the Muslim shrine, the Dome of the Rock stands today.

The wall surrounding the temple was 5,085 feet long, only 195 feet short of a full mile. Some of the stones in the walls measured twenty to forty feet in length and weighed more than a hundred tons each. Around six to seven million Jews lived in the Roman Empire during that time period with another million living in Persia. These Israelites often traveled to Jerusalem for the three festivals of Passover, Shavuot, and Sukkot. The huge temple was built to accommodate such a large number of people, perhaps as many as several hundred thousand at the time ("King Herod the Great, Herod Temple–Aish.com").

The historian Josephus described Herod's temple as follows:

"Viewed from without, the Sanctuary had everything that could amaze either mind or eyes. Overlaid all round with stout plates of gold, the first rays of the sun it reflected so fierce a blaze of fire that those who endeavored to look at it were forced to turn away as if they had looked straight at the sun. To strangers as they approached it seemed in the distance like a mountain covered with snow, for any part not covered with gold was dazzling white. From the very top rose sharp gold spikes to prevent birds from perching on the roof and soiling it. Of the stones in the building, some were 67.5 feet long, 9 wide and 7.5 deep." ("The Jewish War," 2, p. 259-260").

Not only was this the temple that Jesus knew, but it was also the place where the angel Gabriel and Zacharias conversed in regard to the birth of Zacharias' son, John the Baptist (Luke I:5-80). It was the temple where Jesus was taken as an infant (Luke 2:21-33) and, later at the age of twelve, where he confounded the wise men with his knowledge of the Scriptures (Luke 2:42-47). From it, he drove out the money changers (Luke19:45-46), and it was where he proclaimed that he was the Son of God (John 5:14-19). It was also the seat of the mighty Sanhedrin that condemned him to death (Mark 14:53-64). ("Herod's Temple–Contractor Sales") Please note that the Sanhedrin was an assembly or council of all of the chief priests and the elders and the scribes, as recorded in the above Scripture.

Inside Herod's temple was a veil, described as being not only lovely with its beautiful colors and cunning handiwork but also very large and heavy. I have read that it was sixty feet in height, thirty feet wide, the thickness of the palm of a hand, and requiring three hundred priests to manipulate it. Yet, at Jesus' death, this tremendous veil was torn from top to bottom (Mark 15:38). Truly, this was done by the hand of God ("The Thickness of the Temple Veil/ Orchard Keeper"). Tertullian (c.160 A.D.- 220 A.D.), Christian author and ardent defender of Christianity, who lived in northern Africa, stated that the Holy Spirit which dwelt in the temple prior to Christ's death departed afterwards. His words are the following:

"He deserted the Temple [leaving it] desolate, rending the veil and taking away from it the Holy Spirit." ("Cross and destruction of the Temple in one breath")

Eight wonders or signs occurred within a decade prior to the destruction of the Jewish temple in Jerusalem. The historian Josephus recorded these signs in his "Wars of the Jews" (Book VI, Chapter V, Section 3, p. 581-583). Please see below:

These signs included a star resembling a sword, which hovered over the city of Jerusalem, and a comet which could be seen a whole year. A great light, which lasted half an hour, shone around the altar and the "holy house." Also, a high priest led a cow into the temple to be sacrificed, and the heifer gave birth to a lamb in the middle of the temple.

A strange miracle occurred at the very heavy eastern gate of the inner court of the temple. Heretofore, the large and heavy brass gate had to be shut with great difficulty by twenty men. This gate, according to Josephus, "opened of its own accord about the sixth hour of the night." The learned men of the town knew that their holy temple was no longer secure and that the gate was opened "for the advantage of their enemies." Armored troops of soldiers and chariots moved rapidly among the clouds and surrounded cities, according to Josephus.

Another phenomenon occurred when the priests entered the inner court of the temple to perform their sacred duties. They first felt a quaking and heard a loud noise, followed by the sound of a great multitude, saying, "Let us remove hence."

Perhaps the most unusual and frightening sign recorded by Josephus was the behavior of a certain man whom no one knew, who went about, day and night, in all the streets of the city, uttering a doleful lament about Jerusalem and the Jewish temple, thereby angering the populace to the extent that they severely beat him. Crying out loud, the man intoned, "A voice from the east, a voice from the west, a voice from the four winds, a voice against Jerusalem and the holy house, a voice against the bridegrooms and the brides, and a voice against this whole people!"

Though they continued to beat him, he persisted with his dire cry, saying the words over and over. The rulers then brought him to the Roman procurator, where he was beaten until his bones were laid bare, but he didn't plead for mercy nor shed any tears. Rather, at every lash of the whip, he cried out, " Woe, woe to Jerusalem!"

The procurator asked the man who he was and from where did he come. Also, he asked him why he uttered such words, but the wretched man kept screaming his words of woe, as though they were his "premeditated vow." "Woe, woe to Jerusalem!" The procurator thought him a mad man and dismissed him. Though the man was beaten each day, he never spoke ill words to his tormentors, nor good words to those who brought him food.

He continued his odd behavior and words of woe for seven years and five months. He neither grew tired nor hoarse and only ceased his mission when the siege upon Jerusalem and the temple was complete. As he went around the city wall, he cried out in his loudest voice yet, "Woe, woe to the city again and to the people, and to the holy house." Then, as he shouted his last words which were, "Woe, woe to myself, also," a stone (perhaps launched as a missile during the siege of Jerusalem) flew out and smote him, causing his death.

* * * * * * * * * * * * *

In 457 B.C., Ezra went to Jerusalem with 1754 men, one hundred talents of gold, and 750 talents of silver (*Halley's*, p. 229). This was the second return of the Jews to their homeland after their seventy-year exile. Ezra was heartsick when he arrived in Jerusalem, for his people had intermarried with their idolatrous neighbors (Ezra 9:1-3), something that God had strictly forbidden them to do. Idolatry had been the cause of their captivity. According to Ezra 9:3, when Ezra heard of these abominations, he: **"...rent my garment and my mantle, and plucked off the hair of my head and of my beard, and sat down astonied."**

The Israelites who had remained in their homeland had egregiously broken God's commandments. Ezra wept, as did his people. He asked them to put away their idolatrous wives, something that was very difficult to do, as many of the men had children by these wives. However, the distraught people with much weeping obeyed God (Ezra 10). These two groups of Jewish people formed the remnant that would rebuild Jerusalem. More will be written about the "remnant" later.

The third return of the Jews occurred in 444 B.C., when Nehemiah came to Jerusalem as a civil governor with orders from the king of Persia to rebuild the wall and to restore Jerusalem as a fortified city (*Halley's*, p. 229). Old enemies of the Jews, who were then in possession of the land, such as the Moabites, Ammonites, Ashdodites, Arabians, and Samaritans bitterly opposed the restoring of the wall around Jerusalem. Though they harassed the Jews as they rebuilt the wall, the work was accomplished in 52 days under the leadership of Nehemiah (Book of Nehemiah, entire book). Can we not see the hand of God, and the nature of God, in bringing about this accomplishment?

Chapter Five

Another book of the Old Testament that gives us insight into the nature of God is the Book of Job, which deals with human suffering. The French writer, Victor Hugo, said, "The Book of Job is perhaps the greatest masterpiece of the human mind." *(Halley's, p. 240)* It is a book that we all can relate to, for we all suffer. However, I disagree with Victor Hugo to the extent that no "human mind" conceived it. All Scripture is inspired by God, himself.

In the Book of Job, God speaks to Satan who has been **"...going to and fro in the earth, and from walking up and down in it."** (Job I:7) When God exalts his servant Job as **"...none like him in the earth, a perfect and upright man, one that feareth God, and escheweth evil?"** (Job 1:8), Satan tells God that Job is good because Job is blessed with everything. If everything is taken away from him, Satan says, Job will curse God to his face.

God challenges Satan about this, giving Satan the power to take away Job's many blessings, everything except his life, for God wants to prove to Satan that Job cannot be persuaded to denounce him. Satan takes everything away from Job, except his life - his sons, servants, oxen, sheep, and camels - and afflicts him with a loathsome disease. Through all of his heartache and suffering, Job refuses to curse God, but he longs for death to end his pain. In his distress, he asks the immortal question, **"If a man die, shall he live again?"** (Job 14:14).

Unflinchingly, Job also answers his friends who have mocked him, **"For I know that my redeemer liveth, and that he shall** stand at the latter day upon the earth: And though after my skin worms destroy this body, yet in my flesh shall I see God..."** (Job 19:25-26)

Job also utters the truism: **"...Behold, the fear of the Lord, that is wisdom; and to depart from evil is understanding."** (Job 28:28)

Here, again, we note that fear of God is mentioned. He is God, and we are in awe of him, because we know that he is all-powerful and all-knowing. It is akin to the fear that a child has of his godly parents who threaten punishment for not obeying them. The tremendous difference, of course, lies in the fact that the immortal destiny of our very souls will be decided by God, who will be the final judge of our disobedience. Also, the fear is much greater and far more profound than simple awe.

During my in-depth study of the Bible for the writing of this treatise, I realized as never before, in my reading of the Scriptures, the many times we are exhorted – even commanded – to fear God. I skimmed through the entire Bible and found this command some 220 times in most of the books of the Bible and in both the Old Testament and the New Testament. Also, seemingly contradictory, the words, **"Fear not,"** occur some 365 times in the Bible.

In other words, we are to fear God to the extent that our fear of his punishment for our sins outweighs our temptation to commit these sins. However, we are not to live in fear of anything or anyone else, for **"...perfect love casteth out fear..."** (I John 4:18). We are safe in God's love, if we obey God's commandments.

God rewarded Job with twice as much as he had before, according to the Book of Job 42:10, because he remained true to God throughout his ordeal. The man Job represents every mortal who ever lived, for we deal likewise with illness and sorrow almost every day of our lives.

* * * * * * * * * * * * * *

The Old Testament writings ceased around 430 B.C. Four hundred years lapsed between the Old Testament and the writings of the New Testament. During this time, not much was known about Jewish history (*Halley's,* p. 402).

Just when the group of thirty-nine books in the Old Testament was completed and acknowledged as the Word of God is somewhat obscure. The Jewish tradition, according to Halley, is that Ezra reassembled scattered copies of the Scripture after the Jews' return from their captivity and restored them to their rightful place in the temple. Other copies were then made for synagogues from the temple copies. Christians tend to believe that these books were recognized as the inspired Word of God during the time of Moses *(Halley's,* p. 405-406), who wrote the first five books of the Old Testament.

During the final two centuries before Christ, the Jews were so numerous in Egypt, especially at Alexandria, that they formed around two-fifths of the entire population. Most of them ceased to use – and even forgot – the Hebrew language. Since the possibility existed of their forgetting the Law, it became customary to read in the synagogues the Law as interpreted in Greek. Greek was the language of the world during this time period ("CATHOLIC ENCYCLOPEDIA: Septuagint Version–New Advent")

This led to the compilation of a Greek translation from the Hebrew of the Old Testament, which was called the Septuagint. Translated between 300-200 B.C., the Septuagint (sometimes abbreviated LXX) was written by seventy to seventy-two Jewish scholars. In Latin, the term "Septuagint" means seventy, which alludes to the seventy translators. Not only was it used by Hellenistic Jews (after the death of Alexander the Great), but it was also a source of the Old Testament for early Christians who spoke Greek, during the first few centuries A.D. ("Septuagint").

It's of great interest to note that *Ekklesia,* the Greek word translated "church" in the New Testament, is used often to refer to Israel in the Septuagint (What Is the Meaning of Ekklesia?: *Christian Courier*), though I saw conflicting articles about this on the internet. In Acts 7:38, when the first Christian martyr, Stephen, is expounding his beliefs before the Jewish rulers, he tells about Moses when he met with God on Mount Sinai, as he says in the words: **"This is he, that**

was in the church in the wilderness with the angel which spake to him in the mount Sina, and with our fathers: who received the lively oracles to give unto us..."

Though many dispensationalists have said, "Israel is not the Church and the Church is not Israel," many doctrines and eschatology are founded upon this premise. Since this is lending itself to theology, which is not the purpose of this book, I will not delve into this idea further. However, without a doubt, early Christians were well aware of the biblical idea that God's church in the Old Testament was the nation of Israel ("The Word 'Church' in the Old Testament–Pickle Publishing").

The Jewish historian, Josephus (A.D. 37-A.D. 100), born in Jerusalem of priestly aristocracy, had much to say about the validity of these early Scriptures. Educated extensively in Jewish and Greek culture, he was governor of Galilee and military commander in the wars with Rome. He also was present at the destruction of Jerusalem. Here are the words of Josephus:

"We have but 22 books, containing the history of all time, books that are believed to be divine. Of these, 5 belong to Moses, containing his laws and the traditions of the origin of mankind down to the time of his death. From the death of Moses to the reign of Artaxerxes the prophets who succeeded Moses wrote the history of the events that occurred in their own time, in 13 books. The remaining 4 books comprise hymns to God and precepts for the conduct of human life. From the days of Artaxerxes to our own times every event has indeed been recorded, but these recent records have not been deemed worthy of equal credit with those which preceded them, on account of the failure of the exact succession of prophets. There is practical proof of the spirit in which we treat our Scriptures; for, although so great an interval of time has now passed, not a soul has ventured to add or to remove or to alter a syllable, and it is the instinct of every Jew, from the day of his birth, to consider these Scriptures as the teaching of God, and to abide by them, and, if need be, cheerfully to lay down his life in their behalf." (*Halley's*, p. 405-406)

If one questions Josephus' numbering of twenty-two books, as opposed to our thirty-nine books of the Old Testament, one must realize that by combining the two books each of Samuel, Kings, and Chronicles into one; Ezra and Nehemiah into one; and the twelve Minor Prophets (Hosea through Malachi) into one, these twenty-four books are the same as our thirty-nine. Josephus further reduces the number of books to twenty-two by combining Ruth with Judges and Lamentations with Jeremiah. They are all there, only combined differently (*Halley's,* p. 26).

The above words of Josephus, speaking to us from two thousand years ago, ring true to us today. They are unquestionable testimony to the belief of Jews during Jesus' day that the Hebrew Scriptures had been completed and determined for 400 years prior to his time (*Halley's,* p. 406). This exemplifies God's hand and nature in the formation of the Scriptures and in the preservation of Israel and the Scriptures through the ages.

Josephus also had these words to say about Jesus, placing the Son of God in an historical perspective:

"Now, there was about this time Jesus, a wise man, if it be lawful to call him a man, for he was a doer of wonderful works, a teacher of such men as receive the truth with pleasure. He drew over to him both many of the Jews, and many of the Gentiles. He was [the] Christ; and when Pilate, at the suggestion of the principal men amongst us, had condemned him to the cross, those that loved him at the first did not forsake him, for he appeared to them alive again the third day, as the divine prophets had foretold these and ten thousand other wonderful things concerning him; and the tribe of Christians, so named from him, are not extinct at this day." (Josephus, "The Antiquities of the Jews," p. 379)

At the end of the Book of Malachi, the last book of the Old Testament, the Jewish people were back in their land which God had given them, but they were subjects of the Persian Empire. The ensuing years were fraught with hopelessness insofar as their becoming a nation again. They were, instead, subjugated by other nations, one after the other (*Halley's,* p. 402-406).

The Persian Empire lasted about a hundred years, followed by the Greek Period (331-167 B.C.). Alexander the Great's empire included lands formerly under the dominion of Egypt, Assyria, Babylon, and Persia. By 331 B.C., the entire world lay at his feet.

When the great Greek conqueror invaded Jewish territory in 332 B.C., he spared Jerusalem and showed much consideration to the Jews. He offered immunities to Jews to settle in Alexandria, Egypt, which became an influential center of Judaism. However, upon Alexander's death, Palestine was reconquered by the Greek kings of Syria, who were not as benevolent toward the Jews (*Halley's,* p. 402-403).

Antiochus Epiphanes, a Greek king of Syria (175-164 B.C.), hated the Jews with a passion. He made a violent effort to exterminate the Jews and their religion. He ravaged Jerusalem (168 B.C.), defiled the temple where he erected an altar to Jupiter, and forbade temple worship. He forbade circumcision with the threat of death and sold thousands of Jewish families into slavery. He destroyed all copies of Scripture and killed everyone in possession of such copies. He used horrible methods of torture to force Jews to renounce their religion (*Halley's,* p. 403-404).

Infuriated at this attempt to annihilate his people, a priest named Mattathias led a revolt against the Syrian desecration. Fearless and intensely patriotic, Mattathias gathered a loyal band around him, including his five heroic and courageous sons. When Mattathias died in 166 B.C., his son Judas Maccabaeus, a fighter of extraordinary military genius, won battle after battle with unbelievable and almost impossible odds against the Syrians. In 165 B.C. Judas Maccabaeus recaptured Jerusalem and cleansed and rededicated the Temple (*Halley's,* p. 402-404). This is another indication of God's nature in regard to his use of certain people to perform his will and his extraordinary determination and protection in regard to Israel.

In 63 B.C., Palestine was conquered by the Romans under Pompey. Antipater, an Edomite and descendant of Esau, was appointed ruler of Judea. His son, Herod the Great, succeeded him and was ruler when Jesus was born (37-3 B.C.). It was this Herod who slew the children of Bethlehem, during which time Joseph and

Mary carried the very young Jesus to Egypt to avoid the slaughter. A cruel and brutal man, Herod nonetheless rebuilt the temple of the Jews to curry their favor. It was being rebuilt when Jesus walked the earth (*Halley's,* p. 404).

A general feeling of expectancy soared throughout the Middle East during this time period, especially among the Jewish people, for the long-promised Messiah. Heathen empires were disintegrating. People were sick of the polytheism and emptiness of their pagan faiths. When the unusual star rose over Bethlehem, the wise men of the East, who had long been looking for answers to their yearnings and their unflagging hope, recognized it immediately and followed it to the promised Messiah ("The 400 Years between the Old and New Testaments").

According to *Halley's Bible Handbook*, p. 421, the following Old Testament prophecies in regard to the Messiah came to fruition in the New Testament. It is obvious that they relate to only one person in the history of the world. This culmination of truth in the person of Jesus is evidence of God's master plan for his son since the beginning of the world, further insight into the nature of God. See below:

> He was to be of David's family. (Matthew 22:44; Isaiah 9:6)
> He was to be born of a virgin. (Matthew 1:23; Isaiah 7:14)
> He would be born in Bethlehem. (Matthew 2:6; Micah 5:2)
> He would sojourn in Egypt.(Matthew 2:15; Hosea 11:1)
> He would live in Galilee. (Matthew 4;15; Isaiah 9:1,2) at Nazareth (Matthew 2:23; Isaiah 11:1)
> His coming would be announced by an Elijah-like herald. (Matthew 3:3; Isaiah 40:3-5)
> His coming would occasion a massacre of Bethlehem's children. (Matthew 2:18; Jeremiah 31:15)
> He would proclaim a jubilee to the world. (Luke 4:18-19; Isaiah 58:6)
> His mission would include Gentiles. (Matthew 12:18-21; Isaiah 42:1-4)
> His ministry would be one of healing. (Matthew 8:17; Isaiah 53:4)

He would teach by parables. (Matthew 13:14; Isaiah 6:9-10)
He would be disbelieved and rejected by the rulers. (Matthew 15:8; Psalms 69:4)
He would make a triumphal entry into Jerusalem. (Matthew 21:5; Isaiah 62:11)
He would be like a smitten shepherd. (Matthew 26:31; Zechariah 13:7)
He would be betrayed by a friend for thirty pieces of silver. (Matthew 27:9-10; Zechariah 11:12-13)
He would die with malefactors. (Luke 22:37; Isaiah 53:9)
He would be buried by a rich man. (Isaiah 53:9; Matthew 27:57-60)
He would be given vinegar and gall. (Matthew 27:34; Psalm 69:21)
They would cast lots for his garments. (John 19:24; Psalm 22:18)
Even his dying words were foretold. (Matthew 27:46; Psalms 22:1)
Not a bone would be broken. (John 19:36; Exodus 12:46)
His side would be pierced. (John 19:37; Zechariah 12:10)
He would rise from the dead the third day. (Matthew 12:40; Luke 24:46)
His rejection would be followed by the destruction of Jerusalem and great tribulation. (Matthew 24:15; Daniel 9:27)
He himself realized that his death would be a fulfillment of Scripture. (Matthew 26:54-56)

Chapter Six

The whole tone of the Bible and of the revealing of God's nature changed from the Old to the New Testament. Whereas God revealed himself as fearsome and vengeful throughout the Old Testament, his personhood in the flesh of Jesus is tender and loving. His entrance into life on planet earth as a human being was lowly and nondescript by standards of the world. His parents were neither wealthy nor prominent.

When the time arrived for his birth and there was no room for his mother to have her child in one of the inns in Bethlehem, his father carried his mother to a stable, where she gave birth amid the lowing of cattle and the stench of animals. God allowed himself to be born as a small, defenseless baby, as we all enter the world (Matthew 2:1-6; Luke 2: 1-7). Of course, Adam and Eve were fully grown when they were placed on the earth, but everyone else has arrived as a tiny baby, including Jesus, himself.

Not much is known about the childhood of Jesus. However, at the age of twelve, while visiting the temple in Jerusalem, Jesus astounded the great religious leaders with his knowledge of the Scriptures (Luke 2:42-49). Since the New Testament had not yet been written, he was speaking of the Old Testament. Jesus said that he had come to fulfill the Scriptures (Matthew 5:17-18).

It should be noted here that Christianity had its birth in the eastern, or Greek, part of the Roman Empire. Therefore, Greek was the language of Christianity for the first two hundred years of its existence. Whereas the Old Testament was written in Hebrew, the New Testament was first written in Greek (*Halley's,* p. 753-754).

If we closely study the genealogy of Mary and Joseph, Jesus's parents, we will see that Jesus's birth was planned from the beginning of the world and documented throughout the Scriptures (*Halley's,* p. 415), even back to Noah whose immediate family survived the great flood. Of course, Noah can be traced back to Seth who was the third son of Adam and Eve. Noah himself had three sons, but only one son, Shem, has his lineage and progeny documented in the Bible up until the time of Jesus (Matthew I:1-16; Luke 3:23-38).

To know the nature of God is to know the nature of Jesus Christ as revealed in the New Testament. Though the word "Trinity" is not found in the Bible, its meaning is manifested in John 5:7, which states:

"For there are three that bear record in heaven, the Father, the Word, and the Holy Ghost: and these three are one."

Each entity of the divine Trinity was present at the baptism of Jesus. The Father spoke, saying, "...**This is my beloved Son, in whom I am well pleased."** (Matthew 3:17) Jesus in the flesh was there, being baptized, and the Holy Spirit descended like a dove to be with him (Matthew 3:16).

For those who have difficulty envisioning God as three individual components, I suggest that they consider that man himself was created as three beings - in one body - in the very image of God. Man himself is the father; he has the seed for a separate being which is the child; and he has a soul which can be filled with the Holy Ghost. Another analogy involves the three forms of water as a solid, a liquid, and a gas, Christ symbolically being the solid; God the liquid; and the Holy Spirit the gas.

The commonly accepted knowledge of the New Testament is that the Gospel of Matthew gives Jacob's lineage, whereas the Gospel of Luke gives Mary's ancestry, showing Jesus's blood descent (*Halley's,* p. 415). The four Gospels may be viewed as ancient biographies of Jesus. Matthew was a publican or collector of Roman taxes (Matthew 9:9). We don't know Mark's occupation, but Luke was a physician (Colossians 4:14) and John a fisherman (Matthew 4:21). Matthew and John were disciples of Jesus (Matthew 10:1-4), who spent several years of their lives in his divine presence.

Though Mark was not a disciple of Jesus, he was a companion of Paul (Acts 12:25) and also of Peter who was one of Jesus's original twelve disciples (Matthew 10:1-4). Mark relied on his conversations with Peter, who told him about Jesus's three years of ministry to the world. John Mark was son of a Mary whose home was a meeting place for Jesus's disciples (Acts 12:12). Mark's mother, Mary, was an influential leader in the early church in Jerusalem (Acts 12:12). Since Luke didn't actually meet Jesus, he relied on his close associations with Paul and Mark (*Halley's,* p. 485) and James (Jesus' blood brother) and possibly even Jesus's mother, Mary, for accurate information in regard to Jesus' life and ministry (*Halley's,* p. 486).

Written around 60 A.D., some thirty years after Jesus' death and resurrection, the Book of Matthew begins the New Testament. If the Bible is the most widely read book in the whole world, then Matthew is known to be the most widely read book of the Bible (*Halley's,* p. 413). The genealogy of Jesus, as recounted in Matthew 1:1-16, is continued from that found in the first nine chapters of I Chronicles. Carefully protected through long centuries of uncertain vicissitudes, this lineage contains a "family line through which a Promise was transmitted 4,000 years ago, a fact unexampled in history." (*Halley's,* p. 415)

As earthly parents, we try to teach our children the way that we would like for them to live, in accordance with the guidance of the Lord. As a shining light revealing his true nature as our heavenly Father, whose Son has been sent to teach his will, God speaks through Jesus in the following Beatitudes, found in Matthew 5:3-12:

> **"Blessed are the poor in spirit: for theirs is the kingdom of heaven.**
> **"Blessed are they that mourn: for they shall be comforted.**
> **"Blessed are the meek: for they shall inherit the earth.**

> "Blessed are they which do hunger and thirst after righteousness: for they shall be filled.
>
> "Blessed are the merciful: for they shall obtain mercy.
>
> "Blessed are the pure in heart: for they shall see God.
>
> "Blessed are the peacemakers: for they shall be called the children of God.
>
> "Blessed are they which are persecuted for righteousness' sake: for theirs is the kingdom of heaven.
>
> "Blessed are ye when men shall revile you, and persecute you, and shall say all manner of evil against you falsely, for my sake.
>
> "Rejoice, and be exceeding glad: for great is your reward in heaven: for so persecuted they the prophets which were before you."

For three years, Jesus walked throughout the countryside, teaching and healing. He used parables as his way of teaching. A parable is a short fictitious story that illustrates a moral attitude or a religious principle.

Matthew 13:34-35 reads, **"All these things spake Jesus unto the multitude in parables; and without a parable spake he not unto them: That it might be fulfilled which was spoken by the prophet, saying, I will open my mouth in parables: I will utter things which have been kept secret from the foundation of the world."**

This is certainly an attribute of God's nature, his affinity for keeping secret what he is not ready to divulge.

The disciple John was known as one of Jesus's closest friends on earth. He is named five times as the disciple **"whom Jesus loved"** (John 13:23; 19:26; 20:2; 21:7). He is the disciple who stood at the cross during Jesus's crucifixion and the one whom Jesus asked, looking down from the cross, to care for his mother, Mary (John 19:26-27).

The Gospel of John opens with the following words which give insight into the nature of God: **"In the beginning was the Word and the Word was with God and the Word was God."** The **"Word,"** of course, is Jesus.

In John 13:4-9, we read about the humility of Jesus, another trait of the nature of God: **"He riseth from supper, and laid aside his garments; and took a towel, and girded himself. After that he poureth water into a bason, and began to wash the disciples' feet, and to wipe them, with the towel wherewith he was girded. Then cometh he to Simon Peter: and Peter saith unto him, Lord, dost thou wash my feet?**

"Jesus answered and said unto him, What I do thou knowest not now; but thou shalt know hereafter. Peter saith unto him, Thou shalt never wash my feet. Jesus answered him, If I wash thee not, thou hast no part with me. Simon Peter saith unto him, Lord, not my feet only, but also my hands and my head."

John 14:6 records that Jesus says: **"...I am the way, the truth, and the life: no man cometh unto the Father, but by me."**

(Note: This is clear to me that only by Christ can we gain entrance into the kingdom of heaven.)

In John 17:8, we read: **"For I have given unto them the words which thou gavest me..."**

In Chapter 17:14, Jesus said: **"I have given them thy word; and the world hath hated them, because they are not of the world, even as I am not of the world."**

In Chapter 17:17, Jesus prays: **"...thy word is truth."**

Isn't truth what we all yearn for and wrestle with each moment of each day? Are we truthful in our dealings with others and in the way we live our lives? In John 18:37, Pontius Pilate asks Jesus: "Art thou a king then? Jesus answers Pilate in John 18:37:

"Thou sayest that I am a king. To this end was I born, and for this cause came I into the world, that I should bear witness unto the truth. Everyone that is of the truth heareth my voice."

Then, after Jesus' words, we note the question from Pilate that has resounded throughout the ages in every beating heart: **"What is truth?"**

We who have found it now have comfort and peace of mind. We need search no longer.

* * * * * * * * * * * * *

Though the New Testament does not give us a physical description of Jesus, hundreds of icons, paintings and even coins exhibit a common quality that enables us to have an idea of Jesus's appearance. Beginning in the sixth century, artists' depictions of Jesus may have been inspired or even copied from a single source. I looked at several websites and found early descriptions of Jesus. Several were considered fraudulent, but I found some which if not totally authentic, are interesting.

The *Archko Volume,* possibly unauthoritative, contains court documents from the days of Jesus (Yeshua). It was translated by Drs. McIntosh and Twyman of the Antiquarian Lodge, Genoa, Italy, from manuscripts in Constantinople and the records of the Senatorial Docket secured from the Vatican of Rome (1896) 92-93. The description is surprising, since it depicts Jesus as having blue eyes and golden hair. Jesus's description is found in a chapter entitled "Gamaliel's Interview." It is as follows:

"I asked him to describe this person to me, so that I might know him if I should meet him. He said: 'If you ever meet him [Yeshua] you will know him. While he is nothing but a man, there is something about him that distinguishes him from every other man. He is the picture of his mother, only he has not her smooth, round face. His hair is a little more golden than hers, though it is as much from sunburn as anything else. He is tall, and his shoulders are a little drooped; his visage is thin and of a swarthy complexion, though this is from exposure. His eyes are large and a soft blue, and rather dull and heavy....' This Jew [Nazarite] is convinced that he is the Messiah of the world. ...this was the same person that was born of the virgin in Bethlehem some twenty-six years before..."

Under "Other Data," listed on this same website, I found the following information about Jesus's appearance:

"The Problem of the life passion of St. C? us, and the external appearance of Jesus possessed but minor interest for the Church Fathers, although the Catholic Acts of the Holy Apostles ascribe to him an olive complexion, a beautiful beard, and flashing eyes. Further details are first found in a letter to the Emperor Theophilus attributed to John of Damascus (in MPG, xcv.349), which speaks of the brows which grew together, the beautiful eyes, the prominent nose, the curling hair, the look of health, the black beard, the wheat-colored complexion, and the long fingers, a picture which almost coincides with a hand-book on painting from Mt. Athos not earlier than the sixteenth century. In like manner, Nicephorus Callistus, who introduced his description of the picture of Christ (MPG, cxlv. 748) with the words, 'as we have received it from the ancients,' was impressed with the healthful appearance, with the stature, the brown hair which was not very thick but somewhat curling, the black brows which were not fully arched, the sea-blue eyes shading into brown, the beautiful glance, the prominent nose, but brown beard of moderate length, and the long hair which had not been cut since childhood, the neck slightly bent, and the olive and somewhat ruddy complexion of the oval face. A slight divergence from both these accounts is shown by the so-called letter of Lentils, the ostensible predecessor of Pontius Pilate, who is said to have prepared a report to the Roman Senate concerning Jesus and containing a description of him. According to this document Christ possessed a tall and handsome figure, a countenance which inspired reverence and awakened love and fear together, dark, shining, curling hair, parted in the center in Nazarene fashion and flowing over the shoulders, an open and serene forehead, a face without wrinkle or blemish and rendered more beautiful by its delicate ruddiness, a perfect nose and mouth, a full red beard of the same color as the hair and worn in two points and piercing eyes of a grayish-blue."

Below is a reprinting of a letter from Pontius Pilate to Tiberius Caesar describing the physical traits of Jesus. Copies are in the Congressional Library in Washington, D.C.

"TO TIBERIUS CAESAR:

"A young man appeared in Galilee preaching with humble unction, a new law in the Name of the God that had sent Him. At first I was apprehensive that His design was to stir up the people against the Romans, but my fears were soon dispelled. Jesus of Nazareth spoke rather as a friend of the Romans than of the Jews.

One day I observed in the midst of a group of people a young man who was leaning against a tree, calmly addressing the multitude. I was told it was Jesus. This I could easily have suspected so great was the difference between Him and those who were listening to Him. His golden colored hair and beard gave to his appearance a celestial aspect. He appeared to be about 30 years of age. Never have I seen a sweeter or more serene countenance. What a contrast between Him and His bearers with their black beards and tawny complexions! Unwilling to interrupt Him by my presence, I continued my walk but signified to my secretary to join the group and listen. Later, my secretary reported that never had he seen in the works of all the philosophers anything that compared to the teachings of Jesus. He told me that Jesus was neither seditious nor rebellious, so we extended to Him our protection. He was at liberty to act, to speak, to assemble and to address the people. This unlimited freedom provoked the Jews–not the poor but the rich and powerful.

"Later, I wrote to Jesus requesting an interview with Him at the Praetorium. He came. When the Nazarene made His appearance I was having my morning walk and as I faced Him my feet seemed fastened with an iron hand to the marble pavement and I trembled in every limb as a guilty culprit, though he was calm. For some time I stood admiring this extraordinary Man. There was nothing in Him that was repelling, nor in His character, yet I felt awed in His presence. I told Him that there was a magnetic simplicity about Him and His personality that elevated Him far above the philosophers and teachers of His day.

"Now, Noble Sovereign, these are the facts concerning Jesus of Nazareth and I have taken the time to write you in detail concerning these matters. I say that such a man who could convert water into wine, change death into life, disease into health; calm the stormy seas, is not guilty of any criminal offense and as others have said, we must agree–truly this is the Son of God.

"Your most obedient servant,
Pontius Pilate" ("Evidence That Jesus Existed-Ecclesia.org")

As for my thoughts regarding the appearance of Jesus, I had

always pictured him like the Warner Sallman portrait, only with more olive skin. We are pretty much certain that our own family has some Jewish lineage, and I have a sister who has olive skin of the sort that I believe Jesus had.

Also, I believe Jesus would have had brown eyes, not the colors mentioned above, and I don't believe He would have had a red beard. Regardless, I'm certain He was perfect, however He looked.

* * * * * * * * * * * * *

Around A.D. 30, on the fiftieth day after Jesus's resurrection and the tenth day after his ascension into heaven, the disciples and their followers from some fifteen nations gathered together for an occurrence known as Pentecost. In Acts 2:1-21, we read of this time which is recognized today as the birthday of the church. However, I have included below only the first few verses:

"And when the day of Pentecost was fully come, they were all with one accord in one place. And suddenly there came a sound from heaven as of a rushing mighty wind, and it filled all the house where they were sitting. And there appeared unto them cloven tongues like as of fire, and it sat upon each of them. And they were all filled with the Holy Ghost, and began to speak with other tongues, as the Spirit gave them utterance. And there were dwelling at Jerusalem Jews, devout men, out of every nation under heaven. Now when this was noised abroad, the multitude came together, and were confounded, because that every man heard them speak in his own language. And they were all amazed and marveled, saying one to another, Behold, are not all these which speak Galileans? And how hear we every man in our own tongue, wherein we were born?"

Of course, this speaking and understanding all of the different languages by the assembled people is a great reversal from what occurred in the Old Testament, when the people erected the Tower of Babel and God confounded all of the languages, so that all of the languages were different, and no one could speak the languages of other nations. God even scattered people across the earth, so that they wouldn't know the languages of other nations. At Pentecost, not only could everyone speak everyone else's language, but all of the people experienced the unifying power of the Holy Ghost, when it appeared as cloven tongues of fire which sat upon each one in the room.

* * * * * * * * * * * * * *

In attempting to understand the nature of God, how many of us have wondered about people who are born blind or lame or with other defects? What is the meaning of this? In John 9:1-6, we read about a man who was born blind. When Jesus and his disciples walked by the blind man, the disciples questioned Jesus as to whether the man or his parents had sinned, resulting in the man's blindness. Below is the Scripture which explains Jesus's response:

"Jesus answered, Neither hath this man sinned, nor his parents: but that the works of God should be made manifest in him." (John 9:3)

Again, it substantiates the fact that we can't know and appreciate perfection until we witness imperfections. Jesus, of course, healed the blind man.

* * * * * * * * * * * * * *

God's nature in the New Testament is also revealed in the life and works of a man named Saul of Tarsus, whom God chose to explain and enlarge upon his son's life and teachings. Saul appeared to be an unlikely choice to promulgate the Gospel, as he is first mentioned in the Bible as a Pharisee who consented to the stoning of Stephen, the first Christian martyr. Saul in fact **"...made havock of the church, entering into every house, and haling men and women committed them to prison."** (Acts 8:3) However, when Saul left to go to Damascus to bring back more Christians for persecution, the risen Jesus himself spoke to him along the way, and Saul's whole life was changed. He was struck blind and neither ate nor drank for three days. Then, instead of arresting Christians, Paul became one of them, willing to suffer great persecutions because of his acceptance of Jesus Christ as the promised Messiah (Acts 9:1-27).

In the thirteenth chapter of Acts, verse 9, Saul's name becomes Paul, likely reflecting the change from being an unbeliever and a persecutor of Christians to becoming the greatest advocate of Jesus Christ and Christianity in the history of the world. Paul gave his life for what he knew to be the truth.

Well educated and multilingual, Paul was a tentmaker by trade (Acts 18:1-3). He made missionary journeys to many places, including Corinth, Gallacia, Ephesus, Philippi, Colossae, and Thessalonica, where he established churches. He also traveled to Rome, where he later sent a letter to the Romans. The letters which he later wrote to those churches comprise a large part of the New Testament and they further reveal God's nature. The letter which he wrote to the Romans from Corinth, in the winter of 57-58 A.D., was called by the English writer Samuel Taylor Coleridge, "The most profound work in existence." (*Halley's,* p. 584) This letter or book of the New Testament is Paul's most complete explanation of his understanding of the Gospel.

All of the verses from the Book of Romans reveal not only the wisdom and powerful belief of its author, Paul, but also the reason that this book is considered Paul's finest and that it has always been so well beloved by its readers. Some of these verses appear below:

"Who shall separate us from the love of Christ? shall tribulation, or distress, or persecution, or famine, or nakedness, or peril, or sword? As it is written, For thy sake we are killed all the day long; we are accounted as sheep for the slaughter. Nay, in all these things we are more than conquerors through him that loved us. For I am persuaded, that neither death, nor life, nor angels, nor principalities, nor powers, nor things present, nor things to come, Nor height, nor depth, nor any other creature, shall be able to separate us from the love of God, which is in Christ Jesus our Lord." (Romans 8:35-39)

* * *

"That if thou shalt confess with thy mouth the Lord Jesus, and shall believe in thine heart that God hath raised him from the dead, thou shalt be saved." (Romans 10:9)

* * *

"For whosoever shall call upon the name of the Lord shall

be saved." (Romans 10:13)

"So then faith cometh by hearing, and hearing by the word of God." (Romans 10:17)

* * *

"The night is far spent, the day is at hand: let us therefore cast off the works of darkness, and let us put on the armour of light." (Romans 13:12)

* * *

"For none of us liveth to himself, and no man dieth to himself. For whether we live, we live unto the Lord; and whether we die, we die unto the Lord: whether we live therefore, or die, we are the Lord's. For to this end Christ both died, and rose, and revived, that he might be Lord both of the dead and living. But why dost thou judge thy brother? Or why dost thou set at nought thy brother? For we shall all stand before the judgment seat of Christ. For it is written, As I live, saith the Lord, every knee shall bow to me, and every tongue shall confess to God. So then every one of us shall give account of himself to God.

"Let us not therefore judge one another any more: but judge this rather, that no man put a stumblingblock or an occasion to fall in his brother's way." (Romans 14:7-13)

* * *

"Now the God of hope fill you with all joy and peace in believing, that ye may abound in hope, through the power of the Holy Ghost. And I myself also am persuaded of you, my brethren, that ye also are full of goodness, filled with all knowledge, able also to admonish one another. Nevertheless, brethren, I have written the more boldly unto you in some sort, as putting you in mind, because of the grace that is given to me of God. That I should be the minister of Jesus Christ to the Gentiles, ministering the gospel of God, that the offering up of the Gentiles might be acceptable, being sanctified by the Holy Ghost." (Romans 15:13-16)

William Tyndale, the great English reformer and translator, referred to the Book of Romans as "the principle and most excellent part of the New Testament." He went on to say the following in his prologue to Romans that he wrote in the 1534 edition of the English New Testament: "No man verily can read it too oft or study it too well; for the more it is chewed the pleasanter it is, and the more groundly [sic] it is searched the preciouser [sic] things are found in it, so great treasures of spiritual things lieth hid therein." ("Tyndale's Prologue to the Epistle of Paul to the Romans")

Martin Luther, the eminent and courageous leader of the Protestant Reformation, wrote the following commendation of this epistle: "[Romans] is worthy not only that every Christian should know it word for word, by heart, but occupy himself with it every day, as the daily bread of the soul. It can never be read or pondered too much, and the more it is dealt with the more precious it becomes, and the better it tastes." ("A Gospel, Unashamed–Downline Ministries")

* * * * * * * * * * * * * *

In the Book of I Corinthians 12:7-10, written to the church which Paul established in Corinth, he lists the gifts of the Spirit, which include wisdom, knowledge, faith, healings, miracles, prophecy, spirits, tongues, and interpretation of tongues. Also, in I Corinthians13 is the beautifully written chapter on love, which ends with these words (verses 12-13): **"For now we see through a glass darkly; but then face to face: now I know in part; but then shall I know even as also I am known. And now abideth faith, hope, charity, these three; but the greatest of these is charity."** (also translated as "love")

Paul also states in I Corinthians 15:6 that after Christ's crucifixion, he was seen alive by above "...**five hundred brethren at once**...." Deploring his earlier persecution of Christians, Paul states in I Corinthians 15:9, **"For I am the least of the apostles, that am not meet to be called an apostle, because I persecuted the church of God."** This terrible compunction and regret on the part of Paul are evident in all of his writings.

The nature of God is further revealed in the words of Paul in his letter to the Galatians, when he speaks about the **"...works of the flesh..."** in Galatians 5:19-21, which are: **"...Adultery, fornication,** uncleanness, lasciviousness, idolatry, witchcraft, hatred, variance, emulations, wrath, strife, seditions, heresies, envyings, murders, drunkenness, revellings, and such like: of the which I tell you before, as I have also told you in time past, that they which do such things shall not inherit the kingdom of God."

After this, he speaks of the "...**fruit of the Spirit...,**" which includes: "**...love, joy, peace, longsuffering, gentleness, goodness, faith, meekness, temperance...**" Gallatians 5:22-23)

In Ephesians, written to the church at Ephesus, Paul speaks of the universal church, not just a church for the Jews but also for Gentiles (Ephesians 3:6-8). Chapter 11 of the Book of Romans enlarges upon this. Since the Jews had, in essence, rejected Christ, Paul feels it is his mission to bring the Gospel to the Gentiles. This describes the all-inclusive nature of God. Salvation is open to all of mankind, regardless of one's standing in the world, whether one is a Jew or a Gentile, master or slave. However, Paul does say in Romans 11:1-36 that Israel's rejection of Christ is temporary, as he explains in verses 25-27 of this same chapter:

"**For I would not, brethren, that ye should be ignorant of this mystery, lest ye should be wise in your own conceits, that blindness in part is happened to Israel, until the fulness of the Gentiles be come in. And so all Israel shall be saved: as it is written, There shall come out of Sion the Deliverer, and shall turn away ungodliness from Jacob: For this is my covenant with them, when I shall take away their sins.**"

Paul also plainly states in Ephesians 1:22-23 that the church is Christ's body. Knowing that Christians will be faced with insurmountable temptations and persecutions, Paul exhorts the Ephesians in Chapter 6, verses 11-19, of which I have included the verses that follow:

"**Put on the whole armor of God that ye may be able to stand against the wiles of the devil. For we wrestle not against flesh and blood, but against principalities, against powers, against the rulers of the darkness of this world, against spiritual wickedness in high places. Wherefore take unto you the whole armor of God, that ye may be able to withstand in the evil day,** and having done all, to stand."

In Philippians 4:8, written to the church established by Paul at Philippi, Paul expresses his understanding of the Gospel in another way when he writes, **"Finally, brethren, whatsoever things are true, whatsoever things are honest, whatsoever things are just, whatsoever things are pure, whatsoever things are lovely, whatsoever things are of good report; if there be any virtue, and if there be any praise, think on these things."**

Paul's two letters to the Thessalonian Christians at Thessalonica are generally regarded as among the earliest written New Testament books (*Halley's,* p. 627). In these letters he is consumed with Jesus's return to the earth, which he claims will be sudden and unexpected (*Halley's,* p. 628). His letters are also words of comfort for his fellow Christians who were suffering terrible persecutions, even death (*Halley's,* p. 626). He exhorts his people, who only a short while earlier were worshiping idols, to **"...serve the living and true God..."** (I Thessalonians 1:9).

In I Thessalonians 4:16-18, Paul describes the way that Jesus will return to the earth: **"For the Lord himself shall descend from heaven with a shout, with the voice of the archangel, and with the trump of God: and the dead in Christ shall rise first: Then we which are alive and remain shall be caught up together with them in the clouds, to meet the Lord in the air: and so shall we ever be with the Lord. Wherefore comfort one another with these words."**

He also states in Chapter 5:2 that the **"...day of the Lord so cometh as a thief in the night."**

In verse 23 of the same chapter, he exhorts Christians at Thessalonica to be **"...blameless unto the coming of our Lord Jesus Christ,"** by living according to the following precepts in I Thessalonians 5:16-22: **"Rejoice evermore. Pray without ceasing. In everything give thanks: for this is the will of God in Christ Jesus concerning you. Quench not the Spirit. Despise not prophesyings. Prove all things; hold fast that which is good. Abstain from all appearance of evil."**

* * * * * * * * * * * * * *

Paul wrote two letters to a young man named Timothy who became the first bishop of the Ephesus church (*Halley's*, p. 631-632). Timothy accompanied Paul on his second missionary journey (*Halley's*, p. 574). He was a close friend and convert of Paul, whom Paul called his **"...dearly beloved son..."** (II Timothy I:2) Though often used interchangeably, the designations of "bishop" and "deacon" ("Difference Between Deacons and Elders/Difference Between") as officers in the fledgling churches, are not the same. The Greek word for bishop, or elder, is "episkope," while the Greek word for the one who holds the office is "episkopos."

"A bishop is the superintendent or officer in general charge or the overseer of the congregation. Our English word "episcopal" means "governed by bishops." (Episcopal dictionary definition/ episcopal defined–YourDictionary)

A deacon is one who serves others, especially those in a local church congregation. The word "serve" in Greek is "diakonos," which derives from a word that means an attendant, a waiter, or one who ministers to another. From this word comes the word "deacon."

The earliest Christians felt the need to create the offices of bishop and deacon, as recorded in Acts 6:1-6, when they realized they were unable to promote the word of God effectively, because of everyday responsibilities that sapped their time and energy. This is when they searched for **"seven men of honest report, full of the Holy Ghost and wisdom, whom we may appoint over this business."** These men actually became the first officers of the fledgling church.

God's nature is evident in the qualifications of bishops, or elders, and deacons of the churches which Paul had founded, as they appear in I Timothy 3:2-15. Below are some of these verses: **"A bishop then must be blameless, the husband of one wife, vigilant, sober, of good behaviour, given to hospitality, apt to teach; Not given to wine, no striker, not greedy of filthy lucre; but patient, not a brawler, not covetous; One that ruleth well his own house,** having his children in subjection with all gravity;

"For if a man know not how to rule his own house, how shall he take care of the church of God? Even so must their wives be grave, not slanderers, sober, faithful in all things.

"Let the deacons be the husbands of one wife, ruling their children and their own houses well. For they that have used the office of a deacon well purchase to themselves a good degree, and great boldness in the faith which is in Christ Jesus.

"These things write I unto thee, hoping to come unto thee shortly; But if I tarry long, that thou mayest know how thou oughtest to behave thyself in the house of God, which is the church of the living God, the pillar and ground of the truth."

In Paul's second letter to Timothy 3:1-5, he wrote to Timothy about the "**last days**" of time, when he penned the following words: "**This know also that in the last days perilous times shall come, For men shall be lovers of their own selves, covetous, boasters, proud, blasphemers, disobedient to parents, unthankful, unholy, Without natural affection, truce-breakers, false accusers, incontinent, fierce, despisers of those that are good, Traitors, heady, highminded, lovers of pleasures more than lovers of God; Having a form of godliness, but denying the power thereof: from such turn away.**"

In the same chapter of this letter, verse 12, Paul also writes,

"**Yea, and all that will live godly in Christ Jesus shall suffer persecution.**"

God's nature is further revealed in verses 16-17 of this chapter, which states: "**All Scripture is given by inspiration of God, and is profitable for doctrine, for reproof, for correction, for instruction in righteousness: That the man of God may be perfect, throughly furnished unto all good works.**"

In Paul's letter to the Hebrews, chapter 4, verse 12, we gain more insight into the nature of God, when he writes: "**For the word of God is quick and powerful, and sharper than any twoedged sword, piercing even to the dividing asunder of soul and spirit, and of the joints and marrow, and is a discerner of the thoughts** and intents of the heart."

In the chapter 6:18, Paul writes that it is **"impossible for God to lie."** In Hebrews 9:15-28, Paul speaks of Christ and his nature, and I included a few of these verses: **"And for this cause he is the mediator of the new testament, that by means of death, for the redemption of the transgressions that were under the first testament, they which are called might receive the promise of eternal inheritance. For where a testament is, there must also of necessity be the death of the testator. For a testament is of force after men are dead: otherwise it is of no strength at all while the testator liveth."**

When Paul speaks of Christ being the **"mediator of the new testament**," this distinguishes the two divisions of the Bible - the Old Testament and the New Testament. The Old Testament was based on laws written on stone tablets, whereas Christ's teachings are written not only in the New Testament but also on our hearts (II Corinthians 3:3 and *Halley's,* p. 603). Whereas the Jews of the Old Testament offered blood sacrifices of bulls and goats, Christ gave his body as the final sacrifice (Hebrews 9:11-16).

In chapter 10 of the Book of Hebrews, verse 31, Paul writes:**"It is a fearful thing to fall into the hands of the living God."** Here again, we read of the association of fear with the nature of God.

In Hebrews 11, verse 1, Paul writes: **"Now faith is the substance of things hoped for, the evidence of things not seen."** Isn't this the perfect definition of faith?

In this same chapter he names many of the great people of the Old Testament who had remained true to their faith in spite of terrible adversities, from Abel to Zechariah. In Hebrews 11:32-37, he recounts the trials and tribulations of these early believers and their staunch faith:

"And what shall I more say? for the time would fail me to tell you of Gideon, and of Barak, and of Samson, and of Jephthae; of David also, and Samuel, and of the prophets: Who through faith subdued kingdoms, wrought righteousness, obtained promises, stopped the mouths of lions, Quenched the

violence of fire, escaped the edge of the sword, out of weakness were made strong, waxed valiant in fight, turned to flight the armies of the aliens. Women received their dead raised to life again: and others were tortured, not accepting deliverance; that they might obtain a better resurrection:

"And others had trial of cruel mockings and scourgings, yea, moreover of bonds and imprisonment: They were stoned, they were sawn asunder, were tempted, were slain with the sword: they wandered about in sheepskins and goatskins; being destitute, afflicted, tormented...."

After the close of Paul's letters in the New Testament, the short epistle of James appears. Though two disciples were named James, one the brother of John and son of Zebedee and the other the son of Alphaeus, this epistle was written by James, the oldest brother of Jesus. Though Jesus was his parents' first-born, he had brothers and sisters, as recorded in Matthew 13:55-56:

"Is not this the carpenter's son? Is not his mother called Mary? And his brethren, James, and Joses, and Simon, and Judas? And his sisters, are they not all with us?"

Also, in Mark 6:3, we read the following in regard to other siblings of Jesus: **"Is not this the carpenter, the son of Mary, the brother of James, and Joses, and of Juda, and Simon? and are not his sisters here with us?"**

This also offers more understanding of the nature of God, in that two of Jesus' blood brothers, James and Jude, believed that he was the Son of God!

James was an uncommonly good man and the leading overseer of the Judaean Church, as recounted by the historians, Josephus, Hegesippus, Eusebius, and the modern-day H. H. Halley. According to *Halley's*, James suffered death as a Christian martyr during the mid-60s, when the Sanhedrin (supreme council of the Jews) assembled and commanded James, "the brother of Jesus who was called Christ," to proclaim from one of the galleries of the Temple that Jesus was not the Messiah. Instead, James shouted that Jesus was the Son of God and judge of the world. As his enraged enemies stoned him to death, he uttered the same words that Jesus spoke from the cross: **"Father, forgive them, they know not what they do."** (*Halley's,* p. 657)

James defines religion in the following words (James 1:27): **"Pure religion and undefiled before God and the Father is this, To visit the fatherless and widows in their affliction, and to keep himself unspotted from the world."**

Being a widow, myself, I can especially appreciate and relate to the above verse.

He also speaks of the tongue in the following manner in James:3:8-10: **"But the tongue can no man tame; it is an unruly evil, full of deadly poison. Therewith bless we God, even the Father; and therewith curse we men, which are made after the similitude of God. Out of the same mouth proceedeth blessing and cursing. My brethren, these things ought not so to be."**

The disciple Peter wrote two epistles in the New Testament. Referred to as **"this rock"** by Jesus in Matthew 16:18, Peter was considered a leader of the twelve disciples. His letters were written to the churches in Asia Minor which had been founded by Paul and which were undergoing terrible persecutions (*Halley's*, p. 662).

The church, being only about thirty-five years old and being blamed by the Emperor Nero of Rome for the fire which nearly destroyed Rome in 64 A.D., was undergoing horrifying persecution by Nero and Imperial Rome (*Halley's*, p. 662-663). The Roman historian Tacitus who witnessed these persecutions, because of the fire in Rome, ultimately wrote about these in his book *Annals* 15, 44, which was published a few years after the events. In telling about the fates of these early Christians, Tacitus wrote:

"But all human efforts, all the lavish gifts of the emperor, and the propitiations of the gods, did not banish the sinister belief that the conflagration was the result of an order. Consequently, to get rid of the report, Nero fastened the guilt and inflicted the most exquisite tortures on a class hated for their abominations, called Christians by the populace. Christus, from whom the name had its origin, suffered the extreme penalty during the reign of Tiberius at the hands of one of our procurators, Pontius Pilatus, and a most mischievous superstition, thus checked for the moment, again broke out not only in Judaea, the first source of the evil, but even in Rome, where all things hideous and shameful from every part of the world find their centre and become popular.

"Accordingly, an arrest was first made of all who pleaded guilty; then, upon their information, an immense multitude was convicted, not so much of the crime of firing the city as of hatred against mankind. Mockery of every sort was added to their deaths. Covered with the skins of beasts, they were torn by dogs and perished, or were nailed to crosses, or were doomed to the flames and burnt, to serve as a nightly illumination when daylight had expired. Nero offered his gardens for the spectacle, and was exhibiting a show in the circus while he mingled with the people in the dress of a charioteer or stood aloft on a car. Hence, even for criminals who deserved extreme and exemplary punishment, there arose a feeling of compassion, for it was not, as it seemed, for the public good but rather to glut the cruelty of one man that they were being destroyed." ("Cornelius Tacitus–Early Christian Writings")

In an attempt to strengthen and comfort these Christians, Peter wrote in his first epistle, Chapter 3:14: **"But and if ye suffer for righteousness' sake, happy are ye: and be not afraid of their terror, neither be troubled...."**

In Chapter 4:12, he wrote:**"Beloved, think it not strange concerning the fiery trial which is to try you, as though some strange thing happened to you...."**

In Chapter 5:8, he wrote: **"Be sober, be vigilant; because your adversary the devil, as a roaring lion, walketh about, seeking whom he may devour..."**

In his second epistle, written around six years later, just before his own impending martyrdom, Peter again wrote to strengthen the faith of those Christians who were suffering persecutions and martyrdom. During his three years of daily association with Jesus, Peter had seen with his own eyes the miracles of Jesus. He had seen him heal multitudes of sick people (Matthew 4:24-25). He had seen him walk on water (Mark 6:48) and still a menacing storm (Luke 8:22-25). He had seen him transfigured, with Moses and Elijah from the Old Testament Scriptures appearing on either side of him (Matthew 17:1-8). He had seen Jesus raising people from the dead (Luke 8:41-56). After Jesus' crucifixion, Peter saw him alive (John 21:1-12). The following words in II Peter 1:16-21 bear testament to Peter's unshakable faith. I am including the first three verses below:

"For we have not followed cunningly devised fables, when we made known unto you the power and coming of our Lord Jesus Christ, but were eyewitnesses of his majesty. For he received from God the Father honour and glory, when there came such a voice to him from the excellent glory, This is my beloved Son, in whom I am well pleased. And this voice which came from heaven we heard, when we were with him in the holy mount."

To quell the naysayers about the time element in regard to God's timetable for his plans in regard to mankind and to give us more insight into the nature of God, Peter states in II Peter:3:8: **"But, beloved, be not ignorant of this one thing, that one day is with the Lord as a thousand years, and a thousand years as one day."**

In the same chapter, verses 10-14, he writes: **"But the day of the Lord will come as a thief in the night, in the which the heavens shall pass away with a great noise, and the elements shall melt with fervent heat, the earth also and the works that are therein shall be burned up. Seeing then that all these things shall be dissolved, what manner of persons ought ye to be in all holy conversation and godliness, Looking for and hasting unto the coming of the day of God, wherein the heavens being on fire shall be dissolved, and the elements shall melt with fervent heat?**

"Nevertheless we, according to his promise, look for new heavens and a new earth, wherein dwelleth righteousness. Wherefore, beloved, seeing that ye look for such things, be diligent that ye may be found of him in peace, without spot, and

blameless."

* * * * * * * * * * * * * * *

According to well-regarded tradition, after the destruction of Jerusalem by the Roman army of Titus in 70 A.D., the disciple John resided at Ephesus, which had become the hub of Christian population. Here he lived to great age and wrote his Gospel, his Three Epistles, and the Book of Revelation.

In John's first Epistle, he opens his letter with these words: **"That which we from the beginning, which we have heard, which we have seen with our eyes, which we have looked upon, and our hands have handled, of the word of life; For the life was manifested, and we have seen it, and bear witness, and shew unto you that eternal life, which was with the Father, and was manifested unto us..."**

Can we even imagine what it must have been like to have lived when Jesus lived? How blessed were those disciples who saw him, heard him, touched him, walked with him, and even ate with him! Here again, in John's own writing, he refers to the "word" of life. Remember, Jesus is the **"Word."** He is the embodiment of God's nature. In fact, in the Gospel of John 10:30, Jesus said, **"I and my Father are one."**

Only in John's first two epistles is the word **"antichrist"** mentioned. It occurs nowhere else in the Scriptures. John uses the word in reference to any of a group of anti-Christian teachers (2:18; 4:3), but the gist of his writing is that the spirit of antichrist would manifest itself in many ways, finally culminating toward the end of the Christian era in one person or an institution or both (*Halley's,* p. 673).

John writes in his first epistle, Chapter 4:2-3: **"Hereby know ye the Spirit of God: Every spirit that confesseth that Jesus Christ is come in the flesh is of God: And every spirit that confesseth not that Jesus Christ is come in the flesh is not of God: and this is that spirit of antichrist, whereof ye have heard that it should come; and even now already is it in the world. Ye are of God, little children, and have overcome them: because greater is he that is in you, than he that is in the world."**

In verse 7, he writes: **"Beloved, let us love one another for love is of God; and everyone that loveth is born of God, and knoweth God. He that loveth not knoweth not God; for God is love."**

John also writes in verses 20-21 of the same chapter: **"If a man say, I love God, and hateth his brother, he is a liar: for he that loveth not his brother whom he hath seen, how can he love God, whom he hath not seen? And this commandment have we from him, That he who loveth God love his brother also."**

Chapter Seven

The last book of the Bible, The Revelation, was written by St. John "the Divine" around 96 A.D (Revelation I:9). The quotes around "the Divine" are my own, added because none of the other Gospel writers had these words added to their names. Indeed, none of the writers of any of the books of the Bible had these words after their names.

Perhaps they augment the fact that God himself is the author who used the disciple John as the vessel to write his words with totality and irrefutability. John had been banished to the Isle of Patmos during the persecution of the Roman emperor, Domitian, around 95 A.D. Upon his return to Ephesus, he wrote God's Revelation (*Halley's*, p. 683-684).

God, through John, first greets the seven churches of Ephesus, Smyrna, Pergamos, Thyatira, Sardis, Philadelphia, and Laodicia, all of which were in Asia. Then, he proceeds to speak to the angels of each church, describing the churches as good, bad, and lukewarm. Two of the churches, Smyrna and Philadelphia, are determined by God to be good churches. Two other churches, Sardis and Laodicia, are characterized as bad churches, and the other three churches are said to be lukewarm (Revelation 2-3). God says he even knows where Satan's seat is in the Pergamos church (Revelation 2:13).

To the angel of the church of Laodicia, God writes in Revelation 3:15-16:

"I know thy works, that they are neither cold nor hot: I would thou wert cold or hot. So then because thou art lukewarm, and neither cold nor hot, I will spew thee out of my mouth."

Surely, the messages to these ancient churches are just as true today as they were then, for we have the same problems and shortcomings in our modern-day churches as they had in the early churches. The sins that John wrote about, that were rampant in the early church, such as fornication, false teachers, idol worship, and heathen practices can be found in many of today's twenty-first century churches.

John uses many numbers and colors to make known God's revelation, including especially the number "seven" and the color "white" (or lack of color). The Bible begins with seven days of creation and ends with a book of sevens involving the final destiny of God's creation. The Seven Beatitudes of Revelation include the following:

"Blessed is he that readeth, and they that hear the words of this prophecy..." (1:3)

"Blessed are the dead which die in the Lord..." (14:13)

"Blessed is he that watcheth..." [for the Lord's coming] (16:15)

"Blessed are those called unto the marriage supper of the Lamb." (19:9)

"Blessed and holy is he that has part in the first resurrection:..." (20:6)

"Blessed is he that keeps the sayings of the prophecy of this book." (22:7)

"Blessed are they that do his commandments, that they may have right to the tree of life, and may enter in through the gates into the city." (22:14)

The eternity of God's being is a major emphasis of Revelation. Below are the passages that reveal this part of God's nature. What a comfort these words must have been to the early Christians who were facing martyrdom, as they are to us today!

"...I am the first and the last: I am he that liveth, and was dead; and, behold, I am alive forevermore, Amen; and have the keys of hell and of death." (1:17; 18) **"...Lord God Almighty,**

which was, and is, and is to come." (4:8) "...Him that liveth forever and ever..." (4:10)

"I am Alpha and Omega, the beginning and the end, the first and the last." (22:13)

The color **white** (or the lack of color) is often mentioned in connection with heaven. We who overcome will be dressed in **white** (Rev. 3:5). Robes were made **white** (symbolically sinless) by the blood of the Lamb. Jesus, of course, is the Lamb. Jesus's garments at his Transfiguration were **white.**

Halley's Bible Handbook lists some Bible verses which mention "**white**," in keeping with Jesus and sinlessness and heaven. All are from the Book of Revelation. They are the following:

Jesus' head and hair, in the vision (I:14), were "**white**" as wool and snow.
He that overcomes shall be arrayed in "**white**" raiment (3:5).
Heaven's citizens will be clothed in "**white**" (3:18).
The 24 elders were arrayed in "**white**" (4:4).
The martyrs wore "**white**" robes (6:11).
Redeemed multitudes were arrayed in "**white**" robes (7:9).
Robes were made "**white**" in the blood of the Lamb (7:14).
The Lord will come on a "**white**" horse (19:11).
His armies, clothed in "**white**" linen, will be on "**white**" horses, clothed in fine "**white**" linen (18:14).

In Rev. 3:20, we read about Christ standing outside his church and knocking on the door, asking to be let in. This is likely true of many modern-day churches which effectively keep Christ out of their church services. This again demonstrates God's humbleness in knocking on his own church door.

The first part of Chapter Seven of Revelation focuses on the "sealing" of 144,000 people from the twelve tribes of Israel, with 12,000 from each tribe being included. This stresses the fact that God will always protect Israel. You may remember reading in Romans 11:26:

"And so all Israel shall be saved: as it is written, There shall come out of Sion the Deliverer, and shall turn away ungodliness

from Jacob." (Remember that Jacob's name was changed to Israel by God.)

The latter part of this chapter (Revelation 7:9) speaks of the **"great multitude which no one could number, of all nations, and kindreds, and peoples, and tongues,"** who stand before Jesus, clothed in white robes. These had come out of the "**great tribulation**" (verse 14). God says in verses 16 and 17: **"They shall hunger no more, neither thirst anymore; neither shall the sun light on them, nor any heat. For the Lamb which is in the midst of the throne shall feed them, and shall lead them unto living fountains of waters: and God shall wipe away all tears from their eyes."**

How beautiful and comforting these words are, exemplifying the compassion and love of God.

In Chapter Ten, John writes at God's command that **"...there should be time no longer..."** (verse 6). and **"...the mystery of God should be finished..."** (verse 7). Can we even begin to imagine living in a world where time no longer exists? Can we imagine how we might understand the "**mystery**" of God? This book is an attempt to learn, if only a tiny bit, of the nature - and thereby the mystery - of God.

* * * * * * * * * * * * * *

God's nature induced him to allow animals to assume human attributes in the Bible. In Genesis 3:1-24, the entire chapter, the serpent beguiled Eve into eating of the tree of knowledge of good and evil, which God had forbidden her to do. The serpent may have stood upright in the beginning of human life, as the Bible verse below implies. It could also speak, as it talked to Eve, insisting that she eat of the forbidden fruit of the tree. Because of its disobedience, God told the serpent that it was cursed above all cattle and every beast of the field. God further stated in verse 14: **"...upon thy belly thou shalt go, and dust shalt thou eat all the days of thy life: And I will put enmity between thee and the woman, and between thy seed and her seed; it shall bruise thy head, and thou shalt bruise his heel."**

Another instance of an animal exhibiting human qualities

occurred in the entire chapter of Numbers 22, as the Israelites continued their exodus from Egypt toward the promised land. Balak, king of the Moabites, feared the Israelites as they approached his land. He sent word to Balaam, a Gentile prophet or soothsayer, that he wanted Balaam to curse the Jewish people who threatened to overrun the king's land. God gave Balaam the words to speak, but instead of a curse, his words were a blessing for the Israelites.

When Balaam saddled his donkey to go with the Moabite princes, this angered God to the extent that he sent an angel to stand in the donkey's path. Balaam could not see the angel, and as the donkey tried to turn aside, away from the angel, Balaam struck the animal repeatedly with his staff in an attempt to keep the donkey on a straight path.

The donkey finally fell down under Balaam who became angry and whipped the animal again. At this point, God opened the mouth of the donkey and she said unto Balaam: **"What have I done unto thee, that thou hast smitten me these three times?"**

The donkey continued, in verse 30: **"Am I not thine ass, upon which thou hast ridden ever since I was thine unto this day? Was I ever wont to do so unto thee?"**

The Lord opened Balaam's eyes and he saw the angel of God standing in the pathway, his sword drawn in his hand. Balaam bowed his head and fell flat on his face before God (verse 31). This is a mystery that the donkey could see the angel, but Balaam could not.

Of course, the entire Book of Jonah tells of God's using a **"great fish"** to swallow the prophet, when he is cast into the sea. The Bible does not say what type of fish it was, but it was likely a whale. Jonah 2:10 reads: **"And the Lord spake unto the fish, and it vomited out Jonah upon the dry land."**

In 1 Kings 17:4-6, God commanded ravens to bring the prophet Elijah bread and flesh in the morning and bread and flesh in the evening. This occurred when God told Elijah to flee from the wicked King Ahab and to live by the brook Cherith. He was to drink water from the brook and to eat food which the ravens brought.

It is possible, even very likely, that God used the lowly mouse to rout the Assyrian army of Sennacherib (II Kings 19:35-36), in 701 B.C., when that king and his mighty army were at the very gates of Jerusalem. The Bible states that 185,000 men of his army were suddenly slain, and the city of Jerusalem was saved.

Herodotus, the Greek historian who lived several hundred years after the event, recorded that God sent thousands of mice into the camp, which gnawed through the bow-strings, the quivers, and the shields of the Assyrians, rendering the army helpless. It's possible, also, that the mice brought the plague to the enemy army, thus killing that many men ("Sennacherib's hexagonal Prism–Biblical Archaeology in Ancient..."). It's also recorded in the Bible, in I Samuel (5:6- 6:5), that God "smote" the idolatrous people of Ashdod with plagues, including painful hemorrhoids and a terrible visitation of field mice. God indeed moves and works in mysterious ways, often using animals to fulfill his purposes.

A modern-day wonder in regard to almost all of the books of the Old Testament occurred in 1947 near the northwestern shore of the Dead Sea in Qumran Valley in Palestine (*The World Book* "D," p. 56) when some wandering Arab Bedouins, searching for a lost goat, came upon a partially collapsed cave, in which were a number of large clay jars with protruding scrolls. One of these scrolls was identified as the Book of Isaiah, written 2,000 years ago, a thousand years older than any known Hebrew Old Testament book ("The Dead Sea Scrolls–Discovery and Publication"). This is especially remarkable when one considers that a lowly goat led to this discovery. This is another characteristic of God's nature – his use of ordinary creatures to bring about extraordinary events. Also, the age of miracles is not past.

* * * * * * * * * * * * * *

God's nature in the New Testament is further exemplified in the lowly creatures that represented certain characteristics of his divinity. The dove, the lamb, and the lion all symbolized these facets of God's nature. At Jesus's baptism, recorded in John I:32, John the Baptist said, **"...I saw the Spirit descending from heaven like a dove, and it abode upon him."** The dove represented gentleness, peacefulness, and rest. In Genesis 8:8-12, Noah sent forth a dove which finally found a resting place to perch. Again, the dove symbolized rest. Oh, how we all long to rest! Psalm 55:6 expresses this beautifully, as we read: **"And I said, Oh that I had wings like a dove! For then would I fly away, and be at rest."**

Sometimes, we like David yearn to fly away and be at rest. We feel just as David felt several thousand years ago!

Much can be said about the need to rest. Have you ever been bone-tired, exhausted to the point that you long to lie down and rest? When your body is in such a weary state, rest supercedes hunger and every other need of the body. Not only the body but also the mind needs rest.

God himself needed or wanted to rest, as noted in Genesis 2:2: **"And on the seventh day God ended his work which he had made; and he rested on the seventh day from all the work which he had made."**

God also tells us to rest in Exodus 23:12: **"Six days thou shalt do thy work, and on the seventh day thou shalt rest: that thine ox and thine ass may rest, and the son of thy handmaid, and the stranger, may be refreshed."**

Jesus is referred to as the Lamb of God many times in the Bible, for he exhibited many traits of the lamb in his absolute refusal to fight back or in any way resist the evil that ultimately resulted in his death. As the lamb is utterly dependent upon the shepherd for his protection, so Jesus totally relied on his Father. As the Scripture from Isaiah 53:7 states: **"He was oppressed, and he was afflicted, yet he opened not his mouth: he is brought as a lamb to the slaughter, and as a sheep before her shearers is dumb, so he openeth not his mouth."**

John the Baptist said in John 1:29: **"...Behold the Lamb of God, which taketh away the sin of the world."**

In Revelation 13:8, Jesus is referred to as the **"...Lamb slain from the foundation of the world."** In other words, Christ was the sacrificial Lamb whose mission was to give his life for the world.

Another animal whose characteristics Jesus inculcated is the majestic lion. Jesus's lineage derives from Judah who was the fourth son of Jacob (Genesis 49:9). When Jacob blessed his twelve sons, he gave Judah in part the following blessing: **"Judah is a lion's whelp: from the prey, my son, thou art gone up: he stooped down, he couched as a lion, and as an old lion; who shall rouse him up?"**

In Revelation 5:5, a scene in heaven unfolds before the throne of God. A book remains sealed, as no man or angel or any other creature is worthy of opening it. The disciple John who wrote Revelation weeps at first because no one is worthy of opening the book, but he is comforted when the **Lion of Judah** comes forth to open the book. The **"Lion of Judah**," of course, is Jesus. He has conquered death.

Jesus is now the conqueror who has risen from the dead. He is strong like a lion. He allowed himself to be put to death on the cross, but he rose from the dead and now is in heaven with the Father. This is where we all aspire to be, as Christians, when we leave this earthly life.

Chapter Eight

Perhaps the most difficult part of God's nature to perceive and to attempt to understand is the Holy Spirit. The opening words of the Bible in the Book of Genesis (verse 2) mention the **"...Spirit of God"** which **"moved upon the face of the waters."** Dear Reader, before you read further in this book, please know that I can attest to the presence and the power of the Holy Spirit, for I have known both its absence and its presence. Perhaps I should say "His absence" and "His presence," for the Bible uses the masculine pronoun "He" in reference to the Holy Spirit. The indwelling of the Holy Spirit not only comforts but it also allows one to face and handle life's storms and battles with equanimity, knowing that He who indwells you will help you!

The Holy Spirit moved in a different way in the Old Testament, as opposed to the New Testament, for in the Old Testament, it **"came upon"** certain people such as Othniel (Judges 3:9-10), Gideon (Judges 6:34), Samson (Judges 14:5-6), David (I Samuel 16:13), and others. The prophet Joel, speaking the words of God in Joel 2:28, said, **"...I will pour out my spirit upon all flesh."** This pouring out was prophetic, in that it happened during New Testament times. "Coming upon" and "pouring out" are very different. This "pouring out" of the Holy Spirit occurred in the New Testament at Pentecost, some fifty days after Jesus's resurrection, as recorded in Acts 2:1-21. This was the beginning of the Christian Church. A Scripture that probably many people have overlooked in their reading of the Bible is found in Matthew 12:31, when Jesus says:

"Wherefore I say unto you, All manner of sin and blasphemy shall be forgiven unto men: but the blasphemy against the Holy Ghost shall not be forgiven unto men."

Also, in Mark 3:29, Jesus says: **"But he that shall blaspheme against the Holy Ghost hath never forgiveness, but is in danger of eternal damnation."**

In John 4:24, Jesus says: **"God is a Spirit: and they that worship him must worship him in spirit and in truth."**

* * * * * * * * * * * * * *

Dear Reader, do you think often about your soul and your existence on earth? In Genesis 2:7, we read: **"And the Lord God formed man of the dust of the ground, and breathed into his nostrils the breath of life; and man became a living soul."**

From this, we infer that the soul is God's breath. It is this part of the Trinity that gives us a direct line to God the Father. We cannot see Jesus or God, but we can commune with them through our soul which can be filled with the Holy Spirit, if we accept Jesus as our Lord and Savior.

Do you realize that God has a soul? In Leviticus 26:11, we read a verse which expressly states that the Lord also has a soul. It records as follows: **"And I will set my tabernacle among you: and my soul shall not abhor you."**

It is our soul that allows us to communicate with others. It is what exists in us that proves we are alive. How often have we viewed a corpse, half expecting a flicker of an eyelid or a twitch of an arm or leg, only to note the flat absence of life – no movement at all – nothing. Where is the spark of life, the movement that we want to see - the rise and fall of breathing? The body is dead, the soul having left it. In Ecclesiastes 12:7, in his writing about death, Solomon intones: **"Then shall the dust return to the earth as it was: and the spirit shall return unto God who gave it."**

As I understand it, the spirit and the soul are the same, but the Holy Spirit, or Holy Ghost, is different. It can inhabit the spirit so that the spirit of a professing Christian becomes closer to God and allows the person whom it indwells to be stronger in the face of adversity. Also, the Holy Ghost and the Holy Spirit are capitalized in the Bible.

According to I Timothy 4:1, **"...the Spirit speaketh expressly..."** In Revelation 2:7, we read: **"He that hath an ear, let him hear what the Spirit saith unto the churches."** The Holy Spirit also teaches, as recorded in Luke 12:12: **"For the Holy Ghost shall teach you in the same hour what ye ought to say."** As proof that the Holy Spirit commands authority, we read in Acts 13:2: **"...the Holy Ghost said, Separate unto me Barnabas and Saul for the work whereunto I have called them."**

As a Christian, have you ever felt bereft of the Holy Spirit? Probably all of us who profess to being Christians have at times felt that we were not filled with this wonderful Spirit of Truth and Comfort. What we need to do when our spirit is low and empty is to pray that we will be filled with the Holy Spirit. Yes, Jesus himself referred to the Holy Spirit as the **"Comforter"** (John15:26).

In John 14:16, Christ says: **"And I will pray the Father, and he shall give you another Comforter, that he may abide with you forever."**

In John 14:26, we read: **"But the Comforter, which is the Holy Ghost, whom the Father will send in My name, He shall teach you all things..."**

In other words, Christ himself would not be with us in the flesh, but a part of him, the Holy Spirit, also called the Comforter, would be with us.

Also, in John 16:7-16, as Jesus prepared his disciples for his leaving the earth, he said these words: **"Nevertheless, I tell you the truth; It is expedient for you that I go away: for if I go, not away, the Comforter will not come unto you; but if I depart, I will send him unto you. And when he is come, he will reprove the world of sin, and of righteousness, and of judgment: Of sin, because they believe not on me; Of righteousness, because I go to my Father, and ye see me no more; Of judgment, because the prince of this world is judged.**

"I have yet many things to say unto you, but ye cannot bear them now. Howbeit, when he, the Spirit of truth, is come,

he will guide you into all truth: for he shall not speak of himself; but whatsoever he shall hear, that he shall speak: and he will shew you things to come. He shall glorify me: for he shall receive of mine, and shall shew it unto you. All things that the Father hath are mine: therefore said I, that he shall take of mine, and shall shew it unto you. A little while, and ye shall not see me: and again, a little while, and ye shall see me, because I go to the Father."

Did you know that God needs to be comforted? In Ezekiel 5:13, God speaks to the Israelites who are in captivity in Babylonia through the prophet, Ezekiel. He tells his people about the terrible things that will befall them, because they have worshiped gods other than Himself. God needs to be comforted, as expressed in the following lines: **"Thus shall mine anger be accomplished, and I will cause my fury to rest upon them, and I will be comforted: and they shall know that I the Lord have spoken it in my zeal, when I have accomplished my fury in them."**

* * * * * * * * * * * * * *

As we live our lives, we all experience the obstacles of temptations and mental and physical pain. What do we need when we succumb to these temptations, only to feel remorse later, rather than the fulfillment which we sought? What do we need when we are in physical or emotional pain? We want and need to be comforted. The Holy Spirit is the Comforter, one of the parts of the Trinity, the three in one, a part of Jesus himself.

We can find in the Bible parallels in regard to the coming of Christ and the coming of the Holy Spirit to earth. Both of these advents were predicted in the Old Testament. The predictions of Christ's bodily appearance on earth are listed earlier in this treatise.

Some Old Testament predictions in regard to the descent of the Holy Spirit are found in the following verses:

Proverb 1:23, which reads: **"...I will pour out my spirit unto you..."**

Isaiah 32:15, which states:: **"...until the spirit be poured upon us from on high..."**

Can We Fathom the Nature of God?

Ezekiel 36:26-28 reads... **"A new heart will I give you, and a new spirit will I put within you: and I will take away the stony heart out of your flesh, and I will give you an heart of flesh. And I will put my spirit within you, and cause you to walk in my statutes, and ye shall keep my judgments and do them. And ye shall dwell in the land that I gave to your fathers; and ye shall be my people, and I will be your God."**

Ezekiel 39:29 continues with the theme of the conversion of the Jewish people: **"Neither will I hide my face anymore from them: for I have poured out my spirit upon the house of Israel, saith the Lord God."**

Just as John the Baptist announced the incarnation of Jesus and prepared his way, so Jesus spoke of the coming of the Holy Spirit and prepared the hearts of his followers for the Spirit's descent. When the **"...fullness of the time was come..."** that Jesus was born (Galatians 4:4), so it was that when the **"...day of Pentecost was fully come..."** (Acts 2:1), God sent forth his Spirit.

As Jesus was born in the Holy Land, so did the Spirit descend in Jerusalem. Also, as the coming of Christ into the world was marked by unusual and mighty signs and wonders, such as the angel choir (Luke 2:13), the **"...cloven tongues like as of fire..."** (Acts 2:3) which came with the Holy Spirit also displayed God's divine presence and power and nature.

The short chapter of Isaiah 53 predicted that when Christ appeared on earth, he would be unrecognized and unappreciated. Christ declared, in like manner, that the Spirit of truth would not be well received by the world (John 14:17). The analogy between the two is even clearer, for Christ was declared a **"...winebibber..."** (Matthew 11:19), while those who were filled with the Holy Spirit were said to be **"full of new wine."** (Acts 2:13)

The unusual and magnificent star that indicated the abode of the Christ Child may also be compared to the divine shaking of the house where the followers of Jesus were gathered at Pentecost (Acts 2:2). These supernatural occurrences bespoke of God's divine presence and mission and his intervention into the affairs of mankind on planet earth.

The sealed book in Chapter 5 of the Book of Revelation, according to *Halley's Bible Handbook,* p. 709, contains the secrets of the future couched in mystical language that only God can interpret. The "future" during that time period would have been from around 96 A.D., when John wrote the Book of Revelation on up until the present age and beyond.

Another book that is mentioned throughout the Bible and also in Revelation is the **"book of life"** or the Lamb's book. The verses which mention this book include Exodus 32:32-33; Daniel 12:1; and Revelation 3:5; Rev. 13:8; 20:12; 20:15; and 22:19.

As Christians, we all want our names and the names of others to be written in the book of life. Revelation 20:12-15 gives the meaning of this book. The disciple John who wrote the Book of Revelation records as follows:

"And I saw the dead, small and great, stand before God; and the books were opened: and another book was opened, which is the book of life: and the dead were judged out of those things which were written in the books, according to their works. And the sea gave up the dead which were in it; and death and hell delivered up the dead which were in them: and they were judged every man according to their works. And death and hell were cast into the lake of fire. This is the second death. And whosoever was not found written in the book of life was cast into the lake of fire."

In a manner of earthly concepts, these books are akin to a diary and/or a ledger kept by God with a recording of names of people and all that they accomplished during their tenure on planet earth. I don't believe the accomplishments will be of a secular nature, such as fame or fortune. Rather, I believe they will be such accomplishments as kindness, compassion, humility, and love. Dear Reader, I pray that our names are written in this book. If we have any doubts, then now is the time to live in such a way that we can remove all doubt and know that our names are there!

This gives us further comprehension of the nature of God. It also gives us a great sense of worth when we realize how important we are to God. In Matthew 6:26, we read, **"Behold the fowls of** the air: for they sow not, neither do they reap, nor gather into barns; yet your heavenly Father feedeth them. Are ye not much better than they?"**

Also, in Matthew 10:29-30, Jesus said: **"Are not two sparrows sold for a farthing? And one of them shall not fall on the ground without your Father. But the very hairs of your head are all numbered."**

In other words, our God is a wondrous Being who knows the details of everything in the world. Imagine his even knowing the number of hairs on our heads! Our finite minds cannot grasp the sheer magnitude of God and his creation, but he has given us the Bible as a road map for our lives. He actually reveals something of his nature to us in the Bible, if we will only read it! We also need to know what is expected of us as we live our day-to-day lives. The Bible tells us unequivocally how to live our lives.

* * * * * * * * * * * * * *

The nature of God is such that, basically, all of life revolves around our needs of food and water. When we die, will we still want food and water? The answer may be "yes," if we experience what Jesus did when he died and rose from the dead. He made ten appearances to people on earth after his resurrection, before being carried up into heaven. Later, he made a special appearance to Paul on the road to Damascus (*Halley's*, p. 526). During several of these visits, he ate bread and fish and even a honeycomb (Luke 24:30,42 and John 21:12-13). In Matthew 14:19-21 and Acts 27:35, Jesus thanked God for the food he was about to eat, thereby setting an example for us to say a blessing each time we eat.

According to Luke 22:29-30, we will indeed eat and drink with the Master: **"Ye are they which have continued with me in my temptations. And I appoint unto you a kingdom, as my Father hath appointed unto me; That ye may eat and drink at my table in my kingdom, and sit on thrones judging the twelve tribes of Israel."**

However, though Jesus's body retained the horrible imprints of the nails in his hands and feet and the wound where the spear pierced his side, the substance of his body was changed, for he walked through closed doors (John 20:19 and 26). During one of his post-resurrection appearances, he walked with two of his followers on the road to Emmaus, a town several miles from Jerusalem. Jesus's visage must have been altered, for the two followers did not recognize him. However, when they reached their home in the village and he sat down to eat with them, **"...their eyes were opened, and they knew him; and he vanished out of their sight."** (Luke 24:31)

When these same two followers returned to Jerusalem to meet with the eleven disciples and other believers, they told of their experience on the road to Emmaus and later at supper with the risen Christ. As they spoke, Jesus stood in their midst, saying, **"...Peace be unto you."** (Luke 24:36)

The verses below (Luke 24:37-43) depict the believers' reaction: **"But they were terrified and affrighted, and supposed that they had seen a spirit. And he said unto them, Why are ye troubled? And why do thoughts arise in your hearts? Behold my hands and my feet, that it is I myself: handle me, and see; for a spirit hath not flesh and bones, as ye see me have. And when he had thus spoken, he shewed them his hands and his feet. And while they yet believed not for joy, and wondered, he said unto them, Have ye here any meat? And they gave him a piece of a broiled fish, and of an honeycomb, And he took it, and did eat before them."**

This verse puzzles me, because Jesus very pointedly explained to his disciples that he was not a spirit, as quoted above: **"...for a spirit hath not flesh and bones, as ye see me have."** The marks and bruises on his body were still apparent, yet he could move through a closed door. When we die, will we retain the marks on our bodies which are the results of our illnesses or mishaps during life? Will those who have hip and/or knee replacements, for example, still have the metal in their bodies? Will people who die of cancer still have the ravages of the disease prevalent in their bodies? Will we, indeed, rise as Jesus did with bones and flesh and the open wounds of life intact?

I suppose the answer is that Jesus had risen from the grave,

Can We Fathom the Nature of God?

but he had not yet ascended into heaven. We don't know whether we will experience this transition.

Also, when Jesus appeared to all of the disciples, except Thomas, after his resurrection, the doubting Thomas said:**"...Except I shall see in his hands the print of the nails, and put my finger into the print of the nails, and thrust my hand into his side, I will not believe."** (John 20:25)

Later, in verses 26-31, Jesus reappears to the disciples, when Thomas is also present. It reads, as follows: **"And after eight days again his disciples were within, and Thomas with them: then came Jesus, the doors being shut, and stood in the midst, and said, Peace be unto you. Then saith he to Thomas, Reach hither thy finger, and behold my hands; and reach hither thy hand, and thrust it into my side: and be not faithless, but believing. And Thomas answered and said unto him, My Lord and my God. Jesus saith unto him, Thomas, because thou hast seen me, thou hast believed: blessed are they that have not seen, and yet have believed.**

"And many other signs truly did Jesus in the presence of his disciples, which are not written in this book: But these are written, that ye might believe that Jesus is the Christ, the Son of God; and that believing ye might have life through his name."

Of course, there are instances in the Bible where people, some of them long dead, come forth from their graves. After Jesus died from his ordeal on the cross and rose from the dead, we read in Matthew 27:52-53: **"And the graves were opened; and many bodies of the saints which slept arose, And came out of the graves after his resurrection, and went into the holy city, and appeared unto many."**

Jesus brought his friend Lazarus back, alive, from the grave in John 11:41-44, as follows: **"Then they took away the stone from the place where the dead was laid. And Jesus lifted up his eyes, and said, Father, I thank thee that thou hast heard me. And I knew that thou hearest me always: but because of the people which stand by I said it, that they may believe that thou hast sent me. and when he thus had spoken, he cried with a loud**

voice, Lazarus, come forth. And he that was dead came forth, bound hand and foot with graveclothes: and his face was bound about with a napkin. Jesus saith unto them, Loose him, and let him go."

At Jesus's transfiguration on a high mountain with three of his disciples, Peter, James, and John, as recorded in Matthew 17:1-5, he appeared with two great men from the Old Testament, Moses and Elijah (also called Elias in the New Testament). Five hundred years had lapsed between the lives of these two men (*Halley's*, p. 127), yet they appeared together in bodily form with Jesus at his transfiguration (Matthew 17:1-8). Moses and Elijah talked with Jesus, and the three disciples recognized them, though they all lived on the earth during different periods of time. According to scriptural commentaries I have read, Moses represented the law and Elijah the prophets. ("Why Moses and Elijah at the Transformation?–Drive Thru History")

Perhaps my favorite of Jesus's appearances after his resurrection is the third appearance he made to the disciples, as recorded in John 21:1-14. Some of his disciples were fishing in the Sea of Tiberias, also known as the Sea of Galilee, where they had fished all night and had caught nothing. When morning came, Jesus stood on the shore and called out to them, asking whether they had any meat. Not recognizing Jesus, the disciples answered, **"No."** Jesus told them to cast their net on the right side of their ship, and they were not able to draw in the net because of the multitude of fish. John then recognized Jesus and said to Peter: **"It is the Lord."** (John 21:7)

The disciples headed for the shore, dragging the net laden with fish. On the shore, Jesus had prepared a fire of coals with fish and bread cooking thereon. Jesus told them to bring their fish, which numbered one hundred and fifty-three, and to **"Come and dine."**(John 21:12) What a loving father he was, attending to his disciples' basic need of food. How wonderful it would have been to sit down with the Savior and eat a meal that he had prepared! Maybe we will indeed eat and drink in heaven with Jesus, after we die.

My understanding of heaven is that it is a place where the

saved will experience joy, fulfillment, and peace. Our greatest joys on earth will undoubtedly be magnified in heaven. In 1 Corinthians 2:9, Paul says: **"But as it is written, Eye hath not seen, nor ear heard, neither have entered into the heart of man, the things which God hath prepared for them that love him."**

What Paul is referring to in the Old Testament is the verse in Isaiah 64:4, which reads: **"For since the beginning of the world men have not heard, nor perceived by the ear, neither hath the eye seen, O God, beside thee, what he hath prepared for him that waiteth for him."**

* * * * * * * * * * * * * *

God used mountains for some of his most important interactions with men on earth. Maybe this is why we use the term "mountain-top experience" to refer to a moment of transcendence or epiphany when we sense a revelation given to us by God. Though mountains and hills are mentioned over five hundred times in the Scriptures ("What Is the Significance of Mountains in the Bible/Busted Halo"), let's just consider several events that occurred on certain mountains in the Bible.

In the Old Testament, Noah's Ark came to rest on Mt. Ararat after the Flood (Genesis 8:4). Here, God made a covenant with Noah (Genesis 9:11-17). On Mt. Sinai, God met with Moses and gave him the Ten Commandments (Exodus 19:18-20; 20:1-17). Elijah challenged the 450 false prophets of Bael on Mt. Carmel to see which God would answer by fire ((I Kings 18:19-40).

In the New Testament, Jesus **"went up into a mountain"** (Matthew 5:1) to give his Sermon on the Mount. Jesus taught his disciples on the Mount of Olives (Matthew 24:3-Matthew 25) and was transfigured on a mountain (Matthew 17:1-7). Mount Zion is where King David built Jerusalem and where God is said to dwell ("8 Bible verses about God Lives in Jerusalem–Knowing Jesus"). Jesus's final discourse with his disciples took place on the Mount of Olives (Matthew 26:30-56). Yes, God's usage of the mountainous topography of the Judaean landscape gives another hint of his divine nature.

* * * * * * * * * * * * * *

The nature of God is revealed in his creation and use of angels throughout the Bible to carry out his work on earth. Angels are mentioned over three hundred times in the Bible ("Angels–God's Servants"). The Hebrew word for angel is "malach," while the Greek word "angelos," from which the word "angel" derives, means "messenger." ("Malach–The Jewish Chronicle") Angels appeared in the Old Testament and also the New Testament.

Thomas Aquinas, the great medieval theologian, wrote about angels extensively in his book, *Summa Theologia,* published in 1274 A.D. Quoting from Scripture, he named nine orders of angels in three groups. According to Aquinas, the highest hierarchy includes the seraphim (Isaiah 6:2), the cherubim (Genesis 3:24 and Ezekiel 10:1-22) and thrones (Colossians I:16; also Thrones-Wikipedia). The middle hierarchy which involves governments includes dominions (Colossians 1:16)) and powers (Colossians 1:16). The third hierarchy which is involved in work includes principalities (Colossians 1:16), archangels (1Thessalonians 4:16), and angels ("ANGELS– Teachings of St. Thomas Aquinas").

Several Bible verses appear to substantiate the size of the cherubim. In I Kings 6, King Solomon was building the temple, using the pattern that God had given to his father, King David. In the twenty-third verse, we read that he had two cherubim chiseled from olive wood, each being ten cubits high. A cubit measures eighteen to twenty-one inches, or the length from the tip of the middle finger to the elbow. These cherubim would have been around sixteen feet tall.

Another Scripture that attests to the size of the cherubim is II Chronicles 3:10-13. The wings of the cherubim, which were being created for the temple, were around seven and a half feet long. In proportion to the rest of their bodies, their size would replicate the appearance of the angels in I Kings 6, mentioned in the paragraph above.

Angels called seraphim, which literally means "burning ones," appear as serpents in Numbers 21:6-8; Deuteronomy 8:15; and several times in the Book of Isaiah (6:2-6, 14:29, and 30:6). Perhaps the association of burning relates to the burning sensation of the serpents' poison. Seraphs or seraphim are described as six-winged beings that fly around God's throne, singing **"holy, holy, holy."** They appear to be caretakers of God's throne (Isaiah 6:1–6). Whereas Christianity places the seraphim in the highest order of angelic hierarchy, they are in the fifth rank of ten in the Jewish angelic hierarchy.

In the second century B.C. Book of Enoch, seraphim or seraphs are designated as *drakones* or "serpents." They are also mentioned, in conjunction with cherubs, as the heavenly beings standing nearest to the throne of God ("Seraph/Seraphim from Hebrew, meaning 'the burning one,' is a ...").

In II Thessalonians 1:7-9, Paul writes the following words, which likely refer to the seraphim: **"And to you who are troubled rest with us, when the Lord Jesus shall be revealed from heaven with the mighty angels, In flaming fire taking vengeance on them that know not God, and that obey not the gospel of our Lord Jesus Christ:**

"Who shall be punished with everlasting destruction from the presence of the Lord, and from the glory of his power..."

According to the Bible and different sites I visited on the internet ("The Prose Works of John Milton: Christian Doctrine," p.186), the mighty seraphim were more powerful than the cherubim which had six wings and were likely fifteen to eighteen feet tall (I Kings 6:23–26; remember, a cubit was about 20 inches, so the cherubim would have been over 16 feet tall.). Isaiah 6:1-2 corroborates the size of the seraphim, for it tells of two of their wings which covered their faces, two which covered their feet, and two which enabled them to fly. In Isaiah's vision, they stood above God's throne, so likely they were tall, in keeping with the magnitude of God and his throne.

Angels are spirit beings. They are not composed of physical matter. They are neither male nor female ("The Angels: Morning Stars of Creation–EWTN"). However, when they take human form, they always appear as a man, as were the angels Gabriel and Michael.

Nowhere in the Bible are angels described as babies or

beautiful women with wings. Never are they depicted as effeminate or helpless. Rather, they are powerful and formidable, as agents of God ("Appearing in Human Form/United Church of God"). However, the true story below provides a possibly different type of angel.

In his book *Angels: God's Secret Agents,* Billy Graham stated that he had never seen an angel, but he had talked to people who had. He related the story of an apparent angel coming to the aid of a woman in Philadelphia. On a cold, wintry night a little girl visited Dr. S. W. Mitchell, a well-known neurologist, and begged him to go and help her mother who was desperately ill. Dr. Mitchell went, but was astonished to find out that the mother's daughter had been dead for a month. He was even more amazed when he saw the very coat and shoes worn by the little girl in a closet, warm and dry. Was this an angel or was it the young daughter in another form who sought help for her mother?

In Daniel 10:5-6, the prophet describes an angel who appeared before him, as follows: **"Then I lifted up mine eyes, and looked, and behold a certain man clothed in linen, whose loins were girded with the gold of Uphaz: His body also was like the beryl, and his face as the appearance of lightning, and his eyes as lamps of fire, and his arms and his feet like in colour to polished brass, and the voice of his words like the voice of a multitude."**

After reading the above description of an angel, it is no wonder that the angel who descended from heaven and rolled back the stone from Jesus's tomb, then sat upon the stone, affected the keepers of the tomb in such a terrifying way. The Bible says in Matthew 28:2-9:

"And, behold, there was a great earthquake: for the angel of the Lord descended from   heaven, and came and rolled back the stone from the door, and sat upon it. His countenance was like lightning, and his raiment white as snow: And for fear of him the keepers did shake, and became as dead men. And the angel answered and said unto the women, Fear not ye: for I know that ye seek Jesus, which was crucified. He is not here: for he is risen as he said. Come, see the place where the Lord

lay. And go quickly, and tell his disciples that he is risen from the dead; and, behold, he goeth before you into Galilee; there shall ye see him: lo, I have told you. And they departed quickly from the sepulchre with fear and great joy; and did run to bring his disciples word. And as they went to tell his disciples, behold, Jesus met them, saying, All hail. And they came and held him by the feet, and worshiped him."

The entire Book of Revelation was dictated by an angel to Jesus's disciple, John (Revelation 1:1). In Revelation 5:11, "**ten thousand times ten thousand, and thousands of thousands**" of angels sing praise to the Lamb (Jesus). Twenty-seven different references to the activities of angels are found in the Book of Revelation (*Halley's*, p. 693).

Only three angels are named in the Bible. They are Gabriel, Michael, and Lucifer. (Note: Some commentaries include Raphael as an angel, though he's not mentioned in the canon of the Bible. Also, several bad angels are mentioned, but I won't address those here).

Though the angel, Gabriel, appeared twice to Daniel (Daniel 8:16 and 9:21) during the Babylonian Captivity of the Jews in the Old Testament, he is best known for his appearance to Mary, in the New Testament, when he told her she would be the mother of Jesus, the Son of God (Luke 1:26-31). He also appeared to Zacharias and foretold the birth of his son, John the Baptist ("Luke 1:5-13"). In the book of Daniel, the prophet does not actually identify Gabriel as an angel; rather, Daniel refers to him, in 9:21, as "**the man Gabriel.**"

The angel Michael is known as "Prince" of the heavenly hosts. He is referred to as the archangel in Jude 1:9. He also performs a major role in Chapter 12 of the Book of Revelation, when he fights against Satan, and Satan is cast out of heaven to the earth.

In this chapter, verses 7-10, we read the following: "**And there was war in heaven: Michael and his angels fought against the dragon, and the dragon fought and his angels, And prevailed not; neither was their place found any more in heaven. And the great dragon was cast out, that old serpent, called the Devil, and Satan, which deceiveth the whole world: he was cast out into the** earth, and his angels were cast out with him. And I heard a loud voice saying in heaven, Now is come salvation, and strength, and the kingdom of our God, and the power of his Christ: for the accuser of our brethren is cast down, which accused them before our God day and night."**

In Isaiah 14:12, we read of Lucifer who, some believe, was a fallen angel: **"How art thou fallen from heaven, O Lucifer, son of the morning: how art thou cut to the ground, which didst weaken the nations! For thou hast said in thine heart, I will ascend into heaven, I will exalt my throne above the stars of God: I will sit also upon the mount of the congregation, in the sides of the north: I will ascend above the heights of the clouds; I will be like the most High. Yet thou shalt be brought down to hell, to the sides of the pit."**

Lucifer, or Satan, wanted to be God. In II Corinthians 4:4, we read: **"In whom the god of this world hath blinded the minds of them which believe not, lest the light of the glorious gospel of Christ, who is the image of God, should shine unto them."**

The name "**Lucifer**" only appears once in the King James Version of the Bible in Isaiah 14:12-15. Though some sources state that it is a Latin word which was misused in the Old Testament, since the Old Testament was written in Hebrew, it nonetheless was used in the Latin *Vulgate* and has been understood for hundreds of years to refer to Satan. Different sources state that "**Lucifer**" referred to an ancient king, perhaps even the Babylonian King Nebuchadnezzar. However, other sources, including the Reverend Billy Graham, accepted the premise that "**Lucifer**" indeed refers to the Devil, or Satan (Interview with Billy Graham–CNN.com, June 16, 2005).

Revelation 12:17 explains the constant battle between good and evil that we wage each day of our lives. It reads as follows:

"And the dragon was wroth with the woman, and went to make war with the remnant of her seed, which keep the commandments of God, and have the testimony of Jesus Christ."

Here again, we read about the "remnant." We as Christians are the remnant, as are the Jews who will also be saved. The verse explains the remnant as those who **"keep the commandments of**

God."

Revelation 20:10 reveals that the devil would make war with the remnant who keep God's commandments and would be eternally punished for disobeying God: **"And the devil that deceived them was cast into the lake of fire and brimstone, where the beast and the false prophet are, and shall be tormented day and night for ever and ever."**

Nowhere in Scripture can we find that Satan had a tail and a pitchfork. Rather, Satan was perhaps the most beautiful angel ever created by God, but his pride caused his downfall and his ejection by God from heaven. We read about this in Ezekiel 28:14-17:

"Thou art the anointed cherub that covereth; and I have set thee so: thou wast upon the holy mountain of God; thou hast walked up and down in the midst of the stones of fire. Thou wast perfect in thy ways from the day that thou wast created, till iniquity wast found in thee. By the multitude of thy merchandise they have filled the midst of thee with violence, and thou hast sinned; therefore I will cast thee as profane out of the mountain of God: and I will destroy thee, O covering cherub, from the midst of the stones of fire. Thine heart was lifted up because of thy beauty, thou hast corrupted thy wisdom by reason of thy brightness: I will cast thee to the ground, I will lay thee before kings, that they may behold thee."

"Satan" is a Hebrew word, meaning accuser, adversary, or opponent ("Satan–Wikipedia"). The word **"Satan"** appears fifty-five times in the King James Version of the Bible ("Shocked by the Bible: The Most Astonishing Facts You've Never Been Told"). Satan is referred to as the star which fell from heaven in Revelation 9:1-2:, **"And the fifth angel sounded, and I saw a star fall from heaven unto the earth: and to him was given the key of the bottomless pit. And he opened the bottomless pit; and there was smoke out of the pit, as the smoke of a great furnace; and the sun and the air were darkened by reason of the smoke of the pit."**

In Luke 10:18, Jesus himself says, **"I beheld Satan as lightning fall from heaven."**

Referred to as a **"great red dragon"** which fell from heaven in Revelation 12:3-4, Satan took a third of the stars with him. This signifies that free will gave Satan this option. Here he is depicted as having seven heads and ten horns and seven crowns upon his heads. The angels who followed him (referred to as "stars") became the demons of his kingdom. The fact that two-thirds of the angels remained with God should be comforting to us as Christians.

Below are some of the more noted Scriptural passages on other angels:

The Fall of Adam and Eve
(Genesis 3:23-24)

"Therefore the Lord God sent him forth from the garden of Eden, to till the ground from whence he was taken. So he drove out the man; and he placed at the east of the garden of Eden Cherabims, and a flaming sword which turned every way, to keep the way of the tree of life."

Jacob's Ladder
(Genesis 28:10-12)

"And Jacob went out from Beersheba, and went toward Haran. And he lighted upon a certain place, and tarried there all night, because the sun was set; and he took of the stones of that place, and put them for his pillows, and lay down in that place to sleep. And he dreamed, and behold a ladder set up on the earth, and the top of it reached to heaven: and behold the angels of God ascending and descending on it."

Daniel in the Lion's Den
(Daniel 6:19-22)

"Then the king arose very early in the morning, and went in haste unto the den of lions. And when he came to the den, he cried with a lamentable voice unto Daniel: and the king spake and said to Daniel, O Daniel, servant of the living God, is thy God, whom thou servest continually, able to deliver thee from

the lions? Then said Daniel unto the king, O king, live for ever. My God hath sent his angel, and hath shut the lions' mouths, that they have not hurt me: forasmuch as before him innocency was found in me; and also before thee, O king, have I done no hurt."

The Angel Appears to Joseph.
(Matthew 1:18-21)

"Now the birth of Jesus Christ was on this wise: When as his mother Mary was espoused to Joseph, before they came together, she was found with child of the Holy Ghost. Then Joseph her husband, being a just man, and not willing to make her a publick example, was minded to put her away privily. But while he thought on these things, behold, the angel of the Lord appeared unto him in a dream, saying, Joseph, thou son of David, fear not to take unto thee Mary thy wife: for that which is conceived in her is of the Holy Ghost. And she shall bring forth a son, and thou shalt call his name JESUS: for he shall save his people from their sins."

The Angel Gabriel Appears to Mary.
(Luke 1:26-31)

"And in the sixth month the angel Gabriel was sent forth from God unto a city of Galilee, named Nazareth, To a virgin espoused to a man whose name was Joseph, of the house of David; and the virgin's name was Mary. And the angel came in unto her, and said, Hail, thou that art highly favoured, the Lord is with thee: blessed art thou among women. And when she saw him, she was troubled at his saying, and cast in her mind what manner of salutation this should be. And the angel said unto her, Fear not, Mary: for thou hast found favour with God. And, behold, thou shalt conceive in thy womb, and bring forth a son, and shalt call his name JESUS."

JANE H. WALKER

The Resurrection of Jesus
(John 20:11-15)

"But Mary stood without at the sepulchre weeping: and as she wept, she stooped down, and looked into the sepulchre, And seeth two angels in white sitting, the one at the head, and the other at the feet, where the body of Jesus had lain. And they say unto her, Woman, why weepest thou? She saith unto them, Because they have taken away my Lord, and I know not where they have laid him."

The Book of Revelation
(Revelation 8:1-2)

"And when he had opened the seventh seal, there was silence in heaven about the space of half an hour. And I saw the seven angels which stood before God; and to them was given seven trumpets.

"And another angel came and stood at the altar, having a golden censer and there was given unto him much incense, that he should offer it with the prayers of all saints upon the golden altar which was before the throne."

Chapter Nine

Martyrdom of early Christians helped to spread the truth of the Gospel of Christ like holy wildfire. In the Book of Acts 6:1-15, Luke (author of Acts) recorded the murder of Stephen, the first Christian martyr, which occurred in 34 A.D ("Saint Stephen–Wikipedia"). Stephen, one of seven apostles appointed by the twelve disciples after Jesus's death and resurrection, was arrested by a Jewish council and was forced to appear before the same council, likely, which had sent Jesus to his crucifixion. False witnesses accused Stephen of blasphemy ("Acts 6:1-15"). (Note: Matthias was chosen as a disciple to replace Judas Iscariot who had hanged himself. This is recorded in Acts I:26.)

In attempting to explain his beliefs and to persuade the council members about the truth of the Gospel, Stephen recounted Old Testament history, beginning with Abraham and bringing the Jewish Bible narrative up to their present age in history ("Acts 7:1-53"). When he climaxed the scriptural account with a sharp rebuke for their not following God's word and for their murder of Jesus, they reacted as follows in Acts 7:54-60:

"When they heard these things, they were cut to the heart, and they gnashed on him with their teeth. But he, being full of the Holy Ghost, looked up stedfastly into heaven, and saw the glory of God, and Jesus standing on the right hand of God. And said, Behold, I see the heavens opened, and the Son of man standing on the right hand of God. Then they cried out with a loud voice, and stopped their ears, and ran upon him with one accord. And

cast him out of the city, and stoned him: and the witnesses laid down their clothes at a young man's feet, whose name was Saul. And they stoned Stephen, calling upon God, and saying, Lord Jesus, receive my spirit. And he kneeled down, and cried with a loud voice, Lord, lay not this sin to their charge. And when he had said this, he fell asleep."

Of course, the "**Saul**" mentioned in the above Scripture was Saul of Tarsus, whose name was later changed to "**Paul**" (Acts 13:9). Saul, himself, did not believe in Jesus until Christ spoke to him on the road to Damascus, and his life was forever changed (Acts 9: 1-30). Paul wrote much of the New Testament and was later put to death by Nero around A.D. 67 (*Halley's,* p. 583).

After Jesus's death and resurrection, his followers determined to live their lives in accordance with the Scriptures, which were finally completed around 96 A.D ("When Were the Bible books written?–Grace to You"). At first, meeting wherever two or more could gather together, the early Christians felt the need of a Creed to state together, one which would bind them together and to God, himself. The earliest known creed, The Apostles' Creed, was found in a letter written by Marcellus of Ancyra in Greek to Pope Julius I, about 341 A.D ("The Apostles' Creed: Its History and Origins/Faithlife Blog"). In this letter he penned that the apostles wrote the creed together after Pentecost, before leaving Jerusalem to preach. The Apostles' Creed was formerly called the "Old Roman Creed" and was in use during the second century.

Ferdinand Kattenbusch (1851-1935) was a German church historian and theologian. His principal work was a history of The Apostles' Creed, *Das apostolische Symbol* (two vols., 1894, 1900), grounded on the research of C.P. Caspari. Caspari was a Professor of Theology at the University of Norway. He spoke of the Rule of Faith which the Apostolic Church had received from the Apostles. Kattenbusch dated the Old Roman Creed around 100 A.D ("Ferdinand Kattenbusch/ Free online library at Biblical Training.org").

A widely accepted belief in the fourth century was that each of the Twelve Apostles, under the inspiration of the Holy Spirit, contributed an article of the Creed ("The Apostles' Creed–

Wikipedia"). About the year 390, Ambrose, an early church leader, wrote a letter from a Council in Milan to Pope Siricius, which stated, "let them give credit to the Creed of the Apostles, which the Roman Church has always kept and preserved undefiled." However, this was a shorter statement of belief which did not include the phrase, "maker of heaven and earth," which words may have been added in the seventh century ("Creed of the Apostles–Preparing You").

Though individual articles of belief in The Apostles' Creed are found in various writings by the early Church fathers, including Iranaeus, Tertullian, Ambrose, and Augustine, among others ("The Voice of the Church: Or Selections from the Writings of the…"), the earliest semblance of what we know as The Apostles' Creed was in the "Excerpt from Individual Canonical books of St. Pirminius, written between 710-714 ("The Apostles' Creed–Wikipedia"). (Reader, please note that the dates of Pirminius' life do not coincide with the dates above. I have found this to be true in much of my research for this book.) However, The Apostles' Creed, as we know it, can be found in *A Treasury of Early Christianity* by Anne Freemantle, 1953, p. 327. It is dated around 100 A.D. It appears below:

The Apostles' Creed

"I believe in God the Father Almighty, Maker of heaven and in Jesus Christ, His only son, our Lord, Who was conceived by the Holy Ghost, born of the Virgin Mary, suffered under Pontius Pilate, was crucified, died, and was buried: He descended into hell: the third day He rose again from the dead. He ascended into heaven. And sitteth on the right hand of God the Father Almighty: from thence He shall come to judge the quick and the dead. I believe in the Holy Ghost, the holy Catholic Church; the Communion of saints, the forgiveness of sins: the resurrection of the body, and the life everlasting." (Note that some denominations omit "He descended into hell…")

The Nicene Creed, found in the same book above, p. 328, expresses the mind of the Church at the close of the first Council of Nicaea in 325 A.D. It appears below:

The Nicene Creed

"I believe in one God

"The Father Almighty, Maker of heaven and earth, and all things visible and invisible: And in one Lord Jesus Christ, the only-begotten Son of God; Begotten of his Father before all worlds, God of God, Light of Light, Very God of very God; Begotten, not made; being of one substance with the Father; by whom all things were made: Who for us men and for our salvation came down from heaven, And was incarnate by the Holy Ghost of the Virgin Mary, and was made man: And was crucified also for us under Pontius Plate; He suffered and was buried: And the third day He rose according to the Scriptures: And ascended into heaven, and sitteth on the right hand of the Father: And He shall come again, with glory, to judge both the quick and the dead; whose kingdom shall have no end.

"And I believe in the Holy ghost, the Lord, and Giver of Life, who proceedeth from the Father and the Son; Who with the Father and the Son together is worshiped and glorified; who spake by the prophets:

"And I believe in one Catholic and Apostolic Church:I acknowledge one baptism for the remission of sins: And I look for the resurrection of the dead: And for the life of the world to come."

The last of the three major creeds is *The Athanasian Creed* which is a Latin compilation of the fifth century. All of these creeds are used by Catholics, Orthodox Church members, and some Protestants (same book above, p. 327-329).

In addition to the statements of belief in the Creeds of the early Church, twenty-one Ecumenical (worldwide) Councils were held from 325 A.D. until 1965 (*Halley's,* p. 765). Some would suggest that the first Council was in Jerusalem, attended by the Apostles (Acts 15 and Galatians 2), though the first one listed in reference sources is usually the Council of Nicaea in 325 A.D. The first seven were called by Roman emperors, whereas the remaining fourteen were, for the most part, convened by popes. Most of these councils dealt with dogma and heresies ("Ecumenical Church Councils–Mb–Soft.Com").

Several of these councils espoused dogma that did not derive from the Bible. At the ninth First Lateran Council, held in Rome in the Lateran Basilica in 1123, the Council decided that priests in the Latin rite must be celibate ("A Brief History of Celibacy in the Catholic Church/Future Church"). Nowhere in the Bible is this a requirement. In fact, priests do not even exist in the New Testament Church ("The Office of New Testament Priest–Jimmy Akin").

The epistle to the Hebrews expressed the New Testament belief that priests were no longer necessary (Hebrews 7-10). The only reference to the word is used with a Christian meaning in Revelation 1:6; 5:10; and 20:6. In these verses, it applies to all Christians, not only Christian leaders. Likely, this issue of celibacy in the Catholic Church has brought about problems such as molestation of children within the priesthood of the Catholic Church, along with other perversions.

The Nineteenth Council of Trent, convened by Pope Paul III on December 13, 1545, in the mountain village of Trent in northern Italy, was the greatest and longest of all the major ecumenical councils. Twenty-five major sessions spanned eighteen years under five popes and ended on December 4, 1563 ("Catholic Ecumenical Councils–Wikipedia"). As the Counter-Reformation to the Protestant Reformation, Protestantism was condemned as heretical along with its adherents, Martin Luther and other reformers ("9 Things You Should Know About the Council of Trent").

At the Twentieth First Vatican Council, called by Pope Pius IX in June of 1868 and opening on December 8, 1869, the dogma of infallibility of the Pope was affirmed ("First Vatican Council–Wikipedia). I would certainly question the dogma of infallibility of the pope, especially in light of the corruption of the Papacy during its long history. This is true of Protestant churches, also, for no man has been infallible since Jesus Christ. According to the web site (MAJOR COUNCILS OF THE CHURCH; [councils.htm] –*Daily Catholic*) which I visited for this information, this Council was characterized as follows:

"...the turning point where modernists usurped the true Church with a council they hijacked. Since then the true Church founded by Christ is in eclipse, forgotten by a world intent on instant gratification and political correctness where everything is topsy-turvy today. It will take a miracle to right the ship. Yet we know the true Barque of Peter cannot capsize and, when this interminable interregnum is finally terminated, and we have a true Pope again, then the restoration of the Roman Catholic Church can begin. Until that time, faithful Catholics perpetuate the Faith and persevere in the catacombs throughout the world."

At the Twenty-first Second Vatican Council, convened by John XXIII on October 11, 1962 and continued by his successor, Paul VI, for three more years, ending on December 8, 1965, Paul himself ascribed the unleashing of the "Smoke of Satan into the sanctuary."According to the same web site, mentioned above, "Since then errors have spread universally and the Church has been in turmoil, hurtling more souls toward the darkness thanks to the heretical administrations of Bishop Karol Wojtyla from 1978 to 2005 and since then Father Joseph Ratzinger." (MAJOR COUNCILS Of The CHURCH: (Councils.htm–*Daily Catholic*)

Once again, dear Reader, I certainly do not render judgment about one church over another. Though I am a Methodist, I believe that anyone who believes that Jesus Christ is the Messiah and Savior will have salvation. Only God knows what the true Church is. I think it behooves all of us, as Christians, to live as Christ taught us and to make our respective churches the purest, in God's eyes, they can be. I believe all churches should be Scripture-based.

I was stunned, however, to hear recently that Pope Francis wanted to change certain words of "The Lord's Prayer," which begin "**Lead us not into temptation**," as he stated that God would not lead anyone into temptation. I believe he is misunderstanding the meaning of the words. To me, it means that when we are faced with temptation, we want God to lead us away from it. I don't know how it could be construed differently. Pope Francis is mortal, as we all are. We don't need to change the words of Jesus!

Protestant churches have had their own problems, also, which we read and hear about, so we too need to get back to the Scriptures in living our daily lives. I believe the nature of God can be discerned in the efforts of certain people and churches to remind us to trust the Scriptures alone as a model for our lives.

* * * * * * * * * * * * * *

The continuation of the Church and Christianity through the centuries and up until the present day has been marked by certain people and events for over two thousand years. God's nature runs like a cohesive thread in the lives of these people and the historical events that God used to shape the church and the Christian faith. Let's look first at the lives of other people who lived near the time of Christ and were so convinced of the truth of Christianity that they sacrificed their lives as testaments of their faith.

According to John Foxe (1516/1517 A.D.-1587 A.D.), who wrote *Foxe's Book of Martyrs* also known as *The Actes and the Monuments* ("John Foxe–Wikipedia"), the number of Christians who died martyrs' deaths during the first three hundred years after Jesus's death and resurrection was astronomical. Foxe quoted Jerome, early church father of the fourth century, as stating, "There is no day in the whole year unto which the number of five thousand martyrs cannot be ascribed, except only the first day of January." (*Foxe's Book of Martyrs,* W. Grinton Berry, editor, Spire, 1998; Revell, a division of Baker Publishing Group, 2009, p. 12). It behooves us to know more about Foxe and his book, *Foxe's Book of Martyrs.*

John Foxe was born at Boston in Lincolnshire, England, of fairly prominent parents. He married Agnes Randall in 1547 and they had six children. By the time he was twenty-five, he had read the Latin and Greek writers, the canon law, the schoolmen, and had acquired skill in the Hebrew language. He was a lecturer in logic at Magdalen College School, but resigned his post after becoming a Protestant and subscribing to beliefs which were condemned by the Church of England under King Henry VIII.

He was especially opposed to clerical celibacy, which he described in letters to his friends as self-castration ("John Foxe–Wikipedia"). Foxe personally witnessed the martyrdom by burning of William Cowbridge in September of 1538. William Cowbridge was a devout Christian from a prominent English family. With the accession of Edward VI to the throne in 1547, the Protestant cause improved, and Foxe's life was not in danger. However, he did witness two burnings for religion during the reign of Edward VI.

Foxe's Book of Martyrs went through four editions during Foxe's lifetime and was the largest publishing project ever undertaken in England. The first edition, published in 1563, was a huge tome of 1800 pages, over a foot long and could not be lifted with only one hand (*Foxe's Book of Martyrs*–IPFS). The second edition, produced in 1570, was in two volumes with over 2,300 very large pages of double-columned text ("John Foxe–Wikipedia"). The full title of Foxe's work was a paragraph long, as follows:

Actes and Monuments of these latter and perilous dayes, touching matters of the Church, wherein are comprehended and described the great persecutions and horrible troubles that have been wrought and practised by the Romishe Prelates, speciallye in this Realme of England and Scotland, from the yeare of our Lorde a thousande unto the tyme nowe present: Gathered and collected according to the true Copies and Wrytinges certificatorie, as well of the Parties themselves that Suffered, as also out of the Bishops' registers, which were the Doers thereof, by John Foxe. ("PDF THE ACTS AND MONUMENTS OF THE CHRISTIAN...Ex-Classics")

Actes and Monuments was summarily attacked by Catholics, including Thomas Harding, Thomas Stapleton, and Nicholas Harpsfield. Harding called *Actes and Monuments* "that huge dunghill of your stinking martyrs...full of a thousand lies." ("John Foxe–Wikipedia") Foxe responded by removing any offending passages, but where he could rebut his critics, he published a vigorous counterattack with documents offered as proofs.

His second edition was well received by the English Church, however. In 1571, the upper house of the convocation of Canterbury ordered that a copy of the Bishop's Bible and "that full history entitled *Monuments of Martyrs*" be placed in cathedrals and select churches. It was also stipulated that church officials place copies in their houses for their use and the use of their servants and visitors (*Foxe's Book of Martyrs*–Wikipedia).

Though *Foxe's Acts and Monuments* had its detractors

throughout succeeding years, in 2009, *Encyclopaedia Britannica* noted that Foxe's work was "factually detailed and preserves firsthand material on the English Reformation unobtainable elsewhere." (*Foxe's Book of Martyrs* - Main Index Page) March, 2013, marked 450 years since the publication of Foxe's first edition in 1563 A.D. This date is about midway from the beginning of the Roman Catholic Inquisition until our own time period of 2018. It serves to refresh the minds of Christians about the suffering of early martyrs who gave their lives, so that we might believe. I see the nature of God in the very fabric of John Foxe's meticulously compiled *Book of Martyrs*. It is not easy reading, but the Holy Spirit leaps from its pages.

Though the publication of his book made Foxe famous, he received no royalty from its sales, as no royalties were given during that time period. The book sold for more than ten shillings, which was three weeks' pay for a skilled craftsman during that time period. The fourth edition of his book was nearly four times the length of the Bible ("John Foxe–Wikipedia").

The fourth edition was "the most physically imposing, complicated, and technically demanding English book of its era. It seems safe to say that it is the largest and most complicated book to appear during the first two or three centuries of English printing history." The noted writer John Bunyan who wrote *Pilgrim's Progress,* cherished his copy of *Foxe's Book of Martyrs* to the extent that it was one of the few books that he kept with him while in prison (*Foxes' Book of Martyrs*–Bridge Logos"). It continues to be reprinted up until this present day. John Burrow referred to it, after the Bible, as "the greatest single influence on English Protestant thinking of the late Tudor and early Stuart period." (*Foxe's Book of Martyrs*–Wikipedia).

According to Foxe, all of Jesus's disciples, except John (who wrote the Gospel of John; First, Second, and Third Epistles of John; and The Revelation), died martyrs' deaths. However, though a footnote in his book states that the accounts of the martyrdoms of the apostles were mainly "traditional,"they nonetheless could certainly be true. We realize the fact that in the ancient world, tradition was a way of passing down truths to succeeding generations, as this was more than a thousand years before the invention of the printing press. According to John Foxe, p. 6-13 of the 2009 edition of his book, named above and edited by W. Grinton Berry, the following disciples of Jesus were all martyrs who died in different ways:

James and John, the sons of Zebedee, were beheaded in A.D.36.

Thomas preached to the Parthians, Medes, Persians, Carmanians, Hyrcanians, Bactrians, and Magians. In Calamina, a city of India, he was slain with a dart.

James, the son of Alpheus, was crucified in a city of Egypt at the time of Trajan, the Roman emperor.

Simon, called Zelotes (also Peter), preached in Mauritania, Africa, and Britain. He was crucified head down by Nero, as he felt himself unworthy to be crucified as Jesus was.

Mark, the evangelist and first bishop of Alexandria, preached the gospel in Egypt where he was drawn with ropes to the fire and burned to death. He was buried there in a place called "Bucolus," under the reign of Trajan, the Roman emperor.

Bartholomew preached to the Indians and translated the Gospel of Matthew into their language. In Albinopolis, a city of greater Armenia, he was beaten with staves, excoriated (his skin abraded), and finally beheaded.

Andrew preached in 80 A.D. to the Scythians, the Sogdians, the Sacae, and in a city called Sebastopolis, inhabited by the Ethiopians. Aegeas, governor of the Edessenes, insisted that Andrew sacrifice unto idols, which Andrew refused to do. He died as a martyr on a cross.

Matthew converted Ethiopia and Egypt to the Christian faith. He also wrote his Gospel to the Jews in the Hebrew language. Hircanus, the king of Egypt, had him run through with a spear.

Philip, the apostle, preached salvation to the barbarous nations where he was crucified and stoned to death. He was buried in Hierapolis, a city of Phrygia, along with his daughters.

Paul, the apostle who wrote a large part of the New Testament, was beheaded by Nero.

Dear Reader, these deaths of the martyrs are not easy reading, nor is it easy writing for me. However, I think it is incumbent upon us to realize that the belief of these early Christians was so strong and so certain that they willingly - even eagerly - gave their lives as testaments of their faith. They were totally convinced of the truth of Christianity.

Foxe lists in his book the terrible ways that these ancient saints were killed. He states: "whatsoever the cruelness of man's invention could devise for the punishment of man's body, was practised (sic) against the Christians - stripes and scourgings, drawings, tearings, stonings, plates of iron laid unto them burning hot, deep dungeons, racks, strangling in prison, the teeth of wild beasts, gridirons, gibbets and gallows, tossing upon the horns of bulls."

He further states: "Moreover, when they were thus killed, their bodies were laid in heaps, and dogs there left to keep them, that no man might come to bury them, neither would any prayer obtain them to be interred. And yet, notwithstanding all these continual persecutions and horrible punishments, the Church daily increased, deeply rooted in the doctrine of the apostles and of men apostolical, and watered plenteously with the blood of saints." (same *Foxe* edition as last noted, p.18-20)

An early martyr included in *Foxe's Book of Martyrs* was Ignatius, also known as Theophorus, who lived from 35 A.D. to 108 A.D. It is believed that Peter himself appointed Ignatius to the office of bishop of Antioch, Peter being the first bishop, followed by Evodius, then Ignatius ("Ignatius of Antioch–Wikipedia"). You may remember that the disciples were first called **"Christians"** in Antioch, (Acts 11:26). However, Antioch was formerly of Syria. It is now called Antakya, which is in southern Turkey, near the border of Syria ("Antakya–Wikipedia").

Ignatius retained the office of bishop of Antioch for forty years, until it was reported to the Roman Emperor Trajan that he was blasphemous toward the Roman gods. Trajan sentenced Ignatius to die, but tradition survives that before his death, the Roman Emperor had occasion to winter in Antioch, at which time, he questioned Ignatius about his beliefs ("FaithND–St. Ignatius of Antioch"). Below is the conversation that Trajan purportedly had with Ignatius:

"Who are you, spirit of evil, who dare disobey my orders and goad others on to their destruction?"

"No one calls Theophorus a spirit of evil," the bishop replied.

"Who is Theophorus?"

"He who bears Christ within him."

"And do we not bear within ourselves the gods who help us against our enemies?"

"You are mistaken when you call gods those who are no better than devils. There is but one God, who created heaven and earth and all that in them is; and one Jesus, made Christ, into whose kingdom I earnestly desire to be admitted."

"Do you mean Him who was crucified under Pontius Pilate?"

"Yes, the same, who by His death has crucified both sin and its author, and who has proclaimed that every malice of the devil shall be trodden underfoot by those who bear Him in their hearts."

"Do you then," asked the Emperor, "bear Christ within you?"

"Yes," said Ignatius, "for it is written, 'I will dwell in them and will walk with them.'"

("Ignatius of Antioch–Martyr–Marianne Dorman's Homestead")

Trajan decreed that Ignatius should be carried to the Coliseum in Rome, where he was to be fed to the lions ("Ignatius of Antioch–Wikipedia"). Ignatius was taken to a ship, where he was bound and guarded by ten soldiers, whom he referred to in his writings as "ten leopards," because of their cruelty. The guards were anxious to reach Rome with their prisoner before the popular public games were over, for important prisoners were always a special attraction to the crowds in the Coliseum. During this time, Ignatius wrote seven letters to the Ephesians, the Magnesians, the Trallians, the Romans, the Philadelphians, the Smyrnaeans, and one to Polycarp, Bishop of Smyrna. These letters he sent to their destinations by the faithful Christians who gathered near him to receive his benediction at the various places along the route to Rome ("General Audience of

14 March 2007: Saint Ignatius of Antioch").

The letters of Ignatius give us insight into the development of Christian theology during the early years of the church and the very nature of God, whom he served. They appear, however, to have been written in great haste with run-on sentences and without a proper plan ("Ignatius of Antioch–Wikipedia"). This is understandable, considering his dire circumstances as he traveled by boat to his certain martyrdom.

In his letter to the Christians in Rome, he entreated them to do nothing to prevent his martyrdom. He said he longed to die for Christ. Below is part of his letter to his Christian friends in Rome:

"Now I begin to be a disciple. I care for nothing, of visible or invisible things, so that I may but win Christ. Let fire and the cross, let the companies of wild beasts, let breaking of bones and tearing of limbs, let the grinding of the whole body, and all the malice of the devil, come upon me; be it so, only may I win Christ Jesus! (*Foxe*, Berry edition, p.19)

Another quote from his letter to the Roman Christians is as follows: "I write to all the Churches, and impress on them all, that I shall willingly die for God, unless ye hinder me. I beseech of you not to show an unseasonable goodwill towards me. Suffer me to become food for the wild beasts, through whose instrumentality it will be granted me to attain to God. I am the wheat of God, and am ground by the teeth of the wild beasts, that I may be found the pure bread of Christ. Rather entice the wild beasts, that they may become my tomb, and may leave nothing of my body; so that when I have fallen asleep [in death], I may not be found troublesome to any one. Then shall I be a true disciple of Jesus Christ, when the world shall not see so much as my body. Entreat Christ for me, that by these instruments I may be found a sacrifice to God. I do not, as Peter and Paul, issue commandments unto you. They were apostles of Jesus Christ, but I am the very least [of believers]: they were free, as the servants of God; while I am, even until now, a servant. But when I suffer, I shall be the freedman of Jesus Christ, and shall rise again emancipated in Him. And now, being in bonds for Him, I learn not to desire anything worldly or vain." *(The Anti-Nicene Fathers,*

p. 75)

Ignatius is credited with the first known use of the Greek word "katholikos," meaning "universal," "complete," and "whole" to describe the Church ("Catholic [term]–Wikipedia"). Below is an excerpt from his letter to the Smyrnaeans in this regard:

"Wherever the bishop shall appear, there let the multitude [of the people] also be; even as, wherever Jesus Christ is, there is the catholic church. It is not lawful without the bishop either to baptize or to celebrate a love-feast; but whatsoever he shall approve of, that is also pleasing to God, so that everything that is done may be secure and valid." (*The Ante-Nicene Fathers,* p. 90)

It's difficult to imagine the horrors that Ignatius was about to face, on the route to his martyrdom, yet he managed to write letters to various groups of Christians about the ongoing work of the Church. When the guards arrived at Rome, they carried Ignatius to the Flavian Amphitheatre (known today as the Coliseum), the largest amphitheatre ever built, where lions were released, and Ignatius died a martyr's death ("Coliseum–Wikipedia").

Polycarp, a disciple of John the Apostle, according to the historian, Tertullian ("Biography: Polycarp: the Apostolic Legacy–Vision.org"), was born 1n 69 A.D. in Smyrna, a port on the west coast of Asia Minor. He became bishop of Smyrna. As you may remember, Smyrna was one of the "good" churches addressed in the Book of Revelation. Because Polycarp refused to burn incense to the Roman Emperor, he was burned at the stake around 155 A.D ("Biography: Polycarp: The Apostolic Legacy"). He was recorded as saying on the day of his death, "Eighty and six years have I served Him, and He never did me any injury: how then can I blaspheme my King and my Savior?" (*The Ante-Nicene Fathers,* p. 41)

Iranaeus (A.D. 130-200), another early church father, was a pupil of Polycarp. Iranaeus also died a martyr's death. Below is his written memory of Polycarp:

"I remember well the place in which the holy Polycarp sat and spoke. I remember the discourses he delivered to the people, and how he described his relations with John the apostle, and others who had been with the Lord, how he recited the sayings of Christ and the miracles he wrought; how he received his teachings from eyewitnesses who had seen the Word of Life, agreeing in every way with the Scriptures." (*Halley's*–"Church History,"p. 764)

* * * * * * * * * * * * * *

Justin Martyr was a pagan philosopher who lived from circa 100-114 A.D.-165 A.D. in Nablus, Palestine, known today as the West Bank area of Israel. He converted to Christianity at the age of thirty after reading the Scriptures and witnessing the courage and faith of Christian martyrs ("Justin Martyr, Philosopher, Apologist, and Martyr 1 June 167"). He was a Christian apologist who taught and defended Christianity in Asia Minor and Rome. Refusing to sacrifice to idols, he was beheaded in Rome, Italy, in 167 A.D. He said that the "seeds of truth could be found in all religions but only Christianity taught the whole truth." ("Church History Timeline, [The Apologists: 120-220]")

Searching for truth in a succession of philosophical schools, such as Stoicism, Aristotelianism, Pythagorism, and Platonism, Justin Martyr could not find the illusive "truth" in any of these philosophies. Finally, he met an old man on the seashore at Ephesus, who discussed with him the great truths found in the Bible and how the Old Testament predicted the coming of Christ. Accepting this revelation as the truth he had been seeking, Justin devoted the rest of his life to defending the truth of Christianity against its philosophical opponents. He wrote the *Apologies* which defended orthodox Christianity ("Justin Martyr, Philosopher, Apologist, and Martyr 1 June 167").

His is the oldest non-New Testament record of how the early Christians worshiped. In Chapter 62 of this writing, it is implied that the early Christians removed their footwear before worship. According to a website I researched, when church buildings came into existence, footwear was removed upon entering. This continued until around 632 A.D. (" Justin Martyr: On Christian Worship - 150 A.D. (The Prayer Foundation")

The oldest church buildings date back to 230 A.D. *Halley's Bible Handbook* states on page 760 that the "First Church Building was erected in the reign of Alexander Severus (A.D. 222-235)." According to a website I visited ("World's 'oldest Christian church' discovered in Jordan"), it's possible that another church, dating back to 33 A.D. to 70 A.D., has been found in northern Jordan near the Syrian border. "We have uncovered what we believe to be the first church in the world, dating from 33 A.D. to 70 A.D.," Abdul Qader al-Husan, head of Jordan's Rihab Center for Archaeological Studies, said. "We have evidence to believe this church sheltered the early Christians–the 70 disciples of Jesus Christ." A mosaic in the church depicted these Christians as "the 70 beloved by God and Divine." However, the article suggests there is no clear holder of the title of the earliest Christian church, as various sites purport to claim the title with no true evidence.

Justin Martyr wrote the interesting *Dialogue with Trypho the Jew* in which he attempts to convince Trypho, a learned rabbi who had fled from Israel, and other Jews, of the Messiahship of Jesus Christ. I found this in *A Treasury of Early Christianity* which is an anthology of the works of early Christian writers. This dialogue took place ("if it really did"...quote by the compiler, Anne Fremantle) between 132-135 A.D., p.264).

The dialogue begins with Trypho accosting St. Martin as the latter paced the walks of the xystus (a Greek architectural term for a gymnasium at Ephesus ["The Early Christians in Ephesus from Paul to Ignatius"]). Trypho introduces himself by name, then adds, "I am a Hebrew of the circumcision, who have made my escape from the late war, and I live at present in Greece, and chiefly at Corinth." They talk back and forth about philosophical ideas of the times, such as Platonism, Stoicism, Peripateticism, Theoreticism, and Pythagoreanism, which they both have discarded in their own minds as being unsatisfactory in their pursuit of knowledge. Finally, Trypho gives a synopsis of his Jewish beliefs with the following words on page 272:

"There once lived men called prophets, who were anterior to any of those who are considered philosophers, and who were blessed, just, and beloved by God. These spoke by the Holy Ghost, and foretold what should happen thereafter, and what is now taking place. And they alone knew and taught the truth, neither regarding nor fearing any man, nor being themselves carried away by the love of glory, but declaring those things alone which they saw and heard when filled with the Holy Ghost. And their writings still remain to us, and whoever reads them will derive much instruction about the first principles and the end of things, together with all that a philosopher ought to know when he believes them...."

Justin Martyr answers Trypho with the following grand assertion on p. 274-275: "There never will be any other God, Trypho, nor has there even been any from eternity, but the One who created and ordered everything that we see; nor do we hold your God to be one and our own to be another, but we acknowledge one and the same, even Him who brought up your forefathers from the land of Egypt with a mighty hand and a stretched-out arm, nor do we put our trust in any other - for there is no other - but only in Him whom you also adore, the God of Abraham, the God of Isaac, and the God of Jacob. Our hope is, however, not through Moses, nor through the Law, or there would be no difference between you and ourselves; but I have read that there should hereafter be a final law, and a covenant more mighty than all others, which everyone who hopes for the inheritance of God should henceforth observe. The law given at Horeb has become obsolete, and was for you Jews only, but the one of which I speak is for all men alike. A new law passed upon a law abrogates that which is old, and in like manner does a subsequent covenant annul a former one. An everlasting and perfect law, and a faithful covenant, is given to us, even Christ, after which there shall be no other law, or ordinance, or command..."

The short dialogue between the two does not establish whether Trypho is convinced of the truth of Christianity, though he appears to be almost persuaded. However, the final words of Justin Martyr are powerful, signifying his own devout conviction:

"I cannot wish you, sirs, any greater benefit than that, knowing that through this way wisdom is given to every man, you may assuredly believe with us that ours is the Christ of God." (*A Treasury of Early Christianity*, p.276)

During Justin Martyr's time, Christians worshiped out of

doors, in homes, and in catacombs. The catacombs, most often associated with the Roman Empire, were subterranean passageways, made by humans for burial sites and for religious practice. Most of the early worship services focused on the Eucharist ("Where Did Christians Worship/Church History"). Below is a description of early Christian worship, as written in Chapter 67 of *First Apology* by Justin Martyr:

"And on the day called Sunday, all who live in cities or in the country gather together to one place, and the memoirs of the apostles or the writings of the prophets are read, as long as time permits; then, when the reader has ceased, the president verbally instructs, and exhorts to the imitation of these good things.

"Then we all rise together and pray, and, as we before said, when our prayer is ended, bread and wine and water are brought, and the president in like manner offers prayers and thanksgivings, according to his ability, and the people assent, saying Amen; and there is a distribution to each, and a participation of that over which thanks have been given, and to those who are absent a portion is sent by the deacons.

"And they who are well to do, and willing, give what each thinks fit; and what is collected is deposited with the president, who succours the orphans and widows and those who, through sickness or any other cause, are in want, and those who are in bonds and the strangers sojourning among us, and in a word takes care of all who are in need.

"But Sunday is the day on which we all hold our common assembly, because it is the first day on which God, having wrought a change in the darkness and matter, made the world; and Jesus Christ our Saviour on the same day rose from the dead.

"For He was crucified on the day before that of Saturn (Saturday); and on the day after that of Saturn, which is the day of the Sun, having appeared to His apostles and disciples, He taught them these things, which we have submitted to you also for your consideration." (*The Ante-Nicene Fathers,* Vol. 1, Page 186)

St. Justin and six of his devout Christian companions were condemned to death by the Roman prefect, Rusticus, for their refusal to bow down to "the gods" of Rome. In doing research for this book, I found on the internet the examination of Justyn Martyr and these six other early Christians by the Roman prefect, Rusticus. It is horrifying to read, especially when we consider that we, too, as Christians in the year 2018, may one day find ourselves in the same situation as Justin Martyr. Below is the text of the examination of Justin and his six Christian friends ("St. Justin Martyr–Saints and Angels–Catholic Online"):

"The Prefect Rusticus says: approach and sacrifice, all of you, to the gods. Justin says: No one in his right mind gives up piety for impiety. The Prefect Rusticus says: If you do not obey, you will be tortured without mercy. Justin replies: that is our desire, to be tortured for Our Lord, Jesus Christ, and so to be saved, for that will give us salvation and firm confidence at the more terrible universal tribunal of Our Lord and Saviour. And all the martyrs said: Do as you wish; for we are Christians, and we do not sacrifice to idols. The Prefect Rusticus read the sentence: Those who do not wish to sacrifice to the gods and to obey the emperor will be scourged and beheaded according to the laws. The holy martyrs glorifying God betook themselves to the customary place, where they were beheaded and consummated their martyrdom confessing their Saviour."

Justin Martyr was put to death in 165 A.D., during the reign of Marcus Aurelius Antoninus (161-180 A.D.) who, however, was considered one of the best men of heathen antiquity. Known for his philosophical interests, Marcus Aurelius' greatest intellectual pursuit was Stoicism, which emphasized reason, fate, and self-restraint ("St. Justin the Martyr [105-165 A.D.] –Catholic Faith and Reason"). M. Martha, historian of the Roman moralists, stated in regard to Marcus Aurelius Antoninus that "the philosophy of Heathendom grows less proud, draws nearer to a Christianity which it ignored or which it despised, and is ready to fling itself into the arms of the Unknown God." (*CATHOLIC ENCYCLOPEDIA*: Marcus Aurelius Antonius–New Advent)

Though Marcus Aurelius was wary of Christianity, and he branded Christians with obstinacy – the greatest social crime in the eyes of Roman authority ("Marcus Aurelius Antonius-Encyclopedia

Volume-Catholic") – he nonetheless wrote an epistle to the Roman Senate, which appears to substantiate the quotation in the paragraph above. In the letter, he testifies that the Christians were the cause of his military victory ("Letter of Emperor Marcus Aurelius on the Christian–ResearchGate").

* * * * * * * * * * * * *

According to Foxe, the first Christian to die a martyr's death in England was a man named Alban, who was a soldier in the Roman army, stationed at Verulamium, a city about twenty miles northeast of London, now called St. Albans in honor of his martyrdom. His birth date is unknown, and the date of his death isn't certain, but it's believed to be around 209 A.D. ("Saint Alban– Wikipedia"). Though first known to be an infidel, Alban received in his home a clerk who was fleeing from the persecutions of the Roman Emperor Septimius Severus. Alban was greatly moved by the invincibility and sincerity of his guest, whom he often saw in prayer, to the extent that his own life was changed, and he became an ardent Christian, himself.

When the soldiers came to remove the doomed man, Alban dressed himself in the apparel of his house guest and offered himself, instead, as a prisoner of the soldiers. When the soldiers brought him before the pagan judge who was at the altar, offering sacrifice to his false gods, the judge was enraged at Alban's audacity and proceeded to question him, as follows:

"Of what stock or kindred art thou come?"

Alban answered, "What is that to you, of what stock I come? If you desire to hear the verity of my religion, I do you to wit, that I am a Christian, and apply myself altogether to that calling."

Then said the judge, "I would know thy name, and see thou tell me the same without delay."

Then said he, "My parents named me Alban, and I worship the true and living God, Who created all the world."

Then said the judge, fraught with fury, "If thou wilt enjoy the felicity of prolonged life, do sacrifice (and that out of hand) to the mighty gods."

Alban replieth, "These sacrifices which ye offer unto devils, can neither help them that offer the same, neither yet can they accomplish the desires and prayers of their suppliants."

At the command of the judge, Alban was whipped unmercifully. When he persisted in his refusal to sacrifice to the false images, the judge commanded that he be beheaded *(Foxe's Book of Martyrs,* p. 31-33). The reputed place of his beheading is where St. Albans Cathedral now stands.

Several legends are associated with St. Alban's execution. He had to cross a river on his way to his execution, and finding the bridge full of people, he made the waters part and crossed over on dry land. This impressed the executioner so much that he also converted to Christianity and refused to kill Alban. Another executioner was found, whose eyes dropped from his head when he performed the execution. The first executioner was then killed after Alban, thereby becoming the second British Christian martyr.

Many churches and cathedrals in the world are dedicated to St. Alban. The Washington National Cathedral, an Episcopal Church in Washington, D.C., in the United States, is located on Mount St. Alban. The St. Albans School for Boys, which is affiliated with the Cathedral, is also named for him ("Saint Alban –Wikipedia").

John Foxe recorded the martyrdom of Romanus of Antioch (also known as Romanus of Caesarea), which occurred around 303-313 A.D. in the city of Antioch. At Antioch the Christians were all congregated together, when Romanus ran toward them, declaring that wolves in the forms of Emperor Galerius and his grand prefect Asclepiades were invading the city of Antioch. By force, they intended to make all Christians renounce their religion.

When the prefect heard from his armed soldiers that Romanus encouraged the assembled Christians to be strong in the face of Roman authority, the prefect said, "Seek out that rebel and bring him to me, that he may answer for the whole sect." Romanus was arrested and brought before the emperor who with great wrath engaged him in the following conversation:

"What! Art thou the author of this sedition? Art thou the cause why so many shall lose their lives? By the gods I swear thou shalt smart for it, and first in thy flesh shalt thou suffer the pains whereunto thou hast encouraged the hearts of thy fellows."

Romanus answered, "Thy sentence, O prefect, I joyfully embrace; I refuse not to be sacrificed for my brethren, and that by as cruel means as thou mayest invent"and whereas thy soldiers were repelled from the Christian congregation, that so happened, because it lay not in idolaters and worshipers of devils, to enter into the holy house of God, and to pollute the place of true prayer."

Furious with this unrepentant answer Asclepiades ordered that Romanus be bound and "his bowels drawn out." The executioners, however, answered, "Not so, sir, this man is of noble parentage; unlawful it is to put a nobleman to so unnoble a death."

"Scourge him then with whips,"quoth the prefect, "with knaps of lead at the ends."

"Not the blood of my progenitors," said he (Romanus), "but Christian profession maketh me noble."The more the martyr spoke, the greater the fury of the prefect, who commanded that Romanus' sides be lanced with knives, until the bones appeared to be white. When Romanus continued preaching the living God, the Lord Jesus Christ His well-beloved Son, and eternal life through faith in His blood, Asclepiades ordered the tormentors to strike Romanus on the mouth, so that his teeth were knocked out and his pronunciation impaired. Romanus' whole face was tortured, his eyelids torn, his cheeks cut with knives, and his beard plucked little by little from the flesh.

Meekly, the martyr said, "I thank thee, O prefect, that thou hast opened unto me many mouths, whereby I may preach my Lord and Saviour Christ. Look; how many wounds I have, so many mouths I have lauding and praising God."

The prefect said, "Thy crucified Christ is but a yesterday's God; the gods of the Gentiles are of most antiquity." (*Foxe's Book of Martyrs*, p. 34-35)

It is clear from reading the last sentence of the prefect that he nor probably others of his time period thought that Christianity would survive. Indeed, he referred to Christ as "but a yesterday's God," p.35. They would likely be amazed to know that Christianity is alive and well in the year 2018, over 1700 years later. Also, we as

CAN WE FATHOM THE NATURE OF GOD?

Christ's followers intend to carry it forward during our lifetimes, as others will who are later born. The false gods of the grand prefect fell by the wayside not many years after his words were spoken.

Dear Reader, it was with horror that I continued reading about Romanus in the next few pages of *Foxe's Book of Martyrs*, for the unspeakable - the unthinkable - was recorded on these pages. It was the martyrdom of a small child! I had never known that such occurred, but Foxe recorded it for posterity. Without teeth to facilitate his speaking, because of his torture, Romanus somehow made a long oration on the eternity of Christ and his salvation of all who believed in Him. Having done this, he asked that a small child be brought to him. Below are his words, as written by Foxe:

"Give me a child, O prefect, but seven years of age, which age is free from malice and other vices wherewith riper age is commonly infected, and thou shalt hear what he will say."

A little child was called from the multitude who stood before the martyr.

"Tell me, my babe," quoth the martyr, "whether thou think it reason that we should worship one Christ, and in Christ one Father, or else that we worship many gods?"

The child replied, "That certainly (whatsoever it be) which men affirm to be God, must needs be one; and that which pertains to that one, is unique: and inasmuch as Christ is unique, of necessity Christ must be the true God; for that there be many gods, we children cannot believe."

The amazed prefect said, "Thou young villain and traitor, where, and of whom learnedst thou this lesson?"

"Of my mother," quoth the child, "with whose milk I sucked in this lesson, that I must believe in Christ."

The child was tortured as Romanus had been, but never did he flinch. In fact, according to Foxe, he received the stripes with "smiling countenance." The mother took her child in her arms and said, "Farewell, my sweet child; and when thou hast entered the kingdom of Christ, there in thy blest estate remember thy mother."

As the hangman held his sword to the child's neck, the mother sang the song below:

"All laud and praise with heart and voice,
O Lord, we yield to thee:
To whom the death of this thy saint,
We know most dear to be."

Romanus and the child were led to the execution where the child was beheaded. Romanus was led back to prison where he was strangled (*Foxe's Book of Martyrs*, p. 35-38).

CHAPTER TEN

Though not much has been written about Jesus in the context of history, other than the Bible itself, we do have the few writings of certain historians who lived near the time that Jesus walked the earth. Aside from Josephus, other historians who briefly mentioned Jesus in their works were *Clement* (30-100 A.D.) (*The Ante-Nicene Fathers*, Vol. 1, p.5), *Cornelius Tacitus* (ca. 55 A.D.-ca. 120 A.D) (*A Treasury of Early Christianity,* p. 251-252); *Pliny the Younger* (61 A.D.-113 A.D.) (*A Treasury of Early Christianity,* p. 253-255); and *Tertullian* (c.160 -230 A.D.) (*A Treasury of Early Christianity,* p. 277-279).

According to an "Introductory Note" p. 1-3, to the *First Epistle of Clement to the Corinthians,* which I read in the informative book entitled *The Ante-Nicene Fathers* by Alexander Roberts and James Donaldson, Clement was likely a Roman and a Gentile, who seemed to have been with St. Paul at Philippi in 57 A.D. The book also states that though Clement's identity cannot definitely be ascertained, the general opinion is that he is the Clement mentioned by St. Paul in Philippians 4:3. This letter of his to the Corinthians was held in great esteem by the early Church.

The Roman historian, Eusebius (260/265 - 339/340 A.D.), wrote about this epistle, on p. 2 of the "Introductory Note," mentioned above, the following words:

"There is one acknowledged Epistle of this Clement (whom he had just identified with the friend of St. Paul), great and admirable, which he wrote in the name of the Church of Rome to the Church at Corinth, sedition having then arisen in the latter Church. We are aware that this Epistle has been publicly read in very many churches both in old times, and also in our own day." ("First Epistle of Clement to the Corinthians–Christian Classics Ethereal")

The selection below is a lasting tribute to Clement, for it speaks of his earnest belief in his Saviour, Jesus Christ. We must remember that Clement was born around the time that Christ was put to death on the cross. Please note the beauty and sincerity of his words in his letter, on p. 10-11 of "The First Epistle of Clement to the Corinthians":

"Chap. XX – The Peace and Harmony of the Universe"

"The heavens, revolving under His government, are subject to Him in peace. Day and night run the course appointed by Him, in no wise hindering each other. The sun and moon, with the companies of the stars, roll on in harmony according to His command, within their prescribed limits, and without any deviation. The fruitful earth, according to His will, brings forth food in abundance, at the proper seasons, for man and beast and all the living beings upon it, never hesitating, nor changing any of the ordinances which He has fixed. The unsearchable places of abysses, and the indescribable arrangements of the lower world, are restrained by the same laws. The vast unmeasurable sea, gathered together by His working into various basins, never passes beyond the bounds placed around it, but does as He has commanded.

"For He said, 'Thus far shalt thou come, and thy waves shall be broken within thee.' The ocean, impassible to man, and the worlds beyond it, are regulated by the same enactments of the Lord. The seasons of spring, summer, autumn, and winter, peacefully give place to one another. The winds in their several quarters fulfil, at the proper time, their service without hindrance. The ever-flowing fountains, formed both for enjoyment and health, furnish without fail their breasts for the life of men. The very smallest of living beings meet together in peace and concord. All these the great Creator and Lord of all has appointed to exist in peace and harmony; while He does good to all, but most abundantly to us who have fled for refuge to His compassions through Jesus Christ our Lord, to whom be glory and majesty for ever and ever. Amen."

Cornelius Tacitus (55?-120 A.D.) was a Roman historian and senator (*A Treasury of Early Christianity*, p. 251) who referred to Christ in his final work, *Annals* (written ca. 116 A.D.), Book 15, chapter 44. He first describes the six-day Great Fire of Rome that burned much of that city in July of 64 A.D. Since much of the blame for the fire was placed on the new group of people called Christians, Tacitus addresses this, as follows:

"Consequently, to get rid of the report, Nero fastened the guilt and inflicted the most exquisite tortures on a class hated for their abominations, called Christians by the populace. Christus, from whom the name had its origin, suffered the extreme penalty during the reign of Tiberius at the hands of one of our procurators, Pontius Pilatus, and a most mischievous superstition, thus checked for the moment, again broke out not only in Judaea, the first source of the evil, but even in Rome, where all things hideous and shameful from every part of the world find their centre and become popular. Accordingly, an arrest was first made of all who pleaded guilty, then, upon their information, an immense multitude was convicted, not so much of the crime of firing the city, as of hatred against mankind. Mockery of every sort was added to their deaths.

"Covered with the skins of beasts, they were torn by dogs and perished, or were nailed to crosses, or were doomed to the flames and burnt, to serve as a nightly illumination, when daylight had expired. Nero offered his gardens for the spectacles, and was exhibiting a show in the circus, while he mingled with the people in the dress of a charioteer, or stood aloft on a car. Hence, even for criminals who deserved extreme and exemplary punishment, there arose a feeling of compassion, for it was not as it seemed, for the public good, but to glut one man's cruelty, that they were being destroyed." ("Cornelius Tacitus–Early Christian Writings")

Pliny the Younger (62-c. 113) was an augur which was a lifetime priesthood or soothsayer of Rome's official religion. He was supposed to interpret the will of the gods for the Roman people. He was also a writer whose *Epistulae (Letters)* are collected in ten books. These writings describe the life of a Roman gentleman, philanthropist, and scholar. His letter to the historian, Tacitus, describes in detail the eruption of Vesuvius and also the death of his uncle, Pliny the Elder. His letters are the earliest records of Christians, written by a pagan. A good orator, he was thought to be one of the most learned men of his time ("Pliny the Younger–Wikipedia").

In the letters that he wrote to the Emperor Trajan, he described the Christians and asked what should be done about them. He also said that he had forced Christians to curse Christ. In one letter (*Epistulae X:96*) he describes these early Christians:

"They asserted, however, that the sum and substance of their fault or error had been that they were accustomed to meet on a fixed day before dawn and sing responsively a hymn to Christ as to a god, and bound themselves to a solemn oath, not to any wicked deeds, but never to commit any fraud, theft, adultery, never to falsify their word, not to deny a trust when they should be called upon to deliver it up. When this was over, it was their custom to depart and to assemble again to partake of a meal - but ordinary and innocent food." ("Meeting with the Early Church–Pliny's Letter")

The testimony of Pliny the Younger that Christians died for their beliefs is as follows:

"Meanwhile, in the case of those who were denounced to me as Christians, I have observed the following procedure: I interrogated these as to whether they were Christians; those who confessed I interrogated a second and a third time, threatening them with punishment; those who persisted I ordered executed. For I had no doubt that, whatever the nature of their creed, stubbornness and inflexible obstinacy surely deserve to be punished. There were others possessed of the same folly; but because they were Roman citizens, I signed an order for them to be transferred to Rome." ("Pliny the Younger and Trajan on the Christians–Early Christian Writings")

The writer Tertullian (c. 155-c. 240 A.D.) lived in Carthage in the Roman province of Africa. A scholar with an excellent judicial training, his conversion to Christianity occurred around 197-198 A.D. The event must have happened suddenly and decisively. In his *Apol. XVIII*, he stated, "Christians are made, not born." He also said, "The blood of the martyrs is the seed of the Church." Without martyrdom, according to Tertullian, the Church would never have taken root. Tertullian coined the word "Trinity," which word does not appear anywhere in the Bible. However, the threefold parts of our God, i.e. the Father, the Son, and the Holy Spirit definitely comprise the Trinity, which word has come forward to us from many centuries of long ago ("Tertullian – Wikipedia").

Origen Adamantius (184/185 A.D. - 253/254 A.D.) of Alexandria, Egypt (and later, Caesarea, Palestine) and Eusebius, (263 A.D. - 339 A.D.) of Caesarea in Palestine, were two early writers whose works influenced the continuance of Christianity. Origen was a Roman historian and interpreter of Christian beliefs ("Origen–Wikipedia"). We must realize that Christianity had not yet developed a system of theology, so some of Origen's thoughts are strange to us today.

His concept of Apokatastasis, or "restoration of all things," according to a site I visited on the internet, espoused the belief that every person - and even the devil and his demons - would be saved ("Satan and God reconciled?–His Grace Is Enough"). This, of course, contradicted the teachings and actions of the apostles. Though his writings are included in the general collection of the early Church Fathers, Origen was never canonized by the Catholic Church because of his controversial beliefs ("Is Origen a saint and a Church Father?–Ask an Apologist").

However, because of Origen, Caesarea became a center of Christian learning. Important themes in Origen's philosophy emerged, such as free will and the value of education and history, even though some of his concepts seem foreign to our understanding of the Scriptures in this twenty-first century. Origen is credited with being responsible for the collection of information regarding the texts of our New Testament ("Origen–Wikipedia"). On his deathbed, Origen bequeathed his personal library to the Christian community in Caesarea ("Eugammon of Cyrene– WikiVisually").

Though the church historian, Eusebius, never knew Origen, he too lived in Caesarea which by the third century had a population of around 100,000 people. Eusebius compiled a *Collection of Ancient Martyrdoms* which alluded to the fact that many of the Caesarean martyrs lived together in the city. In the 290s, Eusebius began working on his *magnum opus, the Ecclesiastical History.* This was a history of the church and Christian community from the Apostolic Age to Eusebius' own time. About the same time, he worked on his *Chronicle,* a universal calendar of events from creation to Eusebius' time period.

In his *Ecclesiastical History,* Volume 1, pages 85-97, Eusebius wrote a chronologically-ordered account of the Christian Church. It is the first surviving history of the Church. According to an article in *Wikipedia* about Eusebius, he is remembered as the "Father of Church History." ("Eusebius of Caesarea–*Wikipedia*") Though he has had some modern-day (and other) detractors, I think the fact that he lived so close to the time of Christ makes him believable to me.

It is fascinating to read words written by a historian who lived so near the time period of Christ. I feel led to include certain parts of his records, for I believe that you, dear Reader, will also find them fascinating and worthwhile to include. In his *Ecclesiastical History,* Volume 1, pages 85-97, he tells about a man named Abgar.

An Arab by ethnicity, known as Abgar V in Greek (and Acbarus in Latin), was the king of a small Syriac kingdom called Osroene, with its capital at Edessa. Edessa was a major center of the early Christian church in Syria. Abgar V first came to power in 4 B.C. lost his throne in 7 A.D., and regained it five years later. He was king for the next 37 years. His personal rival was Herod the Tetrarch.

Abgar is alleged by several ancient authors to have corresponded by letter with Jesus Christ around 30 A.D. Later, he converted to Christianity, becoming the first ruling monarch in the world to do so. First mention of this is in Eusebius' *History of the Church*, written three hundred years later after the events described. Abgar V contracted a chronic illness which was life-threatening. Having heard about this man called Jesus who could perform miraculous healings, he contacted Jesus via courier.

Eusebius reported that he personally examined both Abgar's letter to Jesus and Jesus' response which were preserved in the Record Office in Edessa. They were written around 30 A.D. He translated them from Syriac (Aramaic) to Greek and published both of them in his *History*. Eusebius states unequivocally that he had seen the letters, one from Abgar and the return letter from Jesus, in the archives at Edessa ("The Letters of Abgar V/Gates of Nineveh: An Experiment in Blogging..."). Abgar's letter to Jesus was sent by courier. It appears below:

"Abgar Uchama the Toparch to Jesus, who has appeared as a gracious savior in the region of Jerusalem–greeting.

"I have heard about you and the cures which you perform without drugs or herbs. If report is true, you make the blind see again and the lame walk about; you cleanse lepers, expel unclean spirits and demons, cure those suffering from chronic and painful diseases, and raise the dead. When I heard all of this about you, I concluded that one of two things must be true–either you are God and came down from heaven to do these things, or you are God's son doing them. Accordingly I am writing to you to come to me, whatever the inconvenience, and cure the disorder from which I suffer. I may add that I understand the Jews are treating you with contempt and desire to injure you; my city is very small, but highly esteemed, adequate for both of us."

Eusebius records that the apostle Thaddaeus (one of the 72 disciples commissioned by Jesus in the middle of his ministry, mentioned in the Gospel of Luke), was sent to Abgar by Jesus, and Abgar was healed. *Halley's Bible Handbook* suggests that Thaddaeus was one of the twelve disciples of Jesus on page 466, who attended Abgar. Eusebius states unequivocally that he had seen the letters, one from Abgar and the return letter from Jesus, in the Record Office at Edessa ("The Letters of Abgar V/Gates of Nineveh: An Experiment in Blogging"). According to Eusebius, the reply from Jesus to Abgar, the Toparch, and carried back by the same courier is as follows:

"Happy are you who believed me without having seen me! For it is written of me that those who have seen me will not believe in me, and that those who have not seen me will believe and live. As to your request that I should come to you, I must complete all that I was sent to do here, and on completing it must at once be taken up to the One who sent me. When I have been taken up I will send you one of my disciples to cure your disorder and bring life to you and those with you."

In Volume 1, page 269, Eusebius mentions Clement who stated that the apostle Paul had a wife whom "he did not take about with him in order to facilitate his mission." ("Eusebius Collection [6 Books]:–Google Books Result") This appears to refute the verses in the New Testament which suggest that Paul did not have a wife ("The Apostles that were married. Bible Hub"). Also, Eusebius matter-of-factly mentions that Paul wrote the Epistle to the Hebrews but that Luke or Clement translated it from the Hebrew into the Greek language ("Authorship of the Epistle to the Hebrews–*Wikipedia*"). I include this tidbit because there is some dissension in regard to the author of Hebrews in our Bible.

In Volume 2, beginning with page 421, Eusebius gives the earliest account we have of the structure and furniture of the first Christian church. The first church in the Bible is mentioned in Acts 2:46 as a part of the Jewish temple in Jerusalem, where the early Christians met. They also met in small groups **"from house to house,"** (Acts 2:46) as in the house of Mary, mother of Mark (Acts 12:12).

Usually, one bishop in a city became the center of unity for Christians in his city. The eucharistic bread was sent from the bishop's church in Rome to other assemblies of Christians. ("Why and when did Christians start constructing specia..../Christian") According to Halley, the first church building was built during the reign of Alexander Severus (A.D. 222-235). After the Edict of Constantine, when Christianity was legitimized, they were built everywhere (*Halley's*, p. 760).

As the body of Christian believers grew, they felt the need of joint assemblies and meeting places. Not only did a church building provide a place for daily Bible teaching, the distribution of gifts to the poor, and baptisms, it also gave a visible sign of permanence. However, for the most part, the early church was dependent upon members or patrons who owned larger homes which could accommodate groups of believers.

Whereas Origen had non-Biblical ideas about the salvation of every person ("The School of Alexandria–Origen–Ch 1–Origen's Life"), Eusebius had his own controversial ideas about the relationship of God and Jesus. He subscribed to the unorthodox belief that Jesus the Son was subordinate to God the Father. This theory was espoused by Arius (c. A.D. 256-336). ("Subordinationism–*Wikipedia*") Again, we must remember that the Church was young and was trying to find its way through the maze of many different interpretations of the Scriptures.

Arius was a Christian presbyter in Alexandria, Egypt. Because of his heretical concept concerning the relationship between Father and Son, which was in opposition to the Church's teaching in regard to the Trinity, the first Ecumentical Council of Nicaea was called by the Roman Emperor Constantine on July 4, 325 A.D. (Isn't it unusual that July 4th in America is the date of the signing of the Declaration of Independence?) The Council of Nicaea emphasized the trinity of the Godhead, and anyone not accepting this belief was exiled or put to death by Constantine.

The Arian controversy was one of the foremost disagreements within the Christian Church, and it still has its proponents, even in this twenty-first century. According to the *Wikipedia* website I researched in regard to Arianism, the Jehovah's Witnesses church is regarded as Arian, along with that of the Church of God ("Arianism–*Wikipedia*"). For several decades, Arianism thrived, even within the family of the emperor, the nobility, and high-ranking clergy ("Arianism/-Theology Wiki/FANDOM Powered by Wikia").

In 303 A.D., the Roman Emperor Diocletian called for the destruction of all Scriptures of the Christians. This compelled Christians to salvage as many of their books as possible by turning over to the Roman authorities less important texts that were not considered sacred. Those who handed over sacred Scriptures to the soldiers were called "traitors" or "traditores." ("Traditors–*Wikipedia*") Those who refused were called confessors and martyrs, for they were imprisoned and killed. This was an effort by Diocletian to destroy Christianity ("Diocletian's destruction and Constantine's production of Scripture").

For ten years, Christians were hunted in forests and caves. They were thrown to wild beasts, burned, and put to death by every device evil could devise. This was the last and worst of the Imperial persecutions ("Supernatural Immunity: Exploring God's Keeping Power from Psalm 91"). Listed below are some of the emperor's orders: "Christians holding office were to be put out of office; All accusations against Christians were to be welcomed and received; Christians were to be tortured for their faith; Scriptures were to be confiscated and burned immediately; Church buildings were to be destroyed; Presidents, bishops, and leaders of churches were to be arrested in order to sacrifice to the gods." ("The Great Persecution began in Rome in A.D. 303–Sermon Index")

The Caesarean historian Eusebius wrote the following words about the Christian persecution under the emperor, Diocletian: "We saw with our own eyes the houses of prayer thrown down to the very foundations, and the Divine and Sacred Scriptures committed to the flames in the market-places, and the shepherds of the churches basely hidden here and there, and some of them captured ignominiously, and mocked by their enemies." (*The Church History of Eusebius*:– Google Books Result)

Chapter Eleven

Constantine was the first emperor of Rome to become a Christian. He was born around A.D. c. 272 in Naissus, now Nisch in Serbia, and died in 337 A.D. (Note: The information about Constantine can be found online under numerous titles. Some include "Constantine the Great–*Wikipedia*"; "Constantine/Biography, Accomplishments, Death, & Facts"; and "Constantine/Christian History." They all differ about his birth date.) Though he was a pagan who murdered his wife and son, during his reign the Christian church became legal.

On his way to Rome in 312 A.D., to fight against the evil Roman emperor, Maxentius, who vied for victory as the sole emperor of the Roman Empire, Constantine, toward evening time, saw a great brightness in the sky, which was in the form of a cross. On it was the Latin inscription *In Hoc Signo Vinces*, which meant "With this sign you shall win." The battle would be lopsided, for Maxentius had a military which was double the size of Constantine's ("Constantine the Great– Wikipedia").

Later, while asleep at night, Jesus appeared to him with the sign of the same cross which he had seen in the sky, telling him to make a likeness of it and to carry it before him when he went to war. This would bring about his victory. This was God's way of ensuring that Christianity would grow and would be strengthened.

On the day following this vision, Constantine commanded that a cross be made of gold and precious stones, which was to be borne ahead of him, instead of his usual standard. It was alleged that, upon his orders, his soldiers' shields were to be marked in Greek with the first two letters of Christ's name ("In *Hoc Signo Vinces*–Church Militant"). When he was victorious, he became a strong advocate of Christianity and was baptized a Christian on his deathbed ("Deathbed Conversion–Wikipedia").

His Edict of Milan in A.D. 313 granted to "Christians and to all others Full Liberty of following the Religion which each may choose," the first act of its kind in history ("General History–Page 219–Google books Result"). This was the beginning of the legitimacy of Christianity. Constantine favored Christians by filling offices with them, exempting Christian ministers from taxes and military service, encouraging and assisting in building churches, and exhorting all of his subjects to embrace Christianity. When the Roman aristocracy continued to adhere to their pagan religions, Constantine moved his capitol to Byzantium and called it Constantinople or "New Rome," capital of the New Christian Empire (*Halley's*, p. 759).

For the churches of Constantinople, the king ordered fifty Bibles, to be prepared under the direction of the Roman historian, Eusebius, by skillful artists and on the finest vellum. He then commissioned two public carriages for their swift conveyance to the Emperor (*Halley's*, p. 745).

He also made Sunday the day of Christians' assembly, forbidding ordinary work (*Halley's*, p. 760). Later, in 380 A.D., though known for brutal excesses in ridding the Roman Empire of paganism, Emperor Theodosius (A.D. 378-398) made Christianity the state religion of the Roman Empire and made church membership compulsory (*Halley's*, p. 760).

* * * * * * * * * * * * * *

God's nature is such that he chose a man named Aurelius Augustinus, or Saint Augustine, who lived from 354-430 A.D., to influence the people of his time period to keep alive the flame of Christianity. Born in Thagaste, a city in Algeria, in Roman Africa, Augustine wrote *The City of God* which attracted many pagans to Christianity. He was converted to Christianity in a garden in Milan, Italy, when he heard a child's voice say, "Take up and read!" He picked up the Bible and read the first Scripture that appeared when he opened the book. It was Romans 13:13-14, which states: **"Let us walk honestly, as in the day; not in rioting and drunkenness, not in chambering and wantonness, not in strife and envying. But put ye on the Lord Jesus Christ, and make not provision for the flesh, to fulfil the lusts thereof."** ("St. Augustine of Hippo–Wikipedia")

Since Augustine had been leading something of a profligate life, he felt that the words were expressly meant for him. They completely changed his life and he gave up the lusts that had controlled his life up until that time. An apocryphal story about Saint Augustine is that before his conversion to Christianity, he used to frequent the prostitutes in his town. A few months after his life-altering encounter with Christ, he passed a prostitute on the street and did not speak to her. She yelled at him, "Augustine, didn't you see me? It is I." His response to her was, "Yes, but it is not I." ("Did St. Augustine say this to a prostitute?–Truth Challenge") He was indeed a changed man, seeking the will of God and not his own. His life and his prolific writings greatly aided in spreading Christianity throughout the world.

Ambrose (340?-397 A.D.) was a fourth-century church father and preacher. Born in Rome, he was an aristocratic statesman whose administrative ability influenced the liturgy of public worship. His advice to Saint Augustine was to follow local customs as far as liturgy was concerned. He said, "When I am at Rome, I fast on a Saturday; when I am at Milan, I do not. Follow the custom of the church where you are." Thus, Ambrose refused to be drawn into a conflict over which particular local church had the "right" liturgical form, where there was no substantial problem ("Ambrose–Wikipedia").

Ambrose wrote many scriptural works, treatises, and letters, of which ninety-one survive. Some of his hymns are still in use. In his writing "On the Death of Theodosius," he tells about Helen, mother of the Roman Emperor Constantine, who was a devout Christian. Helen (250–330 A.D.) longed to find the manger of Christ, so she traveled to the Holy Land on her quest. Though she didn't find the manger, she drew near to Golgotha, where Jesus had hung on the cross. Here, she exclaimed, "Behold the place of combat. Where is thy victory? I seek the standard of salvation, and I do not find it. I, among kings, and the Cross of my Lord in the dust? I in golden ornaments, and the triumph of Christ among ruins?"

Opening the ground, she found three fork-shaped gibbets (gallows) which the debris had covered. Then, she sought the middle wood which would have held the body of Jesus. After returning to the text of the Gospel, she found on the middle gibbet a title which was displayed. It read: "Jesus of Nazareth, King of the Jews." (*A Treasury of Early Christianity,* "St. Ambrose," p. 111-114)

Dear Reader, I checked my Bible to see whether these were the words on the cross, recorded in the four Gospels. The first three Gospels were worded differently. Then, I checked the Gospel of John, and the wording was exactly the same. Remember, John was the only disciple who was an eyewitness at the hanging of Jesus. The words were written in Hebrew, Greek, and Latin ("Jesus, King of the Jews – Wikipedia")

* * * * * * * * * * * * * *

Living from 340-420 A.D., Jerome was another early church father who translated the Latin *Vulgate* around 405 A.D. He was commissioned by Pope Damascus in 382 A.D. to make a revision of old Latin translations. For the Old Testament, he used Hebrew and Greek texts and Latin translations; for the New Testament, he used Greek texts and Latin translations. This was the standard Bible for over one thousand years and is still an important text in Catholicism (*Vulgate*– Wikipedia–History). We must remember that this was before the inventions of the typewriter and the printing press, so this labor on his part took years to complete. God used Jerome to propagate the seed of Christianity.

The period following the decline of the Roman Empire is often referred to as the "Dark Ages." Roughly lasting from the fifth to the fifteenth century, it was a period of religious struggle between Catholicism and emerging Protestantism within the Church and also the warlike religion of Islam. These centuries are shrouded in darkness insofar as intellectual and other achievements were

CAN WE FATHOM THE NATURE OF GOD?

concerned ("Middle Ages–Wikipedia").

During this time period, however, beautiful cathedrals and basilicas were built. The Christian monastic life also took hold, with men living as hermits in the desert, devoting themselves to lives of simplicity and prayer. As men banded together to surrender their lives to prayer and worship, monasteries came into existence, some of which later became centers of learning, such as Oxford and Cambridge ("Medieval University–Wikipedia"). In between prayers, monks worked on their projects of writing, copying and decorating books ("Monastery–Wikipedia").

Mohammed was born around 570 A.D. and died in 632 A.D. What he taught and espoused is the antithesis of Christianity. As horse and camel warriors, his followers rode through the fallen empire with years of vast conquests ("The Dark Ages–AllAboutHistory.org"). The age-old conflict between Christianity and Islam remains until this day. The conflict began with the two half brothers who were the sons of Abraham - Isaac and Ishmael (*Halley's*, p. 102; Genesis 16:1-16; and Genesis 21:1-20).

God made it clear in Genesis 21 that Isaac was his chosen seed, the one whose family would, around 1900 years later, produce his own Son. Abraham and Sarah were the parents of Isaac, whereas Abraham and Hagar, Sarah's Egyptian bondwoman, were the parents of Ishmael (Genesis 16). However, when God saw that Hagar was distraught because she and her son were turned away from the home of Abraham, God promised her that a great nation would derive from her son. The Bible even says that God was with Ishmael who lived in the wilderness and became an archer (Genesis 21). Yet, it is abundantly clear that God's chosen one of the two was Isaac.

I heard someone make the simple but astute observation that Islam, with its Shariah (and other) laws, is comparable to the torturous Inquisition of the Middle Ages, brought about by the Catholic Church. The church cleansed itself of the anti-scriptural Inquisition, while the Shariah sect of Islam is in the throes of unspeakable punishments perpetrated against its believers for almost any infraction against its tenets. Atrocities are still committed and condoned in the name of Islam in this twenty-first century. In the words of *Halley's Bible Handbook,* page 766, Mohammedanism was "a revolt against the idolatry of the 'Christian world,' a judgment on a corrupt and degenerate Church."

Also according to *Halley's Bible Handbook,* page 766, the Battle of Tours, France (A.D. 732), was one of the greatest battles ever won, when Charles Martel, ruler of Gaul from 719 A.D.-791 A.D., defeated the Moslem army and saved Europe from Mohammedanism, which was sweeping the world in its conquests (*Halley's,* p. 717). Gaul was a region of Europe which included the present-day countries of France, part of Germany, Luxembourg, and Belgium ("Gaul During the Roman Empire–French History–Discover France"). The continuing domination of the world by Mohammedanism brought about the seven Crusades which occurred from 1095 A.D.-1272 A.D. *(Halley's,* p. 766).

Simply stated, the Crusades were military expeditions formed, in part, to recapture Palestine from the Moslems who were then in control. Thousands of knights, kings, peasants and townspeople took part in the Crusades. Though the goal of freeing the Holy Land was a lofty one, many of the travelers also fought to increase their riches and territory and power ("How the Crusades Began").

* * * * * * * * * * * * * *

In 1215, a document known as the Magna Carta was prepared on parchment with the seal of King John of England and publicly read to all free men throughout his kingdom. This charter was created by a group of barons who assembled on the plains of Runnymeade, a meadow not far from where Windsor Castle is located today ("The Magna Carta–Wikipedia"). The Magna Carta stated the following:

"No freeman shall be taken, imprisoned, disseised, outlawed, banished, or in any way destroyed, nor will We proceed against or prosecute him, except by the lawful judgment of his peers or by the law of the land." ("The Magna Carta/National Archives")

Surely, God planted this seed of democracy in the thoughts and hearts of the barons who persuaded a wayward king to affix his seal to the powerful charter. This was an acknowledgment that even the king was not above the law. The 800th anniversary of the birth date of the Magna Carta was celebrated in England and acknowledged in America in 2015 ("National Archives Celebrates 800th Anniversary of the Magna Carta"). God is continuing to move among the Gentiles.

JANE H. WALKER

Chapter Twelve

God's nature is such that he allowed the great Italian poet and scholar, Petrarch, to be born (1304 A.D.-1374 A.D.) ("Petrarch–Wikipedia"), whose life furthered the spread of Christianity and ushered in the Renaissance. Francesco Petrarch described his own birth with the following words: "I was born to this world in the Via dell' Orto of the city of Arezzo, just at dawn on Monday, July 20, in the thirteen hundred and fourth year of this latest age which takes its name from Jesus Christ, fountain and author of all my hope." (" Petrarch–Institute for the Study of Western Civilization")

After reading his words, oh Reader, don't you sense something of the nature of God?

Petrarch believed in returning to the ancient writings of Greek and Roman authors, such as Cicero, Virgil, and his mentor, St. Augustine. He disdained the centuries of darkness and ignorance which preceded his birth. He is known to have developed the concept of those unenlightened years as the "Dark Ages" ("Petrarch–Wikipedia").

A simple event in his life wrought a complete reversal in regard to his philosophy of life, when he climbed to the top of Mont Ventoux, a mountain which rises over six thousand feet in the Provence region of southern France. Geologically, it is a part of the Alps, but it is considered separate from them. This mountain has gained fame in modern times because of its use in the *Tour de France* cycling race. The summit is very windy, as its name suggests. Ventoux means "windy" in French. Winds as high as 200 mph have been recorded, and the wind blows at 56 mph 240 days a year ("Mont Ventoux–Wikipedia").

Upon reaching the summit of Mont Ventoux, Petrarch took from his pocket a volume of St. Augustine's *Confessions* and as the book fell open, he read the words that appeared on the open page:

"And men go about to wonder at the heights of the mountains, and the mighty waves of the sea, and the wide sweep of rivers, and the circuit of the ocean, and the revolution of the stars, but themselves they consider not." ("Petrarch–Wikipedia")

Petrarch felt that these words spoke personally to him, and he later responded with the following written words:

"I closed the book, angry with myself that I should still be admiring earthly things who might long ago have learned from even the pagan philosophers that nothing is wonderful but the soul, which, when great itself, finds nothing great outside itself. Then, in truth, I was satisfied that I had seen enough of the mountain; I turned my inward eye upon myself, and from that time not a syllable fell from my lips until we reached the bottom again.... We look about us for what is to be found only within. How many times, think you, did I turn back that day, to glance at the summit of the mountain which seemed scarcely a cubit high compared with the range of human contemplation..." ("Petrarch–Wikipedia")

Petrarch has been called the father of the Renaissance. Metaphorically, the Renaissance did not begin with his "ascent" of Mont Ventoux but with his subsequent "descent," when Petrarch realized the importance of man's soul ("Petrarch's testamentum–WikiVisually"). He was a prolific writer who wrote the words below, while sitting at his desk, and they give us insight not only into his thoughts but into the very nature of God:

"I had got this far, and was thinking of what to say next, and as my habit is, I was pricking the paper idly with my pen. And I thought how, between one dip of the pen and the next, time goes on, and I hurry, drive myself, and speed toward death. We are always dying. I while I write, you while you read, and others while they listen or stop their ears, they are all dying." ("Petrarch– Institute for the Study of Western Civilization by W.H. Fredlund")

Can We Fathom the Nature of God?

An introspective man, Petrarch struggled with the proper balance between the active and the contemplative life. He tended to embrace the importance of solitude and study. He felt that God meant for man to use all of the talents and abilities that the Lord gave him, and he set about to fulfill this belief, giving rise to the very essence of the Renaissance. He was a prolific writer of poetry with the sonnet being his favored method of expression. The Petrarchan sonnet still bears his name. He wrote 366 poems, of which 317 were sonnets. The term Renaissance literally means "rebirth," or a return to the classical values of the golden age of Greek and Roman culture. He was the progenitor of many of the great writers of the Renaissance ("Petrarch–Wikipedia").

A great event occurred in 1440 A.D. when Johannes Gutenberg (1398 A.D.?-1468 A.D.?) developed movable type or the printing press. Born in Mainz, Germany, Gutenberg invented the type mold which made printing from movable metallic type practical for the first time. The Gutenberg Bible was one of the first products of movable type, which set the stage for many Bibles in different languages to be printed ("Johann Gutenberg–Greatsite.com").

Paper, long known to the Chinese, was made of rags in 1319 ("The Bromley Record and Monthly Advertiser"). Printing on paper made all knowledge available to everyone, especially after the invention of the printing press. This also aided in bringing about the Protestant Reformation of the Church ("Gutenberg's Legacy"). It is certain that God brought this about.

* * * * * * * * * * * * *

During the many centuries of the "Dark Ages," the papacy ruled the Church. As papal power grew, corruption became prevalent within the hierarchy of the Church, even among the Popes themselves. The English Catholic historian, politician, and writer, Lord Acton, who lived from 1834-1902 A.D., said, "All power tends to corrupt and absolute power corrupts absolutely." ("John Dalberg–Acton, 1st Baron Acton") This certainly describes the Popes of that period. According to *Halley's Bible Handbook,* p. 774, "the 200 years between Nicholas I and Gregory VI (870-1050 A.D.) are called by historians the MIDNIGHT OF THE DARK AGES.

Bribery, corruption, immorality and bloodshed make it just about the blackest chapter in the whole history of the Church."

Nicolas I (858-867 A.D.) was the first pope to wear a crown. To exalt his papal authority, he used a book that appeared around 857 A.D., called *Pseudoisidorian Decretals,* purportedly containing letters and decrees of bishops and councils of the second and third centuries, all tending to glorify the Pope. These were forgeries and corruptions of ancient historical documents, which were found to be heretical some centuries later (*Halley's*, p. 773).

Many popes bought the office of Pope for themselves, an immoral and unethical procedure called simony, which is the purchase or sale of church office with money (*Halley's*, p. 774). Again, according to *Halley's Bible Handbook,* Sergius III (A.D. 904-911) was said to have a mistress, Marozia. She, her mother Theodora, and her sister "filled the Papal chair with their paramours and bastard sons, and turned the Papal Palace into a den of robbers." This era has been called by historians "The Rule of the Harlots (904-963 A.D.)." (*Halley's*, p. 774)

Benedict IX (1033 A.D.-1045 A.D.) at the age of twelve was made Pope through a money bargain with the powerful families that ruled Rome. According to *Halley's Bible Handbook,* p. 774, he "surpassed John XII in wickedness, committed murders and adulteries in broad daylight, robbed pilgrims on the graves of martyrs, a hideous criminal, the people drove him out of Rome." He is called by some the worst of all of the Popes (*"Halley's,* p. 775").

Material abounds about the corruption of the Papacy during this time period, and it upsets me to write about it. It is in stark contrast to the simple yet powerful beginnings of the Church after Jesus's death and resurrection. The Church had lost its way.

Perhaps just as unbelievable as we find the papal corruption to be was the effort by the Roman Catholic Church to seek out and punish heretics (persons who opposed Church teachings). Pope Gregory IX (1227 A.D.-1241 A.D.) created a special court to investigate and force heretics to change their beliefs. This was called the Inquisition, a term which brought dread and terror into the hearts of those who had any doubts about their faith (*Halley's,* p. 776-777).

Also on page 777 is the information that no fewer than 900,000 Protestants were put to death between the years 1540–1570 in the Pope's war for the extermination of the Waldenses. The Waldenses were named after a devout Christian named Waldo who was a rich merchant of Lyons in southern France. He was anti-papacy and taught the Bible as the sole authority in life. Though the Waldenses were tortured and persecuted, they are the only medieval sect surviving and now are the leading Protestant body in Italy. The term **"inquisition"** can be found in Deuteronomy 19:18, but I don't believe that God meant for it to be as misused as it was for over five hundred years (*Halley's,* p. 776-777 and p. 785).

Judges, or "Inquirers," were usually priests or monks (*Halley's,* p. 777) from some of the surrounding monasteries. Working in secret, the Inquisition often abused its power. Suspects were tortured and heretics who refused to change their beliefs were burned at the stake. Catholics now condemn the Inquisition for its terrible excesses ("Vatican Looks Back at Inquisition–*CBS News*"). The following are two examples of the sheer madness of those who suffered under the Inquisition:

Joan of Arc was a young peasant girl who lived from 1412? - 1431 A.D. She was born in Domremy, Duch of Bar, Kingdom of France. At the age of thirteen she began experiencing revelations from God, she said, through the voices of Saint Michael, Saint Catherine and Saint Margaret. For five years these voices instructed her to drive out the invading English troops. She persuaded the king of France to let her lead an army against the English. When not dressed in white armor, which was commissioned by Charles VII, king of France ("Joan of Arc–Maid of Heaven– Armor of Joan of Arc"), she dressed in men's clothes as a disguise. She was given a sword, a banner and a steed to ride. After winning many battles for France, which altered the course of French history, she was taken prisoner by the English and was tried for witchcraft and heresy.

At the trial she was asked, "Do you know if you are in the grace of God?" She answered, "If I am not, may God place me there; if I am, may God so keep me. I should be the saddest in all the world if I knew that I were not in the grace of God." She was nineteen years old at the time (Joan of Arc–Wikipedia). Six hundred people, who knew her, were called upon as witnesses in court, but no word was spoken against her ("100 Decisive Battles: From Ancient Times to the Present, p. 160–164"). She was described as modest in conduct, a virgin, who ate and drank little. Only good could be said of her. Still, she was condemned to death by the Inquisition and was ordered to be burned at the stake.

Over ten thousand people witnessed her execution (Joan of Arc Biography/Biography Online). The authorities tied her to a tall pillar above the crowd. She asked for a cross, and a sympathetic English soldier carved a small one out of wood. Someone then brought a crucifix from a nearby church and held it in front of her, as the flames rose around her. Several eyewitnesses said she repeatedly screamed the holy name of Jesus until death finally came (Joan of Arc Biography).

Joan of Arc embodied religious devotion with great bravery and humility. The schism between the Catholic Church and the early Protestant Reformation was beginning. Joan of Arc is now a French national heroine and saint of the Roman Catholic Church. In 1920, nearly five hundred years after her martyrdom, Pope Benedict XV read the bull of canonization, declaring Joan of Arc a saint. Over 60,000 people attended the ceremony, along with 140 descendants of Joan's family ("Canonization of Joan of Arc–Wikipedia"). In 1923, the acclaimed Irish-born playwright, George Bernard Shaw, wrote his famous play *Saint Joan*, which portrays Joan as a woman with Protestant beliefs (*St. Joan The Preface*–Cliffs Notes).

Another instance of the misplaced judgments of the Inquisition involved the life of Galileo, Italian astronomer, mathematician and physicist who lived from 1564-1642 A.D. Galileo believed that the Polish astronomer, Copernicus (1473-1543 A.D.), was correct in advancing the theory that the earth is a moving planet (*The World Book*, [CI-CZ] p. 1039). Some 1400 years earlier, the Greek astronomer Ptolemy (A.D. 100?-165?) had formulated the theory that the earth was at the center of the universe and was motionless ("Copernican heliocentrism–Wikipedia"). This misconception, though challenged by other scientists through the years, was accepted by the Church for hundreds of years (After 350 Years, Vatican Says Galileo Was Right - It Moves–*NYTimes*).

In essence, Galileo was going against Church beliefs when he verified Copernicus's theories and published in a book his ideas about the earth and its position in space. In 1613, Galileo wrote a letter stating his belief that the Copernican theory was consistent with both Catholic doctrine and proper Bible interpretation. Several times, he was summoned before the dreaded Inquisition in Rome and was finally sentenced to life imprisonment in a villa outside Florence, where he lived in relative isolation until he died ("Galileo Affair–Wikipedia")..

In 1979, Pope John Paul II declared that the Roman Catholic Church may have been mistaken in condemning Galileo. A church commission studied the case and, in 1983, it concluded that Galileo should not have been convicted of heresy. In 1992, Pope John Paul II publicly endorsed the commission's finding that the Church made a mistake in censuring Galileo (*The World Book*, "G" p.11-12).

* * * * * * * * * * * * * *

Some thirty years after the trial of Galileo, as people began to abandon superstitious beliefs, an important professorship of mathematics, the Lucasian Chair, originated at Cambridge University in England. Henry Lucas (©. 1610-1663), a Member of Parliament for the university from 1639-1640, left instructions in his will for an annual income to support the professorship. In December, 1993 ("Henry Lucas [politician]–Wikipedia"), the Lucasian Chair celebrated the 330th anniversary of its founding ("Biographical Topics: The Lucasian Chair–Mathematics").

Known as the most famous academic chair in the world, it has been headed by some of the greatest thinkers on earth, including Sir Isaac Newton (1642-1727) who was the second holder of the chair in 1669. Newton expanded upon Galileo's ideas and brought about an explosion of scientific knowledge that continues today ("Isaac

Newton–Wikipedia").

The Lucasian Chair is one of mathematics which is the foundation of science and engineering. The contribution of Newton was enormous. His monumental work, *Philosophiae Naturalis Principia Mathematica* (1687) provided the groundwork for the modern understanding of the universe (*The World Book*, [N-O], p. 388-390).

Arguably, the *Principia* is the most important book published in modern European history. Newton believed the entire universe, including every planet, star, moon, and comet, was held together in a network of gravitational pulls. His work contained no wild speculations, but actual calculations that proved his hypotheses beyond reasonable doubt.

Newton felt that the whole universe was explainable by a law – subject to the application of mathematics and the human mind. He offered the reader three basic principles which have become known as Newton's three laws of motion. They are the following:

1. Every body continues in its state of rest, or of uniform motion in a straight line, unless it is compelled to change that state by forces impressed upon it.

2. The change in motion is proportional to the motive force impressed, and is made in the direction of the straight line in which that force is impressed.

3. To every action there is always opposed an equal reaction (Isaac Newton's *Principia Summary & Preface*–Sir Isaac Newton Online).

"Even today, these three laws are the basic axioms on which physics rests and the first principles that every student of physics learns." (Isaac Newton's *Principia Summary and Preface*–Sir Isaac Newton Online).

Published in 1687, the *Principia* excited European intelligentsia like a bombshell. Written and published in Latin, the first edition sold rapidly. When Newton published a second edition in 1713, he commented on the role of God in creating the universe. He said, "this most beautiful system of the sun, planets, and comets could only proceed from the counsel and dominion of an intelligent and powerful being."

The order that he found in the cosmos proved, rather than disproved, the idea of a benevolent and all-powerful creator. He felt that his scientific research was a way to glorify God by revealing the complexity, greatness, and underlying order of creation. Since God was beyond human understanding, "as a blind man has no idea of colors," Newton wrote, "so we have no idea of the manner by which the all-wise God perceives and understands all things." He added, "But the structure of the universe provides a clue, enabling us to know (God)...by his most wise and excellent contrivances of things, and final causes." Truly, God's nature is revealed not only in the magnificent structure of the universe but also in each of us, who are created in his own image (Spark Notes: Isaac Newton: *Principia*).

To grasp the magnitude of Newton's contributions to science, one need only read the following quotation by Alexander Pope, in regard to Sir Isaac Newton: "Nature and nature's laws lay hid in the night; God said, 'Let Newton be; and all was light.'" ("Alexander Pope and Philosophy–The Victorian Web") This is in keeping with the perspective of this book, that God's nature is such that he places certain people on earth at different times in history, who reveal his handiwork.

Newton's first great achievement was the invention of fluxions, which resulted in calculus. He used this foundation to advance his other precepts. His second great achievement was the discovery of the composition of light, used later in the development of optics. His third great discovery of the universal force of gravity was the seed for his *Principia*, his most profound achievement ("Newton–17th Century Mathematics–The Story of Mathematics").

Chemistry did not materialize until the late eighteenth century ("The Emerging Networks of Modern Chemistry [1680-1860]"). During Newton's lifetime, alchemy and chemistry were still intertwined ("Rediscovering the Alchemy of Isaac Newton–History in the Headlines"). Alchemy is defined as "a philosophical system containing a complex and mobile core of rudimentary science and elaborated with astrology, religion, mysticism, magic, theosophy and many other constituents."

"Alchemy dealt not only with the mysteries of matter but also with those of creation and life; it sought to harmonize the human individual with the universe surrounding him." This is the definition found in the *World Book Dictionary,* 1988, p. 50. Another dictionary, the *Webster's New Collegiate Dictionary,* 1981, p. 27, defined alchemy as a "medieval chemical science and speculative philosophy aiming to achieve the transmutation of the base metals into gold, the discovery of a universal cure for disease, and the discovery of a means of indefinitely prolonging life...a power or process of transforming something common into something precious."

Alchemists of the day kept a low profile and were very secretive because of the risks involved in going against church policy and beliefs. Magic was linked with the devil, and any infraction, whatsoever, could prompt punishment at the pillory or ruination of alchemists' homes. Newton obviously attempted to search through jibberish for the real basis of chemistry and the understanding it would bring ("Isaac Newton's occult studies"). Though the word "occult" is used in the resource, it actually should be "alchemy."

Though Newton kept his thoughts about organized religion to himself, he felt that his service in the name of religion was his scientific discoveries. In keeping with the thinking of the Renaissance, he believed in a return to the ancient classics, including the earlier forms of Christianity. He studied the oldest Biblical works he could find for authentic and true doctrines ("Isaac Newton Before the Ocean of Truth–1601-1700 Church History").

Newton was a devout Christian who said, "Atheism is so senseless. When I look at the solar system, I see the earth at the right distance from the sun to receive the proper amounts of heat and light. This did not happen by chance." ("Isaac Newton–Foundations of Liberty") Also, he said, "I have a fundamental belief in the Bible as the Word of God, written by men who were inspired. I study the Bible daily.("Sir Isaac Newton–Nobel Scientist & God–Does God Exist? JanFeb12") He stated the following about God, the Supreme Being: "This most beautiful system of the sun, planets, and comets, could only proceed from the counsel and dominion of an intelligent Being...This Being governs all things, not as the soul of the world but as Lord over all; and on account of his dominion he is wont to be called "Lord God," or "Universal Ruler"; The Supreme God is a Being eternal, infinite, absolutely perfect." ("Religious Views of Isaac Newton–Wikipedia")

When not working on scientific quests, Newton spent time and effort working out the chronology of the world. Using Biblical sources, he applied his knowledge of mathematics in establishing the dates of important events in history, especially focusing on the beginning of time, as we know it. However, he finally agreed with Bishop James Usher's date for creation as 4004 B.C. His own calculations were only a few years off from those of Usher ("Biblical Chronology/Bible Science Forum"). More about Bishop James Usher is included later in this book.

According to a website ("Lucasian Chair") which I found about the Lucasian Chair, the following is enlightening: "For 100 pounds, the world has received quite a bit of knowledge: calculus, gravity, laws of motion, optics, fluid mechanics, quantum mechanics, eye-glasses for astigmatism, the computer, programming languages, and black holes are illustrations...Science and religion have been intertwined for as long as we can remember, at times with great animosity. The holders of the chair have had varying degrees of involvement with religion.

"To become a professor at Cambridge in 1664, one had to have taken holy orders...The problem was not between religion and other things, but rather between particular forms of religion, because religion was very political in nature...Newton was not public about his religious beliefs, but did leave documents on the topic...The religious issues were quiet for the rest of the 18th century, but the last man to take office in the 1700s was in fact Reverend [Isaac] Milder. The men who followed him were not ordained, but most were quite religious."

Stephen Hawking, born in 1942 (300 years after Galileo's death), died in the spring of 2018. He occupied the Lucasian Chair during the years 1979-2009. His specialty in regard to the Lucasian Chair professorship was listed as theoretical physics ("Lucasian Professor of Mathematics– Wikipedia"). His book entitled *A Brief*

History of Time was on the London *Sunday Times* best-seller list for 237 weeks, longer than any book, other than the Bible and the writings of Shakespeare. It has been translated into forty languages and still continues to sell well (*A Briefer History of Time* by Stephen Hawking/Science/The Guardian).

I happened to turn to a television program perhaps a year ago, in which Stephen Hawking attempted to explain time and evolution. At the end of the program, he all but discounted God's hand in creation. I felt sorry for him not only for the disability that he manages with such grace and courage but also for the fact that with all of his brilliance, he cannot know the truth. He spoke of a beginning that somehow just occurred. Well, who began it? He didn't even try to answer that obvious question. I did notice that Hawkings' funeral service was conducted in a Christian church, so maybe he became a believer before his death.

Also, I never hear evolutionists try to explain light. How did light come about? I would like to hear Hawking's explanation of light. Yes, we receive it from our sun, but how did light begin? We Christians don't need an explanation. We know how it began in the first book of the Bible, Genesis. Dr. Jerry Vines, past president of the Southern Baptist Convention from 1988-1990, wrote a book called *24/7 The Genesis Account of Creation*, in which he included the following words on page 66: "Science cannot offer an explanation on the origin of light. Only the Bible can. God commanded light to exist, and it did in all of its mystery. Light can be bent. Light can be twisted. Yet, light will bounce off a polished surface. Light will go through a solid surface like glass without changing its nature or its speed. How? Why? Light is potent like its originator, God."

At least 21 verses in the Bible speak of light, and below are some of them:

Psalm 27:1 **"The Lord is my light and my salvation; whom shall I fear? The Lord is the strength of my life; of whom shall I be afraid?"**

Psalm 119:105 **"Thy word is a lamp unto my feet, and a light unto my path."**

Matthew 4:16 **"The people which sat in darkness saw a

great light; and to them which sat in the region and shadow of death light is sprung up."

Matthew 5:16 "Let your light so shine before men, that they may see your good works, and glorify your Father which is in heaven."

John 1:5 "And the light shineth in darkness; and the darkness comprehended it not."

John 8:12 "Then spake Jesus again unto them, saying, I am the light of the world: he that followeth me shall not walk in darkness, but shall have the light of life."

John 12:35-37 "Then Jesus said unto them, Yet a little while is the light with you. Walk while ye have the light, lest darkness come upon you: for he that walketh in darkness knoweth not whither he goeth. While ye have light, believe in the light, that ye may be the children of light."

James 1:17 "Every good gift and every perfect gift is from above, and cometh down from the Father of lights, with whom is no variableness, neither shadow of turning."

1 John 1:5-7 "This then is the message which we have heard of him, and declare unto you, that God is light, and in him is no darkness at all. If we say that we have fellowship with him, and walk in darkness, we lie, and do not the truth: But if we walk in the light, as he is in the light, we have fellowship one with another, and the blood of Jesus Christ his Son cleanseth us from all sin."

Revelation 21:23-25 "And the city had no need of the sun, neither of the moon, to shine in it: for the glory of God did lighten it, and the Lamb is the light thereof. And the nations of them which are saved shall walk in the light of it: and the kings of the earth do bring their glory and honour into it."

* * * * * * * * * * * * *

Since the beginning of time, man has wondered about the age of the earth and the beginning of time, itself. Several early men of vision worked out their own chronologies of the earth, including Jose ben Halafta, a Jewish scholar of the second century A.D. (3761 B.C.);

Venerable Bede, living from 672/673-735 A.D. (3952 B.C.); Joseph Scaliger, French religious leader and scholar who lived from 1540-1609 A.D. (3949 B.C.); Johannes Kepler, German mathematician, astronomer and astrologer who lived from 1571-1630 A.D. (3992 B.C.); and Sir Isaac Newton, who lived from 1642-1727 A.D. (4000 B.C.), in addition to Bishop James Usher, who lived from 1581-1656 A.D. (4004 B.C.). ("Ussher chronology–WikiVisually")

The widely held belief during that time period was that the Earth's potential duration was 6,000 years (4,000 before the birth of Christ and 2,000 after), in keeping with the six days of creation of the Bible which states that **"one day is with the Lord as a thousand years, and a thousand years as one day."** (II Peter 3:8) Though many modern-day theologians discount Usher's chronology, many others accept it, even today ("Ussher chronology–WikiVisually").

James Usher (1581-1656) was Archbishop of Armagh, Primate of All Ireland, and Vice-Chancellor of Trinity College in Dublin. He was a gifted linguist ("James Ussher–Wikipedia"). Using the Bible as the basis for his chronology, Usher first wrote a complete history of the world in Latin. This 1600-page volume was published in 1650 A.D. An English translation entitled *The Annals of the World* was published in 1658, two years after his death ("The World.: Born in 4004 B.C.? / Answers in Genesis"). It has recently been translated into modern English and republished ("Can the Ussher Chronology Be Trusted?/The Institute for Creation").

Usher began his work with the assumption that the Bible is the only reliable source of chronological information for the time periods it covers. Relying on the dates of the Persian Empire (approximately the sixth to the third centuries B.C.), he knew that little was known about the sources of Greek, Roman and Egyptian history or the history of other nations. For events before the dates of the Persian Empire, Usher relied solely on Bible data to establish his historical framework. He used the death of King Nebuchadnezzar to establish all earlier Biblical dates ("The World: Born in 4004 B.C. / Answers in Genesis"). One can find more about Usher and his work by visiting sites on the internet.

The following excerpt from Usher's *The Annals of the World* gives us an idea of his thinking and his writing. His spellings are kept much as they were when he wrote it in 1654:

"For as much as our Christian epoch falls many ages after the beginning of the world, and the number of years before that backward is not only more troublesome, but (unless greater care be taken) more lyable to errour; also it hath pleased our modern chronologers, to adde to that generally received hypothesis (which asserted the Julian years, with their three cycles by a certain mathematical prolepsis, to have run down to the very beginning of the world) an artificial epoch, framed out of three cycles multiplied in themselves; for the Solar Cicle being multiplied by the Lunar, or the number of 28 by 19, produces the great Paschal Cycle of 532 years, and that again multiplied by fifteen, the number of the indiction, there arises the period of 7980 years, which was first (if I mistake not) observed by Robert Lotharing, Bishop of Hereford, in our island of Britain, and 500 years after by Joseph Scaliger fitted for chronological uses, and called by the name of the Julian Period, because it conteined a cycle of so many Julian years.

"Now if the series of the three minor cycles be from this present year extended backward unto precedent times, the 4713 years before the beginning of our Christian account will be found to be that year into which the first year of the indiction, the first of the Lunar Cycle, and the first of the Solar will fall. Having placed therefore the heads of this period in the kalends of January in that proleptick year, the first of our Christian vulgar account must be reckoned the 4714 of the Julian Period, which, being divided by 15. 19. 28. will present us with the 4 Roman indiction, the 2 Lunar Cycle, and the 10 Solar, which are the principal characters of that year. [Notation from the modern republishing of Usher's work: *The 19 year lunar cycle times 28 year solar cycle times 15 year indiction cycle equals 7980 years.*]

"We find moreover that the year of our forefathers, and the years of the ancient Egyptians and Hebrews were of the same quantity with the Julian, consisting of twelve equal moneths, every of them conteining 30 days, (for it cannot be proved that the Hebrews did use lunary moneths before the Babylonian Captivity) adjoying to the end of the twelfth moneth, the addition of five dayes, and every four year six. And I have observed by the continued succession of these years, as they are delivered in holy writ, that the end of the great Nebuchadnezar and the beginning of Evil-merodach (his son's) reign, fell out in the 3442 year of the world, but by collation of Chaldean history and the astronomical cannon, it fell out in the 186 year c Nabonasar, and, as by certain connexion, it must follow in the 562 year before the Christian account, and of the Julian Period, the 4152, and from thence I gathered the creation of the world did fall out upon the 710 year of the Julian Period, by placing its beginning in autumn: but for as much as the first day of the world began with the evening of the first day of the week, I have observed that the Sunday, which in the year 710 aforesaid came nearest the Autumnal Equinox, by astronomical tables (notwithstanding the stay of the sun in the dayes of Joshua, and the going back of it in the days c Ezekiah) happened upon the 23 day of the Julian October; from thence concluded that from the evening preceding that first day of the Julian year, both the first day of the creation and the first motion of time are to be deduced)." ("Bishop Ussher Dates the World: 4004 B.C.–Loch Haven University")

Dear Reader, I do not presume to understand Bishop James Usher's chronology, and I am certain that even if I read his entire account, I would come no closer to understanding it. However, it is fascinating to read, and the fact that Sir Isaac Newton and other mathematicians and great thinkers of that time period agreed with him is enough for me to accept his reasoning. If you would like to read more of his illuminating work, then ask your library to get his book *The Annals of the World* for you. When he died in 1658, a magnificent state funeral was held for him. He was buried in Westminster Abbey ("Westminster Abbey–James Ussher").

* * * * * * * * * * * * *

Turning from the Church and its problems throughout the Middle Ages, one must also be aware of other difficulties that beset the entire world during this extended time period. Throughout history, people have been subjected to an illness called the plague.

CAN WE FATHOM THE NATURE OF GOD?

Caused by rats and the fleas that feast on them, the plague likely struck the city of Ashdod in 1,000 B.C., as recorded in I Samuel. Around 542 A.D., it struck the city of Constantinople, now known as Istanbul, Turkey, where it killed half the population of the city ("The Bubonic Plague–Black Death").

From 1347 A.D. until 1352 A.D., the Black Plague (which is what it is now called) visited the earth again, taking the lives of a third of the population of Europe at the time. Millions and millions of people died. Some towns were totally wiped out ("The Black Death–Academic Sites"). Was this a punishment from God for the waywardness of the Church and its people? People called flagellants stood in the streets and whipped themselves in an attempt to cleanse their sins, thinking this would stop the spread of the disease ("The Flagellants Attempt to Repel the Black Death, 1349").

Medieval writers told of the horrors of the plague, from the gruesome symptoms of purplish splotches on the body to the delirium of its victims who turned on one another and even abandoned their children and families. Pandemonium ensued, for no one knew what to do to treat the illness. The sick vomited and coughed up blood. Their sores oozed pus and blood ("The Black Death/ HowStuffWorks").

Another pandemic of the Bubonic Plague began in China in the mid-1800s. During the next seventy-five years, some 20,000,000 people died from the disease. Finally, in 1896, the first plague vaccine was developed. The illness occasionally still occurs in the world (The *World Book*, [P], p. 508).

Only recently, I read an article in a newspaper, written in 2011, with the title, "Deadly Black Death Bug Hasn't Changed But We Have." The article stated that scientists have discovered the genetic code of the Black Death, which hasn't changed much during the past 600 years. According to the article, 30,000,000 – 50,000,000 people died of the plague, about one out of three Europeans.

However, modern man is better able to cope with the plague, if it should strike again. Our immune systems are stronger and we have antibiotics such as tetracycline which can cure the disease. Also, our improved sanitation and medical treatment of the sick would dramatically curtail the effects of a modern-day pandemic

("Deadly black death bug hasn't changed–*NY Daily News*, October 13, 2011").

In 1918, the Spanish Flu pandemic occurred, leaving fifty million people dead. Within months it had killed more people than died in World War I. It killed more people than any other illness in recorded history ("The Influenza Epidemic of 1918–National Archives"). What will come next? We keep reading of "superbugs" that are mutating, which might do us harm.

Along with diseases that have swept the world, it seems that we have experienced more severe weather than usual during the past few years. Several violent hurricanes, especially the hurricanes Camille, Andrew, Katrina, Sandy, Harvey, and Irma have lashed the United States coasts and caused the deaths of many, along with vast devastation of homes and businesses.

The island of Puerto Rico, as I write this, is experiencing one of the worst humanitarian crises ever recorded in the wake of the hurricane Maria. The recent tsunamis and earthquakes have taken their tolls in human and animal suffering and ruin. Is God trying to tell us something, as he did the people during Bible times? The books of the prophets, from Isaiah to Malachi, are filled with examples of the wrath of God upon his own chosen people.

I remember when the hurricane Katrina hit the Gulf Coast that a certain evangelical television personality warned that it was the judgment of God on a wicked nation. He was laughed at and scorned for such a pronouncement, but those who know the Scriptures concede that God uses his awesome power in ways that are beyond our comprehension. The Bible states over and over that we are to fear him. How often in the Scriptures have we read of the dire consequences that the Israelites brought upon themselves because of their disobedience to God? I don't doubt for a minute that some, or perhaps all, of the terrible catastrophes of the past few years, and throughout history, were examples of the wrath of God. My friend, wrath is a component of the nature of God!

The Bible is filled with warnings and testaments of God's anger, from the first Book of Genesis to the last book of the Bible. Indeed, the Book of Revelation (Revelation 15:7) speaks of the

"seven golden vials full of the wrath of God, who liveth forever and ever." These vials include painful sores, extreme burning heat, earthquakes, and even darkness over the land. Some of these vials have already been used and may be used upon the earth again, during our lifetime.

Though we speak of the Dark Ages as though they were years in the distant past, the sad irony is that we today are living in a Dark Age insofar as the Church is concerned. Though we are living in an age when technology abounds and gets "smarter" with each passing year, this era has a dearth of morality and decency. Whereas school children once had Scriptures read to them every day by their school teachers, today it is against the law to do such. Prayer has also been removed from the school systems of America. Whereas once our great nation was a beacon of Christian light to the rest of the world, we now have leaders who apologize for our country and refuse to recognize that we are a Christian nation founded upon Christian principles, though we are tolerant of the beliefs of others.

* * * * * * * * * * * * *

During the early 1300s, the great cultural movement known as the Renaissance (1300 A.D. - 1600 A.D) began in Italy, then spread to England, France, Germany, and the Netherlands. The term Renaissance literally means "rebirth," which was characterized by a revival of interest in the classics of Roman and Greek civilizations (*The World Book*–"QR", pages 232-239). Italians with a thirst for antique culture, and others who treasured old manuscripts of classic literature, founded libraries for their accumulation and storage, such as Pope Nicholas V (1397-1455), who founded the Vatican Library sometime between 1447-1455 ("Pope Nicholas V–Wikipedia").

The writings of Homer (850 B.C.?) were reprinted in 1488; Plato (424/423 B.C.-348/347 B.C.) in 1512; Aristotle (384 B.C.-322 B.C.)in 1498; and Virgil (70 B.C.-19 B.C.) in 1470 ("History of the Renaissance in Europe: A Rebirth, renewal, rediscovery"). This made them available to the general public and became the rightful heritage of all of mankind not only for that time period but for the centuries ahead ("History of the Renaissance in Europe: A rebirth, renewal, rediscovery"). Our schools and universities still propagate the extraordinary thinking of these ancient writers and inculcate them into their curricula ("Classical Education in America by David Walker Howe–Spring").

Whereas the Middle Ages had subjugated the mind and body of man, the Renaissance resurrected, freed, and even glorified man in literature and art and discoveries. The Bible, in its original tongues, was rediscovered during this time period ("History for Ready Reference"). Great writers of the Renaissance included William Shakespeare (1564-1616); John Milton (1608-1674); Thomas More (1478-1535), Elizabeth I (1533-1603), John Calvin (1509-1564, and Edmund Spenser. Many of these literary works focused on man's religious nature, which mirrored God's own nature ("Renaissance Literature Periods & Movements").

Well-known artists of the Renaissance included Sandro Botticelli (1445-1510); Leonardo da Vinci (1452-1519); Michelangelo Buonarroti (1475-1564); Raphael Sanzio (1483-1520), Titian (1485-1576), among many others (List of Renaissance artists–Simple English Wikipedia, the free..."). Many of the greatest works of art had Christian motifs, such as da Vinci's *The Last Supper;* Michelangelo's *Pieta* sculpture; and Raphael's *Madonna and Child.*

Only a few years later than this time period, in 1741, George Frederic Handel(1685-1759), born in Germany, composed the English-language oratorio, *Messiah*. Though Handel created the heavenly music for *Messiah*, Charles Jennens compiled the scriptural text from the King James Bible and from the Psalms included with the (1662 A.D.) Book of Common Prayer. The early music scholar Richard Luckett described Handel's *Messiah* as "a commentary on Jesus Christ's Nativity, Passion, Resurrection and Ascension," beginning with God's promises as predicted by the prophets and ending with Christ's glorification in heaven.

According to the musicologist Donald Burrows, much of the text is largely incomprehensible to those who are ignorant of the biblical passages. Though born in Germany, Handel became a naturalized British subject in 1727. His original manuscript for

Messiah is held in the British Library's music collection (*Messiah* [Handel]– Wikipedia).

Handel completed the music for *Messiah* in twenty-four days of swift composition. At the end of his manuscript, he wrote the letters *"SDG–Soli Deo gloria*, "To God alone the glory." The apocryphal story about this inscription and the speed of composition was that Handel wrote the music in a state of divine inspiration in which, as he wrote the "Hallelujah" chorus, "he saw all heaven before him."("Handel's *Messiah* Inspires Listeners, Transcends Time/*CBN News"*) Surely, God used these devout Christians... Handel and Jennens...to draw us nearer to Him each time we hear this glorious and powerful oratorio.

Chapter Thirteen

Dear Reader, the second part of the title of this book bespeaks of the exceptionalism of America. Its beginning is shrouded in the ideas and lives of certain people who lived hundreds of years ago in other countries. The United States was the culmination of these developments. The rest of this book will reveal the roots of our country's exceptionalism.

Though the Age of Discovery, sometimes called the Age of Exploration, was a period of global history ranging from the fifteenth to the seventeenth centuries, a Portuguese prince named Prince Henry (Henrique) the Navigator (1394-1460) actually ushered in the era. Prince Henry, born in Porto, Portugal, sent many sailing expeditions down Africa's west coast for the purposes of creating maps of the West African coast, defeating the Muslims, spreading Christianity, and establishing trade routes ("Henry the Navigator– Prince– Biography. com").

The scientific and technical advances of the Renaissance led to more seaworthy ships that were capable of surviving in the Atlantic Ocean. Navigation and shipbuilding progressed by leaps and bounds during this age. Though many Europeans explored the East on overland routes, such as the Silk Road, these travels were blocked when the Ottoman Empire took control of Constantinople in 1453. This also stopped access to North Africa and the Red Sea, two important trade routes to the Far East ("2 Age of Exploration/ History Hub").

Many nations built and sailed ships during the Age of

Exploration, including England, Spain, Portugal, Italy, France, and several Scandinavian countries. Also, in addition to discovering two new continents, North and South America, these nations formed colonies all over the world. From their earlier overland trips to the Far East, explorers had brought back unique and unusual goods, such as cinnamon, nutmeg, and cloves. The demand for these items, and others, led to the quest for a sea route to the Far East. Though many nations were searching for silver and gold, they also wanted to trade for spices and silk ("Age of Discovery [Exploration]/Europe, 15th Century–17th Century").

The Portuguese conducted the first journeys associated with the Age of Discovery. Their sailors' early voyages relied on portolan charts which were maps created for navigators based off of land features. Portuguese ships called caravels hugged the African coast, carrying spices, slaves, gold and other goods from Asia and Africa to Europe. Sailors had to stay within sight of land to steer their ships. Under the rule of Prince Henry the Navigator (1394-1460), the Portuguese improved their methods of navigation to the extent that they could sail out of sight of land and discover other places, such as the Madeira Islands in 1419 and the Azores in 1427 ("Age of Discovery–Wikipedia").

Around 1418, Prince Henry began the first school for oceanic navigation at Sagres, Portugal, where people were trained in navigation, map-making, and science, in order to navigate the west coast of Africa. During this time, no Europeans had sailed past the treacherous Cape Bojador and returned alive. Cape Bojador had strong currents and violent storms. The ocean beyond that point was called the "Sea of Darkness."

The Portuguese explorer Gil Eannes was the first European to sail beyond the dangerous Cape Bojador, in 1434, and return ("Prince Henry the Navigator–EnchantedLearning.com"). In 1488, the Portuguese explorer Barthomeu Dias (1450-1500) reached the Cape of Good Hope, which he called the "Cape of Storms" (Cabo das tormentas). It was later renamed by John II of Portugal as "Cape of Good Hope" (*Cabo da boa Esperanca*), presumably because of the wonderful optimism brought about by the opening of a sea route to India and the East ("Bartolomeu Dias/Portuguese explorer/*Britannica*.com"). Other important voyages that took place during this time period were Ferdinand Magellan's attempt to circumnavigate the globe, in the search for a trade route to Asia through the Northwest Passage, and Captain James Cook's voyages which were conducive to his mapping various areas as far as Alaska ("Anchorage History–Cook Inlet Historical Society").

This was an age of many discoveries which helped in the freedom of man's spirit in conquering new worlds, not only in the aesthetic realms of literature and art, but also in the geography of the earth. The mariners' compass, discovered by Flavius Giojo of Naples, Italy, in 1302 A.D., was used by Columbus during his voyage to the West in 1492 A.D ("A History of the United States on a New Plan: Adapted to the..."). The telescope, known to Arabians in the Middle Ages and described by Roger Bacon in 1250 A.D., was used by Copernicus to prove the revolution of the earth in 1530 A.D. It was also used by Galileo to verify his theory of the planetary system. ("The Renaissance of Modern Europe: A Review of the Scientific,....")

* * * * * * * * * * * * * *

As the world was experiencing a revival insofar as intellectual and artistic pursuits were concerned, the Church was undergoing a cleansing in what is now referred to as the Protestant Reformation. "Protestant" derives from the root word "protest," as people began to protest against the beliefs and actions of the Roman Catholic Church. Because of papal excesses and the grandiose style of church leaders and government within the papacy, the church was always trying to raise money to meet these expenses.

In Italy the popes and other papal leaders lived like secular princes. They built costly palaces and engaged in corrupt methods of obtaining money. The church became farther and farther removed from the humble and loving example that Jesus set when he walked the earth ("Leo X Facts; information, pictures/ *Encyclopedia*.com articles about"); also, "Half Windsor Full Throttle: Popes and Papal History sheds light on...").

For a thousand years, from Theodosius' legitimacy of the

Christian faith in the fourth century until the fourteenth century, the church experienced peace insofar as set persecution of Christians was concerned (*Foxe's Book of Martyrs,* 2009, W. Grinton Berry, editor, p. 47). However, the schism within the church, brought about by the Protestant Reformation, which had its genesis during the 1300s, again brought about persecution within the Catholic Church of those who did not adhere to the exact tenets of the Catholic Church. Whereas the early persecution was brought about by pagan Roman authorities, this later persecution was Roman Catholic against Protestant, or Christian against Christian. It was called the Inquisition, which has already been mentioned in this book ("What were the Inquisitions?–Got Questions").

Many critics of the church began speaking out against the flagrant abuses that constantly emanated from the papacy. Among these were John Wycliffe in England, John Hus in Bohemia and Girolamo Savonarola in Italy. However, their protests did not bring about a change in the ongoing abuses of papal power. Rather, charges of heresy were leveled against these men ("HISTORY OF THE REFORMATION").

During the middle of the fourteenth century, Europe was shaken by a series of earthquakes and pestilence. Many, many people lost their lives. John Wycliffe sounded an alarm to a careless and profane generation with the publication of his first writing, a small treatise entitled "The Last Age of the Church." In this publication he described the corruptions of the church, which he felt were the cause of the punishment bestowed on Europe by God ("Writings and Examinations of Brute, Thorpe, Cobham, Hilton, Pecock,...").

John Wycliffe (c.1330-1384) has been called "the Morning Star of the Reformation," for he was one of the earliest opponents of papal authority superceding secular power. Wycliffe was an English philosopher, theologian, lay preacher, translator and university teacher at Oxford in England. He was an early dissident in the Roman Catholic Church, who preached and wrote about anticlerical and biblically-centered reforms. He believed that the Bible should be translated into the common language of the people, which he accomplished himself in 1382, when the Wycliffe's Bible was completed, translated into English directly from the Latin *Vulgate* ("John Wycliffe– Wikipedia"). The later King James Version, which borrowed heavily from Wycliffe's New Testament translation, retained its beauty, strength, and clarity ("John Wycliffe–*New World Encyclopedia*").

Hoping to do away with the existing hierarchy of the church and to replace it with poor priests who lived in poverty, Wycliffe believed that these priests should spread the Gospel in the way that he envisioned it. The priests wearing long, dark, red robes and carrying a staff went barefoot, two by two, preaching the sovereignty of God. These followers of Wycliffe were called Lollards ("The Knights Templar & the Protestant Reformation").

Wycliffe was disillusioned with the state of the church, for he felt that the Scriptures should be the authoritative center of Christianity. He believed the papacy was unhistorical, the monasteries and the priesthood corrupt. He felt that the church could exist without a visible leader. He also opposed the possessions of the church, believing these to be unbiblical, also. What would he think of the Vatican today, and even certain Protestant churches with their wealth and possessions?

Believing that the church was in dire need of reform, Wycliffe propagated his ideas for this reform in his *Summa Theologica* and *De civili dominio*, in regard to the authority of rulers and Popes and his outrage concerning unbiblical papal excesses. He saw a great contrast in what the church was and what it should be ("Daily Medieval: Wycliffe the Reformer").

For over seventy years, the Papal Palace was at Avignon, France (1305-1377). The avarice of the Avignon Popes knew no bounds. To fill the coffers of the Popes and to support the luxuries of the immoral papal court, burdensome taxes were imposed. Every church office was sold for money and many new offices were created to be sold. From 1377-1417, there were two sets of Popes, one at Rome and the other at Avignon, each claiming to be the "Vicar of Christ," while hurling insults and curses upon the other ("Evil Popes–Grace Gems"). Wycliffe wrote that "it is not necessary to go either to Rome or to Avignon in order to seek a decision from the Pope, since the triune God is everywhere. Our pope is Christ." ("John Wycliffe–GREATSITE.COM") Finally, however, with the selection of) Pope Martin V (1369-1431), the papacy was returned to Rome, Italy ("Pope Martin V–Wikipedia").

From 1377-1382, Wycliffe was summoned to appear before several convocations of his ecclesiastical superiors to answer to charges of holding and publishing erroneous and heretical doctrines. Though he was neither excommunicated nor deprived of his living, he was nevertheless a marked man. The Pope bided his time in trying to decide what to do with him.

While Wycliffe was saying Roman Catholic Mass in the parish church on December 28, 1384, he suffered a stroke and died within only a few days. In 1415, The Council of Constance declared John Wycliffe a heretic who was banned by the church. It was decided that his books should be burned and his body exhumed. In 1428, his remains were exhumed at the command of Pope Martin V, who decreed that the proclaimed heretic's remains be burned and the ashes cast into the River Swift ("John Wycliffe–Wikipedia").

John Foxe, author of *Foxe's Book of Martyrs,* said of Wycliffe, "though they digged up his body, burnt his bones, and drowned his ashes, yet the Word of God and the truth of his doctrine, with the fruit and success thereof, they could not burn." (*Foxe's Book of Martyrs,* p. 69) According to many historical accounts I have read, *John Foxe's Book of Martyrs* was so revered by the early Protestant church that it was often chained alongside the Holy Bible for those who could read (*Foxes's Book of Martyrs and Early Print Culture,* p. 277).

The persecution and martyrdom of a follower of John Wycliffe, named Sir John Oldcastle, knight, Lord Cobham, is also recounted in *Foxe's Book of Martyrs.* These pages about Lord Cobham (1360-1378 A.D.-1417 A.D.) give the reader great insight into the turmoil and agony of the church during this time period. The struggle between the Roman Catholic Church and the Protestant Reformation was borne out in the life of Lord Cobham.

Prefacing his account of the ordeal of Lord Cobham, Foxe wrote the following:

"No small number of godly disciples left that good man behind him, to defend the lowliness of the gospel against the exceeding pride, ambition, simony, avarice, hypocrisy, sacrilege, tyranny, idolatrous worshippings, and other filthy fruits, of those stiff-necked pharisees; against whom Thomas Arundel, the Archbishop of Canterbury (as fierce as ever was Pharaoh, Antiochus, Herod, or Caiaphas) collected, in Paul's church at London, a universal synod of all the papistical clergy of England, in the year of our Lord 1413 (as he had done divers others before), to withstand their most godly enterprise.

"The principal cause of the assembling thereof, was to repress the growing and spreading of the Gospel, and especially to withstand the noble and worthy Lord Cobham, who was then noted to be a principal favourer, receiver, and maintainer of those whom the bishop named Lollards; especially in the dioceses of London, Rochester, and Hereford, setting them up to preach whom the bishops had not licensed, and sending them about to preach: holding also and teaching opinions of the sacraments, of images, of pilgrimage, of the keys and church of Rome, repugnant to the received determination of the Romish Church. It was concluded among them, that, without any further delay, process should be awarded out against him, as against a most pernicious heretic." (*Foxe's Book of Martyrs,* p. 70)

Sir John Oldcastle (Lord Cobham) lived in Cowling Castle near Rochester, Kent. He was not only a devout Christian but also one of the most powerful Englishmen of his time. Being a wealthy man, he maintained a school at his estate in Kent, where men studied to preach the Gospel. Since he was not licensed by the Catholic Church to do this, he was marked as a heretic and was urged to conform to the beliefs of the Catholic Church. Because he was of noble birth and outstanding among the hierarchy of English government, the Catholic authorities were hesitant in bringing charges of heresy against him. They therefore appealed to the king to bring Lord Cobham back into the fold of the Catholic Church ("Sir John Oldcastle/Herefordshire Past").

King Henry V met personally with Lord Cobham and

admonished him to change his views in regard to the papacy and the Roman Catholic Church. However Lord Cobham refused to alter his deeply held beliefs. His answer to the king was as follows:

"You, most worthy prince, I am always prompt and willing to obey, forasmuch as I know you a Christian king, and the appointed minister of God, bearing the sword to the punishment of evil doers, and for safeguard of them that be virtuous. Unto you, next my eternal God, owe I my whole obedience, and submit thereunto, as I have done ever, all that I have, either of fortune or nature, ready at all times to fulfil whatsoever ye shall in the Lord command me. But, as touching the Pope and his spirituality, I owe them neither suit nor service, forasmuch as I know him, by the Scriptures, to be the great Antichrist, the son of perdition, the open adversary of God, and the abomination standing in the holy place." (*Foxe's*, p. 72)

This angered the king to the extent that he, like Pontius Pilate, washed his hands of the fate of Lord Cobham and gave the archbishop Thomas Arundel authority to examine Lord Cobham and his beliefs and to punish him, according to decrees called "The Laws of Holy Church." Lord Cobham, however, refused to appear on the appointed day before the archbishop. Rather, he took paper and pen in hand and wrote a confession of his faith, which he signed and sealed and carried to the king, hoping to find favor and mercy from the monarch.

Again, the king contended that Lord Cobham would be examined by Arundel, the Archbishop, the time period's own Caiaphas who sat in judgment of Jesus. On the day of his examination, Lord Cobham was brought from the Tower, where he had been imprisoned, to appear before Archbishop Arundel and other legates of the Roman Catholic Church. The Archbishop Arundel opened the examination with the following words:

"Sir John, in the last convocation of the clergy of this our province, ye were detected of certain heresies, and, by sufficient witnesses, found culpable: whereupon ye were, by form of spiritual law, cited, and would in no case appear. Upon your rebellious contumacy ye were both privately and openly excommunicated.

Notwithstanding we neither yet showed ourselves unready to have given you absolution (nor yet do to this hour), would ye have meekly asked it."

To this, Lord Cobham replied that he desired no absolution. Rather, he wanted to read his confession of faith regarding certain articles wherein he was accused. He then read his confession before them, as follows:

"As for images, I understand that they be not of belief, but that they were ordained since the belief of Christ was given by sufferance of the Church, to represent and bring to mind the passion of our Lord Jesus Christ, and martyrdom and good living of other saints: and that whoso it be, that doth the worship to dead images that is due to God, or putteth such hope or trust in help of them, as he should do to God, or hath affection in one more than in another, he doth in that, the greatest sin of idol worship.

"Also, I suppose this fully, that every man in this earth is a pilgrim toward bliss, or toward pain; and that he that knoweth not, ne will not know, ne keep the holy commandments of God in his living here (albeit that he go on pilgrimages to all the world, and he die so), he shall be damned: he that knoweth the holy commandments of God, and keepeth them to his end, he shall be saved, though he never in his life go on a pilgrimage, as men now use, to Canterbury, or to Rome, or to any other place."

Upon hearing this, the disdainful archbishop counseled among the other papal representatives who were in attendance. They concluded that Lord Cobham must explain his beliefs further. The major charge of heresy involved the Catholic Church's belief in transubstantiation, which held that the bread and wine served at communion actually became the body and blood of Jesus. The Protestant churches did not adhere to this doctrine. The archbishop addressed Lord Cobham, as follows:

"Come hither, Sir John: ye must declare your mind more plainly. As thus, whether ye hold, affirm, and believe, that the sacrament of the altar, after the consecration rightly done by a priest, remaineth material bread, or not? Moreover, whether ye do hold, affirm, and believe, that, as concerning the sacrament of penance (where a competent number of priests are), every Christian man is necessarily bound to be confessed of his sins to a priest ordained by the church, or not?" Lord Cobham reminded the archbishop that he had written his confession of beliefs and they still held. He would change nothing that he had written.

"Sir John," the archbishop said, "beware what ye do; for if ye answer not clearly to those things that are here objected against you, the law of holy church is that we may openly proclaim you a heretic."

"Do as ye shall think best," Lord Cobham said.

The papal bishops and prelates in attendance were amazed at Lord Cobham's reply and "wonderfully disquieted," according to John Foxe, whose book about the martyrs I quoted. The archbishop finally declared to his prisoner that he must follow the teachings of the Holy Church of Rome and abide by the words of St. Augustine, St. Jerome, and St. Ambrose, "which determination all Christian men both to believe and to follow." John Foxe noted that no mention was made here of abiding by the words of Jesus!!

At this, the archbishop commanded that Lord Cobham be returned to the Tower where he could consider his errant beliefs until another meeting time within the next few days. He especially wanted Lord Cobham to answer to his belief regarding the bread which was served at Communion. After the words of consecration, did it remain "material bread"?

When the next convocation was held, even more priests, canons, monks, friars, parish clerks, bell ringers and pardoners were in attendance. Sir Robert Morley, knight and officer of the Tower prison, brought Lord Cobham to the meeting. There, he was left as a lamb among wolves.

"Sir John," said the archbishop, "we sent you a writing concerning the faith of the blessed sacrament, clearly determined by the Church of Rome, our mother, and by the holy doctors."

Lord Cobham answered, "I know none holier than is Christ and His apostles. And as for that determination, I wot it is none of theirs; for it standeth not with the Scriptures, but manifestly against them."

"What is your belief concerning Holy Church," said one of the papist lawyers.

"My belief," replied Lord Cobham, "is that all the Scriptures of the sacred Bible are true. All that is grounded upon them I believe thoroughly, for I know it is God's pleasure that I should so do; but in your lordly laws and idle determinations have I no belief. For ye be no part of Christ's Holy Church, as your open deeds do show; but ye are very Antichrists, obstinately set against His holy law and will. The laws that ye have made are nothing to His glory, but only for your vain glory and abominable covetousness. And as for your superiority, were ye of Christ, ye should be meek ministers, and no proud superiors."

"Swift judges always are the learned scholars of Wickliff!" said one of the papal legates.

"As for that virtuous man Wickliff," answered Lord Cobham, "I shall say here, before God and man, that before I knew that despised doctrine of his, I never abstained from sin. But since I learned therein to fear my Lord God, it hath otherwise, I trust, been with me: so much grace could I never find in all your glorious instructions." (Note to you, my Reader: The rest of this interrogation of Lord Cobham is found in *Foxe's Book of Martyrs,* p. 70-89.)

In December of 1417, Lord Cobham was taken to the fields near Lincoln's Inn, now part of modern day London. Though bound as a traitor, he managed to kneel and pray for his enemies, then told all in attendance to obey the Scriptures and them, only. According to the website I found about his execution, he "was drawn (stomach cut open, for punishment) hanged gently between two gallows by metal chains (for being a traitor) and then slowly burned to death (for heresy). Throughout this appalling ordeal he constantly prayed, staying steadfast to the end." ("John Oldcastle, Lord of Cobham, Preacher") The strange word in the foregoing quotation is the word "gently." How is a person "hanged gently"? Maybe it was just common wordage of that era.

A fascinating reminder of the ordeal of Sir John Oldcastle

(Lord Cobham) occurred some four centuries later, when the gifted author Alfred, Lord Tennyson wrote a lengthy poem about that brave and good man, entitled Sir John Oldcastle, Lord Cobham ("Sir John Oldcastle, Lord Cobbam by Alfred Tennyson/Poetry Cat"). Tennyson lived from 1809-1892. He was Poet Laureate of the United Kingdom during much of Queen Victoria's reign ("Alfred Tennyson–Poet–Biography. com"). He is the ninth most frequently quoted writer in *The Oxford Dictionary of Quotations* ("100 Inspiring Quotes by Alfred Lord Tennyson That Will Brighten Up...").

Chapter Fourteen

John Huss (also known as John Hus or Jan Hus), who lived from 1369 to 1415 A.D., was a Czech priest, early church reformer and master at Charles University in Prague, Czechoslavakia. He was born to peasant parents in Husinec, Kingdom of Bohemia, and traveled to Prague at a young age, where he supported himself by singing and serving in churches. In 1400 A.D., he was ordained a priest and became rector of the University of Prague. Greatly influenced by the writings of John Wycliff, he received the appointment of preacher at Bethlehem Chapel. Huss translated Wycliff's Trialogus into the Czech language and helped to distribute it. Stirred and strengthened by the writings of Wycliff, he preached his sermons in the Czech language, rather than Latin, as the papacy demanded.

Though he as a young man spent some time with other derelict young people, whom he called "a foolish sect," John Huss finally discovered the Bible, and his life was forever changed. He said, "When the Lord gave me knowledge of Scriptures, I discharged that kind of stupidity from my foolish mind." He further stated that he began more and more to trust the Scriptures, "desiring to hold, believe, and assert whatever is contained in them as long as I have breath in me."

John Huss and other early church reformers believed in placing more emphasis on the Bible, expanding the authority of church councils and lessening that of the Pope, and promoting the moral reform of the clergy. A fearless preacher, Huss attacked the corruption of the church and the vices of the clergy. With passionate vehemence, he condemned the sale of indulgences, the idea of purgatory, the worship of saints, and worship in a foreign language. He believed in the Scriptures, rather than the dogmas and ordinances of the church. In the year 1413, he completed *On the Church*, a view of the church which borrowed heavily from the writings of John Wycliff ("John Huss/Christian History").

Because of his going against the authority of the Roman Catholic Church, Huss was imprisoned in 1414 by the Archbishop of Constance, Germany, at his castle, Gottlieben, on the Rhine. Here, he was chained day and night, poorly fed, and ill. In 1415, he was transferred to a Franciscan monastery, where he spent the last weeks of his life.

Huss believed that the church was not the hierarchy designated as the church by the Roman papacy. Rather, he believed that the church was the entire body of those who believed in Jesus Christ. Christ, not the Pope, was the church's head. No article of faith stated that one must obey the Pope to be saved, he asserted.

During several of his trials before papal legates, he was asked to recant all that he was teaching and preaching, in order to save his life. Huss stated he could not recant the truth that he had found in the Scriptures. Huss refused with the words, "God is my witness that the things charged against me I never preached. In the same truth of the Gospel which I have written, taught, and preached, drawing upon the sayings and positions of the holy doctors, I am ready to die today." ("Jan Hus–Wikipedia")

The horribly captivating *Foxe's Book of Martyrs* recounts the final trial of John Huss at the Council of Constance, which I feel compelled to include in this writing, for it sets before us the courage and sincerity of a man over six hundred years ago, who gave his life so that we might better understand the truths found only in the Scriptures and not look for them elsewhere. I also sense the nature of God in the defense that John Huss gave to those interrogating him. Huss was especially condemned for the ideas he expressed in *On the Church* and for supporting the writings of John Wycliff. Being brought before the papal council, which included the Emperor Sigismund in his imperial robes and habit, and being commanded not to speak, Huss nonetheless knelt before them and committed his treatment to God with the following words:

"O Lord Jesu Christ! Whose Word is openly condemned here in this Council, unto Thee again I do appeal, Who when Thou wast evil entreated of Thine enemies, didst appeal unto God Thy Father, committing Thy cause unto a most just Judge; that by Thy example, we also being oppressed with manifest wrongs and injuries, should flee unto Thee." (*Foxe's*, p. 126)

The sentence of condemnation was read against him, as follows: "Forasmuch as one John Huss, the disciple of John Wickliff, hath taught, preached, and affirmed the articles of Wickliff, which were condemned by the Church of God; especially resisting in his open sermons, and also with his adherents and accomplices in the schools, the condemnation of the said articles of Wickliff, and hath declared him, the said Wickliff, for the favour and commendation of his doctrine, before the whole multitude of the clergy and people, to be a catholic man, and a true evangelical doctor.

"Wherefore, this most sacred and holy Council of Constance, doth condemn and reprove all those books which the said John Huss wrote; and doth decree, that they all shall be solemnly and openly burned in the presence of the clergy and people of the city of Constance, and elsewhere; adding, moreover, that all his doctrine is worthy to be despised and eschewed of all faithful Christians. This sacred Synod doth straitly command, that diligent inquisition be made for such treatises and works; and that such as are found, be consumed with fire.

"Wherefore, this most sacred and holy synod, determineth, pronounceth, declareth, and decreeth that John Huss was and is a true and manifest heretic, and that he hath preached openly errors and heresies, despising the keys of the church, and ecclesiastical censures. In the which his error, he hath continued with a mind altogether indurate and hardened by the space of many years, much offending the faithful Christians by his obstinacy and stubbornness, when he made his appeal unto the Lord Jesus Christ, as the Most High Judge.

"Whereupon the said synod judgeth him to be condemned as a heretic; and reproveth the said appeal as injurious, offensive, and done in derision unto the ecclesiastical jurisdiction; and judgeth the said Huss not only to have seduced the Christian people by his writings and preachings, neither to have been a true preacher of the Gospel of Christ, but also to have been an obstinate and stiffnecked person, such a one as doth not desire to return again to the lap of our holy mother the Church, neither to abjure the errors and heresies which he hath openly preached and defended. Wherefore this most sacred Council decreeth that the said John Huss shall be deposed and degraded from his priestly orders and dignity."

Though John Huss was forbidden to speak, he notwithstanding often interrupted the condemnation against him, especially when his writings were condemned.

"Wherefore have you condemned those books, when you have not proved that they are contrary to the Scriptures?" he asked.

When his sentence and judgment were ended, he knelt down and prayed for those in judgment of him, even as they mocked and derided him.

"Lord Jesus Christ! Forgive mine enemies, by whom Thou knowest that I am falsely accused, and that they have used false witness and slanders against me; forgive them, I say, for Thy great mercy's sake."

Desiring to degrade Huss of his priesthood, the seven papal bishops who sat in judgment of him ordered Huss to put on the garments which he wore as a priest. When putting on the albe, John Huss remembered the beautiful vesture with which Herod mockingly clothed Jesus, and he did comfort himself by the example of Christ. (The "albe" or "alb" was a liturgical vest worn by priests, consisting of a full-length, close-sleeved tunic usually of linen, gathered at the waist with a cincture. A cincture is a girdle or belt.) When he stood before them in the priestly vestment, the bishops yet again commanded him to recant of his "heresy," which he answered as follows:

"These lords and bishops do exhort and counsel me, that I should here confess before you all that I have erred; which thing to do, if it were such as might be done with the infamy and reproach of man only, they might peradventure easily persuade me thereunto; but now truly I am in the sight of the Lord my God, without Whose great ignominy and grudge of mine own conscience, I can by no means do that which they require of me. With what countenance then should I behold the heavens? With what face should I look upon them whom I have taught, whereof there is a great number, if, through me, it should come to pass that those things, which they have hitherto known to be most certain and sure, should now be made uncertain? Should I, by this my example, astonish or trouble so many souls, so many consciences, endued with the most firm and certain knowledge of the Scriptures and Gospel of our Lord Jesu Christ and his most pure doctrine, armed against all the assaults of Satan? I will never do it, neither commit any such kind of offence, that I should seem more to esteem this vile carcase appointed unto death, than their health and salvation." (*Foxe's*, p. 128-129)

One of the bishops then took away the chalice which Huss held, saying the following: "O cursed Judas! Why hast thou forsaken the counsel and ways of peace? We take away from thee this chalice of thy salvation."

John Huss then replied, as follows: "I trust unto God, the Father omnipotent, and my Lord Jesus Christ, for Whose sake I do suffer these things, that He will not take away the chalice of His redemption, but have a steadfast and firm hope that this day I shall drink thereof in His kingdom."

With curses, the bishops began in order to remove the vestments which they had only a short while before put upon John Huss. Hearing their curses, the great church reformer said that he did willingly embrace their blasphemies for the name of "our Lord Jesus Christ."

The bishops contended among themselves how to cut the crown of John Huss' shaven head, whether to use a razor or a pair of shears. Huss turned toward the emperor and said the following words: "I marvel that forasmuch as they be all of like cruel mind, yet they cannot agree upon their kind of cruelty."

Finally agreeing upon the use of shears, they cut off the skin on the top of Huss' head. With this accomplished, they had the following words to say: "Now hath the Church taken away all her ornaments and privileges from him. Now there resteth nothing else, but that he be delivered over unto the secular power."

However, the bishops were not yet done with their prisoner. They made a crown of paper, about a cubit (18-22 inches) in height, on which were painted three ugly devils with the title of *"Heresiarcha"* (meaning the leader of a heretical movement) set over their heads. When John Huss saw the hat, he responded with the following words:

"My Lord Jesus Christ, for my sake, did wear a crown of thorns; why should not I then, for His sake, again wear this light crown, be it ever so ignominious? Truly I will do it, and that willingly."

When the paper hat was placed upon Huss' head, the bishop said, "Now we commit thy soul unto the devil."

Lifting his eyes toward heaven, John Huss said:

"But I do commend into Thy hands, O Lord Jesu Christ! my spirit which Thou hast redeemed."

"This most sacred synod of Constance leaveth now John Huss," said one of the bishops, "who hath no more any office in the Church of God, unto the civil judgment and power."

The emperor then commanded Louis, Duke of Bavaria, to deliver John Huss to the place of execution. According to *Foxe's Book of Martyrs*, the Duke stood before them, attired in his robes and "holding the golden apple with the cross in his hand." The place of Huss' execution was at the gate of Gottlieben, near the gardens. As the Duke guided Huss toward his execution, accompanied by a group of armed men, they passed a fire wherein the books of the great reformer were burning. Foxe states that the whole city of Constance followed the procession to the execution.

Upon reaching the Gottlieben gate, between the garden and the gates of the suburbs, John Huss fell to his knees and lifting his eyes to heaven, he prayed the thirty-first and fifty-first Psalms, followed by the verse, **"Into thine hand I commit my spirit."** When his tormentors pulled him up from his place of prayer, he uttered the following words:

"Lord Jesu Christ! help me, that with a constant and patient mind, I may suffer this cruel and ignominious death, whereunto I am condemned for the preaching of Thy most holy Gospel and Word."

The hangman stripped him of his garments, then tied his hands with wet ropes behind his back to a stake. Noticing that he was facing east, someone in the crowd called out that he shouldn't be facing east, since he was a heretic. Immediately, he was turned at the stake, so that he faced west. His neck was tied with a chain to the stake, and straw and wood were piled around him, up to his chin.

Before the wood was set on fire, John Huss was once again exhorted to be mindful of his salvation and to renounce his errors. To this, the great reformer answered, as follows:

"What error should I renounce, when I know myself guilty of none? For this was the principal end and purpose of my doctrine, that I might teach all men repentance and remission of sins, according to the verity of the Gospel of Jesus Christ: wherefore, with a cheerful mind and courage, I am here ready to suffer death."

As the fire was kindled, John Huss began to sing with a loud voice, "Jesu Christ! The Son of the living God! have mercy upon me." The fire at first produced smoke which caused Huss to gag and cough, but it soon consumed his body. At his death, those of authority in attendance then mistreated his body, making a new fire and burning the head which was first cut into small gobbets, in order for it to burn more speedily. The heart was beaten with staves and clubs, before being pricked with a large stick and roasted in the fire.

Gathering the ashes together, they took all that was left of John Huss and cast it into the River Rhine. Thusly, this martyr for Christ left the earth on July 6, 1415 (*Foxe's,* p. 130-134).

* * * * * * * * * * * * *

After John Huss' death, trouble broke out in different parts of Bohemia, as the followers of Huss sent a protest to the Council of Constance which had executed their leader. This protest, known as the *protestatic Bohemorum,* condemned the execution of Huss in powerful language. Many Catholic priests were driven from their parishes. Sigismund, the Holy Roman Emperor, threatened to drown the followers of John Wycliff and John Huss.

During the years of 1419-1434, wars broke out between the adherents of John Huss and the Roman Catholic Church. These were known as the Hussite or Bohemian Wars. Gunpowder, discovered around 1320 A.D., revolutionized the waging of war. The Hussites used hand-held gunpowder weapons such as hand cannons in defeating the larger armies of the papacy, which involved heavily armored knights.

A staunch follower of the Church of Rome, the Emperor Sigismund collaborated with Pope Martin V, who issued a bull (a solemn papal letter) on March 17, 1420, which announced a crusade for the destruction of the Wycliffites, Hussites, and all other heretics in Bohemia. Though they at first besieged the city of Prague, this army of the papacy abandoned this when negotiations took place for a settlement of the opposing sides' religious differences. The united Hussites issued their demands in a paper called the "Four Articles of Prague." The contemporary chronicler, Laurence of Brezoria, listed these, as follows:

1. The word of God shall be preached and made known in the kingdom of Bohemia freely and in an orderly manner by the priests of the Lord.

2. The sacrament of the most Holy Eucharist shall be freely administered in the two kinds, that is bread and wine, to all the faithful in Christ who are not precluded by mortal sin - according to the word and disposition of Our Saviour.

3. The secular power over riches and worldly goods which the clergy possesses in contradiction to Christ's precept, to the prejudice of its office and to the detriment of the secular arm, shall be taken and withdrawn from it, and the clergy itself shall be brought back to the evangelical rule and an apostolic life such as that which Christ and his apostles led.

4. All mortal sins, and in particular all public and other disorders, which are contrary to God's law shall in every rank of life be duly and judiciously prohibited and destroyed by those whose office it is.

Apparently not accepting the Hussites' "Four Articles of Prague," the Roman Church instigated five battles or crusades against the Hussites. Legend survives that upon seeing the Hussite banners and hearing the Hussite battle hymn *"Ktozjsu bozi bojovnici"* ("Ye Who Are Warriors of God"), the invading papal armies immediately took to flight. However, the Hussites were finally defeated at the Battle of Grotniki, bringing the Hussite Wars to an end. The Church of Rome then accepted a modified form of the Articles of Prague, known as "the compacts." These declared the following:

1. The Holy sacrament is to be given freely in both kinds to all Christians in Bohemia and Moravia, and to those elsewhere who adhere to the faith of these two countries.

2. All mortal sins shall be punished and extirpated by those whose office it is so to do.

3. The word of God is to be freely and truthfully preached by the priests of the Lord, and by worthy deacons.

4. The priests in the time of the law of grace shall claim no ownership of worldly possessions. ("Hussite Wars–Wikipedia")

JANE H. WALKER

Chapter Fifteen

The Age of Discovery continued with the voyages of Christopher Columbus (1451-1506) at the end of the fifteenth century. Born in Genoa, Italy, Columbus traveled to Lisbon, Portugal, where he studied cartography, mathematics, navigation, and astronomy. Realizing how difficult and arduous the land and sea routes to Asia were, Columbus had a different idea about reaching the Far East. Why not sail west across the Atlantic, instead of around the massive and treacherous African continent? After receiving negative reactions to his plan from officials in Portugal and England, he finally found a sympathetic audience from the Spanish monarchs, Ferdinand of Aragon and Isabella of Castile. Columbus wanted fame and fortune, along with the desire to spread the Christian faith to the heathens which surely lived in the West. Ferdinand and Isabella agreed with these goals, as they were also theirs. This plan in the mind of Columbus would change the world forever.

On August 3, 1492, Columbus and his men sailed from Spain in three ships...the *Nina,* the *Pinta,* and the *Santa Maria.* On October 12, they made landfall, not in Asia, as Columbus had thought, but on one of the Bahamian islands. For months Columbus sailed what we now know as the Caribbean, going from island to island, looking for precious stones, pearls, silver, gold, spices and other desired merchandise. However, he found very little. He did not discover the land area of the United States, as most of us believed in our grammar school days. However, he led the way for many other explorers who came after him ("Christopher Columbus–Exploration–HISTORY.com").

During the time period of Columbus' voyages, William Tyndale (1492-1536 A.D.) was following in the footsteps of Wycliffe. Best known for his translation of the Bible directly from Hebrew and Greek texts into English, Tyndale was another great leader in the Protestant Reformation. An English scholar and ordained priest, Tyndale was a gifted linguist, fluent in French, Hebrew, Greek, German, Italian, Latin, and Spanish, in addition to his native English. Tyndale believed that the Bible should be available to everyone, for he was convinced that the way to God and to salvation was through God's word in the Bible.

In 1409, Archbishop Thomas Arundel had held a church council at Oxford, which determined that the translation of the Bible into English or any other language was heretical. Reading aloud the Bible in English and even the mere presence of a Bible in English were grounds of heresy. Those found guilty were turned over to the state for burning.

After Tyndale completed his translation of the New Testament, while on the continent where he had fled for his life, it was smuggled into England and Scotland. The Durham bishop, Cuthbert Tunstall, condemned the English translation in 1526, warning booksellers not to sell the books and having copies burned in public. Cardinal Wolsey, London bishop, condemned Tyndale as a heretic in 1529.

A true story in regard to Tyndale was told by John Foxe (1517-1587), the English historian and author of *Foxe's Book of Martyrs,* who related that an educated but blasphemous clergyman told Tyndale that, "We had better be without God's laws than the Pope's." Charged with spiritual indignation, Tyndale replied, "I defy the Pope, and all his laws, and if God spares my life, ere many years, I will cause the boy that driveth the plow to know more of the Scriptures than thou dost."

In 1530, Tyndale wrote *The Practyse of Prelates,* denouncing Henry VIII's planned annulment from Catherine of Aragon in favor of Anne Boleyn. The irate Henry VIII attempted to have Tyndale apprehended and returned to England, but Charles I of Spain, who became Holy Roman Emperor Charles V, refused this request, insisting that formal evidence was needed before extradition.

However, Tyndale in 1535 was betrayed by local authorities and seized in Antwerp, then held in the castle of Vilvoorde near Brussels, Belgium. On a cold day in October, he was led to a huge cross in a large circular space in Vilvoorde, where his executioners tied his feet to the cross and placed a chain of iron around his neck. Because of his indictment for heresy, he was sentenced to strangulation and burning.

As the cold chain tightened around his neck, Tyndale cried out to the crowd witnessing his execution, "Lord! Open the King of England's eyes." The iron chain crushed his neck, and the flames consumed his body ("William Tyndale–Wikipedia"). Another martyr had given his life for Christ!

* * * * * * * * * * * * *

During this time, Pope Leo X (1475-1521) initiated a massive construction project to beautify St. Peter's Basilica at the Vatican. His tastes were expensive. He spent lavishly on himself and voluptuous entertainment. People with low morals swarmed the papal court where wit mattered more than Christian witness. In order to finance the beautification of St. Peter's Basilica, Pope Leo signed certificates which offered pardon of all sins to buyers and their friends without any confession or repentance. Below is the wording on these certificates: "(I) absolve you...from all thy sins, transgressions, and excesses, how enormous soever they be...and remit to you all punishment which you deserve in purgatory on their account and I restore you...to the innocence and purity which you possessed at baptism, so that when you die the gates of punishment shall be shut...and if you shall not die at present, this grace shall remain in full force when you are at the point of death." ("Infamous Indulgence Led to Reformation–1501-1600 Church History")

A man named Johann Tetzel, a Dominican priest, traveled through Germany, selling these certificates, which people gladly bought, finding it easier to give money than to live their lives as Jesus had taught them to live. Tetzel was a criminal, having been convicted of terrible offenses against society and God, but who had managed to escape punishment for his crimes.

Before Tetzel entered a town, a messenger traveled before him, announcing, "The grace of God and of the holy father is at your gates." Being denied access to the word of God in their own language by the papacy, the people of the town welcomed Tetzel as the emissary of the Pope and listened as he assured them that the indulgences had power to save not only the living but also the dead. Since the people were unable to read the Bible in their own language, they did not know that the Pope could neither pardon them for their sins nor save them.

I found some words of Tetzel in an article on the internet with the title ("Two Beasts, Three Deadly Wounds and Fourteen Popes"). Some of these are recounted below: Tetzel said, "There is no sin so great that an indulgence cannot remit, and even if anyone (which doubtless is impossible) had offered violence to the blessed Virgin Mary, mother of God, let him pay–only let him pay well and all will be forgiven him." ("D'Aubigne, Book III, Chapter 1, p. 86")

He added, "I would not change my privileges for those of St. Peter in heaven; for I have saved more souls by my indulgences than the apostle by his sermons." (Ibid)

Defying the words of God, Tetzel said, "Indulgences avail not only for the living, but for the dead. For that repentance is not even necessary. Priest! noble! merchant! wife! youth! maiden! Do you not hear your parents or your other friends who are dead; and who cry from the bottom of the abyss; we are suffering horrible torments! A trifling alms would deliver us; you can give it, and you will not!" (Ibid)

Maybe Tetzel got what he deserved in an incident reported by William Cathcart D.D. in his book, *The Papal System.* The incident, according to Cathcart, underscored the potential to incite men to criminal acts upon receipt of indulgences for sins yet to be committed and their costs. Below are the sins and their payment for particular indulgences:

"Kings, queens, princes and bishops had to pay twenty-five ducats for an ordinary indulgence. Abbots paid ten. All with an income of five hundred florins paid six. Those who had 200 florins a year paid one; others only a half, a still smaller sum might be taken from poorer persons.

"There was a tax for particular sins. Polygamy nine ducats and magic two ducats. For thirty crowns Tetzel sold a Saxon gentleman an indulgence, giving him pardon for a nameless sin which he was about to commit. The Saxon flogged and robbed him, and was discharged by Duke George without penalty when he showed his indulgence." ("Ferguson and Woodburn, Philadelphia, 1872, p. 276, 277")

When Martin Luther (1483 A.D. - 1546 A.D.), a humble monk living in Germany, heard of the sale of these certificates, or indulgences, he was outraged. On All Saints Day, October 31, 1517 A.D., he nailed his *Disputation of Martin Luther on the Power and Efficacy of Indulgences,* more commonly known as his *Ninety-five Theses*, or arguments for church reform, to the Castle Church door at Wittenberg, Germany, accusing the Roman Catholic Church of heresy. This marked the beginning of the Protestant Reformation ("Martin Luther and the *95 Theses*–Facts & Summary– HISTORY. com"). While at Wittenberg, Martin Luther also wrote in longhand a very lengthy letter on September 6, 1520, to the dissolute Pope Leo X. This letter may be found at the website: ("Letter of Martin Luther to Pope Leo X. Luther, Martin. 1909-14").

"Thesis 86" of Luther's *Ninety-five Theses* asks: "Why does not the pope, whose wealth today is greater than the wealth of the richest Crassus build the basilica of Saint Peter with his own rather than with the money of poor believers?" ("Martin Luther's *95 Theses*–Luther.de") "Crassus" was a Roman statesman, financier and military leader, also called "the Rich." ("PDF Roman Leader Information")

A side note about the gloriously beautiful Saint Peter's basilica is that it was basically constructed to flatter the egos of arrogant monarchs who are memorialized more than the apostles Peter and Paul, in whose honor the church was dedicated. The great artist Michelangelo contributed to the magnificent beauty of the basilica with his *Pieta* sculpture and his design of its dome ("View Article; Michelangelo's Contributions to Saint Peter's"). Catholic scholars today admit that the selling of indulgences to finance the building of St. Peter's was outrageous and should never have occurred ("The Roman Catholic Church–A Critical Appraisal," p.111).

Luther's *Ninety-five Theses* were written in Latin. In January of 1518, friends of Luther translated the *Ninety-five Theses* from Latin into German, then printed and widely copied them for circulation. This was greatly aided by the invention of the printing press in 1440 A.D ("How Gutenberg Changed the World"). Though Martin Luther initially believed in purgatory, his thinking changed with time. He said a person is not a heretic for denying purgatory, since "The Scriptures know nothing of it." The 1522 version of Luther's *Personal Prayer Book* contains the petition: "Have mercy upon all poor souls in purgatory," but these words are removed in the 1524 edition ("Did Martin Luther accept or reject the existence of Purgatory..").

Luther was consumed with the non-biblical selling of indulgences by the Pope. Certainly, we can see the hand of God in bringing about the Reformation, his nature being such that the seed of truth was preserved through a man called Martin Luther. When he appeared before the Diet of Worms, in Worms, Germany, on April 17, 1521, Luther was shown a table filled with copies of his writings. When asked whether he still believed what he had written, he boldly stated, "Unless I am convinced by proofs from Scriptures or by plain and clear reasons and arguments, I can and will not retract, for it is neither safe nor wise to do anything against conscience. Here I stand. I can do no other. God help me. Amen."

On May 25, some five weeks later, the Holy Roman Emperor Charles V issued his Edict of Worms, which declared that Martin Luther was an outlaw. Knowing that Luther's life was in danger, his powerful friends among the princes of Germany arranged for him to be seized by a group of masked horsemen who carried him to the protection of Wartburg Castle, where he lived for a year. While there, he changed his appearance, growing a full beard and wearing the garb of a knight. During this period of his life, Luther translated and published the New Testament in the common dialect of the German people in 1522. This was followed by his translation of the

Old Testament in 1534, resulting in the entire Bible being translated into German ("Martin Luther– Greatsite.com").

The final two days of Martin Luther's life are recorded in *Foxe's Book of Martyrs*. Miraculously, Luther had escaped execution for his heretical beliefs and writings. In 1546 at the age of sixty-three, the reformer was called home to the Lord he had loved and served for some twenty-nine years. Foxe described Luther's final hours as follows:

"Wednesday last past, and the 17th of February, Dr. Martin Luther sickened of his accustomed malady, to wit, of the oppression of humours in the orifice or opening of the stomach. This sickness took him after supper, with which he vehemently contending, required secess into a by-chamber, and there he rested on his bed two hours, all which time his pains increased; and as Dr. Jonas was lying in his chamber, Luther awaked, and prayed him to rise, and to call up Ambrose his children's schoolmaster, to make a fire in another chamber; into which when he was newly entered, Albert, Earl of Mansfield, with his wife, and divers others at that instant came into his chamber. Finally, feeling his fatal hour to approach, before nine of the clock in the morning, on the 18th of February, he commended himself to God with this devout prayer: 'My heavenly Father, eternal and merciful God! Thou hast manifested unto me Thy dear Son, our Lord Jesus Christ. I have taught Him, I have known Him; I love Him as my life, my health, and my redemption; Whom the wicked have persecuted, maligned, and with injury afflicted. Draw my soul to Thee.'

"After this he said as ensueth, thrice:'I commend my spirit into Thy hands, Thou hast redeemed me, O God of Truth!' 'God so loved the world, that He gave His only Son, that all those that believe in Him should have life everlasting.' Having repeated oftentimes his prayers, he was called to God. So praying, his innocent ghost peaceably was separated from the earthly corpse." (*Foxe's*, p. 186-187)

* * * * * * * * * * * * *

John Calvin (1509-1564) was one of the great leaders of the Protestant Reformation, beginning a movement that revolutionized the Christian Church in Europe, America, and ultimately the rest of the world. He believed in predestination, the idea that God had already chosen who would and would not be saved. He also felt that the state should enforce church laws.

Born in Noyon, France, he initially began studying for the priesthood, but changed his major to civil law when he began to reject Catholicism. Because of his association with church reformers, Calvin had to flee Catholic Paris. The Catholic Church was hunting heretics and, in 1534, burned twenty-four heretics at the stake ("John Calvin Biography–ThoughtCo").

Calvin spent his last years in French-speaking Geneva, Switzerland, which was ripe for church reform. Soon, three immediate breaks from the Catholic Church took place: monasteries were closed, the Mass was banned, and papal authority was rejected. However, when liberal forces took over the city, Calvin escaped to Strasbourg. In 1540, he returned to Geneva, where he instituted many church reforms. The city was edging toward theocracy, a religious government. In Geneva, the moral code became the criminal law, wherein sin was a punishable crime. Being thrown out of the Church meant being exiled from the city. Lewd singing could bring about the guilty person's tongue being pierced. Blasphemy was punished by death.

Calvin established primary and secondary schools and also the University of Geneva. His followers included John Knox (1514-1572), who brought Calvinism to Scotland where the Presbyterian Church has its roots. George Whitefield (1714-1770) took the Calvinist message to the American colonies ("John Calvin Biography–ThoughtCo").

During this time period of the church, one of the major controversies that drove a wedge between the Roman Catholic Church and the reformers or Protestants was the meaning of Holy Communion. The Roman Catholic Church believed in transubstantiation, meaning that the bread and wine used in Communion actually became the body and blood of Christ. Anyone deviating from this belief was charged with heresy and faced execution either by burning or beheading. ("The Unholy Inquisition

- Preserved Word Ministries"). Reformers believed that Jesus was sacrificed once and that the bread and juice were to be ingested in remembrance of Him ("The main differences between Catholics and Protestants/Culture/Arts").

The Roman Catholic Church also believed in pomp and pageantry and icons. Some of their churches were magnificent, even when built among people who lived in dire poverty. The Pope was the final word in matters of doctrine, which encouraged pilgrimages to shrines ("The Role of Indulgences in the Building of New Saint Peter's Basilica"). Even today, the rift between the Roman Catholic Church and Protestant churches remains, though no Christians are being put to death by other Christians, as happened only several hundred years ago.

According to several articles I read on the internet, the Vatican officially teaches that "For the Roman Pontiff, by reason of his office as Vicar of Christ, and as pastor of the entire church has full, supreme, and universal power over the whole Church, a power which he can always exercise." ("THE POPE OR THE HOLY SPIRIT –Who is the true 'Vicar of Christ...'")

Joseph Ratzinger was elected as Pope Benedict XVI in April of 2005. Before this, he was head of the Congregation for the Doctrine of the Faith (formerly called the Office of the Roman Inquisition). In the year 2000, he issued a document called "Dominus Iesus," in which he decreed that the Roman Catholic Church was the "only instrument for the salvation of all humanity." ("Vatican declares only the Roman Catholic Church brings salvation.")

The Protestant belief is that **"there is one God, and one mediator between God and men, the man Jesus Christ."** (I Timothy 2:5) The Catholic Church has countered that it is the unified church and that Protestantism has splintered into many different factions such as Methodists, Baptists, Presbyterians, and others. This is true, but it is also true that Catholicism has had its own splinter groups, including the Eastern Orthodox Church, the Anglican Church, and other factions. ("The Ecumenical Movement–The Restored Church of God") The schism involving the tri-fold papacy lasted a number of years ("Western Schism–Wikipedia").

My point in mentioning these schisms of Christianity is not to weaken the church. Rather, it is to highlight the ongoing struggle of the church to purify itself. The Protestant belief is that each person must decide what he or she believes and must join with the group which most nearly espouses his or her beliefs. It is incumbent upon each of us to meditate, to pray, and to study the Scriptures to determine what we believe. Of course, all of this is predicated upon one's belief that the Bible is the Word of God. If we don't accept the Bible as the Word of God, then what do we have in its place? The Bible has been in existence for thousands of years. This is surely a testament of the nature of God and his Church.

* * * * * * * * * * * * *

In August of 1588, an armada of 130 ships left Spain, sailing under the authority of Philip 2, husband of the deceased English Queen Mary 1, also known as "Bloody Mary," because of the many executions of Protestants during her reign. At Mary's death, her sister Elizabeth 1 became Queen of England. While Mary was Catholic, Elizabeth was Protestant. Both were daughters of Henry V111. The purpose of the armada was to invade England, overthrow Queen Elizabeth 1, and defeat the establishment of Protestantism in England.

Being composed of 130 ships, the fleet had 8,000 sailors and 18,000 soldiers, 1,500 brass guns and 1,000 iron guns. Though the English fleet outnumbered the Spanish, 200 ships to 130, the Spanish fleet outgunned the English – its firepower was 50% more than that of the English. However, the English ships were more maneuverable, allowing the fleet to stay out of range of Spanish gunners.

Robert Dudley, Earl of Leicester, headed a force of 4,000 soldiers at West Tilbury, Essex, to defend the Thames Estuary against any incursion by the Spanish, up-river towards London. Queen Elizabeth traveled to Tilbury on August 8 to encourage her military and to give to them her famous speech, as follows:

"My loving people, we have been persuaded by some that are careful of our safety to take heed how we commit ourselves to armed multitudes for fear of treachery, but I do assure you, I do not desire to live to distrust my faithful and loving people. Let tyrants fear. I have always so behaved myself, that under God I have placed my chiefest strength and safeguard in the loyal hearts and goodwill of my subjects, and therefore, I am come amongst you as you see at this time, not for my recreation and disport, but being resolved, in the midst and heat of battle, to live or die amongst you all – to lay down for my God, and for my kingdoms, and for my people, my honour and my blood even in the dust. I know I have the body of a weak and feeble woman, but I have the heart and stomach of a king – and of a King of England too, and think foul scorn that Parma or Spain, or any prince of Europe, should dare to invade the borders of my realm, to which, rather than any dishonour should grow by me, I myself will take up arms - I myself will be your general, judge, and rewarder of every one of your virtues in the field.

"I know already, for your forwardness, you have deserved rewards and crowns, and, we do assure you, on the word of a prince, they shall be duly paid you. In the mean time, my lieutenant general shall be in my stead, than whom never prince commanded a more noble or worthy subject, not doubting but by your obedience to my general, by your concord in the camp, and your valour in the field, we shall shortly have a famous victory over those enemies of my God, of my kingdom, and of my people."

In September of 1588, the battered Spanish ships sailed the lengthy route around Scotland and Ireland into the North Atlantic. Strong storms damaged the fleet further, preventing many of the ships from returning to Spain. Around 5,000 men died by drowning, starvation and slaughter by the English forces, after being driven ashore in Iceland.

Only 67 ships and less than 10,000 men of the Spanish armada survived. Many of the men were near death from diseases. Food and water were scarce. It was said that when Philip 2 learned of the fate of the armada, he declared, "I sent the Armada against men, not God's winds and waves." This battle resulted in the continued Protestantism of England.

The victory of England denoted a shift in the balance of naval power in favor of the English. By 1588, according to historian and author, Geoffrey Parker, "the capital ships of the Elizabethan navy constituted the most powerful battlefleet afloat anywhere in the world." English ship yards were leaders in technical innovation. The full-rigged ship was one of the greatest technological advances of the century, and it permanently transformed naval warfare.

The legacy of the English victory over the Spanish Armada was the boost to national pride that continued for years, also contributing to the legendary greatness of Elizabeth 1. It seemed to give heart to the Protestant cause across Europe and the belief that God supported the Protestant faith. Commemorative medals were struck that bore variations on the inscription "1588 Flavist Jehovah et *Dissipati Sunt*" with "Jehovah" in Hebrew letters (God blew, and they are scattered"). ("Spanish armada–Wikipedia") In 1888, the Armada Memorial was constructed at Plymouth Hoe, Plymouth, Devon, England, to celebrate the tercentenary of the Armada ("Armada Memorial– Wikipedia").

Chapter Sixteen

The first European colonies in North America were Spanish. St. Augustine, Florida, became a Spanish settlement in 1565. Please note the Christian name given to this first colony. Before this, the land mass of North America was visited by the Norseman, Leif Erickson, and possibly even the early Phoenicians ("Who First Discovered America?/Owlcation"). However, for around 115 years after Columbus discovered the New World, only Spain had colonies in North America.

Though most of North America was inhabited only by the native Indians, by 1607, more than 150,000 Spanish settlers had come to the New World. From Africa, the Spanish brought a large number of black slaves. Historians claim that there were at least 150,000 black slaves in the New World before the English came to live in America ("Chapter III The Early European Colonies").

Many European fishermen sailed to the waters off the coasts of the United States and Canada to fish, but did not settle there ("The First Voyages of the European/Site for Language Management"). The British tried to establish a colony in Roanoke, Virginia, in 1585, but it did not survive. It became known as the Lost Colony, since no one could determine what happened to the settlement ("Roanoke Colony–Wikipedia"). However, the first permanent English colony in America was the settlement of Jamestown in 1607 ("Jamestown, Virginia–Wikipedia").

In December of 1606, three ships–*the Susan Constant, the Godspeed,* and *the Discovery*–reached the New World with 105 men and boys and thirty-nine crew members. No women were aboard these ships. The first shipment of women came in October, 1608. Sponsored by the Virginia Company of London and led by Captain Christopher Newport, the vessels arrived at the southern edge of Chesapeake Bay in April of 1607. Venturing inland upstream along the James River, the settlers ultimately chose Jamestown Island for their settlement. Jamestown (originally "James His Towne") was named in honor of King James I.

Jamestown at first appeared to be a good location, because it could easily be defended from ships of other European countries that were also establishing New World colonies and were periodically at war with England. These included the Dutch Republic, France, and especially Spain. Also, the site of Jamestown was not inhabited by the Virginia Indians, most of whom were affiliated with the Powhatan Confederacy.

However, the settlement was in a swampy area, infested with mosquitoes. The resulting malaria killed over 135 colonists. Many people died from drinking the brackish water of the tidal James River, but most died from disease and starvation ("History of Jamestown, Virginia [1607-99]–Wikipedia").

Investors of the Virginia Company hoped to reap rewards from their speculative investment in the colony of Jamestown. They demanded that the colonists send sufficient commodities to pay the cost of the voyage–a piece of gold, certainty that they had found the South Sea, and one member of the lost Roanoke Colony. The ever-bold John Smith, leader of the Jamestown Council, delivered what surely was a wake-up call to the far-removed investors in London, who knew little of the colonists' everyday struggles to survive. Below is John Smith's answer to the Virginia Company:

"I humbly intreat your Pardons if I offend you with my rude Answer..." "When you send again I entreat you rather send but thirty carpenters, husbandmen, gardiners, fishermen, blacksmiths, masons and diggers up of trees, roots, well provided; than a thousand of such as we have: for except wee be able both to lodge them and feed them, the most will consume with want of necessaries before they can be made good for anything." ("Sea Venture– Wikipedia")

When the English colonists arrived in Virginia in May of 1607, they soon were informally introduced to an Indian child of the age of eleven or twelve, named Pocahontas. According to an article I found on the internet, one colonist told of her turning cartwheels with the boys of the settlement, through the marketplace of the fort... while naked ("PDF Pocahontas").

Though some historians discredit the story about Chief Powhatan's young daughter, Pocahontas, saving John Smith's life, she did become an emissary to the colonists at Jamestown Island. She brought food and clothing to the colonists when their fort was destroyed by fire in 1608. She later asked Smith for the release of Virginia Indians captured by the colonists during a raid to acquire English weaponry. In 1616, Smith wrote an account of Pocahontas which describes her attempt to save his life. Below is a sentence from that writing:

"At the minute of my execution, she hazarded the beating out of her own brains to save mine; and not only that, but so prevailed with her father that I was safely conducted to Jamestown." ("Smith's 1616 Letter to Queen Ann-Digital History")

Pocahontas and her husband, Kocoum, lived at Passapatanzy, a village of the Patawomecks, a Powhatan Confederacy tribe which did some bartering with Powhatans. She was kidnapped by Samuel Argall, longtime resident of Jamestown and deputy governor of Virginia, and carried about ninety miles south to the English settlement of Henricus on the James River. Argall hoped to establish an alliance between the Patawomecks and the Virginians, which her capture might ensure. He also held her as ransom, demanding the release of English prisoners and supplies, held by Powhatan. While at the English settlement, under the tutelage of Reverend Alexander Whitaker who had arrived in Jamestown in 1611, she converted to Christianity and took the name "Rebecca."

From late 1609 to early 1610, a period of poor crops for natives and colonists became known as "the Starving Time." Of 500 English colonists, only sixty survived. Their hardship was compounded by the loss of their most skillful leader, Captain John

Smith. Being injured in a gunpowder accident in 1609, he had to return to England for medical attention in October of that year.

The starving colonists abandoned Jamestown and were sailing back to England when they came upon a fleet of three supply ships, arriving from England and commanded by a new governor, Thomas West, 3rd Baron De La Ware. Known as "Lord Delaware," Governor West brought with him a doctor, food, and greatly needed supplies. He turned around the departing ships and brought the entire group back to Jamestown.

John Rolfe was one of the colonists who returned with the group. A business man whose wife and child had died, he had with him some seeds of a new strain of tobacco and also some untried ideas for its marketing. History records proved that he would account for the success of the colony as much as Lord Delaware's timely arrival had ("History of Jamestown, Virginia [1607-99]–Wikipedia").

By 1611, most of the colonists who had arrived at the Jamestown settlement had died, and the colony had produced no economic value to English investors. However, John Rolfe began planting tobacco which appealed to the taste of the Europeans, and he began exporting it in large quantities. Soon, as other colonists followed suit, windfall profits in tobacco gave Jamestown almost a gold rush atmosphere. Beaver skins also helped to assure the survival of Jamestown. ("The English fur trade in Chesapeake Bay, c–RootsWeb: Freepages")

John Rolfe became a wealthy and prominent man. After the death of his wife, he married the young Virginia Indian woman, Pocahontas, in 1614. Though Rolfe described her as "one whose education hath bin rude, her manners barbarous, her generation accursed, and so discrepant in all nutritive from myself," he stated that he was "in love" with Pocahontas. All of this he told to her father Powhatan and Governor Dale, whose permission he sought to marry her. Both her father and Governor Dale agreed to the marriage, hoping it would heal relations between the colonists and the local Indians. From their marriage began eight years of relative peace, known as the "Peace of Pocahontas."

Their son, Thomas Rolfe, was born in 1615. In 1616, John

Rolfe, Pocahontas, and their young son left their plantation home for a public relations mission to England. Pocahontas was received as visiting royalty by Queen Anne and was presented to King James I. However, as they planned the return trip home, Pocahontas died of an illness at Gravesend in 1617, where she was buried. Many well-known descendants of Thomas Rolfe and Pocahontas include Edith Wilson, wife of Woodrow Wilson, and Thomas Mann Randolph, Jr., husband of Martha Washington Jefferson, who was the daughter of Thomas Jefferson and his wife, Martha Wayles Skelton Jefferson. ("Pocahontas: Mataoka and the Virginia Colonists–ThoughtCo")

By 1618, the colonists were exporting 50,000 pounds of tobacco to England a year and were beginning to realize enough profit to guarantee the economic survival of the colony ("PDF Encounters with Tobacco The Development of the Virginia Colony"). Nevertheless, relations with the native Indians took a turn for the worse after the death of Pocahontas and the return of John Rolfe and other colonial leaders in 1617. Poor harvests, disease, and the growing need for tobacco lands brought about the escalation of hostilities ("Colony of Virginia–Wikipedia").

The Indian Massacre of 1622 left 347 settlers (men, women, and children) dead and brought about the abduction of many others. A letter written by Richard Frethorne to his parents in 1623 stated, "We live in fear of the enemy every hour ("Jamestown Colony: A Political, Social, and Cultural History")." The Second Indian Massacre of 1644 killed nearly 500 colonists. Finally, peace was temporarily restored in 1646, when the first treaties were signed between the Virginia Indians and the English colonists. However, problems with the hostile Indians continued for years ("Colony of Virginia–Wikipedia").

In Virginia, the Indian attacks became even more deadly, and the settlers begged Governor William Berkeley and the Virginia House of Burgesses to protect small landowners from these assaults. When Berkeley refused to come to their aid and even disbanded a volunteer army of three hundred settlers, whom he branded as rebels, sixty of the group followed Nathaniel Bacon (1647-1676) in retaliatory raids on the Indians. Though a new assembly at Jamestown granted Bacon an official commission as an Indian fighter, Berkeley (a representative of the English crown) carried out several military expeditions against Bacon's group. "Bacon's Rebellion" was the first popular revolt in the English colonies against their distant English governance (Nathaniel Bacon/American colonist/*Britannica*.com).

An anonymous article on Bacon's rebellion in Virginia was written in 1705 at the request of a British investigating commission by a colonist known as T.M. It was taken from a source entitled Force I: "The Beginning, Progress, and Conclusion of Bacon's Rebellion in Virginia, in the Years 1675 and 1676." An excerpt appears below, which gives us insight into the trials and fears of the New World:

"My dwelling was in Northumberland, the lowest county on Potomac River, Stafford being the upmost, where having also a plantation, servants, cattle, etc., my overseer there had agreed with one Robt. Hen to come thither and be my herdsman, who then lived ten miles above it. But on a Sabbath-day morning in the summer anno1675, people in their way to church saw this Hen lying athwart his threshold, and an Indian without the door; both chopped on their heads, arms and other parts, as if done with Indian hatchets, the Indian was dead; but Hen when asked who did that, answered, Doegs Doegs, and soon died. Then a boy came out from under a bed, where he had hid himself, and told them Indians had come at break of day and, done those murders.

"From this Englishman's blood did [by degrees] arise Bacon's Rebellion, with the following mischiefs, which overspread all Virginia and twice endangered Maryland, as by the ensuing account is evident....

"In these frightful times the most exposed small families withdrew into our houses of better numbers, which we fortified with palisades and redoubts; neighbors in bodies joined their labors from each plantation to others alternately, taking their arms into the fields, and setting sentinels, no man stirred out-of-door unarmed. Indians were ever and anon espied, three, four, five, or six in a party, lurking throughout the whole land, yet (what was remarkable) I rarely heard of any houses burnt, though abundance was forsaken, nor ever of any corn or tobacco cut up, or other injury done, besides murders, except the killing a very few cattle and swine. Frequent complaints of bloodsheds were sent to Sir Wm. Berkeley (then Governor) from the heads of the rivers, which were as often answered with promises of assistance." ("T.M. The Virginia Rebellion in the Seventeenth Century.Stedman and...")

The gist of the rest of the article was that Bacon was captured by the high sheriff of Jamestown and brought to the Governor who set him free. However, Bacon did not believe that his liberty was to be lengthy. He fled into the country at the head of an army of four hundred men, only to return to Jamestown after several days. There, his people burned the entire town, including the church and statehouse. After this, Bacon called a convention at Middle Plantation, fifteen miles from Jamestown, in August of 1676. One proclamation commanded that all men in the land, "on pain of death," should join with him to oppose the forces who were due to arrive from England to subdue him.

However, Bacon returned from his final expedition, sick of the flux, and died. His followers, including a Mr. Lawrence and a Mr. Drummond, who had led in the burning of the town met untimely deaths. It was said that the Governor, a pawn of the English crown, would have hanged half the country, if he had his way. These events shed light on the early struggles of the settlers to be free of the yoke that bound them to England.

By 1662, Jamestown's status as mandatory port of entry for Virginia had ended. At the suggestion of five students at the College of William and Mary, a proposal was submitted to the colony's leaders to move the capital to higher ground. The change would bring about an escape from the mosquitoes and resulting malaria that had plagued the swampy Jamestown site. With this accomplished, the new site was renamed Williamsburg, in honor of King William III ("History of Jamestown, Virginia [1607-99]–Wikipedia").

* * * * * * * * * * * * * *

Though the first colonists came to America for many different reasons, i.e. to make money, to explore, to practice their religion freely, and to live on their own land, the Pilgrims and the Puritans came to the New World basically to have religious freedom. When

England broke away from the Roman Catholic Church in the 1500s and created a new church, called the Church of England, everyone in England had to belong to the new church. However, a group of people known as Separatists decided to leave, or "separate" from the Church of England, which they thought still retained too much adherence to the Roman Catholic Church ("The Pilgrims and the Puritans Come to America").

Under the leadership of William Bradford (1590-1657), these Separatists, also called Pilgrims, planned to leave England in 1608 to settle in Holland. For them, II Corinthians 6:17 made their decision the right one, for it stated, **"Wherefore come out from among them, and be ye separate, saith the Lord...."** ("America's First 'War on Christmas'/Mostly True Stories of K. RenaeP.")

After twelve years in Holland, the Pilgrims returned to England to obtain the backing of the Virginia Company to go to America. Again, with William Bradford leading them, 102 Pilgrims and a crew of thirty to forty men set sail on the *Mayflower* in September of 1620 ("List of *Mayflower* passengers–Wikipedia"). Only one primary account exists that describes the voyage of the Mayflower, and it was written by William Bradford in his *History of Plymouth Plantation.* I realize it is long, but I thought it interesting enough to include it. I cannot imagine being on that ship and experiencing all that they did, then leaving the ship without anyone or anything to welcome me to a new world. An excerpt is below:

"September 6. These troubles being blown over, and now all being compact together in one ship, they put to sea again with a prosperous wind, which continued divers days together, which was some encouragement unto them; yet according to the usual manner many were afflicted with sea sickness. And I may not omit here a special work of God's providence. There was a proud and very profane young man, one of the seamen, of a lusty, able body, which made him the more haughty; he would always be condemning the poor people in their sickness, and cursing them daily with grievous execrations, and did not let to tell them, that he hoped to help to cast half of them overboard before they came to their journey's end, and to make merry with what they had; and if he were by any gently reproved, he would curse and swear most bitterly. But it pleased God before they came half seas over, to smite this young man with a grievous disease, of which he died in a desperate manner, and so was himself the first that was thrown overboard. Thus his curses light on his own head; and it was an astonishment to all his fellows, for they noted it to be the just hand of God upon him.

"After they had enjoyed fair winds and weather for a season, they were encountered many times with cross winds, and met with many fierce storms, with which the ship was shroudly shaken, and her upper works made very leaky, and one of the main beams in the mid ships was bowed and cracked, which put them in some fear that the ship could not be able to perform the voyage. So some of the chief of the company, perceiving the mariners to fear the sufficiency of the ship, as appeared by their mutterings, they entered into serious consultation with the master and other officers of the ship, to consider in time of the danger; and rather to return than to cast themselves into a desperate and inevitable peril. And truly there was great distraction and difference of opinion among the mariners themselves; fain would they do what could be done for their wages sake, (being now half the seas over), and on the other hand they were loath to hazard their lives too desperately.

"But in examining of all opinions, the master and others affirmed they knew the ship to be strong and firm under water; and for the buckling of the main beam, there was a great iron screw the passengers brought out of Holland, which would raise the beam into his place, the which being done, the carpenter and master affirmed that with a post put under it, set firm in the lower deck, and otherways bound, he would make it sufficient. And as for the decks and upper works they would caulk them as well as they could, and though with the working of the ship they would not long keep staunch, yet there would otherwise be no great danger, if they did not overpress her with sails. So they committed themselves to the will of God, and resolved to proceed.

"In sundry of these storms the winds were so fierce, and the seas so high, as they could not bear a knot of sail, but were forced to hull, for divers days together. And in one of them, as they thus lay at hull, in a mighty storm, a lusty young man called John Howland coming upon some occasion above the gratings, was, with a seele of the ship thrown into the sea; but it pleased God that he caught hold of the topsail halyards, which hung overboard, and ran out at length; yet he held his hold (though he was sundry fathoms under water) till he was hauled up by the same rope to the brim of the water, and then with a boat hook and other means got into the ship again, and his life saved; and though he was something ill with it, yet he lived many years after, and became a profitable member both in church and commonwealth. In all this voyage there died but one of the passengers, which was William Butten, a youth, servant to Samuel Fuller, when they drew near the coast.

"But to omit other things, (that I may be brief), after long beating at sea they fell with that land which is called Cape Cod; the which being made and certainly known to be it, they were not a little joyful. After some deliberation had amongst themselves and with the master of the ship, they tacked about and resolved to stand for the southward (the wind and weather being fair) to find some place about Hudson's River for their habitation. But after they had sailed that course about half a day, they fell amongst dangerous shoals and roaring breakers, and they were so far entangled therewith as they conceived themselves in great danger, and the wind shrinking upon them withal, they resolved to bear up again for the Cape, and thought themselves happy to get out of those dangers before night overtook them, as by God's providence they did. And the next day they got into the Cape-harbor where they rid in safety.

"A word or two by the way of this cape; it was thus first named by Captain Gosnold and his company, Anno. 1602, and after by Captain Smith was called Cape James; but it retains the former name amongst seamen. Also that point which first showed these dangerous shoals unto them, they called Point Care, and Tucker's Terror; but the French and Dutch to this day call it Malabar, by reason of those perilous shoals, and the losses they have suffered there.

"Being thus arrived in a good harbor and brought safe to land, they fell upon their knees and blessed the God of heaven, who had brought them over the vast and furious ocean, and delivered them from all the perils and miseries thereof, again to set their feet on the firm and stable earth, their proper element. And no marvel if they were thus joyful, seeing wise Seneca was so affected with sailing a few miles on the coast of his own Italy; as he affirmed, that he had rather remain twenty years on his way by land, than pass by sea to any place in a short time; so tedious and dreadful was the same unto him.

"But here I cannot but stay and make a pause, and stand half amased at this poore peoples presente condition; and so I thinke will the reader too, when he well considers ye same. Being thus passed ye vast ocean, and a sea of troubles before in their preparation (as may be remembered by yt which wente before), they had now no friends to wellcome them, nor inns to entertaine or refresh their weatherbeaten bodys, no houses or much less townes to repaire too, to seek for succoure...

"Let it also be considered what weake hopes of supply & succoure they left behinde them, yt might bear up their minds in this sade condition and trialls they were under; and they could not but be very smale. It is true, indeed, ye affections & love of their brethren at Leyden was cordiall & entire towards them, but they had little power to help them, or them selves; and how ye case stode betweene them & ye marchants at their coming away, hath already been declared. What could not sustaine them but ye spirite of God & his grace? May not & ought not the children of these fathers rightly say: Our fathers were Englishmen which came over this great ocean and were ready to perish in this wildernes; but they cried unto ye Lord, and he heard their voyce, and looked on their adversitie, &c, Let them therfore praise ye Lord, because he is good, & his mercies endure for ever." ("PDF Of Plymouth Plantation Written from 1630-1650 by William Bradford...")

Another contemporary account of the *Mayflower*'s voyage exists, but it was not a first-hand account, as William Bradford's was. It was written in 1624 by Captain John Smith (the same one allegedly rescued by Pocahontas), based on second-hand information he had heard or read in letters which were sent back to England. John Smith wrote the following (with his spelling left intact):

"Upon these inducements some few well disposed Gentlemen and Merchants of London and other places provided two ships, the one of 160 Tunnes (the *Mayflower*), the other of 70 (the *Speedwell*); they left the coast of England the 23 of August, with about 120 persons, but the next day the lesser ship sprung a leake, that forced their return to Plimmoth [England]: where discharging her and 20 passengers, with the great ship and a hundred persons besides sailers, they set saile againe the sixt of September, and the ninth of November fell with Cape James [Cape Cod]; but being pestered nine weeks in this leaking unwholesome ship, lying wet in their cabbins, most of them grew very weak, and weary of the sea." ("The Journey from *Mayflower* steps to Cape Cod")

Beset by autumn storms, the 1620 voyage undertaken by the Pilgrims on the *Mayflower* was more than 3,000 miles ("*Mayflower* Voyage and Passengers*** – Colonial America"). Owned and operated by Captain Christopher Jones, the *Mayflower* was about one hundred feet long with three decks. It carried the essentials needed for its passengers' journey and their future lives in the New World. They would have carried tools and weapons, including gunpowder, shot, and cannon, as well as sheep, dogs, poultry, and goats. Cattle and horses would come later.

The *Mayflower* would also have carried two boats: a long boat and a "shallop," or twenty-one foot dinghy. Twelve artillery pieces (eight minions and four sakers–types of cannons) would have also been transported across the ocean on the *Mayflower*, as the Pilgrims felt they might need to defend themselves against enemy European forces, as well as the native Indians ("Mayflower–Wikipedia").Two deaths occurred on the treacherous voyage across the stormy Atlantic, ill omens of all that awaited them upon their arrival at Plymouth Settlement, Massachusetts ("*Mayflower* Voyage and Passengers***–Colonial America").

The following description of the everyday activities of the transatlantic passengers makes for some interesting reading, which underscores the stalwart character of these brave people who left their comfortable homes in England and Holland to travel to an unknown land, all for their love of God and the freedom to worship Him:

"The passengers mostly slept and lived in the low-ceilinged great cabins. These cabins were thin-walled and extremely cramped. The cabin area was 25 feet by 15 at its largest, and on the main deck, which was 75 by 20 at the most. Below decks, any person over five feet tall would be unable to stand up straight. The maximum possible space for each person would have been slightly less than the size of a standard single bed. The *Mayflower* passengers were the earliest permanent European settlers in New England. During their time, they were referred to as the "First comers." They lived in the perilous times of what was called "the Ancient beginnings" of the New World adventure.

"Passengers would pass the time by reading by candlelight or playing cards and games like Nine Men's Morris. Meals on board were cooked by the firebox, which was an iron tray with sand in it on which a fire was built. This was risky because it was kept in the waist of the ship. Passengers made their own meals from rations that were issued daily and food was cooked for a group at a time. Upon arrival late in the year, the harsh climate and scarcity of fresh food caused many more deaths. Due to the delay in departure, provisions were short. Living in these extremely close and crowded quarters, several passengers experienced scurvy, a disease caused by a lack of the essential nutrient vitamin C (ascorbic acid).

"There was no way to store fruits or vegetables without their becoming rotten, so many passengers did not receive enough nutrients in their diets. Passengers with scurvy experienced symptoms such as rotten teeth, which would fall out; bleeding gums, and stinking breath. Passengers consumed large amounts of alcohol, specifically beer. Beer was thought to be safer than water because the Pilgrims were accustomed to unsafe drinking water. Beer was thought to be part of a healthy, well-balanced diet. William Mullins took 126 pairs of shoes and 13 pairs of boots. These clothes included: oiled leather and canvas suits, stuff gowns and leather and stuff breeches, shirts, jerkins, doublets, neckcloths, hats and caps, hose, stockings, belts, piece goods, and haberdasherie.

"No cattle or beasts of draft or burden were brought on the journey, but there were pigs, goats, and poultry. Some passengers brought family pets such as cats and birds. Peter Browne took his large bitch mastiff and John Goodman brought along his spaniel.

"The seamen on the *Mayflower* had four devices to help them during their journey. They charted their course with a compass. They measured their speed with the log and line system. This system consisted of a board attached to a line, which was tossed over the stern. The line was marked with a knot at regular intervals related to the length of a nautical mile. Time was measured with hour glasses; for example, 'when the hour glass had emptied at the top vessel, a sailor would strike a bell, and another sailor would count how many knots of line had run out.' The speed of the ship in nautical miles per hour (still called "knots") would then be known." ("Isaac Mullins b. Abt 1602: Reid-Shroeder Family Tree")

Upon arriving at the tip of Cape Cod in November of 1621, the settlers wrote a social contract which stated that they would follow the compact's rules and regulations for the sake of survival. Since they had unintentionally not landed in the colony of Virginia, as originally determined and financed by the Company of Merchant Adventurers of London, the colonists had to form their own governance, which initially took the form of the *Mayflower Compact*. It reads, as follows:

"In the name of God, Amen. We whose names are underwritten, by the loyall subjects of our dread soveraigne Lord, King James, by the grace of God, of Great Britaine, Franc, and Ireland king, defender of the faith, etc.

"Haveing undertaken, for the glorie of God, and advancemente of the Christian faith, and honour of our king and countrie, a voyage to plant the first colonie in the Northerne parts of Virginia, doe by these presents solemnly and mutually in the presence of God, and one another, covenant and combine our selves togeather into a civill body politick, for our better ordering and preservation and furtherance of the ends aforesaid; and by vertue hereof to enacte, constitute and frame such just and equall lawes, ordinances, acts, constitutions, and offices, from time to time, as shall be thought most meete and convenient for the generall good of the Colonie, unto which we promise all due submission and obedience. In witness whereof we have hereunder subscribed our names at Cap-Codd the 11 of November, in the year of the raigne of our soveraigne lord, King James, of England, France, and Ireland, the eighteenth, and of Scotland the fiftie-fourth. Anno Dom. 1620." (*Mayflower Compact* by Wheelwright, 32-33 and "Pilgrims and Puritans: Background–Xroads Virginia.edu...")

The *Compact* arose from the need to maintain civic and social adherence to rules which would be determined by later elected officials. Some democratic tendencies are evident in the text, which prescribes the consent of the people as becoming the basis of a society of "just and equall lawes," where leaders and figures of authority would all be elected by the people. However, though they wanted to be independent and to live in accordance with their Separatist beliefs, they also wanted to maintain their ties to England. This *Mayflower Compact* was signed by 41 of the ship's 101 passengers onboard ship the day the settlers arrived at Cape Cod (*Mayflower Compact* – Constitutional Rights Foundation).

The second paragraph makes it plain that those brave people risked the dangerous voyage across the Atlantic Ocean for the glory of God and the advancement of the Christian faith. God had a mighty hand in the settlement of the United States of America by Christian people. America would be the nation that would befriend and protect the tiny country of Israel when it achieved nationhood once again in 1948 ("State of Israel proclaimed–May 14, 1848–HISTORY.com"). The nature of God determined the holy bond that still exists between the United States and Israel.

An exploring expedition set out to search for a settlement site under the leadership of Christopher Jones. Obviously not prepared for the freezing winter weather, the thirty-four persons in the open shallop were forced to spend the night ashore, ill-clad in wet shoes and stockings that became frozen. To underscore the dire circumstances of this expedition, Bradford recorded, "Some of our people that are dead took the original of their death here." Finally, after a difficult encounter with the local natives, the Nausets, the colonists decided to relocate to Plymouth in December of 1620.

During the first winter, the passengers remained onboard the *Mayflower*, suffering an outbreak of a contagious disease which was a mixture of pneumonia, scurvy, and tuberculosis. When this ended only 53 colonists, just over half, were still alive. Half of the crew died, as well. In the spring the settlers built huts on shore and in March of 1621, the surviving passengers finally disembarked from the *Mayflower* (*Mayflower*–Wikipedia).

William Bradford, the contemporary historian of Plymouth, kept a journal of sorts in regard to the tiny colony. He completed Book I of the narrative in 1630, when some one hundred persons reached Plymouth on the *Mayflower*. In 1642, he made the entry below entitled "Wickedness Breaks Forth":

"Marvelous it may be to see and consider how some kind of wickedness did grow and break forth here, in a land where the same was so much witnessed against and so narrowly looked unto, and severely punished when it was known, as in no place more, or so much, that I have known or heard of; insomuch that they have been somewhat censured even by moderate and good men for their severity in punishments. And yet all this could not suppress the breaking out of sundry notorious sins as this year [1642], besides other, gives us too many sad precedents and instances, especially drunkenness and uncleanness. Not only incontinency between persons unmarried, for which many both men and women have been punished sharply enough, but some married persons also. But that which is worse, even sodomy and buggery (things fearful to name) have broken forth in this land oftener than once.

"I say it may justly be marveled at and cause us to fear and tremble at the consideration of our corrupt natures, which are so hardly bridled, subdued, and mortified; nay cannot by any other means but the powerful work and grace of God's Spirit. But (besides this) one reason may be that the devil may carry a greater spite against the churches of Christ and the Gospel here, by how much the more they endeavor to preserve holiness and purity among them and strictly punish the contrary when it arises either in church or commonwealth; that he might cast a blemish and stain upon them in the eyes of [the] world, who use to be rash in judgment. I would rather think thus, than that Satan has more power in these heathen lands, as some have thought, than in more Christian nations, especially over God's servants in them...." ("William Bradford, Of Plymouth Plantation [1642]")

In 1650, the small town still had less than 1,000 inhabitants. Bradford wrote the remainder of the history between 1646 and 1651. Taken from *History Of Plymouth Plantation,* he describes "The Starving Time" below:

"But that which was most sad and lamentable was that in two or three months' time half of their company died, especially in January and February, being the depth of winter, and wanting houses and other comforts; being infected with the scurvy and other diseases which this long voyage and their inaccommodate condition had brought upon them. So as there died sometimes two or three of a day in the aforesaid time, that of one hundred and odd persons, scarce fifty remained. And of these, in the time of most distress, there were but six or seven sound persons who to their great commendations, be it spoken, spared no pains night or day, but with abundance of toil and hazard of their own health fetched them wood, made them fires, dressed them meat, made their beds, washed their loathsome clothes, clothed and unclothed them.

"In a word, did all the homely and necessary offices for them which dainty and queasy stomachs cannot endure to hear named; and all this willingly and cheerfully, without any grudging in the least, showing herein their true love unto their friends and brethren; a rare example and worthy to be remembered. Two of these seven were Mr. William Brewster, their reverend elder, and Myles Standish, their captain and military commander, unto whom myself and many others were much beholden in our low and sick condition. And yet the Lord so upheld these persons as in this general calamity they were not at all affected either with sickness or lameness. And what I have said of these I may say of many others who died in this general visitation, and others yet living; that while they had health, yea, or any strength continuing, they were not wanting to any that had need of them. And I doubt not but their recompense is with the Lord...." ("PDF William Bradford")

Though William Bradford never published his *History of Plymouth Plantation*, the manuscript remained in the Bradford family for nearly a century. It was then used by the Reverend Thomas Prince when he wrote *Chronological History* in 1736. After Prince's death, the manuscript was left in the tower of the Old South Meeting House in Boston ("The Bradford Manuscript–jstor").

During the Revolutionary War, the manuscript was lost for another century. In the 1850s it was discovered in the Bishop of London's library at Fulham Palace. When the Bishop of London, Frederick Temple, realized the historical importance of the book, he sought to have it returned to America. The bishop's court ordered that a photographic copy of the manuscript be made for the court and the original delivered to the Governor of Massachusetts.

On May 26, 1897, the Bradford journal was presented to the Governor of the Commonwealth of Massachusetts during a joint session of the legislature. It is deposited in the State Library of Massachusetts in the State House in Boston. In 1912, the Massachusetts Historical Society published a "final" authorized version of the 400-year old text ("Of Plymouth Plantation–Wikipedia").

According to several websites which I visited on the internet, the first few months were grueling for the Pilgrims. Half of their 102 settlers died. "Of the 17 male heads of families, ten died during the first infection"; of the 17 wives, only three were left after three months ("Pilgrims and Puritans: Background–Xroads.virginia.edu..."). With such devastation, it is no wonder that when conditions improved the following summer, the real meaning of Thanksgiving became most apparent.

Three Indians who helped the Pilgrims during their early struggles to survive were Squanto, Samoset, and Massasoit. Squanto was a member of the Pquotuxet tribe, whereas Samoset was an Abnaki chief from the Maine area. Because of probable smallpox and other epidemics (brought over by the Europeans), both of these tribes had died out. They then joined with the Wampanoag tribe, whose great leader was Chief Massasoit ("Squanto, Samoset, and Massosoit–Everything 2.com").

When Samoset first walked into the Plymouth settlement, he startled the colonists not only by his presence but also by greeting the suffering Pilgrims with "Hello, Englishmen." He had learned English from a fisherman some years before. On his third visit in March of 1621, he brought Squanto and introduced him to the settlers. Squanto had been to England and could communicate well with the colonists ("Times Are Altered with Us: American Indians from First Contact to..."). He taught them "how to set their corn, where to take fish, and to procure other commodities." The Pilgrims looked upon him as "a special instrument sent of God for their good, beyond their expectation ("Squanto:A Special Instrument of God"). Squanto stayed with the Pilgrims for eighteen (some sites say twenty) months and made himself indispensable as interpreter, teacher, and guide. He taught the Pilgrims where and how to fish, how to tread eels from mud, and where in the forest to find herbs. He also taught the settlers how to plant and fertilize Indian corn or maize ("Squanto–Wikipedia").

Squanto introduced the Wampanoag sachem, or chief, Massasoit, to the Pilgrims. Due to a high mortality rate because of disease and war with other tribes, the Wampanoag were a greatly weakened tribe. The Naragansett tribe had escaped many of the epidemics because they mostly lived on islands in the bay named after them. They had become the most powerful tribe in the area, and the Wampanoag were forced to pay them tribute ("Wampanoag–Wikipedia").

The *Mayflower* passenger Edward Winslow described Massasoit in an intriguing way, as follows: "In his person he is a very lusty man, in his best years, an able body, grave of countenance, and spare of speech. In his attire little or nothing differing from the rest of his followers, only in a great chain of white bone beads about his neck, and at it behind his neck hangs a little bag of tobacco, which he drank and gave us to drink; his face was painted with a sad red like murry, and oiled both head and face, that he looked greasily. All his followers likewise, were in their faces, in part or in whole painted, some black, some red, some yellow, and some white, some with crosses, and other antic works; some had skins on them, and some naked, all strong, tall, all men of appearance...[he] had in his bosom hanging in a string, a great long knife; he marveled much at our trumpet, and some of his men would sound it as well as they could." ("Massasoit–*Mayflower*History.com")

Hoping to forge an agreement with the British, in order to escape the yoke of the dominant Naragansett tribe, Massasoit arranged for a treaty between his people and the English. In March of 1621, the treaty was concluded by Massasoit and Plymouth Governor, John Carver, in the presence of Edward Winslow, Myles Standish, and other Pilgrim leaders. Provisions of the treaty were as follows:

1. That neither he nor any of his should injure or do hurt to any of our people.

2. And if any of his did hurt to any of ours, he should send the offender, that we might punish him.

3. That if any of our tools were taken away when our people were at work, he should cause them to be restored; and if ours did any harm to any of his, we would do the like to them.

4. If any did unjustly war against him, we would aid him; if any did war against us, he should aid us.

5. He should send to his neighbor confederates, to certify them of this, that they might not wrong us, but might be likewise comprised in the conditions of peace.

6. That when their men came to us, they should leave their bows and arrows behind them, as we should do our pieces when we came to them.

Lastly, that doing thus, King James would esteem him as his friend and ally ("The Treaty That Saved Plymouth Colony/in Custodia Legis: Law").

The Wampanoag gave the colonists permission to occupy 12,000 acres of the tribe's land, though it is believed that the native Indians did not understand land ownership. Rather, the Indians considered it as sharing land. This land became Plymouth Plantation ("WAMPANOAG.definitiondeWAMPANOAGetsynonymesde...").

Massasoit never broke the treaty that he made with the settlers, whom he called the "coat men." ("Weetamoo: Heart of the Pocassets, Massachusetts--Rhode Island...") He was humane and honest and never violated his word. He tried to imbue his people with a love of peace. The peace treaty lasted fifty years, during which time the Pilgrims were never hurt or attacked by Indians (*The American Cyclopaedia* [1879]/Massasoit–Wikisource, the free...). According to reliable English sources, Massasoit prevented the failure of Plymouth Colony and the certain starvation that the Pilgrims would have encountered without his benevolence ("Massasoit–Wikipedia").

Squanto remained with the Pilgrims for the rest of his life. In the summer of 1621, he traveled with some of the Pilgrim leaders, including William Bradford and Myles Standish, to "the Massachusetts," a tribe living in the Blue Hill area south of Boston. When they offered glass beads and trifles in exchange for beaver furs, the Pilgrims began a beneficial trading relationship with "the Massachusetts," which allowed them to provide furs to their London financial backers. These fur shipments to England became the settlers' economic salvation. Squanto taught the Pilgrims the trading practices of the fur business, since the furs were trapped and the pelts cured by Native Americans ("Squanto, the Free Social Encyclopedia"). These were bartered for English products such as metals and blankets and articles of clothing ("PDF the Pilgrims & the fur trade–Pilgrim Hall Museum").

In 1622, while acting as a scout for the Plymouth colony, Squanto became ill and died. According to William Bradford, who was governor of the colony for thirty years, Squanto asked him on his deathbed to "pray for him, that he might go to the Englishmen's God in heaven." ("Squanto–Bill Petro") Squanto is a revered symbol of Thanksgiving.

Edward Winslow wrote an account of the 1621 Thanksgiving in a letter dated December 12, 1621. It reads, as follows:

"Our corn [i.e. wheat] did prove well, and God be praised, we had a good increase of Indian corn, and our barley indifferent good, but our peas not worth the gathering, for we feared they were too late sown. They came up very well, and blossomed, but the sun parched them in the blossom. Our harvest being gotten in, our governor sent four men on fowling, that so we might after a special manner rejoice together after we had gathered the fruit of our labors. They four in one day killed as much fowl as, with a little help beside, served the company almost a week. At which time, amongst other recreations, we exercised our arms, many of the Indians coming amongst us, and among the rest their greatest king Massasoit, with some ninety men, whom for three days we entertained and feasted, and they went out and killed five deer, which they brought to the plantation and bestowed on our governor, and upon the captain and others. And although it be not always so plentiful as it was at this time with us, yet by the goodness of God, we are so far from want that we often wish you partakers of our plenty." ("Thanksgiving–*MayflowerHistory*.com")

* * * * * * * * * * * * * * *

In 1863, President Abraham Lincoln made Thanksgiving a national holiday with his Thanksgiving Proclamation. Today, Thanksgiving is the fourth Thursday of November. This was set by President Franklin Roosevelt in 1939 and approved by Congress in 1941 ("Lincoln proclaims official Thanksgiving holiday–Oct 03, 1863..."). Truly, God was blessing our nation, and we had national leaders who demonstrated their thankfulness to God. America's destiny and exceptionalism are parts of the plan and the nature of God.

Chapter Seventeen

In 1630, under the leadership of John Winthrop (1606-1676), a group of around a thousand Puritans left England, hoping to find religious freedom in America. Twelve ships made the trip across the Atlantic Ocean, with John Winthrop being aboard the flagship, *Arabella*. John Winthrop was a lawyer and devout Christian. Before debarking the *Arabella*, after his arrival at Salem, Winthrop wrote a statement of Christian principles which he felt the Puritans should adhere to, called "A Model of Christian Charity," in which he called on his fellow emigrants to make their new colony a city upon a hill, using Matthew 5:14-16 as his biblical reference ("America's Covenant with God: John Winthrop's 'City on a Hill' Speech"). The Scripture is below:

"Ye are the light of the world. A city that is set on an hill cannot be hid. Neither do men light a candle, and put it under a bushel, but on a candlestick; and it giveth light unto all that are in the house. Let your light so shine before men, that they may see your good works, and glorify your Father which is in heaven."

John Winthrop wanted their colony to be a model to all of the European nations in regard to what a properly reformed Christian commonwealth should be. This was especially relevant in 1630, since Protestants were suffering defeat during the Thirty Years' War among most of the nations of Europe, while Catholicism was being restored in countries previously subscribing to Protestantism ("Swedish intervention in the Thirty Years' War–Wikipedia").

Below is an excerpt from Winthrop's statement, regarded as one of the best expressions of the ideals of the Puritan Commonwealth in America:

"Thus stands the case between God and us. We are entered into covenant with Him for this work. We have taken out a commission. The Lord has given us leave to draw our own articles, we have promised to base our actions on these ends, and we have asked Him for favor and blessing. Now if the Lord shall please to hear us, and bring us in peace to the place we desire, then He has ratified this covenant and sealed our commission, and will expect strict performance of the articles contained in it. But if we neglect to observe these articles, which are the ends we have propounded, and–dissembling with our God–shall embrace this present world and prosecute our carnal intentions, seeking great things for ourselves and our posterity, the Lord will surely break out in wrath against us and be revenged of such a perjured people, and He will make us know the price of the breach of such a covenant.

"Now the only way to avoid this shipwreck and to provide for our posterity is to follow the counsel of Micah, to do justly, to love mercy, to walk humbly with our God. For this end, we must be knit together in this work as one man; we must hold each other in brotherly affection; we must be willing to rid ourselves of our excesses to supply others' necessities; we must uphold a familiar commerce together in all meekness, gentleness, patience, and liberality. We must delight in each other, make others' conditions our own and rejoice together, mourn together, labor and suffer together, always having before our eyes our commission and common work, our community as members of the same body.

"So shall we keep the unity of the spirit in the bond of peace. The Lord will be our God and delight to dwell among us as His own people. He will command a blessing on us in all our ways, so that we shall see much more of His wisdom, power, goodness, and truth than we have formerly known. We shall find that the God of Israel is among us, and ten of us shall be able to resist a thousand of our enemies. The Lord will make our name a praise and glory, so that men shall say of succeeding plantations: 'The Lord make it like that of New England, For we must consider that we shall be like a City upon a Hill; the eyes of all people are on us." ("The Idea of the Covenant– Digital History")

The Thirty Years' War (1618-1648) redrew the religious and political map of central Europe. The two sides in the war were essentially the leading Protestant states of Great Britain, the Dutch Republic, and Denmark, whereas the German Catholics were led by Bavaria, Spain, and the papacy. In 1618, Ferdinand II, heir to the throne of Bohemia, began to curtail certain Protestant religious privileges, which caused the Protestants to appeal to their brethren in Great Britain, the Dutch Republic, and Denmark for aid.

Only Swedish military intervention in 1630, led by King Gustavus Adolphus, saved the Protestant cause. However, battles were fought throughout the thirty-year period with successes going to both the Catholic and the Protestant sides. This war was the worst catastrophe experienced by Germany until the Second World War. Twenty percent of Germany's population perished during the conflict, with many towns losing not only population but also manufacturing and trade deficits. However, the war helped to bring an end to religious wars ("Thirty Years' War–Facts & Summary–HISTORY.com").

* * * * * * * * * * * * * *

The major difference between the Pilgrims and the Puritans was that the Pilgrims wanted to "separate" from the Church of England, but the Puritans had no intention of breaking with the Anglican Church. The Pilgrims and the Puritans were alike in that both groups were nonconformists who refused to accept any authority in their religion except that revealed in the Bible. Though the Pilgrims' approach to class distinction was close to an egalitarian perspective, the "Puritans considered religion a very complex, subtle, and highly intellectual affair."

Puritan leaders were highly trained scholars who refuted the view that "very few Englishmen had yet broached the notion that a lackey was as good as a lord, or that any Tom, Dick, or Harry...could understand the Sermon on the Mount as well as a Master of Arts from Oxford, Cambridge, or Harvard." Puritans felt that knowledge of Scripture was absolutely essential even among the laity. In 1635, only five years after the founding of the Massachusetts Bay Colony the first "Free Grammar School" was founded in Boston. As John Cotton penned in *Christ the Fountaine of Life,* "zeale is but a wildefire without knowledge." ("Pilgrims and Puritans: Background–Xroads.virginia.edu...")

Massachusetts passed the first American compulsory school law in 1642. In 1647, it passed another law, requiring every town of fifty families to provide free common and grammar school instruction. The excerpt below, known as the "Old Deluder Satan Law," makes it plain that the main thrust of Puritan education was being able to read the Scriptures:

"It being one chief project of that old deluder Satan to keep men from the knowledge of the Scriptures, as in former times by keeping them in an unknown tongue, so in these latter times by persuading from the use of tongues, that so at least the true sense and meaning of the original might be clouded by false glosses of saint-seeming deceivers, and to the end that learning may not be buried in the grave of our fathers in the church and commonwealth, the Lord assisting our endeavors:

"It is therefore ordered that every township in this jurisdiction, after the Lord hath increased them to 50 households, shall forthwith appoint one within their town to teach all such children as shall resort to him to write and read...."

"And it is further ordered that when any town shall increase to the number of one hundred families or householders, they shall set up a grammar school, the master thereof being able to instruct youth so far as they may be fitted for the university...." ("Massachusetts School Laws–Wikipedia")

Though the Puritans in the 1560s were contemptuously referred to as such, they were ardent reformers striving to direct the Church to the state of "purity" that existed during the time of Christ. This involved doing away with residual "popery," such as ceremony, vestments, and the like. To the Puritans, the key to purifying the Church was the Bible. Whatever was not found in the Bible was cast aside.

While the Puritan emphasis on scholarship did create class distinction, it nevertheless touted the importance of education for the entire group and even demanded a level of learning in regard to salvation. As Thomas Hooker observed in *The Application of Redemption*:

"Its with an ignorant sinner in the midst of all means as with a sick man remaining in the Apothecaries shop, ful of choycest Medicines in the darkest night:...because he cannot see what he takes, and how to use them, he may kill himself or encrease his distempers, but never cure any disease."

Regardless of the uncompromising attitude that described the Puritans' entry into New England, their emphasis on education resulted in the establishment of Harvard College which survived because the entire colony was willing to support it. Even the poor farmers "contributed their pecks of wheat" for the promise of a "literate ministry."("Pilgrims and Puritans: Background").

From 1629 through 1643, around 21,000 Puritans emigrated to New England. Between 1630-1640, over 13,000 men, women, and children sailed to Massachusetts. The Puritan family was the rock of New England society, both economically and spiritually. Puritan women took upon themselves the task of rearing children who matured into virtuous Christian adults. A harmonious marriage and godly children were the prescription for successful Puritan colonies ("History of the Puritans in North America–Wikipedia").

To maintain structure within their colony, the early Puritans had to devise ways to govern and discipline themselves in their new settlement. At first they recognized only two factions within their towns. These were gentlemen and freeholders or freemen. Though the term "freeman" originated in twelfth-century Europe, it was common as an English or American colonial expression during the Puritan era.

"Freeman" was a person who possessed all the civil and political rights belonging to people who lived under a free government. Slaves were not considered freemen. A man could attain freeman citizenship after perhaps being an indentured servant who after an allotted period of time satisfied a "payment" due to someone. Many immigrants came to the colonies as indentured servants, with someone else paying their passage to the colonies in return for services later rendered. Native Americans, women, and other non-Puritans were not made "freemen" ("Freeman 'Colonial'– Wikipedia").

To be a freeman, one had to fulfill certain requirements, which I found on the web site ("Freeman's Oath–Babcock–Acres"). They include the following:

"Must of Sworn Allegiance to the Crown

Must be a Male over 21 years of age

Membership in a duly recognized church (note: this varied in the Plymouth and Massachusetts Bay colonies)

Own personal property generally valued at 40 pounds or 40 shillings per year

Must be of a quiet and peaceful manner

Other Freemen in the area endorsed him."

Those who sought to be free had to take *The Oath of Freemen in Massachusetts*, in which they vowed to defend the Commonwealth and not to plot to overthrow the government. The first handwritten version of the "Freeman's Oath" was made in 1634. Stephen Daye in 1639 printed the revised version as a broadside or single sheet of paper, intended to be posted in public places. Being a Freeman gave a person the right to vote in town meetings, to hold public office, to elect deputies to the General Assembly, and to own land ("Freeman 'Colonial'/Wikipedia"). *The Oath of Freemen in Massachusetts* appears below:

Freeman's Oath

"I, (A.B.) Being by Gods providence, an Inhabitant, and Freeman, within the jurisdiction of this Commonwealth; do freely acknowledge my self to be subject to the Government thereof: And therefore do here swear by the great and dreadful Name of the Ever-living God, that I will be true and faithfull to the same, and will accordingly yield assistance & support thereunto, with my person and estate, as in equity I am bound; and will also truly endeavor to maintain and preserve all the liberties and priviledges thereof, submitting my self to the wholesome Lawes & Orders made and established by the same. And further, that I will not plot or practice any and reveal the same to lawfull Authority now here established, for the speedy preventing thereof. Moreover, I doe solemnly bind my self in the sight of God, that when I shal be called to give my voyce touching any matter of this State, in which Freemen are to deal, I will give my vote and suffrage as I shall judge in mine own conscience may best conduce and tend to the publike weal of the body, So help me God in the Lord Jesus Christ."

This oath had much historical significance in that it was the first document printed on a press in America, in 1639. King Charles objected to what he perceived as an independence on the part of the colonists in the oath, which he attempted to subdue in 1665 by decreeing that it be amended to include a pledge of "faith and true allegiance to our Sovereign Lord the King." ("Nobody Remembers the Oath of Freemen/Joyanna Adams")

The "freeman" concept was enlarged upon by John Cotton (1585-1652), an influential Puritan leader who escaped the persecution of Nonconformists by the Church of England. Persecuted because he did not adhere to certain Anglican religion rituals, which resulted in legal action taken against him in 1632, he immigrated to the Massachusetts Bay Colony in 1633. He wrote several works that reveal much about New England Congregationalism, including *The Way of the Churches of Christ in New England* (1645) and *The Way of Congregational Churches Cleared* (1648). In 1646, he wrote a catechism that was used for many years for the spiritual instruction of children in New England, called *Milk for Babes, Drawn out of the Breasts of Both Testaments*.

Educated at Trinity College, Cambridge, Cotton became vicar of the parish church at St. Botolph's in Boston, Lincolnshire, in 1612, and remained there for twenty-one years. However, he became more Puritan in his beliefs during this time (John Cotton/ American colonial leader/ *Britannica.com*).

* * * * * * * * * * * * * *

However, the structure of these colonies began to evolve into a theocracy, something similar to the turmoil which the Puritans had experienced in the mother country of England, from which they had fled. From 1656-1657, Quaker missionaries were active in New Amsterdam (New York City), where its leaders issued proclamations enjoining the missionaries from practicing their faith. Those who defied these injunctions were severely punished. This harsh treatment of fellow Christian brethren aroused the sympathies of twenty-eight citizens of Flushing, Long Island, who wrote a letter, in 1657, to certain colonial authorities, asking them to show tolerance to the Quakers. This was an early plea for the establishment of religious freedom (*The Annals of America* [1493-1754], p. 224). An excerpt from the letter follows:

"The law of love, peace, and liberty in the states extending to Jews, Turks, and Egyptians, as they are considered the sons of Adam, which is the glory of the outward state of Holland; so love, peace, and liberty, extending to all in Christ Jesus condemns hatred, war, and bondage; and because our Savior says it is impossible but that offense will come, but woe be unto him by which they come, our desire is not to offend one of His little ones in whatsoever form, name, or title he appears in, whether Presbyterian, Independent, Baptist, or Quaker; but shall be glad to see anything of God in any of them, desiring to do unto all men as we desire all men should do unto us, which is the true law both of church and state; for our Savior says this is the law and the prophets.

"Therefore, if any of these said persons come in love unto us, we cannot in conscience lay violent hands upon them, but give them free egress into our town and houses as God shall persuade our consciences. And in this we are true subjects both of the church and state; for we are bound by the law of God and man to do good unto men and evil to no man; and this is according to the patent and charter of our town given unto us in the name of the States General, which we are not willing to infringe and violate but shall hold to our patent and shall remain your humble subjects, the inhabitants of Flushing." (*The Annals of America* [1493-1754], p. 224)

King Charles II of England gave the land in Pennsylvania

to William Penn (1644-1718) in 1681. Penn was a Quaker who established the Pennsylvania colony as a place where Quakers and people of other faiths could have religious freedom. Penn believed that civil authorities shouldn't interfere with the religious lives of citizens ("William Penn–Wikipedia"). He drew up laws to protect the civil liberties of "all persons...who confess and acknowledge the one almighty and eternal God to be the creator, upholder, and ruler of the world." ("America, Christianity, And The Forgotten Link"). Between 1659-1661, Massachusetts Puritan magistrates did hang four Quaker missionaries ("Mary Dyer–Wikipedia"). The persecution of the Puritans in England was now manifesting itself, in turn, on those who dissented from the Puritan beliefs in America.

One Puritan leader who could see the danger in this situation was Roger Williams (1603-1683) who arrived in Boston in 1631. He was a "separatist" Puritan minister, meaning that he believed in the complete separation of the colony from the Church of England. Leaders of the Massachusetts Bay Colony were so enraged by Williams' beliefs and conduct that they expelled him from their colony. When blocked by Boston political leaders who objected to his separatism, Roger Williams spent two years with his fellow Separatists in the Plymouth Colony. However, his beliefs came into conflict with theirs to the extent that he resided at Salem.

In 1636, Williams founded the city of Providence, Rhode Island. He was one of the first Puritans to advocate separation of church and state, and Rhode Island was one of the first states in the Christian world to adhere to freedom of religion ("Roger Williams–Wikipedia"). God was surely working among the early American colonists.

However, though the Puritans were earnest in their quest to purify the church in the New World, they still kept to the ancient belief in witches and witchcraft. In February of 1692, a group of young women in Salem Village (now Danvers), Massachusetts, began experiencing delusions and hysteria. When the local doctor could find no physical cause, a conference of ministers decided that the girls were victims of witchcraft ("History of the Salem Witch Trials–History of Massachusetts Blog"). The afflicted girls began accusing certain settlers of being "agents of the devil ("Role of skin lesions in the Salem witchcraft trials–NCBl").

Along with most of the New England Puritans, Increase and Cotton Mather believed in the reality of witches and their witchcraft. Increase Mather (1639-1723) became president of Harvard College in 1692 and was a prominent Boston minister and pastor of the North Church ("Increase Mather-Wikipedia"). His son, Cotton Mather (1663-1728), was also a prominent Puritan minister and author of over 450 books and pamphlets ("Cotton Mather–Wikipedia"). However, though both father and son believed in witches, they were unsettled about what to do about them.

As head of the Puritan Church in Boston, Cotton Mather played a prominent part in the tragic events of the Salem witchcraft trials in the 1690s. Indeed, his 1689 essay, "Memorable Providences Relating to Witchcraft and Possessions" actually fostered the hysteria which surrounded the trials. Below is a passage from this writing:

"Wherefore, the devil is now making one attempt more upon us; an attempt more difficult, more surprising, more snarled with unintelligible circumstances than any that we have hitherto encountered; an attempt so critical, that if we get well through, we shall soon enjoy halcyon days, with all the vultures of hell trodden under our feet. He has wanted his incarnate legions to persecute us, as the people of God have in the other hemisphere been persecuted; he has, therefore, drawn forth his more spiritual ones to make an attack upon us. We have been advised by some credible Christians yet alive that a malefactor, accused of witchcraft as well as murder, and executed in this place more than forty years ago, did then give notice of a horrible plot against the country by witchcraft, and a foundation of witchcraft then laid, which if it were not seasonably discovered would probably blow up and pull down all the churches in the country.

"And we have now with horror seen the discovery of such a witchcraft! An army of devils is horribly broke in upon the place which is the center, and after a sort, the firstborn of our English settlements. And the houses of the good people there are filled with the doleful shrieks of their children and servants, tormented by invisible hands, with tortures altogether preternatural. After the mischiefs there endeavored, and since in part conquered, the terrible plague of evil angels has made its progress into some other places, where other persons have been in like manner diabolically handled." ("Mather, Cotton [1663-1728], The Wonders of the Invisible world: Being...")

Increase Mather felt that justice required "scientific" proof to determine the fate of the accused, rather than the accusations of "bewitched" accusers. In his work of 1693, "Cases of Conscience Concerning Evil Spirits Personating Men," he elaborated upon this belief, as stipulated in the excerpt below (*The Annals of America: 1493-1754*, p.296):

"Some are ready to say that wizards are not so unwise as to do such things in the sight or hearing of others, but it is certain that they have very often been known to do so. How often have they been seen by others using enchantments? Conjuring to raise storms? And have been heard calling upon their familiar spirits? And have been known to use spells and charms? And to show in a glass or in a show stone persons absent? And to reveal secrets which could not be discovered but by the devil? And have not men been seen to do things which are above human strength, that no man living could do without diabolical assistances?...

"The devil never assists men to do supernatural things undesired. When therefore, such like things shall be testified against the accused party, not by specters, which are devils in the shape of persons either living or dead, but by real men or women who may be credited, it is proof enough that such a one has that conversation and correspondence with the devil as that he or she, whoever they be, ought to be exterminated from among men. This notwithstanding I will add: It were better that ten suspected witches should escape than that one innocent person should be condemned."

In 1692, Thomas Brattle, later treasurer of Harvard College, wrote a vivid account of a court case in a letter to an unknown English clergyman. It had the title, "Thomas Brattle: Condemnation of Witchcraft Trials." In it, he spoke out against the superstitions that still held the Puritans in their grip. Below is an excerpt from his letter:

"As to the late executions, I shall only tell you that in the opinion of many unprejudiced, considerate, and considerable spectators, some of the condemned went out of the world not only with as great protestations but also with as good shows of innocence as men could do.

"They protested their innocence as in the presence of the great God, whom forthwith they were to appear before. They wished and declared their wish, that their blood might be the last innocent blood shed upon that account. With great affection they entreated Mr. Cotton Mather to pray with them; they prayed that God would discover what witchcrafts were among us; they forgave their accusers, they spoke without reflection on jury and judges for bringing them in guilty and condemning them; they prayed earnestly for pardon for all their sins, and for an interest in the precious blood of our dear Redeemer...." (*The Annals of America:* 1493-1754, p. 290)

A special court was convened to try these cases which involved several hundred persons being accused of witchcraft. Of these, at least five died in prison, nineteen were hanged, and one, Giles Corey, was pressed to death for refusing to answer charges.

The most infamous trials were held in 1692 in Salem Town, conducted by the Court of Oyer and Terminer. In English law, Oyer and Terminer is a partial translation of the Anglo-French *oyer et terminer* which literally means "to hear and determine." Governor William Phips of Massachusetts signed the commission for the special court of Oyer and Terminer for the Salem witch trials, but it was dissolved in 1693 when the cases were later reviewed and disproved ("William Phips– Wikipedia"). Robert Calef, a contemporary writer, wrote about the results of these trials, as quoted below:

"And now Nineteen persons having been hang'd, and one prest to death, and Eight more condemned, in all Twenty and Eight, of which above a third part were Members of some of the Churches of N. England, and more than half of them of a good Conversation in general, and not one clear'd; about Fifty having confest themselves to be Witches, of which not one Executed; above an Hundred and Fifty in Prison, and Two Hundred more accused; the Special Commission of Oyer and Terminer comes to a period,...." ("The Salem Witch Trials by Tanner Denton on Prezi")

Governor William Phips also wrote his summation of the court cases in the following message, recorded February 21, 1693, in the unusual language and spelling of the time period:

"When I put an end to the Court there ware at least fifty persons in prision in great misery by reason of the extreme cold and their poverty, most of them having only spectre evidence against them and their mittimusses being defective, I caused some of them to be lettout upon bayle and put the Judges upon consideration of a way to reliefe others and to prevent them from perishing in prision, upon which some of them were convinced and acknowledged that their former proceedings were too violent and not grounded upon a right foundation... The stop put to the first method of proceedings hath dissipated the blak cloud that threatened this Province with destruccion;..." ("Daily Life During the Salem Witch Trials")

The witchcraft episode in Massachusetts was a horrifying cautionary tale about the dangers of religious extremism, isolationism, false accusations, and wrongful lapses in due process ("Salem Witch Trials–Wikipedia"). George Lincoln Burr (1857-1938), renowned U. S. historian, professor of history, and librarian at Cornell University, made the insightful statement several hundred years after the wirchcraft trials that, "more than once it has been said, too, that the Salem witchcraft was the rock on which the theocracy shattered." ("Salem Witch Trials–When Cult Beliefs and Group Hysteria Collide")

After the witchcraft hysteria was past, during the early 1700s, Cotton Mather wrote an article about the Puritan Creed, which exhorted the settlers not only to worship but also to work. Using Genesis 47:3 (**"What is your occupation?"**) as his focus, he wrote "A Christian at His Calling," which was first printed in Boston (*The Annals of America* [1493-1754], p. 321). A passage appears below:

"Come, come, for shame, away to your business. Lay out your strength in it; put forth your skill for it; avoid all impertinent avocations. Laudable recreations may be used now and then; but, I beseech you, let those recreations be used for sauce, but not for meat. If recreations go to encroach too far upon your business, give to them that put off.... It may be there are some that neglect their occupation and squander away one hour, and perhaps one day, after another, drinking, and gaming, and smoking, and fooling at those drinking houses that are so sinful as to entertain them. Unto you, O Miserables, I must address a language like that of our Savior: Thou wicked and slothful person, reform thy ways or thou art not far from outer darkness. Is it nothing to thee that by much slothfulness thy money and credit and all is decaying, and by the idleness of thy hands thy house is coming to nothing? Is it nothing to thee that thou art contracting the character of a vagabond and a prodigal?...If the Lord Jesus Christ might find thee in thy storehouse, in thy shop, or in thy ship, or in thy field, or where thy business lies, who knows what blessings He might bestow upon thee?"

Life was hard in the frontier settlements of America. The independence and self-reliance and raw courage of men and women willing to give up the comforts of an established community were the backbone of our great nation. Land was ample and productive for the earliest pioneers of our nation, but labor was scarce. To produce the bare necessities of life, frontier families had to work to the point of exhaustion.

We can gain insight into the struggles of one such family in North Carolina by reading about the family of the Reverend John Urmstone, who wrote a letter to the secretary of the Society for Propagating the Gospel on July 7, 1711. It is an enlightening account of a colonist's determination to provide for himself (*The Annals of America* [1493-1754], p. 329). Below is his letter:

"Workmen are dear and scarce. I have about a dozen acres of clear ground, and the rest woods; in all, 300 acres. Had I servants and money, I might live very comfortably upon it, raise good corn of all sorts, and cattle, without any great labor or charges, could it once be stocked; but for want thereof shall not make any advantage of my land. I have bought a horse some time ago; since that, three cows and calves, five sheep, and some fowls of all sorts, but most of them unpaid for, together with fourteen bushels of wheat, for all which I must give English goods.

"At this rate I might have had anything that either this government or any of the neighboring colonies afford; but had I stock, I need not fear wanting either butter, cheese, beef, or mutton, of my own raising, or good grain of all sorts. I am forced to work hard with axe, hoe, and spade. I have not a stick to burn for any use but what I cut down with my own hands. I am forced to dig a garden, raise beans, peas, etc., with the assistance of a sorry wench my wife brought with her from England. Men are generally of all trades, and women the like within their spheres, except some who are the posterity of old planters and have great numbers of slaves, who understand most handicraft. Men are generally carpenters, joiners, wheelwrights, coopers, butchers, tanners, shoemakers, tallow-chandlers, watermen, and what not; women, soap-makers, starch-makers, dyers, etc. He or she that cannot do all these things, or has not slaves that can, over and above all the common occupations of both sexes, will have but a bad time of it; for help is not to be had at any rate, everyone having business enough of his own. This makes tradesmen turn planters, and these become tradesmen."

* * * * * * * * * * * * * *

From the beginning of the Massachusetts Bay Colony, the Puritans attempted to Christianize the local Indians, despite the difficulty of instilling their strict moral values in people whose culture was so different from their own. John Eliot (1604-1690), renowned as New England's "Apostle to the Indians," brought about the conversion of many Indians in the vicinity of the Massachusetts colony ("John Eliot [missionary]–Wikipedia"). Excerpts from *Eliot's the Day-Breaking, if Not the Sun-Rising of the Gospel with the Indians in New-England* reveal the disciplinary methods used by the Puritans to enforce their beliefs upon the Indians (*The Annals of America* [1493-1754], p. 181-183). Some of these rules are listed below:

"1. That if any man be idle a week, at most a fortnight, he shall pay 5s.

2. If any unmarried man shall lie with a young woman unmarried, he shall pay 20s.

3. If any man shall beat his wife, his hands shall be tied behind him and [he shall be] carried to place of justice to be severely punished.

4. Every young man, if not another's servant and if unmarried, he shall be compelled to set up a wigwam and plant for himself, and not live shifting up and down to other wigwams.

5. If any woman shall not have her hair tied up but hang loose or be cut as men's hair, she shall pay 5s.

6. If any woman shall go with naked breasts, [she] shall pay 2s, 6d.

7. All those men that wear long locks shall pay 5s.

8. If any shall kill their lice between their teeth, they shall pay 5s. This law, though ridiculous to English ears, yet tends to preserve cleanliness among Indians."

* * * * * * * * * * * * * *

After the Protestant Reformation, the Catholic Church began its own purging of its church, which came to be known as the Counter Reformation. The Council of Trent was called in sessions between 1545 and 1563 in Trent, Italy. On questions disputed by Protestant theologians, the Catholic Church defined its own doctrines and attempted to stamp out abuses by the clergy. Many wars broke out, resulting from religious conflicts, as Catholic governments tried to stop the spread of Protestantism within their own countries ("Counter-Reformation–Wikipedia").

However, Protestantism put down strong roots in all of the European countries. Adherents were put to death for daring to question the pope and the church hierarchy ("European wars of religion–Wikipedia"). Martin Luther, himself, was condemned by Pope Leo X of heresy ("Pope Leo X Condemned Luther of Heresy– 1501-1600 Church History").

The purpose of this book is not to judge or condemn the Catholic Church...or any church, for that matter. I truly believe that every person who acknowledges Jesus Christ as his/her Savior and Lord will be saved, regardless of denominational differences. Even today, individual churches of all denominations have problems, and the struggle continues from over 2,000 years ago to mold the church into what God wants it to be.

JANE H. WALKER

Chapter Eighteen

Dear reader, the lives of other lesser known martyrs speak from the pages of *Foxe's Book of Martyrs,* which I feel compelled to reveal to you. Perhaps you, yourself, will feel the urge to check out this perhaps heretofore unknown book, which has opened my eyes to the daunting struggle of the church through the centuries in the very lives of those who suffered to purify it. It's an ongoing struggle, even in this modern-day era, which godly people shoulder and endure each day.

Master John Hooper (1495 A.D.?-1555 A.D.) was born in Somerset, England. He entered Merton College, Oxford, where he received his degree of Bachelor of Arts in 1518 A.D. However, he did not pursue this life of academia. Rather, he became a monk in the Cisterian monastery but quickly wearied of its isolated life of superstitions. Returning to Oxford, he began reading the writing of the Swiss reformers, which led to his conversion as a reformer. He stated, "I became rightly acquainted with the Lord." ("John Hooper–Bishop of Gloucester–Scion of Zion")

Fearing for his life because of his dissident views about the Catholic Church, Hooper escaped to the Continent where he lived for some years among those who shared his reformed faith at Basle and Zurich. There, he married Anna de Tzerclas (or Tserclaes ["John Hooper– Wikipedia"]).

Upon the ascension of Edward VI, who had Protestant leanings, to the English throne, Hooper and many other exiles returned to England where he was appointed Chaplain to the

Protector, the Duke of Somerset. He preached twice every Sunday to overflow crowds. Soon, he was nominated as Bishop of Gloucester, but his consecration was delayed because of his objections to the vestments which he was required to wear ("John Hooper–Bishop of Gloucester–Scion of Zion").

Finally, he was consecrated as bishop of Gloucester on March 8, 1551, when it was said of him, "No father in his household, no gardener in his garden, no husbandman in his vineyard, was more or better occupied than he in his diocese among his flock, teaching and preaching to the people and attending the public duties of his calling, neither failing to bring up his own children in learning and good manners." (*Foxe's*, Berry, Ed., p. 194) The diocese of Worcester was soon united with that of Gloucester.

John Foxe said of Master John Hooper:

"Twice I was, as I remember, in his house in Worcester, where in the common hall, I saw a table spread with good store of meat, and beset full of beggars and poor folk: and I, asking his servants what this meant, they told me that every day their lord and master's manner was, to have to dinner a certain number of poor folk of the said city by course, who were served by four at a mess, with hot and wholesome meats; and, when they were served (being before examined by him or his deputies of the Lord's prayer, the articles of their faith, and the ten commandments), then he himself sat down to dinner, and not before." (*Foxe's*, Forgotten Books' App, London, 2017, p. 619)

His wife, concerned for her husband's health, felt that he should be more moderate in his labours, which continued while the boy king, Edward VI, reigned in England. However, everything changed in the life of John Hooper when Queen Mary (known as Bloody Mary) ascended the English throne in 1553 A.D., for she was an ardent supporter of the Roman Catholic Church. She immediately set out to reverse the changes made during the reigns of Henry VIII and Edward VI. Married priests were driven from their churches, images were replaced and the Mass restored ("John Hooper–Bishop of Gloucester–Scion of Zion").

John Hooper was one of the first to be arrested because of his reformist beliefs. He was sent as a prisoner to the Fleet Prison on September 1, 1553, where he stayed for more than seventeen months. The Fleet was a debtors' prison near the river Fleet in London, having been built in the twelfth century. John Hooper himself wrote of his incarceration in this dreadful, filthy place in something entitled, "The True Report of Master Hooper's Entertainment in the Fleet; written with his own Hand, the 7th of January, 1555." It follows below, nearly five hundred years later, for us to read and reflect upon the terrible suffering of this medieval saint:

"The 1st of September, 1553, I was committed unto the Fleet from Richmond, to have the liberty of the prison; and, within six days after, I paid for my liberty five pounds sterling to the warden, for fees: who, immediately upon the payment thereof, complained unto Stephen Gardiner, Bishop of Winchester; and so was I committed to close prison one quarter of a year in the Tower-chamber of the Fleet, and used very extremely.

"Then by the means of a good gentlewoman, I had liberty to come down to dinner and supper, not suffered to speak with any of my friends; but, as soon as dinner and supper was done, to repair to my chamber again. Notwithstanding, while I came down thus to dinner and supper, the warden and his wife picked quarrels with me, and complained unruly of me to their great friend the Bishop of Winchester.

"After one quarter of a year and somewhat more, Babington the warden, and his wife, fell out with me for the wicked mass; and thereupon the warden resorted to the Bishop of Winchester, and obtained to put me into the wards, where I have continued a long time; having nothing appointed to me for my bed, but a little pad of straw and a rotten covering, with a tick and a few feathers therein, the chamber being vile and stinking, until by God's means good people sent me bedding to lie in.

"On the one side of which prison is the sink and filth of all the house, and on the other side the town-ditch, so that the stench of the house hath infected me with sundry diseases. – During which time I have been sick; and the doors, bars, hasps, and chains being all closed, and made fast upon me, I have mourned, called, and cried for help. But the warden, when he hath known me many times ready to die, and when the poor men of the wards have called to help me, hath commanded the doors to be kept fast, and charged that none of his men should come at me, saying, 'Let him alone; it were a good riddance of him.'

"I paid always like a baron to the said warden, as well in fees, as for my board, which was twenty shillings a week, besides my man's table, until I was wrongfully deprived of my bishopric; and, since that time, I have paid him as the best gentleman doth in his house; yet hath he used me worse, and more vilely, than the veriest slave that ever came to the hall-commons.

"The said warden hath also imprisoned my man William Downton, and stripped him out of his clothes to search for letters, and could find none, but only a little remembrance of good people's names, that gave me their alms to relieve me in prison; and to undo them also, the warden delivered the same bill unto the said Stephen Gardiner, God's enemy and mine.

"I have suffered imprisonment almost eighteen months, my goods, living, friends, and comfort taken from me; the Queen owing me by just account four score pounds or more. She hath put me in prison, and giveth nothing to find me, neither is there suffered any to come at me whereby I might have relief. I am with a wicked man and woman, so that I see no remedy (saving God's help), but I shall be cast away in prison before I come to judgment. But I commit my cause to God, Whose will be done, whether it be by life or death." (*Foxe's,* Berry, Ed., p. 197-199)

According to John Foxe, Hooper was given many opportunities to recant his "heretical" beliefs and to return to the fold of the Catholic Church. Hooper, however, remained steadfast in his reformist beliefs, suffering and languishing in prison under the rule of the infamous Queen Mary. Finally, it was determined that he should be executed for heresy (same source as above, p. 202-207).

When the day arrived for his execution, he was arrested by a great band of men with "bills, glaves, and weapons." Foxe wrote that Hooper was led between two sheriffs, "as it were a lamb to the place of slaughter." He wore the gown of his host, in whose house he had been held a prisoner, with a hat upon his head, and a staff in his hand for balance. The sciatica which had come upon him in prison caused him to walk haltingly (p. 209-210).

Upon reaching the place of his execution, he kneeled to pray, at which time a box was laid upon a stool in front of him with a "feigned" pardon from the Queen, if he would recant. At the sight of this, Hooper cried, "If you love my soul, away with it! If you love my soul, away with it!"

At this, he was removed of his clothes, being left in his shirt. A pound of gunpowder in a bladder was between his legs, and a like quantity was under each arm, delivered by a guard. Standing on a tall stool, he looked below at the weeping and sorrowful people (p. 210-211).

It was stated that three fires were lit to complete the execution of John Hooper who prayed, "O Jesus, the Son of David, have mercy upon me, and receive my soul!" As the last fire was lit, he prayed in a loud voice, "Lord Jesus, have mercy upon me: Lord Jesus receive my spirit." These were his last words (p. 212-213).

John Foxe ended his description of the burning of Master John Hooper with the following words: "But when he was black in the mouth, and his tongue swollen, that he could not speak, yet his lips went till they were shrunk to the gums; and he knocked his breast with his hands, until one of his arms fell off and then knocked still with the other, what time the fat, water, and blood, dropped out at his fingers' ends, until by renewing of the fire his strength was gone, and his hand did cleave fast, in knocking, to the iron upon his breast. So immediately, bowing forwards, he yielded up his spirit.

"Thus was he three quarters of an hour or more in the fire. Even as a lamb, patiently he abode the extremity thereof, neither moving forwards, backwards, nor to any side: but he died as quietly as a child in his bed. And he now reigneth, I doubt not, as a blessed martyr in the joys of heaven, prepared for the faithful in Christ before the foundations of the world; for whose constancy all Christians are bound to praise God." (p. 213)

* * * * * * * * * * * * * *

An understanding of the historical backdrop of the Protestant Reformation, particularly insofar as English-speaking people are concerned, helps in placing John Foxe and his *Book of Martyrs* in the chaos and religious upheaval of the 1500s. Foxe lived during the reigns of five English Tudor monarchs, beginning with Henry VIII and ending with his daughter, Elizabeth I. This was a century rife with presumed heresies on the parts of Catholics and Protestants, even within the Tudor family, itself ("Tudor Period–Wikipedia").

Henry VIII (1491 A.D.-1547 A.D.) was King of England from 1509-1547. Known for his six marriages, Henry is also recognized for his role in the separation of the Church of England from the Roman Catholic Church. Those who sided with the papacy in Rome kept quiet and moved about in secrecy to avoid possible execution.

Henry's break with the Catholic Church came about because the Pope refused to grant the king an annulment from his marriage to his first wife, Catherine of Aragon. Enraged at this, Henry established himself as the Supreme Head of the Church of England in 1534. Anyone who publicly opposed Henry's religious policies was summarily beheaded or burned alive. According to an article I read about Henry VIII, some 72,000 people were put to death because of their allegiance to the papacy and the tenets of the Roman Catholic Church during his reign ("8 Things You May Not Know About Henry VIII–History Lists"). In his attempt to secure power over the papacy, Henry suppressed monasteries and pilgrimage shrines. Any monks who dissented from the king's religious decrees were tortured and executed ("Henry VIII of England–Wikipedia").

The Church of England grew from this separation from the Roman Catholic Church. King Henry ordered the clergy to preach against pilgrimages, miracles, relics and superstitious images. Candles were removed from churches, according to the king's request, and rituals once observed in Latin were changed to English. He ordered the shrines to saints destroyed, and once sacred relics were ridiculed as "worthless old bones." ("Henry VIII–*encyclopedia* article–Citizendium")

The separation of the Church of England from the mother church in Rome evolved slowly from 1533 to 1540. The Act of

Supremacy in 1534 stated that the king was "the only Supreme Head in Earth of the Church of England," and the Treasons Act of 1534 declared that anyone refusing to acknowledge the King as such would be guilty of high treason, which was punishable by death. The Church of England was now completely under Henry's control with no ties to the papacy in Rome ("Reformation Parliament–History of Parliament Online"). Henry was officially excommunicated from the Roman Catholic Church in 1538 A.D. by Pope Paul III ("EWTN.com–Excommunication of Henry VIII").

Henry VIII was obsessed with producing a male heir to the throne, and because two of his wives were unable to have sons, they were beheaded. He considered Jane Seymour his favored wife, since she gave birth to a son, Edward, who became Edward VI (1537-1553). As the king had wished before his death, he was buried at Windsor in the same tomb as his third wife, Jane Seymour, who died from childbirth complications in 1537. Though Edward had Protestant leanings, he was only nine years old when he inherited the crown and could not actually exercise his power. According to King Henry's will, sixteen executors were designated to serve on a regency council until Edward reached the age of eighteen ("Edward VI of England–Wikipedia").

However, Edward died before his sixteenth birthday and left no heirs, so the two older daughters of Henry VIII, who were half sisters of Edward, were next in line to the English throne. Mary, daughter of Catherine of Aragon, was a Roman Catholic, whereas Elizabeth, daughter of Anne Boleyn, was Protestant. The future of the church in England was literally in the hands of these two daughters who had opposing religious beliefs ("King Edward VI Tudor Monarchs Facts, Information and Pictures").

Before Edward's death in 1553, the boy king attempted to remove his half sister, Mary, from succession to the British throne, because of their religious differences. Instead, as the fifteen-year-old king lay dying in 1553, he named his cousin, Lady Jane Grey, in his will as queen, after his death ("BBC–History–Edward VI"). This added to the religious turmoil in England, for Lady Jane Grey was a devout Protestant.

Lady Jane Grey (1537-1554 A.D.) was a tragic figure in English history, as she was executed by her cousin, Queen Mary, after ruling England for only nine days. Regarded as one of the most educated young women of her time, she became a martyr because of her departure from Roman Catholicism. Jane's upbringing was strict, though well-meant and typical of the era. When someone visited her and found her reading Plato, she is said to have complained, as follows:

"For when I am in the presence either of father or mother, whether I speak, keep silence, sit, stand or go, eat, drink, be merry or sad, be sewing, playing, dancing, or doing anything else, I must do it as it were in such weight, measure and number, even so perfectly as God made the world; or else I am so sharply taunted, so cruelly threatened, yea presently sometimes with pinches, nips and bobs and other ways (which I will not name for the honour I bear them)... that I think myself in hell."

Mary contrived to have Jane convicted for treason, and in 1553, Parliament declared Mary the rightful queen. Mary had Jane imprisoned and her sentence was to "be burned alive on Tower Hill or beheaded as the Queen pleases." Jane was taken to the Tower Green, inside the Tower, where she was to be beheaded. According to an account of her execution revealed in the anonymous *Chronicle of Queen Jane and of Two Years of Queen Mary,* Jane said the following words, as she ascended the scaffold:

"Good people, I am come hither to die, and by a law I am condemned to the same. The fact, indeed, against the Queen's highness was unlawful, and the consenting thereunto by me: but touching the procurement and desire thereof by me or on my behalf, I do wash my hands thereof in innocency, before God, and the face of you, good Christian people, this day." ("Lady Jane Grey– Wikipedia")

Wringing her hands, in which she held a book, she continued: "I pray you all, good Christian people, to bear me witness, that I die a good Christian woman, and that I do look to be saved by no other mean, but only by the mercy of God in the blood of His only son

Jesus Christ: and I confess that when I did know the word of God, I neglected the same, loved myself and the world, and therefore this plague and punishment is happily and worthily happened unto me for my sins; and yet I thank God, that of His goodness He hath thus given me a time and a respite to repent. And now, good people, while I am alive, I pray you assist me with your prayers." ("The Execution of Lady Jane Grey: 460 Years Ago Today")

She then recited Psalm 51 **("Have mercy upon me, O God")** in English and gave her handkerchief and her gloves to her maid. When the executioner asked her for forgiveness, she forgave him, but pleaded, "I pray you dispatch me quickly." She also asked him, in regard to her head, "Will you take it off before I lay me down?" The axeman answered, "No, madam." After blindfolding herself, she tried to find the block with her hands, crying, "What shall I do? Where is it?" When someone directed her to it, she laid her head on the block and spoke the last words of Jesus as recounted in the Gospel of Luke 23:46: **"Father, into thy hands I commend my spirit!"** At this, she was beheaded.

Her martyrdom is recorded in *Foxe's Book of Martyrs*. It has been noted that John Foxe began his history of the Christian persecutions at the suggestion of Lady Jane Grey. The fact that a person of royalty had died for her beliefs gave great impetus to the Protestant Reformation. The historian Albert Pollard called her "The traitor-heroine of the Reformation." Lady Jane Grey was around sixteen or seventeen years old at the time of her execution ("Lady Jane Grey–Wikipedia").

* * * * * * * * * * * * *

In the latter fifteenth and early sixteenth centuries, English citizens were speaking and writing more in English every day. Their language had evolved from the invasions of the island of Britain over many hundreds of years. Invaders known as Angles from Germany, Saxons from Lower Saxony in modern Germany, and Jutes from the Jutland peninsula in modern Denmark, crossed the English channel and fought with the Celts who had lived in Britain for thousands of years. This mixture of cultures and languages resulted in Anglo-

Saxon or Old English ("How English Evolved into a Modern Language–VOA Learning English").

Beowulf (which many of us studied in high school and/or college) is the oldest known English poem to survive from this period. It was written in Old English over a thousand years ago. (*"Beowulf*–page 1–The British Library"). Its author is unknown (*"Beowulf*–poet").

Other invasions by the Vikings from the far North and the Normans from Normandy in northern France brought further changes to the language of Great Britain. This resulted in the Middle English language of the period. Nowadays, school children attempt to read Geoffrey Chaucer's *The Canterbury Tales* in Middle English, which sounds more like modern English. Geoffrey Chaucer was one of the first important writers to use what had evolved into the English language ("How English Evolved into a Modern Language–VOA Learning English").

English is the most important language in the world ("These are the most powerful languages in the world/World…"). It is the official language of more than seventy-five countries, including Britain, Canada, the United States, Australia, and South Africa. More people are attempting to learn English than any other language in the world. English is used almost exclusively in international business and political negotiations. It is the international language of medicine and science. Passenger airplane pilots must speak English, according to international treaties ("Where Did the English Language Come From?–VOA Learning English").

I believe the English language was important in God's eyes, since it was brought to America by English-speaking colonists. God intended to use America to solidify his kingdom, for America was destined to protect Israel. Who knew, some five hundred years ago, that Israel would once again become a nation, other than God, himself? His omniscience is total and awesome.

However, the church in England was using a Latin translation of the Bible and its services were being conducted in Latin. Since the leaders of the Protestant Reformation urged people to read and conduct their lives by the teachings of the Bible, the continued use of Latin posed a problem for those who were unable to read the Bible for themselves.

The clergy at that time often used their ability to read the Bible in Latin to lord it over the ordinary citizens, so the English people yearned for a Bible in English that they themselves could read and understand ("They Tried to Keep God's Word From the Masses–Watchtower..."). Because of this need, King Henry VIII of England authorized the printing of the Great Bible (so called because of its large size) in 1539. Prepared by Miles Coverdale, working under commission of Thomas, Lord Cromwell, Secretary to King Henry VIII and Vicar General, this Bible was lacking in direct translation from the original Greek, Hebrew and Aramaic texts ("Great Bible–Wikipedia").

In 1560, the Geneva Bible was published, which became the primary Bible of sixteenth century Protestantism. It was the Bible used by William Shakespeare, Oliver Cromwell, John Milton, John Knox, John Donne, and John Bunyan. It was also one of the Bibles carried to America on the *Mayflower* in 1620. It was called the Geneva Bible because it was published in Geneva, Switzerland. During the reign of the Catholic Queen Mary of England (1553-1558), many Protestant scholars fled from England to Geneva, where John Calvin and later Theodore Beza provided spiritual leadership. The involvement of Knox and Calvin in the creation of the Geneva Bible made it appealing in Scotland, where a law was enacted in 1579 that required every household of sufficient means to purchase a copy ("Geneva Bible–Wikipedia").

Almost simultaneously during this time period, fewer than ten diocesan bishops were working on a Bible translation which was published later in 1568, known aptly as the Bishops' Bible. Though it failed to displace the Geneva Bible, the Geneva Bible nonetheless contained much controversial theology and political undertones ("1568 Bishops' Bible–Greatsite.com"). The time was ripe for a better translation of the Bible.

After the death of Queen Elizabeth I of England, who had no issue, her cousin James VI of Scotland inherited the throne and became James I of England, Scotland and Ireland. King James did not like the Geneva Bible because its annotations were Calvinist and Puritan in character and were obviously anti-royalty. The notes contained in the Geneva Bible even suggested that tyrannical kings should possibly be overthrown and certainly not obeyed. King James saw the need for a new Bible translation, one that would discredit the Geneva Bible and would not threaten the rule of English kings ("Religion Today: Bible Battles: King James vs. the Puritans").

King James summarily held the Hampton Court Conference in 1604 "for the hearing, and for the determining, things pretended to be amiss in the church." Bishops, clergymen, and professors met to consider the complaints of four Puritan leaders. The Puritan president of Corpus Christi College, John Reynolds, "moved his Majesty, that there might be a new translation of the Bible, because those which were allowed in the reigns of Henry the eighth, and Edward the sixth, were corrupt and not answerable to the truth of the Original."

The king replied that he "could never yet see a Bible well translated in English; but I think that, of all, that of Geneva is the worst. I wish some special pains were taken for an uniform translation, which should be done by the best learned men in both Universities, then reviewed by the Bishops, presented to the Privy Council, lastly ratified by the Royal authority, to be read in the whole Church, and none other." A resolution came forth from this meeting that agreed to the following: "That a translation be made of the whole Bible, as consonant as can be to the original Hebrew and Greek; and this to be set out and printed, without any marginal notes, and only to be used in all churches of England in time of divine service."

Though King James appointed fifty-four learned men to translate the Bible, only forty-seven actually took part in the translation. Organized into six groups, the translators met at Westminster, Cambridge, and Oxford. Ten at Westminster worked on Genesis through II Kings, while seven had Romans through Jude. At Cambridge, eight translated I Chronicles through Ecclesiastes, while seven others worked on the Apocrypha. Oxford assigned seven to translate Isaiah through Malachi, while eight translated the Gospels, Acts, and Revelation. The translators stated that they were "poor instruments to make GOD'S holy Truth to be yet more and more known," while at the same time, they felt that "Popish persons" sought to keep the people "in ignorance and darkness."

The King James Bible was completed in 1611. The title page read as follows: "THE HOLY BIBLE, Conteyning the Old Testament, and the New: Newly Translated out of the Originall tongues: & with the former Translations diligently compared and revised, by his Majesties Special Commandment. Appointed to be read in Churches. Imprinted at London by Robert Barker, Printer to the Kings most Excellent Majestie." *ANNO DOM.* 1611.

The New Testament had its own separate title page, which read as follows: "THE NEWE Testament of our Lord and Saviour JESUS CHRIST. Newly Translated out of the Original Greeke: and with the former Translations diligently compared and revised, by his Majesties special Commandment. IMPRINTED at London by Robert Barker, Printer to the Kings most Excellent Majestie. *ANNO DOM.* 1611. *Cum Privilegio.*"

Though the Authorized Version, as it came to be called, went through several editions and revisions, it eclipsed all prior versions of the Bible. Also, though other versions have been printed, such as the Revised Version, the King James Bible is still accepted as the standard by which all other versions are compared. In 1792, Alexander Geddes, a Roman Catholic priest, paid the following tribute to the King James Bible:

"The highest eulogiums have been made on the translation of James the First, both by our own writers and by foreigners. And, indeed, if accuracy, fidelity, and the strictest attention to the letter of the text, be supposed to constitute the qualities of an excellent version, this of all versions, must, in general, be accounted the most excellent. Every sentence, every word, every syllable, every letter and point, seem to have been weighed with the nicest exactitude; and expressed, either in the text, or margin, with the greatest precision."

Brooke Westcott, one of the members of the committee that produced the Revised Version, spoke about the King James Bible, as follows: "From the middle of the seventeenth century, the King's

Bible has been the acknowledged Bible of the English-speaking nations throughout the world simply because it is the best. A revision which embodied the ripe fruits of nearly a century of labour, and appealed to the religious instinct of a great Christian people, gained by its own internal character a vital authority which could never have been secured by any edict of sovereign rulers." ("A Brief History of the King James Bible")

(Note: If you prefer another translation, that is fine, just so it is the Bible! Within my own family, we have many of the other translations preferred over the King James version.)

* * * * * * * * * * * * * *

Though New England was settled, for the most part, by people of Calvinist beliefs, which held that certain people were predestined to be saved, those Puritans who embraced Arminianism felt that a man's righteous living could influence God's attitude toward him. This departure from strict Calvinism encouraged the more liberal ideas of the eighteenth and nineteenth centuries. The Reverend Peter Bulkeley (1583-1659), a preacher and one of the founders of Concord, Massachusetts, believed in the Calvinist principle of predestination but insisted that righteous living could win God's favor and ensure one's acceptance into heaven. Bulkeley's famous sermon "The Gospel-Covenant" was published in 1651. Here again, we read that the settlement of New England was likened to "a city set upon a hill." An excerpt follows:

"And for ourselves here, the people of New England, we should in a special manner labor to shine forth in holiness above other people. We have that plenty and abundance of ordinances and means of grace, as few people enjoy the like; we are as a city set upon a hill, in the open view of all the earth, the eyes of the world are upon us, because we profess ourselves to be a people in covenant with God, and therefore not only the Lord our God, with whom we have made covenant, but heaven and earth, angels and men, that are witnesses of our profession, will cry shame upon us if we walk contrary to the covenant which we have professed and promised to walk in. If we open the mouths of men against our profession, by reason of the scandalousness of our lives, we (of all men) shall have the greater sin....

"Let us study so to walk that this may be our excellency and dignity among the nations of the world among which we live, that they may be constrained to say of us, only this people is wise, a holy and blessed people; that all that see us may see and know that the name of the Lord is called upon us; and that we are the seed which the Lord hath blessed (Deut. 28:10; Isa. 61:9)." (*The Annals of America* [1493-1754], p. 211-212)

Arminianism derived from the theological ideas of the Dutch Reformed theologian Jacobus Arminius (1560-1609). Though Arminianism is related to Calvinism, it differs in its concepts of divine predestination and salvation. In this regard, it is opposed to Calvinism, for Arminianism stresses that all people have the opportunity of salvation through faith, not only the predestined.

The heated discussions between fellow Methodist ministers and friends, John Wesley and George Whitefield, often involved the differences between Calvinism and Arminianism. Wesley defended his beliefs in regard to Arminianism in a periodical entitled *The Arminian* and by writing articles such as "Predestination Calmly Considered." He attacked the set belief that characterized predestination and also held the tenet that man could lose his salvation.

Though Calvinism and Arminianism both may exist today within the same denomination, adherents of both doctrines are found in many Protestant denominations. Churches which embrace Arminianism include Methodists, Free Will Baptists, Christian Churches and Churches of Christ, General Baptists, Seventh-day Adventists, Church of the Nazarene, The Salvation Army, Conservative Mennonites, Old Order Mennonites, Amish and Charismatic denominations. Adherents of the Calvinist doctrine include the Reformed Churches, Particular Baptists, Reformed Baptists, Presbyterians, and Congregationalists. According to an article I read in Wikipedia, which included the data above, Billy Graham and the majority of Southern Baptists accept Arminianism. Lutherans' views in regard to salvation and election are different from both the Calvinist and Arminian schools of soteriology, theology dealing with salvation, especially as effected by Jesus Christ ("Arminianism–Wikipedia").

It's easy to become bogged down in doctrinal differences among the many denominations and splinter groups that have derived from the early churches. Even today, church members sometimes break away and form their own churches. The purpose of this book is not to discuss in detail the beliefs of the many different denominations but rather to focus on the nature of God. We all tend to dwell on the differences among us, rather than the unity that we can only find by returning again and again to God's word in the Bible. It sometimes seems that we have let our imaginations lead us away from the profundity of the message of the Bible, rather than attempting to digest the important words that provide a road map for the living of our lives.

Chapter Nineteen

The fact that Christianity has survived for over two thousand years is miraculous, considering the adversities of its adherents from the outset of its existence. This brings to mind the "remnant," which has been preserved since the time of Noah. The meaning of "remnant," in this regard, would be those who acknowledged God and tried to live according to his commandments. Noah and his family were the remnant who survived the flood. As time moved on, another remnant would have been the Southern Kingdom of Israel, which for the most part worshiped God, as opposed to the Northern Kingdom of Israel, which worshiped Bael.

During the Assyrian and Babylonian conquests of Israel, the remnant would have been those Jews who strived to follow God's commandments, though subjugated by heathen nations. During the Jews' captivity by Persia, the remnant would have been those who returned to their former homeland to rebuild the temple and the wall around Jerusalem. The word "remnant" in our Bible also refers to Christians, then and now, who try to live according to the teachings of Christ. All of the above are included in my understanding of the remnant.

The idea, or wordage, concerning a remnant in the Bible occurs some 540 times ("The Remnant–Refuge in the Heart of God"). In Matthew 7:21-29, Jesus makes it clear that only a remnant will be saved. The Scripture reads, as follows:

"Not every one that saith unto me, Lord, Lord, shall enter into the kingdom of heaven; but he that doeth the will of my

Father which is in heaven. Many will say to me in that day, Lord, Lord, have we not prophesied in thy name? And in thy name have cast out devils? And in thy name done many wonderful works? And then will I profess unto them, I never knew you: depart from me, ye that work iniquity. herefore whosoever heard these sayings of mine, and doeth them, I will liken him unto a wise man, which built his house upon a rock: And the rain descended, and floods came, and the winds blew, and beat upon that house; and it fell not: for it was founded upon a rock And every one that heareth these sayings of mine, and doeth them not, shall be likened unto a foolish man, which built his house upon the sand: and the rain descended, and the floods came, and the winds blew, and beat upon that house; and it fell: and great was the fall of it."

Each of the letters to the seven churches in the Book of Revelation (chapters 2 and 3) contains a special message to the remnant of true believers in every congregation and every age. This minority group is referred to as **"he that overcometh"** or **"him that overcometh."** The final eschatological remnant includes those who keep God's commandments and have the testimony of Jesus.

One of the websites I found on the internet ("The Concept of the Remnant–Lambert Dolphin"), in regard to the remnant featured in the Bible, stated that "There can be little doubt the church in America (and certainly in Europe also) today is fully Laodicean. The age of Philadelphian Christianity has quietly slipped away from us in the past half-century." You may remember from reading the Book of Revelation that the church in Philadelphia is characterized as a good church, whereas the church in Laodicea is depicted as a bad church. The quote continues from this website, stating, "Since the Laodicean church is representative of the church as a whole at the close of our age we should pay special attention to the Lord's analysis of this church and his words of exhortation to the faithful remnant that remains at the end of the age." The following Scripture is the Lord's message to the church in Laodicea, as recorded in Revelation 3:14-22:

"And unto the angel of the church of the Laodiceans write;

These things saith the Amen, the faithful and true witness, the beginning of the creation of God; I know thy works, that thou art neither cold nor hot: I would thou wert cold or hot. So then because thou art lukewarm, and neither cold nor hot, I will spue thee out of my mouth. Because thou sayest, I am rich, and increased with goods, and have need of nothing; and knowest not that thou art wretched, and miserable, and poor, and blind, and naked: I counsel thee to buy of me gold tried in the fire, that thou mayest be rich; and white raiment, that thou mayest be clothed, and that the shame of thy nakedness do not appear; and anoint thine eyes with eyesalve, that thou mayest see. As many as I love, I rebuke and chasten: be zealous therefore, and repent. Behold, I stand at the door, and knock: if any man hear my voice, and open the door, I will come in to him, and will sup with him, and he with me. To him that overcometh will I grant to sit with me in my throne, even as I also overcame, and am set down with my Father in his throne. He that hath an ear, let him hear what the Spirit saith unto the churches."

* * * * * * * * * * * * *

From the 1730s to the 1770s, a great historical movement known as the "First Great Awakening" swept through the American colonies. This revival of religious righteousness was part of a broader evangelical upsurge occurring in England, Scotland, and Germany. This ushered in a new "Age of Faith" that caused men to trust the Bible, rather than their own human reasoning ("The First Great Awakening, Divining America TeacherServe National...").

The genesis of this First Great Awakening appeared among Presbyterians in Pennsylvania and New Jersey. Led by the Tennent family which included the Reverend William Tennent, a Scot-Irish immigrant, and his four sons - all clergymen - the Presbyterians not only conducted religious revivals in those colonies during the 1730s but they also established a seminary to train clergymen whose earnest and fervid preaching brought sinners to evangelical conversion. This seminary was originally known as "the Log College," but is better known today as Princeton University ("DOC The First Great Awakening:).

One might wonder what brought about this awakening or revival. This was an era of extraordinary upheaval and crises for ordinary people. As England was entering the Industrial Revolution, evangelicals such as the Methodists had large numbers of converts among miners and factory workers. England, Scotland, and Germany were ripe for evangelical zeal. In America, the population shift to the South and West brought about changes that caused families to endure hardscrabble, rootless lives along with the persistent threat of Indian attacks. Presbyterians. Baptists, and Methodists depicted their churches as havens of refuge from the evils of social chaos and cultural confusion.

Religious fervor spread quickly from the Presbyterians to the Congregationalists (Puritans) and Baptists of New England. Powerful preachers like Jonathan Edwards evoked terrifying images of the utter corruption of human nature and the terrors that awaited the unrepentant in hell. In his best known sermon, "Sinners in the Hands of an Angry God," Edwards depicted the sinner as a loathsome spider hanging by a slender thread over a pit of seething brimstone.

Some converts in the northern colonies became inspired to become missionaries to the American South. Presbyterian preachers from New York and New Jersey carried the revival to the Virginia Piedmont and, by the 1750s, some members of a group known as Separate Baptists moved to central North Carolina, where they held revivals.

Although George Whitefield was ordained as a minister in the Church of England, he joined with other Anglican clergymen who shared his evangelical views, most notably John and Charles Wesley. Together, they led a movement to reform the Church of England, which resulted in the founding of the Methodist church in the eighteenth century.

However, the dramatic methods of presenting their hellfire and damnation sermons, often accompanied by weeping openly, brought about a polarization along religious lines. Anglicans and Quakers gained new followers among those who disapproved of the revivals' emotionalism and excesses, while the Baptists (and, in the 1770s, the Methodists) made even larger gains among the ranks of radical evangelical converts. Soon, civil governments were brought into the fray. In colonies where one denomination received state support, other churches lobbied legislatures for disestablishment, which brought to an end the favored status of Congregationalism in Connecticut and Massachusetts and of Anglicanism in the southern colonies ("The First Great Awakening, Divining America, TeacherServe...").

* * * * * * * * * * * * * *

During the 1700s, more and more colonists complained about the vise-like grip that England had upon their land. Pastors during that time, who were loyal to the despotic king, were known as "royalists" and "loyalists." They were also called the king's toadies or "Tories." They taught their congregations to have "unlimited submission and passive obedience" to the Crown, regardless of the tyrannical way they were treated by the king.

The pastors who spoke out against the king were known as liberal and radical. King George mocked these nonconformist clergymen by calling them the "Black Regiment," because of the black robes they wore ("Jonathan Mayhew on Romans 13 and submission to higher powers"). In our present day we know that "loyalism' has returned to America's church pulpits. Rare is the pastor who ever speaks out against the misdeeds of our modern-day rulers. Of course, this would likely alienate certain members of the congregation, if he or she did.

However, our nation had a firebrand preacher named Jonathan Mayhew (1720-1766) who did speak out against the injustices and cruelties imposed on the colonists by the king. Mayhew received his D.D. from Harvard in 1747. He was ordained as a Congregationalist Minister and was pastor of the West Church in Boston until his death in 1766.

John Adams, the second president of the United States, called the Reverend Mayhew "a transcendent genius." He also referred to him as "the morning gun of the Revolution," which occurred some ten years after Mayhew's death. Mayhew preached several sermons on Romans 13:1-8, basically using the sentence, **"Let every soul be subject unto the higher powers."**

Mayhew contended that if a ruler were righteous and dealt fairly with his subjects, then he should be obeyed. However, if he mistreated his subjects, as the English king was doing, then his people should rise up and throw off this tyranny. On January 30, 1750, Jonathan Mayhew delivered a sermon entitled "A Discourse Concerning Unlimited Submission and Non-Resistance to the Higher Powers." In it, he preached against the divine right of kings and any type of royal or ecclesiastical absolutism. Mayhew's sermon served to embolden his parishioners to the point that some would give their lives some twenty-six years later to throw off the tyranny of the English crown.

In 1818, John Adams wrote that Mayhew's sermon was as follows: "...was read by everybody; celebrated by friends, and abused by enemies. During the reigns of King George the First and King George the Second, the reigns of the Stuarts - the two James and the two Charles - were in general disgrace in England. In America they had always been held in abhorrence. The persecutions and cruelties suffered by [the colonists'] ancestors under those reigns had been transmitted by history and tradition, and Mayhew seemed to be raised up to revive all their animosity against tyranny, in church and state, and at the same time to destroy their bigotry, fanaticism, and inconsistency." (*The Annals of America* [1493-1754], p. 481)

The prolonged quest for colonial domination in North America, the Caribbean, and India resulted in the French and Indian War which was also called the Seven Years War. It began in 1754. Though the English won the war and secured its rule over the American colonies, it caused a resulting debt so staggering that it nearly destroyed the English government. This was the beginning of open hostilities between the colonies and Great Britain ("French and Indian War/Seven Years' War, 1754-1763").

Though we all have read about Benjamin Franklin's *Poor Richard's Almanac* which he published in the eighteenth century, we are likely not as familiar with Nathaniel Ames' annual publication, *The Astronomical Diary and Almanac*, which he authored from 1726 until his death in 1764. This almanac was almost as popular as

Franklin's, reaching a yearly circulation of 60,000 of the population of around one million colonists during the 1750s and 1760s. An excerpt from the 1758 edition of Ames' almanac appears below:

"As the celestial light of the Gospel was directed here by the finger of God, it will doubtless finally drive the long, long night of heathenish darkness from America; so arts and sciences will change the face of nature in their tour from hence over the Appalachian Mountains to the western ocean. And as they march through the vast desert, the residence of wild beasts will be broken up, and their obscene howl cease forever. Instead of which, the stones and trees will dance together at the music of Orpheus; the rocks will disclose their hidden gems; and the inestimable treasures of gold and silver be broken up. Huge mountains of iron ore are already discovered, and vast stores are reserved for future generations. This metal, more useful than gold and silver, will employ millions of hands, not only to form the martial sword and peaceful share, alternately, but an infinity of utensils improved in the exercise of art and handcrafted among men.

"Nature, through all her works, has stamped authority on this law, namely, 'That all fit matter shall be improved to its best purposes.' Shall not then those vast quarries that teem with mechanic stone - those for structure be piled into great cities; and those for sculpture into statues to perpetuate the honor of renowned heroes, even those who shall now save their country. O! ye unborn inhabitants of America! Should this page escape its destined conflagration at the year's end, and these alphabetical letters remain legible, when your eyes behold the sun after he has rolled the seasons round for two or three centuries more, you will know that in Anno Domini 1758, we dreamed of your times." (*The Annals of America* [1755-1783], p.29)

* * * * * * * * * * * * *

In 1733, England's Parliament levied a tax on molasses or sugar with the Sugar and Molasses Act, which was modified in 1754. Other than sugar, different foreign goods taxed were certain wines, pimiento, coffee, cambric and printed calico. The Act also regulated the export of lumber and iron ("The Sugar Act–USHistory.org").

In 1765, the British Parliament imposed the Stamp Act on the American colonies. Taxes were placed on all printed materials in the colonies, requiring that many printed materials in the colonies be produced in London on paper carrying an embossed revenue stamp. These printed materials were many types of paper used throughout the colonies, including magazines, legal documents, newspapers, and cards. The Stamp Act met with violent resistance by the colonists. By the end of December, 1764, the colonists sent pamphlets and petitions protesting both the Sugar Act and the Stamp Act. However, these protests were mostly ignored by Parliament ("Stamp Act 1765–Wikipedia").

By the 1760s, as relations between England and the American colonists continued to deteriorate, the seal adopted by Massachusetts on the eve of the American Revolution expressed the mood and the will of the colonists - a militiaman with a sword in one hand and the Magna Carta in the other. The colonists believed that in America they were creating a country that adopted the best of the English system combined with the will and aspirations of new settlers in a new place - a place where a person could rise in the world by merit, not birth; a place where free men could voice their opinions and actively be a part of self-government ("The U. S. Has a Rich English History/Beaufort County Now").

* * * * * * * * * * * * * *

On December 10, 1770, King George III issued a proclamation, commanding the governor of Virginia "upon pain of the highest displeasure, to assent to no law by which the importation of slaves should be in any respect prohibited or obstructed." In 1772, the Virginia Assembly earnestly debated the question, "How shall we get rid of the great evil?" The Assembly finally pleaded with the king not to deny their efforts to stop the slave trade, which they termed "a very pernicious commerce." The king evaded a reply and the importation of slaves continued ("History of Slavery– The Civil War").

Patrick Henry (1736-1799), lawyer, politician, fiery orator, and Governor of Virginia, proposed the Virginia Stamp Resolutions which by most accounts were regarded as treason against England.

In a speech he delivered on March 23, 1775, and addressed to the president of a convention gathered at Richmond, he rallied his compatriots to throw off the yoke of the oppressive mother country ("Patrick Henry–Wickipedia"). Below is an excerpt:

"They tell us, sir...that we are weak, unable to cope with so formidable an adversary. But when shall we be stronger? Will it be the next week or the next year? Will it be when we are totally disarmed, and when a British guard shall be stationed in every house? Shall we gather strength by irresolution and inaction? Shall we acquire the means of effectual resistance by lying supinely on our backs and hugging the delusive phantom of hope, until our enemies shall have bound us hand and foot? Sir, we are not weak if we make a proper use of those means which the God of nature has placed in our power. Three millions of people armed in the holy cause of liberty and in such a country as that which we possess are invincible by any force which our enemy can send against us.

"Besides, sir, we shall not fight our battles alone. There is a just God who presides over the destinies of nations, and who will raise up friends to fight our battles for us? The battle, sir, is not to the strong alone; it is to the vigilant, the active, the brave. Besides, sir, we have no election. If we were base enough to desire it, it is now too late to retire from the contest. There is no retreat but in submission and slavery! Our chains are forged. Their clanking may be heard on the plains of Boston! The war is inevitable – and let it come!! I repeat it, sir, let it come!!!

"It is vain, sir, to extenuate the matter. Gentlemen may cry, peace, peace, but there is not peace. The war is actually begun! The next gale that sweeps from the north will bring to our ears the clash of resounding arms! Our brethren are already in the field! Why stand we here idle? What is it that gentlemen wish? What would they have? Is life so dear or peace so sweet as to be purchased at the price of chains and slavery?

"Forbid it, almighty God – I know not what course others may take; but as for me," cried he, with both his arms extended aloft, his brows knit, every feature marked with the resolute purpose of his soul, and his voice swelled to its boldest note of exclamation

– "give me liberty, or give me death!"

"He took his seat. No murmur of applause was heard. The effect was too deep. After the trance of a moment, several members started from their seats. The cry, 'To arms!' seemed to quiver on every lip and gleam from every eye." (*The Annals of America* [1755-1783], p. 322-323). However, I'm sure that the thought of war with the greatest military power on earth by the fledgling colonies caused many to question the national will for such a confrontation.

* * * * * * * * * * * * * *

Abigail Adams, wife of John Adams, second president of the United States, had little formal education, but the fact that she was highly intelligent and broad-minded is reflected in the many letters she wrote to her husband during this time of crisis for the American colonies. In a letter dated November 17, 1775, she cited her concerns for her country:

"I wish I knew what mighty things were fabricating. If a form of government is to be established here, what one will be assumed? Will it be left to our assemblies to choose one? And will not many men have many minds? And shall we not run into dissensions among ourselves?

"I am more and more convinced that man is a dangerous creature; and that power, whether vested in many or a few, is ever grasping, and, like the grave, cries 'Give, give.' The great fish swallow up the small; and he who is most strenuous for the rights of the people when vested with power, is as eager after the prerogatives of government. You tell me of degrees of perfection to which human nature is capable of arriving, and I believe it, but, at the same time, lament that our admiration should arise from the scarcity of the instances.

"The building up a great empire, which was only hinted at by my correspondent, may now, I suppose, be realized even by the unbelievers. Yet, will not ten thousand difficulties arise in the formation of it? The reins of government have been so long slackened that I fear the people will not quietly submit to those restraints which are necessary for the peace and security of the community. If we separate from Britain, what code of laws will be established?

How shall we be governed so as to retain our liberties? Can any government be free which is not administered by general state laws? Who shall frame these laws? Who will give them force and energy? It is true your resolutions, as a body, have hitherto had the force of laws; but will they continue to have?

"When I consider these things, and the prejudices of people in favor of ancient customs and regulations, I feel anxious for the fate of our monarchy or democracy, or whatever is to take place. I soon get lost in a labyrinth of perplexities; but, whatever occurs, may justice and righteousness be the stability of our times, and order arise out of confusion. Great difficulties may be surmounted by patience and perseverance." (*The Annals of America* [1755-1783], p.362-363)

War with the mother country was imminent. When George Washington was appointed commander in chief of the Continental Army, his answer to Congress on June 16, 1775 was as follows: "As to pay, I beg to assure the Congress, that, as no pecuniary consideration could have tempted me to accept this arduous employment, at the expense of my domestic ease and happiness, I do not wish to make any profit from it. I will keep an exact account of my expenses. Those, I doubt not, they will discharge, and that is all I desire." ("George Washington Accepts Appointment as...–Library of Congress")

From 1776 to 1783, Tom Paine wrote a series of patriotic tracts called "The Crisis" papers. The first of these so moved George Washington that he ordered it to read to his troops late in December of 1776, when the American cause seemed to be faltering. Several excerpts of this paper appear below:

"These are the times that try men's souls. The summer soldier and the sunshine patriot will, in this crisis, shrink from the service of his country; but he that stands it now deserves the love and thanks of man and woman. Tyranny, like hell, is not easily conquered; yet we have this consolation with us – that the harder the conflict, the more glorious the triumph. What we obtain too cheap, we esteem too lightly: It is dearness only that gives everything its value. Heaven knows how to put a proper price upon its goods; and it would be strange indeed if so celestial an article as freedom should not be highly rated. Britain, with an army to enforce her tyranny, has declared that she has a right not only to tax but 'to bind us in all cases whatsoever,' and if being bound in that manner is not slavery, then is there not such a thing as slavery upon earth. Even the expression is impious, for so limited a power can belong only to God."

"Not a place upon earth might be so happy as America. Her situation is remote from all the wrangling world, and she has nothing to do but to trade with them. A man can distinguish himself between temper and principle, and I am as confident, as I am that God governs the world, that America will never be happy till she gets clear of foreign dominion. Wars, without ceasing, will break out till that period arrives, and the continent must in the end be conqueror; for though the flame of liberty may sometimes cease to shine, the coal can never expire."

"This is our situation and who will may know it. By perseverance and fortitude we have the prospect of a glorious issue; by cowardice and submission, the sad choice of a variety of evils – a ravaged country – a depopulated city – habitations without safety and slavery without hope – our homes turned into barracks and bawdy houses for Hessians, and a future race to provide for, whose fathers we shall doubt of. Look on this picture and weep over it! And if there yet remains one thoughtless wretch who believes it not, let him suffer it unlamented." (*The Annals of America* [1755-1783], p. 456-461)

Chapter Twenty

The American Revolutionary War began in 1775, between the British in their red coats and their strict battle formations and the colonists, many without uniforms but with zeal enough to put up a splendid fight. Below are some quotes that have come down to us from that time period:

"Stand your ground. Don't fire unless fired upon, but if they mean to have a war, let it begin here." (Captain John Parker, to his Minute Men on Lexington Green, April 19, 1775) (*The Annals of America* [1755-1783], p. 324)

* * *

"To give a particular account of the ravages of the troops as they retreated from Concord to Charlestown would be very difficult, if not impracticable. Let it suffice to say that a great number of the houses on the road were plundered and rendered unfit for use, several were burned, women in childbed were driven by the soldiery naked into the streets, old men peaceably in their houses were shot dead, and such scenes exhibited as would disgrace the annals of the most uncivilized nation.

"These, brethren, are marks of ministerial vengeance against this colony for refusing, with her sister colonies, a submission to slavery; but they have not yet detached us from our royal sovereign. We profess to be his loyal and dutiful subjects, and, so hardly dealt with as we have been, are still ready, without lives and fortunes, to defend his person, family, Crown, and dignity. Nevertheless, to the persecution and tyranny of his cruel Ministry we will not tamely submit – appealing to Heaven for the justice of our cause, we determine to die or be free." (Joseph Warren: The Battles of Lexington and Concord, April 26, 1775.) (*The Annals of America* [1755-1783], p. 325-326)

* * *

"Men, you are all marksmen – don't one of you fire until you see the whites of their eyes."

(Israel Putnam, Battle of Bunker Hill, June 17, 1775.) (*The Annals of America* [1755-1783], p. 334)

* * * * * * * * * * * * * *

Early in the summer of 1776, when the British ships sailed into New York Harbor, they were the largest fleet ever seen in American waters. General William Howe had 32,000 men under his command, which included a powerful naval fleet. "In fact, it was the largest expeditionary force of the 18th century, the largest most powerful force ever sent forth from Britain or any nation" ("Heroes of New York Harbor: Tales from the City's Port"). The odds were stacked against the colonists.

George Washington led a combined army of 19,000 continental soldiers and ragtag militiamen, many of whom did not even own a uniform. However, the guerilla warfare of the back country, which many of the colonists had waged against the native Indians, proved to be in the colonists' favor.

As the war dragged on, desertions among the enlisted men increased and the size of the American army was reduced to as low as 5,000 men during the harsh winter of 1776-1777 at Valley Forge. Sometimes, only 2,000-3,000 soldiers were equipped for battle. Though disease plagued the troops, also, Washington did inoculate the army against smallpox which was rampant during this time period.

With defeatism sweeping throughout the untrained and ill-equipped army, one wonders how the colonists won the war. I believe that God himself intervened and so filled the minds and hearts of his people with such power and courage and self-determination that no force on earth could have prevailed against them. I believe the Lord had great plans for our country, which was created by his divine nature and guidance.

Though the purpose of this book is not to recount the different battles of the American Revolutionary War, I did read an account of the first battle between the colonists and the British troops at Lexington, Massachusetts, that set the tone for the rest of the war. When the British troops met some seventy minutemen, lined up on the Lexington Green, the British major, John Pitcairn, ordered the colonists to disperse, calling them "rebels" and "villains."

As the colonists began backing away, someone fired a single shot. No one knew where the shot came from, but it began the first battle of the war and became known as the "shot heard round the world." When British troops, shouting their battle cry "HUZZA! HUZZA! HUZZA!, charged the minutemen with bayonets, eight colonists died and ten more were wounded. As historians later recorded, "One wounded American patriot, whose wife and son were watching the spectacle, crawled 100 yards to die on his front doorstep ("War in the American Revolution–Shmoop.").

* * * * * * * * * * * * * *

Some months later, the colonists made the final break from the mother country with the immortal words of the Declaration of Independence, written in 1776. Though it is several pages long, its Preamble opens with the following words:

"When in the Course of human events, it becomes necessary for one people to dissolve the political bands which have connected them with another, and to assume among the powers of the earth, the separate and equal station to which the Laws of Nature and of Nature's God entitle them, a decent respect to the opinions of mankind requires that they should declare the causes which impel them to the separation.

"We hold these truths to be self-evident: that all men are created equal, that they are endowed by their Creator with certain inalienable rights, that among these are life, liberty and the pursuit of happiness."

The day of its passage, July 4, 1776, it was signed only by John Hancock of Massachusetts, the presiding officer who, after affixing his bold signature to the document, exclaimed, "There, I guess King George will be able to read that." The Declaration was signed by other members of the Congress on August 2, when a copy engrossed on parchment bore witness to their names.

Though the Declaration of Independence was written by Thomas Jefferson, Jefferson asked Benjamin Franklin and John Adams to review it and to make any changes they thought necessary. They made very few changes in the original document. I ask you, Reader, isn't it evident that God guided these strong, able, and devout men in writing this beautiful declaration? I believe that God was looking ahead several hundred years to the renewed statehood of his beloved Israel, and he wanted America to be the defender and protector of this country where He would return one day. I find it significant that God was called upon by these three great men several times in the document, often being referenced as "God," "Creator," "Supreme Judge," and "Divine Providence." (*The Annals of America* [1755-1783], p. 447-449)

Even as this declaration was being signed by brave men from each of the original thirteen colonies, these signers were being hunted for treason at the order of the British General Thomas Gage. The last sentence of the declaration reveals the terrible crisis of the times, for these men knew their fledgling country would be fighting a war against the largest military force on earth. These men were placing the lives of their families and their own lives at risk by overturning the way that people had been categorized in the world for the past two thousand years. The last sentence is heart-wrenching in its straightforwardness and its valor. These are words acknowledged by men on a battlefield, when they are ready and willing to die for one another and for what they believe: "And for the support of this Declaration, with a firm reliance on the protection of Divine Providence, we mutually pledge to each other our lives, our fortunes and our sacred honor."

At the signing of the Declaration of Independence, Benjamin Franklin stated: "We must, indeed, all hang together, or most assuredly we will all hang separately." ("Franklin's Contribution to the American Revolution as...–USHistory.org")

Dear Reader, I had not originally intended to include a section about the signers of the Declaration of Independence, but I was so moved when I only lately read an article about what happened to each of the signers, that I felt I must include the article in my book. This information comes from ("Destiny of the Signers–nhccs") Please see below:

"Five signers were captured by the British and brutally tortured as traitors. Nine fought in the War for Independence and died from wounds or from hardships they suffered. Two lost their sons in the Continental Army. Another two had sons captured. At least a dozen of the fifty-six had their homes pillaged and burned.

"What kind of men were they? Twenty-five were lawyers or jurists. Eleven were merchants. Nine were farmers or large plantation owners. One was a teacher, one a musician, and one a printer. These were men of means and education, yet they signed the Declaration of Independence, knowing full well that the penalty could be death if they were captured.

"In the face of the advancing British Army, the Continental Congress fled from Philadelphia to Baltimore on December 12, 1776. It was an especially anxious time for John Hancock, the President, as his wife had just given birth to a baby girl. Due to the complications stemming from the trip to Baltimore, the child lived only a few months.

"William Ellery's signing at the risk of his fortune proved only too realistic. In December, 1776, during three days of British occupation of Newport, Rhode Island, Ellery's house was burned, and all his property destroyed.

"Richard Stockton, a New Jersey State Supreme Court Justice, had rushed back to his estate near Princeton after signing the Declaration of Independence to find that his wife and children were living like refugees with friends. They had been betrayed by a Tory sympathizer who also revealed Stockton's own whereabouts. British troops pulled him from his bed one night, beat him and threw him in jail where he almost starved to death. When he was finally released, he went home to find his estate had been looted, his possessions burned, and his horses stolen. Judge Stockton had been so badly treated in prison that his health was ruined and he died before the war's end. His surviving family had to live the remainder of their lives off charity.

"Carter Braxton was a wealthy planter and trader. One by one his ships were captured by the British navy. He loaned a large sum of money to the American cause; it was never paid back. He was forced to sell his plantation and mortgage his other properties to pay his debts.

"Thomas McKean was so hounded by the British that he had to move his family almost constantly. He served in the Continental Congress without pay, and kept his family in hiding.

"Vandals or soldiers or both looted the properties of Clymer, Hall, Harrison, Hopkinson and Livingston. Seventeen lost everything they owned.

"Thomas Heyward, Jr., Edward Rutledge and Arthur Middleton, all of South Carolina, were captured by the British during the Charleston Campaign in 1780. They were kept in dungeons at the St. Augustine Prison until exchanged a year later.

"At the Battle of Yorktown, Thomas Nelson, Jr. noted that the British General Cornwallis had taken over the family home for his headquarters. Nelson urged General George Washington to open fire on his own home. This was done, and the home was destroyed. Nelson later died bankrupt.

"Francis Lewis also had his home and properties destroyed. The British jailed his wife for two months, and that and other hardships from the war so affected her health that she died only two years later.

"Honest John" Hart, a New Jersey farmer, was driven from his wife's bedside when she was near death. Their thirteen children fled for their lives. Hart's fields and his grist mill were laid waste. For over a year he eluded capture by hiding in nearby forests. He never knew where his bed would be the next night and often slept in caves. When he finally returned home, he found that his wife had died, his children disappeared, and his farm and stock were completely destroyed. Hart himself died in 1779 without ever seeing any of his family again.

"Such were the stories and sacrifices typical of those who risked everything to sign the Declaration of Independence. These men were not wild-eyed, rabble-rousing ruffians. They were soft-spoken men of means and education. They had security, but they valued liberty more."

* * * * * * * * * * * * * *

In relating the historical impact and aftereffects of the American Revolution, one must make more than mere mention of the winter of 1777-1778 of Washington's army at Valley Forge, Pennsylvania, some twenty miles northwest of British-occupied Philadelphia. Here, Washington had moved his army of 12,000 men, many of whom – about one in four – had no shoes. From their marching, many had left bloody footprints in the snow ("Valley Forge–Wikipedia"). They lived in crude log huts that they built themselves. On December 23, 1777, Washington wrote, "We have this day no less than 2,873 men in camp unfit for duty because they are barefooted and otherwise naked." ("Public Papers Harry S. Truman 1945-1953–Truman Library")

Though no battle was fought at Valley Forge, it became a proving ground for later battles that were won by the Americans ("Valley Forge–ScienceViews.com"). Without adequate supplies of meat and bread, the soldiers ate "firecake," which was a tasteless mixture of water and flour. Sometimes, they had a black pepper-flavored tripe broth, called "pepper pot soup."

The lack of food became so critical that Washington despaired "that unless some great and capital change suddenly takes place...this Army must inevitably...starve, dissolve, or disperse, in order to obtain subsistence in the best manner they can."("Valley Forge–Wikipedia") He also stated, on April 1, 1778, "To see the men without clothes to cover their nakedness, without blankets to lie upon, without shoes...without a house nor hut to cover them until those could be built, and submitting without a murmur, is a proof of patience and obedience which, in my opinion, can scarcely be paralleled." ("Valley Forge–ScienceViews.com")

An eyewitness account of George Washington on his knees in prayer has come to us from Isaac Potts, a Valley Forge resident who told the following story to the Rev. Nathaniel Randolph Snowden (1770-1851), who then recorded it in his "Diary and Remembrances." The testimony follows:

"I was riding with Mr. Potts near to the Valley Forge where the army lay during the war of ye Revolution, when Mr. Potts said, 'Do you see that woods & that plain?' There laid the army of Washington. It was a most distressing time of ye war, and all were for giving up the Ship but that great and good man. In that woods (pointing to a close in view) I heard a plaintive sound as of a man at prayer. I tied my horse to a sapling & went quietly into the woods. To my astonishment I saw the great George Washington on his knees alone, with his sword on one side and his cocked hat on the other. He was at Prayer to the God of the Armies, beseeching to interpose with his Divine aid, as it was ye Crisis & the cause of the country, of humanity & of the world. Such a prayer I never heard from the lips of man. I left him alone praying. I went home & told my wife. We never thought a man could be a soldier & a Christian, but if there is one in the world, it is Washington. We thought it was the cause of God & America could prevail.'" ("George Washington–Christian Soldier")

Poorly clothed and undernourished, and living in crowded, damp huts, which the soldiers had built, themselves, the Army was wracked by disease and illness. Pneumonia, typhoid, smallpox, typhus, and dysentery brought about the deaths of 2,500 soldiers by the winter's end. Animals fared no better, for by the end of the winter, some 700 horses had died ("Valley Forge–Wikipedia").

The young United States found a lasting bond with France during the Revolutionary War when Marquis de Lafayette (1757-1834) arrived at Valley Forge in 1777, at the age of nineteen, to help the colonists win their independence from England. He also persuaded France to send military aid to the colonists in their struggle. Lafayette endured the terrible winter of 1777-1778, along with Washington and the bedraggled colonists who almost alone provided the fighting force of the United States. Agreeing to serve without pay, Lafayette was made a major general and joined the staff of George Washington.

Lafayette became a "hero in two worlds" when he returned to France in 1782. At the age of twenty-four, he assisted in the negotiations that won America's independence, working closely with Benjamin Franklin and later Thomas Jefferson in behalf of American interests (*The World Book Encyclopedia*–"L"–p. 27-28).

Before sailing home to France, he received a personal letter from George Washington in which the great general wrote: "I owe it to your friendship and to my affectionate regard for you, my dear Marquis, not to let you leave this country without carrying with you fresh marks of my attachment to you and new expressions of the high sense I entertain of your military conduct and other important services in the course of the last campaign, although the latter are too well-known to need the testimony of my approbation, and the former, I persuade myself, you believe is too well riveted to undergo diminution or change."

Lafayette, in return, before leaving from Boston, penned a letter to Washington in which he said: "Adieu, my dear general. I know your heart so well that I am sure that no distance can alter your attachment to me. With the same candour I assure you that my love, my respect, my gratitude for you, are above expression; that, at the moment of leaving you, I feel more than ever the strength of these friendly ties that forever bind me to you, and that I anticipate the pleasure, the most wished-for pleasure, to be again with you and by my zeal and services, to gratify the feelings of my respect and affection." ("The True Story of Lafayette: called the friend of America")

Lafayette spent some $200,000 or more of his own money for "services rendered" during the Revolutionary War. When he returned to the United States in 1824, he began a tour of the country which rivaled the frenzy of audiences at music concerts today. Congress eventually paid Lafayette for his war service. He was given two checks, one for $120,000 and one for $80,000 ("MARQUIS DE LAFAYETTE Autograph Letter Signed–LiveAuctioneers").

In addition to Lafayette, another bright note during the horrible winter at Valley Forge was the arrival of Baron (Freiherr) Friedrich Wilhelm von Steuben, once a member of the elite General Staff of Frederick the Great, King of Prussia. Bearing a letter of introduction from Benjamin Franklin, von Stuben offered his military skills to the colonists' cause "without pay or rank." Since no standard American training manual existed and since von Steuben spoke little English, he drafted his own manual in French. His aides often worked late into the night, translating his manual into English. Known colloquially as "The Blue Book," his work had the title *Regulations for the Order and Discipline of the Troops of the United States*.

Arriving at Valley Forge from France on February 23, 1778, von Steuben was a drill instructor who was full of energy. He taught the Americans how to aim their muskets with accuracy, how to charge with their bayonets, and how to perform together in compact ranks. Washington saw his troops advance from ragtag soldiers to an imposing presence of organized companies, regiments and brigades, moving with military precision under von Steuben's leadership ("Valley Forge– Wikipedia").

Something laudatory must be said, also, about the loyalty of wives, children, mothers and sisters of the soldiers. Martha Washington, wife of George Washington, arrived at Valley Forge on February 10, 1778. She visited soldiers and organized a sewing circle of women who knitted and patched the soldiers' clothing. These women also served as laundresses, cleaning and mending the soldiers' uniforms. Perhaps their greatest service, however, was the spark they gave to the morale of the soldiers with their presence and their help during the freezing winter months. When marching, women were relegated to the back of the column and were forbidden to ride on wagons. Some women lost their lives on the battlefield, while attempting to obtain goods from dead or wounded soldiers ("Valley Forge–Wikipedia").

After the winter, the Continental Army heard that France was going to help their cause by sending monetary and military supplies to the army. France had signed an alliance pact with the thirteen colonies on February 6, 1778. Hearing of this, the American army repeatedly shouted, "Long live France! Long live the friendly powers! Long live the American States!" ("American Revolution: Valley Forge [1777/8]–Geni")

Though the bitter winter at Valley Forge has been relegated to the history books, it imbued the American soldiers with a strong will to endure, persevere, and later triumph over seemingly insurmountable obstacles and bring independence to the United States. Washington always felt that the strengthening of character of the American army at Valley Forge was what made the army stronger and more bound together. It helped the Americans to win the war ("Valley Forge–Wikipedia"). In homage to the fearless and humble and dedicated George Washington, the following inscription appears at his beloved home, Mount Vernon, which is now a national treasure:

> "Washington, the brave, the wise, the good,
> Supreme in war, in council, and in peace.
> Valiant without ambition, discreet without fear,
> confident without presumption.
> In disaster, calm; in success, moderate, in all, himself.
> The hero, the patriot, the Christian.
> The father of nations, the friend of mankind,
> Who, when he had won all, renounced all,
> and sought in the bosom of his family and of nature, retirement,
> and in the hope of religion, immortality."
> ("George Washington–Christian Soldier")

* * * * * * * * * * * * * *

In an attempt to bring cohesion among the thirteen original colonies after the Revolutionary War, the separate states came together to form the Articles of Confederation in 1781. They agreed to call themselves and their country "The United States of America," continuing the name chosen in the Declaration of Independence. These articles were the new nation's basic charter of government until the Constitution of the United States was created in 1789 ("Articles of Confederation - Wikipedia").

From October of 1787 until May of 1788, some eighty-five essays were written under the pen name, "Publius," in regard to the desirability of a proposed Constitution over the Articles of Confederation. Called the *Federalist Papers,* or The Federalist, these essays were written by Alexander Hamilton, James Madison, and John Jay. They were first published in two New York newspapers, but were republished in numerous newspapers in other states. These colonial leaders attempted to persuade the original thirteen states to ratify the United States Constitution and were instrumental in bringing this about ("*The Federalist* Papers–Wikipedia"). Thomas Jefferson called *The Federalist* "the best commentary on the principles of government which ever was written." ("U. S. Senate: *The Federalist*")

The Declaration of Independence and the U. S. Constitution are both based on the Magna Carta. In 1787, the United States Constitution was drafted by members of a constitutional convention held in Philadelphia, Pennsylvania ("Magna Carta in the United States–American Bar Association"). Chaired by George Washington, other members who prominently figured in the drafting of the Constitution were Alexander Hamilton, Benjamin Franklin, James Madison, George Mason, James Wilson, and Gouverneur Morris ("Our Constitutional Founders/What Would the Founders Think?").

The British statesman William E. Gladstone proclaimed the Constitution as "the most wonderful work ever struck off at a given time by the brain and purpose of man." ("The Constitutional Convention of 1787: A Comprehensive Encyclopedia") This precious document affords to every man, regardless of his station in the world, equal protection under the law. In our ever-changing world, this proclamation has guided the United States in its role as leader of the free world.

In a letter to Bushrod Washington (1762-1829), nephew of George Washington and U. S. Supreme Court associate justice for over thirty years), dated November 10, 1787, George Washington wrote the following thought-provoking words: "The warmest friends and the best supporters the Constitution has, do not contend that it is free from imperfections; but they found them unavoidable and are sensible, if evil is likely to arise therefrom, the remedy must come hereafter; for in the present moment, it is not to be obtained; and, as there is a Constitutional door open for it, I think the people (for it is with them to judge) can as they will have the advantage of experience on their side, decide with as much propriety on the alterations and amendments which are necessary as ourselves. I do not think we are more inspired, have more wisdom, or possess more virtue than those who will come after us." ("Letter to Bushrod Washington/Teaching American History")

In another letter, dated August 29, 1788, to Sir Edward Newenham, Irish politician, conservative reactionary and ardent supporter of the American cause, Washington summed up the thoughts and feelings of his compatriots with the excerpt which follows:

"You will permit me to say, that a greater drama is now acting on this theatre than has heretofore been brought on the American stage, or any other in the world. We exhibit at present the novel and astonishing Spectacle of a whole people deliberating calmly on what form of government will be most conducive to their happiness; and deciding with an unexpected degree of unanimity in favour of a system which they conceive calculated to answer the purpose." ("Documentary History of the Constitution of the United States of...")

Though Thomas Jefferson praised the United States Constitution, he felt that it lacked a Bill of Rights. In a letter dated December 20, 1787, which he wrote to James Madison, he helped to convince Madison that the Constitution needed to be amended. Below is an excerpt from his letter: "I like much the general idea of framing a government which should go on of itself peaceably, without needing continual recurrence to the state legislatures. I like the organization of the government into legislative, judiciary, and executive...I will now tell you what I do not like. First, the omission of a bill of rights, providing clearly and without the aid of sophism for freedom of religion, freedom of the press, protection against standing armies, restriction of monopolies, the eternal and unremitting force of the habeas corpus laws, and trials by jury in all matters of fact triable by the laws of the land and not by the laws of nations." (*The Annals of America* [1784-1796], p. 185)

Again, I ask you, dear Reader, don't you think that God had a hand in fashioning these sacred texts through the people that he placed on earth during their time periods? Do you think these great documents were only happenstance? Do you think that these gifted and good men just happened to live at the same time and just happened to meet to create two of the greatest documents the world has ever known? I see the guiding hand of God, and his revealing nature, in the formation of the United States of America and the documents of its governance. God is the reason for the exceptionalism of America!

* * * * * * * * * * * * *

Also occurring in 1776, during the time period of the American Revolution, a man named Adam Smith (1723-1790) published his book entitled *An Inquiry into the Nature and Causes of the Wealth of Nations*. Adam Smith was a Scottish social philosopher and a pioneer of political economy. He is often cited as the father of modern economics and capitalism and is known as the founder of free market economics ("Adam Smith and *The Wealth of Nations*/ Investopedia"). The modern-day economist, Alan Greenspan, stated that *The Wealth of Nations* was "one of the great achievements in human intellectual history." (*The Wealth of Nations*/Biblical Prosperity)

Though capitalism is not a perfect economic system, it has proven to provide food and medicine and comfort not only to the people of the United States but also the people of the world. It has allowed the United States to become the greatest nation on earth. When tragedy strikes anywhere in the world, the United States is usually first to send food and medicine and personnel to assist those in need.

Chapter Twenty-One

The ugly head of slavery reared itself in the American colonies during their earliest existence. Though at first the settlers used indentured servants, Native Americans, and West Africans to work their tobacco and cotton, they later found that Africans were the best answer to agricultural labor needs in the New World. Indentured servants were too costly, and Native Americans were prone to escape into the surrounding wilderness, in which they knew better how to survive than the Africans ("The Birth of Race-Based Slavery").

Though slavery was not expressly forbidden by the Massachusetts constitution, it was tested in a case, involving one Nathaniel Jennison who was indicted for assault on Quock Walker, a Negro. Jennison defended his assault on the grounds that Walker was his slave. However, his defense was rejected by the Superior Court on the basis that slavery was by inference unconstitutional in the Commonwealth of Massachusetts. Though the case was never officially reported, the opinion of Chief Justice Cushing was recorded in his private notebook with a verdict of "guilty" on the part of Nathaniel Jennison. It was a case that was remembered by some, as events led the nation toward the Civil War. Below is an excerpt from the opinion of Chief Justice Cushing:

"As to the doctrine of slavery and the right of Christians to hold Africans in perpetual servitude, and sell and treat them as we do our horses and cattle, that (it is true) has been heretofore countenanced by the province laws formerly, but nowhere is it expressly enacted or established. It has been a usage - a usage which took its origin from the practice of some of the European nations, and the regulations of British government respecting the then colonies, for the benefit of trade and wealth. But whatever sentiments have formerly prevailed in this particular or slid in upon us by the example of others, a different idea has taken place with the people of America, more favorable to the natural rights of mankind, and to that natural, innate desire of liberty, which with heaven (with regard to color, complexion, or shape of noses)...has inspired all the human race.

"And upon this ground our constitution of government, by which the people of this commonwealth have solemnly bound themselves, sets out with declaring that all men are born free and equal – and that every subject is entitled to liberty, and to have it guarded by the laws, as well as life and property – and in short is totally repugnant to the idea of being born slaves. This being the case, I think the idea of slavery is inconsistent with our own conduct and constitution; and there can be no such thing as perpetual servitude of a rational creature, unless his liberty is forfeited by some criminal conduct or given up by personal consent or contract." ("Quock Walker–Wikipedia")

Slavery has existed in different forms throughout most of the world and throughout human history. North American people had enslaved one another long before Europeans arrived. In Africa, blacks were enslaving one another at the time of America's founding ("Six Inconvenient truths about the U.S. and slavery–Michael Medved"). On the eve of the Civil War 3,000 black slave owners – blacks who owned black slaves –owned 20,000 slaves in 1860 ("Viral post gets it wrong about extent of slavery in 1860/PunditFact").

In his 1995 book, The End of Racism, Dinesh D'Souza includes a poignant example from Africa:

"Perhaps the fairest generalization is that no Africans opposed slavery in principle, they merely opposed their own enslavement. One English activist, who led a campaign to suppress slavery in the Sudan, found Africans unreceptive to his pleas and pressures. It was in vain that I attempted to reason with them against the principles of slavery - they thought it wrong when they were themselves the sufferers, but were always ready to indulge in it when the preponderance of power lay upon their side." ("The End of Racism: Finding Values in An Age of Technoaffluence")

America, then, was like most of the countries of the world in allowing slavery to exist. However, when the War of Independence was fought for the principles named in the Declaration of Independence, it became necessary for America to rid itself of the blight of slavery. George Washington was one of the first to do this.

Like many of the founding fathers, George Washington owned slaves, which numbered 317. Other presidents also owned slaves. They are listed below with the number of their slaves following their names:

Thomas Jefferson: 600
James Madison: 100+
James Monroe: 75
Andrew Jackson: <260
Martin Van Buren: 1
William Henry Harrison: 11
John Tyler: 70
James K. Polk: 25
Zachary Taylor: <150
Andrew Johnson: 8
Ulysses S. Grant: 5

("List of Presidents of the United States who owned slaves– Wikipedia")

(Note: I checked several websites, and the numbers of slaves varied considerably for most of the presidents.)

Though the issue of slavery is sometimes used to discredit the moral fiber of our founding fathers, we must remember that slavery was introduced to America nearly two centuries before the earliest colonies were established ("The Road to the Civil War: Division and Compromise on Slavery"). It was sad irony that while America was trying to free herself from the yoke of servitude to England, men, women, and children were being kept in bondage in our own country. This made America's leaders look inwardly, at themselves, and caused many of them to free their slaves.

Indeed, many of the founding fathers found the institution of slavery abhorrent, as is attested by their writings. Below are quotes from some of our country's early leaders who spoke out against slavery:

"Indeed I tremble for my country when I reflect that God is just." (Thomas Jefferson, *Notes on Virginia,* 1781; updated and changed, 1782-85)

"I never mean, unless some particular circumstance should compel me to it, to possess another slave by purchase, it being among my first wishes to see some plan adopted by which slavery in this country may be abolished by law." (George Washington, letter to J. F. Mercer, Sept. 9, 1786)

"We perceive an existing evil which commenced under our Colonial System, with which we are not properly chargeable, or at all not in the present degree, and we acknowledge the extreme difficulty of remedying it." (James Monroe, 1801)

"I have, through my whole life held the practice of slavery in such abhorrence; that I have never owned a negro or any other slave; though I have lived for many years in times when the practice was not disgraceful; when the best men in my vicinity thought it not inconsistent with their character; and when it has cost me thousands of dollars of the labor and subsistence of free men, which I might have saved by the purchase of negroes at times when they were very cheap."(John Adams, letter to Evans, June 8, 1819)

"We cannot emancipate the slaves of the other states without their consent...(except) by producing a convulsion which would undo us all. We must wait the slow but certain progress of those good principles which are everywhere gaining ground, and which assuredly will ultimately prevail." (William Henry Harrison, 1820)

"What can I do for the cause of God and man, for the progress of human emancipation, for the suppression of the African slave trade? Yet my conscience presses me on; let me but die upon the breach." (John Quincy Adams, 1841)

[Note: Eli Whitney (1765-1825] invented the "cotton engine," or the cotton gin in 1793. This machine could clean as much cotton in a day as fifty people could, working by hand. Of course, this invention revolutionized the cotton industry, making the United States the world's leading cotton grower.]

From the sticky green seeds of the cotton boll, Eli Whitney's hand-cranked machine could separate the white cotton fiber. Excited planters used the gin to seed entire fields planted with cotton. As the demand for raw cotton escalated, more labor was needed to pick it. Slavery, which had been on the wane, made a cruel comeback. ("Cotton Gin and Eli Whitney-Invention-History.com")

In his first draft of the Declaration of Independence, Thomas Jefferson condemned the slave trade, but these words were deleted from the final version ("The Deleted Passage of the Declaration of Independence [1776]/The..."). At the Federal convention of 1787, the issue was raised again but was struck down by Southern slave owners and Northern slave traders ("The Constitution and Slavery–Constitutional Rights Foundation"), thereby delaying its resolution for twenty years. When Jefferson became president, he declared in his sixth annual message of 1806:

"I congratulate you, fellow citizens on the approach of the period at which you may interpose your authority constitutionally to withdraw the citizens of the United States from all further participation in these violations of human rights which have been so long continued on the unoffending inhabitants of Africa, and which the morality, the reputation, and the best interests of our Country, have long been eager to proscribe." ("The Writings of Thomas Jefferson: Being His Autobiography,....")

Though Congress in 1808 prohibited any further importation of slaves, the illegal traffic continued, even after Congress declared it piracy in 1820 ("Act Prohibiting Importation of Slaves–Wikipedia"). By 1860, the slave population of the South was four million, comprising a third of the region's inhabitants. In 1790, the approximate price of a field hand was $200; in 1860, it ranged between $1,200 and $1,800 ("Cotton and Race in the Making of America: The Human Costs of...").

From around the late 1700s to 1865, a system called the Underground Railroad helped many slaves escape. Though neither "underground" nor a "railroad," it was called such because of the secret and swift way in which certain people helped the slaves to escape. Of course, all activities in helping fugitive slaves to escape were illegal. (Note: Most of this information about the Underground Railroad comes from "Underground Railroad–Wikipedia." Other information is noted by other sources.)

As early as 1793, the federal government had passed Fugitive Slave Acts which allowed slave catchers to travel north and force runaways back into slavery. When the Fugitive Slave Act was passed in 1850, assisting or helping hide fugitive slaves became a federal offense. The offender was subject to six months in prison and a $1,000 fine ("Fugitive Slave Act of 1850–Wikipedia").

A Quaker named Levi Coffin was called the "president of the underground railroad." His home in Newport, now Fountain City, Indiana, was on three major escape routes. He helped more than 3,000 slaves escape ("Levi Coffin/Biography, Wife Catharine, and House/*Britannica,*com"). The most famous black leader of the Underground Railroad was Harriet Tubman, an escaped slave herself. She made nineteen trips to the South and helped around 300 slaves escape to freedom ("Harriet Tubman–Black History.com").

The usual routes to freedom ran through Ohio, Indiana, and western Pennsylvania. The goal was to reach Canada by way of Detroit or Niagara Falls, New York. Others sailed across Lake Erie to Ontario from Erie, Pennsylvania, and Sandusky, Ohio. Some runaway slaves in the East followed routes from southeastern Pennsylvania through New England to Quebec ("Underground Railroad–Haworth Family").

The trustees of Oberlin College in Ohio voted in 1835 to admit Negro students. Shortly thereafter, the college became an important station on the Underground Railroad ("Oberlin College[1833-]/ The Black Past: Remembered and Reclaimed"). From 1830-1860, some 50,000 slaves escaped to freedom by way of the Underground Railroad ("Underground Railroad–Social Studies for Kids"). By 1860, however, during the time period leading up to the Civil War, 3,953,760 slaves were living in the United States (*The American Cyclopaedia:* A Popular Dictionary of General Knowledge).

Believing that slavery violated Christian principles, eighteenth century Quakers were the first organized abolitionists. People involved with the Underground Railroad used their own terminology in discussing participants, safe places, and other secretive codes. Railroad code words were used, however, to name places along the routes of escape. "Conductors" were those who guided slaves from one place to another. "Safe houses" or "stations" were hiding places where slaves could find food, protection, and a place to sleep. "Station masters" were people who hid fugitive slaves in their own homes, barns, or churches. "Cargo" referred to fugitive slaves who were in the safekeeping of a conductor or station master.

Other code words which enabled fugitive slaves to find their way north included "drinking gourd," which referred to the Big Dipper constellation and "the River Jordan," which referred to the Ohio River. The Ohio River was a hub of activity in regard to the Underground Railroad. Canada, a final safe haven for many fugitive slaves, was called the "Promised Land." ("History/National Underground Railroad Freedom Center") Many notable people participated in the Underground Railroad, including John Fairfield of Ohio, the son of a slaveholding family in Virginia ("John Fairfield [Abolitionist]–Wikipedia").

* * * * * * * * * * * * * *

James Smith, a Methodist minister and a member of a family of wealthy Virginia planters, explored parts of Pennsylvania and Kentucky and Ohio during the years 1783-1797. Though Smith used slaves on his plantation, he felt that it was wrong and added his voice to the anti-slavery movement that had America in its grip, after the Revolutionary War. An excerpt from his journals of 1795 and 1797 appears below:

"Yes, I anticipate, O land, the rising glory of thy unequaled fame. Thy forests, now wild and uncultivated, soon shall the hand of industry sow with the golden grain. Thy unequaled soil, cultivated by the fostering hands of freemen, shall e'er long display its beauties and yield an increase worthy a land of liberty. Thy stately trees, habituated for ages to lie and rot, shall e'er long raise the lofty dome and be fashioned into curious workmanship by the hand of the ingenious artist. Thy large and noble rivers, which silently flow in gentle currents, shall e'er long waft thy rich products to distant markets in foreign climes; and thou, beautiful Ohio, shalt stand an impenetrable barrier to guard this sacred land. And though the tears of the oppressed on thy southeastern border may help increase thy crystal tide, yet the galling yoke, should it attempt to cross thy current, shall sink beneath thy wave and be buried in thy bosom. The voice of the oppressor may spread terror and dismay throughout the eastern and southern states, but farther than thy delightful banks it cannot, it dare not, it shall not be heard. Yes, in thee, O thrice happy land, shall be fulfilled an ancient prophecy.

'The wilderness and the solitary place shall be glad and the desert shall rejoice, and blossom as the rose...the glory of Lebanon shall be given unto it, the excellency of Carmel and Sharon...for in the wilderness shall waters break out, and streams in the desert...There the prisoners rest together; they hear not the voice of the oppressor.' (Isaiah 35; Job 3)

"I must now leave this fair land of happiness with offering to Heaven this humble request: May the foot of pride never come against thee, nor human blood stain thy lovely plains. May the scourge of war never desolate thee, nor cruel tyrants raise their banners here. May the aged never feel the loss of liberty, nor the yoke of slavery rest on the necks of thy children. May thy gates remain open to the oppressed of all nations and may those that flock thither be the excellent ones of the earth; and if the still continued oppressions of enlightened Virginia should at length bring down the just judgments of an incensed Deity, may it be when I or those that pertain unto me have found an asylum in thy peaceful borders..." (*The Annals of America* [1797-1820], p.11)

* * * * * * * * * * * * *

Extraordinary territorial growth of the United States occurred during the early 1800s. During Thomas Jefferson's first term as president of the United States, in 1803, he acquired the Louisiana Purchase, which included part or all of fifteen states. From the time when Jefferson first became president in 1801, he began planning an expedition to chart a route through the Louisiana Territory and the Oregon region. His plan included gathering information about the regions and establishing communication with the Indians who lived in them. (Note: Much of the information about the Lewis and Clark Expedition was found on the website ("Lewis and Clark Expedition").

At the behest of Thomas Jefferson, the Lewis and Clark expedition began in May of 1804 and ended in September of 1806. Sponsored by the government, it was led by U. S. Army officers Meriwether Lewis and William Clark. They traveled around 8,000 miles and explored vast wilderness of what is now the Northwestern United States.

Lewis studied how to classify plants and animals and how to determine geographical position by observing the stars. Clark recruited about fifty skilled woodsmen and hunters, used to manual labor and military discipline. Their large flat-bottomed keelboat carried medicine, food, scientific instruments, weapons and presents for the Indians.

During the winter, a French-Canadian trader named Toussaint Charbonneau and his wife, Sacagawea, a Shoshone Indian, joined the expedition. Sacagawea was expecting a child when she joined the expedition and had hiked and toured with the group up to the day she gave birth. When she began suffering violent labor pains and prolonged labor, Captain Lewis tried to think of something to help her, as no physician was with them. Another French trapper called Jessom crumbled off a small piece of one of the rings from Lewis' prized rattler specimen collection and mixed it with water. This provided the necessary propulsion for the birth of Sacagawea's healthy baby boy ("Sacagawea gives birth to Pompey–Feb. 11, 1805–HISTORY.com").

While watching a television program about the Lewis and Clark expedition, I heard that Sacajawea carried her infant son on her back a thousand miles during the trip. This was also verified in the online ("SparkNotes: Before the Expedition"). She was a remarkable and valuable member of the expedition.

In 1805, the party continued west with thirty-three people in two piroques (dugouts) and six newly-built canoes. The other members of the expedition returned to St. Louis with the keelboat, loaded with plant, animal, and mineral specimens and with maps and reports for President Jefferson. Also included were live magpies and a prairie dog.

The Idaho mountains were the most treacherous part of the journey. The explorers had to lead their horses along rocky, narrow mountain paths. Some of the horses lost their footing and fell to their deaths, taking with them precious supplies and equipment. The explorers were often hungry and finally killed and ate their pack horses ("Lewis and Clark in Idaho").

The United States claimed the Oregon region as a result of the expedition. It also made possible the great pioneer movement that settled the West in the mid-1800s. Lewis' and Clark's journals of the expedition describe the native peoples of the West, the natural resources, and information on scientific matters. Though first published in 1814 in an edited version, they were published in their entirety in 1905 ("The Journals of Lewis and Clark: Almost Home/ Journals of the Lewis..."). As a reward for his service, Meriwether Lewis was appointed governor of the Upper Louisiana Territory by Jefferson in 1807. Clark was appointed Indian agent and brigadier general of militia in the Louisiana Territory. In 1809, Lewis either was murdered or committed suicide. ("Meriwether Lewis–Wikipedia").

* * * * * * * * * * * * *

The population of New York City in 1818 was only about 120,000. Old New York had few street lamps which were filled with poor oil and badly trimmed. William E. Dodge, a merchant of New York, said they looked on a dark night like so many lightning bugs and in winter would often go out entirely before morning.

Policemen didn't exist but there were a few watchmen who patrolled the streets until nearly daylight. They would make a round of the city each hour and as the clock struck, they pounded with their clubs three times on the curb and called out, for example, "twelve o'clock and all is well."

Public dirt carts passed by buildings to pick up trash, whereas in the poorer sections of town, swine would roam the streets and eat the garbage ("Dodge–Academic Home Page").

CAN WE FATHOM THE NATURE OF GOD?

* * * * * * * * * * * * * *

As the new century of the 1800s began and the western frontier of the United States was being settled, families would travel by horseback or wagon some twenty to fifty miles from their home places for "camp meetings," where they would listen to traveling preachers. Here, they would camp together for a number of days. The Methodist preacher Francis Asbury (1745-1816) became one of the best circuit riders in America. Subject to ill health all of his life, he had to be tied to the saddle to remain upright during his horseback riding from one place to another ("Christian History and Biography–Christian History Institute").

During these early revivals, many in attendance succumbed to physical displays of "possession," known as "the jerks." These were manifested by "falling, jerking, rolling, barking, and laughing." Lorenzo Dow, an itinerant evangelist and preacher, left an account for posterity of his journey to Knoxville, Tennessee. Here, he first encountered the phenomenon known as "the jerks." These appeared to be involuntary muscle spasms, apparently induced by religious zeal. In his journal entries of February, 1804, Dow wrote about these manifestations and though these excerpts are lengthy, I found them interesting, and I believe you will, too. Please read below:

"I had heard about a singularity called the "jerks" or "jerking exercise," which appeared first near Knoxville in August last, to the great alarm of the people, which reports at first I considered as vague and false. But, at length, like the Queen of Sheba, I set out to go and see for myself, and sent over these appointments into this country accordingly.

"When I arrived in sight of this town, I saw hundreds of people collected in little bodies, and, observing no place appointed for meeting, before I spoke to any, I got on a log and gave out a hymn; which caused them to assemble around in solemn attentive silence. I observed several involuntary motions in the course of the meeting, which I considered as a specimen of the jerks. I rode seven miles behind a man across streams of water and held meeting in the evening, being ten miles on my way.

"In the night I grew uneasy, being twenty-five miles from my appointment for next morning at 11 o'clock. I prevailed on a young man to attempt carrying me with horses until day, which he thought was impracticable, considering the darkness of the night and the thickness of the trees. Solitary shrieks were heard in these woods, which he told me were said to be the cries of murdered persons. At day we parted, being still seventeen miles from the spot, and the ground covered with a white frost.

"I had not proceeded far before I came to a stream of water, from the springs of the mountain, which made it dreadful cold. In my heated state I had to wade this stream five times in the course of an hour, which I perceived so affected my body that any strength began to fail. Fears began to arise that I must disappoint the people, till I observed some fresh tracks of horses, which caused me to exert every nerve to overtake them in hopes of aid or assistance on my journey; and soon I saw them on an eminence. I shouted for them to stop till I came up. They inquired what I wanted. I replied, I had heard there was a meeting at Seversville by a stranger and was going to it. They replied that they had heard that a crazy man was to hold forth there and were going also; and perceiving that I was weary, they invited me to ride. And soon our company was increased to forty or fifty, who fell in with us on the road from different plantations.

"At length I was interrogated whether I knew anything about the preacher. I replied, 'I have heard a good deal about him and have heard him preach, but I have no great opinion of him.' And thus the conversation continued for some miles before they found me out, which caused some color and smiles in the company.

"Thus, I got on to meeting; and, after taking a cup of tea gratis, I began to speak to a vast audience, and I observed about thirty to have the jerks. Though they strove to keep still as they could, these emotions were involuntary and irresistible, as any unprejudiced eye might discern. Lawyer Porter, who had come a considerable distance, got his heart touched under the word, and, being informed how I came to meeting, voluntarily lent me a horse to ride near 100 miles, and gave me a dollar, though he had never seen me before.

"Hence to Marysville, where I spoke to about 1,500; and many appeared to feel the word, but about 50 felt the jerks. At night I lodged with one of the Nicholites, a kind of Quakers who do not feel free to wear colored clothes. I spoke to a number of people at his house that night. While at tea, I observed his daughter (who sat opposite to me at table) to have the jerks, and dropped the teacup from her hand in the violent agitation. I said to her, 'Young woman, what is the matter?' She replied, 'I have got the jerks.' I asked her how long she had it. She observed, 'A few days'; and that it had been the means of the awakening and conversion of her soul by stirring her up to serious consideration about her careless state, and so forth.

"Sunday, February 19, I spoke to Knoxville to hundreds more than could get into the courthouse, the governor being present. About 150 appeared to have the jerking exercise, among whom was a circuit preacher (Johnson) who had opposed them a little before, but he now had them powerfully; and I believe he would have fallen over three times had not the auditory been so crowded that he could not unless he fell perpendicularly.

"After meeting, I rode eighteen miles to hold a meeting at night. The people of this settlement were mostly Quakers, and they had said (as I was informed): 'The Methodists and Presbyterians have the jerks because they sing and pray so much; but we are a still, peaceable people; wherefore we do not have them.' However, about twenty of them came to the meeting to hear one, as they said, somewhat in a Quaker line. But their usual stillness and silence was interrupted, for about a dozen of them had the jerks as keen and as powerful as any I had seen, so as to have occasioned a kind of grunt or groan when they would jerk.

"It appears that many have undervalued the great revival and attempted to account for it altogether on natural principles; therefore, it seems to me (from the best judgment I can form) that God has seen proper to take this method to convince people that He will work in a way to show His power and sent the jerks as a sign of the times, partly in judgment for the people's unbelief and yet as a mercy to convict people of divine realities.

"I have seen Presbyterians, Methodists, Quakers, Baptists, Episcopalians, and Independents exercised with the jerks – gentleman and lady, black and white, the aged and the youth, rich and poor, without exception; from which I infer, as it cannot be accounted for on natural principles, and carries such marks of involuntary motion, that it is no trifling matter. I believe that those who are most pious and given up to God are rarely touched with it, and also those naturalists who wish and try to get it to philosophize upon it are excepted. But the lukewarm, lazy, halfhearted, indolent professor is subject to it; and many of them I have seen who, when it came upon them, would be alarmed and stirred up to redouble their diligence with God; and after they would get happy, were thankful it ever came upon them.

"Again, the wicked are frequently more afraid of it than the smallpox or yellow fever; these are subject to it. But the persecutors are more subject to it than any; and they sometimes have cursed and swore and damned it while jerking. There is no pain attending the jerks, except they resist it, which if they do, it will weary them more in an hour than a day's labor, which shows that it requires the consent of the will to avoid suffering." (*The Annals of America* [1797-1820], p. 208-210)

Chapter Twenty-Two

As the world continued to watch the American experiment of self-government, writers in European nations began to criticize the character of the American people, stating that thirty years of peace and prosperity, since the American Revolution, had brought about American degeneracy. The writers alleged that American character was strong during the hard-fought Revolution but it had weakened considerably since the war. Charles Ingersoll, a Philadelphia lawyer and ardent patriot, detested these critical assessments of America to the extent that he wrote his own analysis of the national American character. To this work, he gave the title "Inchiquin," which was published anonymously as a series of letters in 1810. Below are some excerpts from his last letter:

"History affords no instance of a nation formed originally on such principles, or of such materials, as the American. It is a common opinion that these materials were of the worst species – vagabonds, mendicants, and convicts. But the fact is that the first settlers were mostly of reputable families and good character, who came to America under the auspices of intelligent and distinguished individuals, in the language of their own epic, 'braving the dangers of untraversed seas,' in an honorable and sacred cause. From these sources, the great currents of American population have proceeded, increased much more partially than is commonly supposed, from foreign streams..."

"According to the common course of events, the genius of the American people should be enhanced, not deteriorated, by the peace and prosperity they have enjoyed since the period of their birth as a nation. By sketches of the present state of their religion, legislation, literature, arts, and society, with an aspect never turned from their national characteristics and embracing no further details than are necessary for their exposition, I propose to endeavor to refute the false opinions inferred from their tranquility, and at the same time to exhibit their national character.

"In this age of infidelity and indifference, to call any people a religious people is a license which nothing but a comparative view of the state of religion in this and in other Christian countries can uphold. It is, however, true that the number of persons devoted to pious exercises, from reflection, independent of education and habit, is greater in the United States than in any other part of the world, in proportion to the population; and religious morality is more general and purer here than elsewhere. The political ordinance of religious toleration is one of those improvements in the science of politics for which mankind will acknowledge their obligations to America; and the divorce of church and state is an inestimable pledge for the purity and stability of republican government (*The Annals of America,* 1797-1820, p. 270-274).

* * * * * * * * * * * * * *

The War of 1812 followed closely on the heels of the American War of Independence. The new nationalism of the American colonies motivated the colonists to stand up for themselves, once again, to thwart their intimidation by Great Britain. Causes of the war included British attempts to restrict American trading policies, the Royal Navy's recruitment of American seamen, and America's desire to expand its boundaries ("War of 1812–Facts and Summary–HISTORY.com").

Actually, the United States began the War of 1812 by invading Canada in June of 1812. Hoping to annex Canada to its lands, the poorly trained U. S. Forces were easily defeated by a much smaller army of British regulars, Canadian militia, and natives. The Americans retreated back over the border, but the angry British captured Washington, D. C. and burned the White House ("A British

Perspective/War of 1812/PBS").

Perhaps unbeknownst to many present-day Americans, around 5,000 - 9,000 American sailors were forced into the English Royal Navy, with the majority being legitimate American citizens. Though the fledgling American government protested this practice, British Foreign Secretary Lord Harrowby wrote contemptuously in 1804:

"The pretension advanced by Mr. [Secretary of State James] Madison that the American flag should protect every individual on board of a merchant ship is too extravagant to require any serious refutation." ("War of 1812–Causes–ThoughtCo")

Around 15,000 Americans died as a result of the War of 1812 ("War of 1812–FAQs/Civil War Trust"). Though American troops did repulse invasions in New York, Baltimore, and New Orleans, the British succeeded in the capture and burning of the nation's capital, Washington, D. C., in August of 1814 ("War of 1812–Facts & Summary–HISTORY.com"). If any single heroism shone forth during the War of 1812, it bloomed upon the personage of Dolley Madison (1768-1849), wife of President James Madison and the first of the president's wives to bear the title of "First Lady." Though ladies were usually relegated to the drawing rooms of their homes, during discussions of any depth, and though women's suffrage was over a century away, Dolley Madison was truly ahead of the times ("Dolley Madison–First Ladies–HISTORY.com").

The British were relentless in their determination to bring America to its knees, once more. Again and again, British landing parties teemed ashore, bent upon robbing homes, raping women, and burning public and private property ("War of 1812: British raiders pillage Hampton–*Daily Press*"). Though many Washington residents began packing up families and furniture, Dolley Madison was determined to stay in the capital in the White House.

On August 17, 1814, some 4,000 veteran English troops began a slow, cautious advance on Washington, without a single trained American soldier in the area to oppose them. By then, thousands of Washington's populace were crowding the roads and fleeing the city. President Madison did call out 6,000 militiamen, however, whom he decided to join on their march to confront the British.

In an attempt to keep herself apprised of the situation, Dolley Madison would go up to the White House roof and scan the horizon with a spyglass. Her husband had urged her to save the cabinet papers and every public document which she could cram into her carriage. In the mounting chaos, she wrote a letter to her sister, Lucy, August 23, 1814, describing her situation:

"Dear Sister:

"My husband left me yesterday morng. to join Gen. Winder. He enquired anxiously whether I had courage, or firmness to remain in the President's house until his return on the morrow, or succeeding day, and on my assurance that I had no fear but for him and the success of our army, he left me, beseeching me to take care of myself, and of the cabinet papers, public and private. I have since recd. two dispatches from him, written with a pencil; the last is alarming, because he desires I should be ready at a moment's warning to enter my carriage and leave the city; that the enemy seemed stronger than had been reported, and that it might happen that they would reach the city, with intention to destroy it.

"I am accordingly ready; I have pressed as many cabinet papers into trunks as to fill one carriage; our private property must be sacrificed, as it is impossible to procure wagons for its transportation. I am determined not to go myself until I see Mr. Madison safe, and he can accompany me, as I hear of much hostility towards him... disaffection stalks around us... My friends and acquaintances are all gone, even Colonel C. with his hundred men, who were stationed as a guard in the enclosure.

"French John (a faithful domestic), with his usual activity and resolution, offers to spike the cannon at the gate, and to lay a train of powder which would blow up the British, should they enter the house. To the last proposition I positively object, without being able to make him understand why all advantages in war may not be taken.

"Wednesday Morng., twelve o'clock. Since sunrise I have been turning my spy glass in every direction, and watchg. with unwearied anxiety, hoping to discover the approach of my dear husband and his friends, but, alas! I can descry only groups of military, wandering in all directions, as if there was a lack of arms, or of spirit to fight for their own firesides.

"Three O'clock – Will you believe it, my Sister? We have had a battle or skirmish near Bladensburg, and I am still here, within sound of the cannon! Mr. Madison comes not; may God protect him! Two messengers, covered with dust, come to bid me fly; but I wait for him...At this late hour a wagon has been procured; I have had it filled with the plate and the most valuable portable articles, belonging to the house. Whether it will reach its destination, the "Bank of Maryland," or fall into the hands of British soldiery, events must determine.

"Our kind friend, Mr. Carroll, has come to hasten my departure, and is in a very bad humor with me, because I insist on waiting until the large picture of Gen. Washington is secured, and it requires to be unscrewed from the wall. This process was found too tedious for these perilous moments; I have ordered the frame to be broken, and the canvas taken out. It is done, and the precious portrait placed in the hands of two gentlemen of New York, for safe keeping. And now, dear sister, I must leave this house, or the retreating army will make me a prisoner in it by filling up the road I am directed to take. When I shall again write to you, or where I shall be tomorrow, I cannot tell!" (Letter from Dolley Madison to Lucy Todd [August 23, 1814]")

(Note: Using several sources for information about Dolley Madison's role in the War of 1812, I noticed several discrepancies. Dolly Madison had three sisters. One source stated that the letter above was written to her sister, Lucy, another to her sister, Anna. Another source stated that Dolley prepared a feast for the President and his staff, which the British later ate on the White House china. A contradicting Smithsonian source refuted this, as I write below.)

As the boom of the cannon came within earshot of the White House, Dolley Madison began packing a wagon with the red silk draperies of the Oval Room, the silver service, and the blue and gold Lowestoft china which she had purchased for the President and his staff. As she feverishly packed treasures of the White House, "two messengers covered with dust" came from the battlefield, urging her to flee. Still, she refused, telling her servants that if she were a man, she would place a cannon in every window of the White House and would fight to the bitter end.

However, with the arrival of Major Charles Carroll, who urged her to leave, she finally agreed. It was then that she ordered servants to retrieve the Gilbert Stuart portrait of George Washington in the state dining room. She told Carroll that it must not be abandoned to the British to be mocked and desecrated. Since the painting was screwed to the wall, and without proper tools to remove it, she ordered that the frame be broken. At this point, two more friends – Jacob Barker, a wealthy ship owner, and Robert G. L. De Peyster – arrived to offer their help. Dolley entrusted the painting of Washington to these two men, hurriedly instructing them to conceal it from the British at all costs. They were to transport the painting to safety in a wagon. As Dolley reached the door of the White House, according to an account she gave to her grandniece, Lucia B. Cutts, she spied a copy of the Declaration of Independence in a display case. With haste, she placed it in one of her suitcases.

Once outside, a free African-American named Jim Smith galloped in from the battlefield on a horse covered in sweat. "Clear out! Clear out!" he shouted. The British were then only a few miles away.

In the middle of a thunderstorm, Dolley left the White House and met her husband at their predetermined meeting place. Here, they watched the burning of the city and the White House, though the rain helped in controlling the flames. Although they returned to Washington only three days later, they could not take up residence in the White House, but lived out the rest of President Madison's term in the city's Octagon House ("When Dolley Madison Took Command of the White House/History…").

* * * * * * * * * * * * *

Battle weary from the war with France, headed by Napoleon, the English finally agreed to a truce with the United States. When the Treaty of Ghent was signed on February 17, 1815, many U. S. Citizens celebrated the War of 1812 as a "second war of independence," beginning an era of patriotism and national pride ("War of 1812–Facts & Summary–HISTORY/.com").

The War of 1812 was also the event which inspired Francis Scott Key to write the words of "The Star-Spangled Banner" on the back of a letter in his pocket. Key was a witness to the last enemy fire at Fort McHenry, as he was being held prisoner on a British ship. As he watched the bombardment of the fort, he waited for some sign of America's victory. When the dawn came, he could see the American flag, battered but still waving over the fort. Though sung for its inspiration during the Civil War and other national crises, "The Star-Spangled Banner" was not adopted as our national anthem until March 3, 1931 ("Francis Scott Key: how 'The Star Spangled Banner' Came to be Written...").

* * * * * * * * * * * * * *

The question of slavery continued to haunt the American colonies, and more and more people urged its abolition. In May of 1818, the General Assembly of the Presbyterian Church took a leading role in issuing an adamant demand for its abolishment. Several excerpts from the report appear below:

"We consider the voluntary enslaving of one part of the human race by another as a gross violation of the most precious and sacred rights of human nature, as utterly inconsistent with the law of God which requires us to love our neighbor as ourselves; and as totally irreconcilable with the spirit and principles of the Gospel of Christ, which enjoin that '**all things whatsoever ye would that men should do to you, do ye even so to them**.' (Matthew 7:12) Slavery creates a paradox in the moral system. It exhibits rational, accountable, and immortal beings in such circumstances as scarcely to leave them the power of moral action. It exhibits them as dependent on the will of others whether they shall receive religious instruction, whether they shall know and worship the true God, whether they shall enjoy the ordinances of the gospel, whether they shall perform the duties and cherish the endearments of husbands and wives, parents and children, neighbors and friends, whether they shall preserve their chastity and purity, or regard the dictates of justice and humanity. Such are some of the consequences of slavery, consequences not imaginary but which connect themselves with its very existence."

"From this view of the consequences resulting from the practice into which Christian people have most inconsistently fallen of enslaving a portion of their brethren of mankind, for 'God hath made of one blood all nations of men to dwell on the face of the earth' it is manifestly the duty of all Christians who enjoy the light of the present day, when the inconsistency of slavery, both with the dictates of humanity and religion, has been demonstrated, and is generally seen and acknowledged, to use their honest, earnest, and unwearied endeavors to correct the errors of former times, and as speedily as possible to efface this blot on our holy religion, and to obtain the complete abolition of slavery throughout Christendom, and if possible throughout the world." (*The Annals of America* [1797-1820], p. 507-508)

During this time period, the slave ships were continuing to bring African slaves over the wide Atlantic Ocean to the American colonies to work the cotton and tobacco fields. A slave named Olaudab Equiano, later named Gustavus Vassa, was one of the few slaves who became educated and kept a journal. In some of his writings of 1791, he described the slave ship which brought him to America. Oh, Reader, I cannot imagine being on such a ship. Yes, it is lengthy, but also enlightening. Below are excerpts from his journal:

"The first object which saluted my eyes when I arrived on the coast was the sea, and a slave ship, which was then riding at anchor and waiting for its cargo. These filled me with astonishment, which was soon converted into terror when I was carried on board. I was immediately handled and tossed up to see if I were sound by some of the crew; and I was now persuaded that I had gotten into a world of bad spirits, and that they were going to kill me. Their complexions, too, differing so much from ours, their long hair, and the language they spoke (which was very different from any I had ever heard) united to confirm me in this belief. Indeed, such were the horrors of my views and fears at the moment that, if 10,000 worlds had been my own, I would have freely parted with them all to have exchanged my condition with that of the meanest slave in my own country. When I looked round the ship, too, and saw a large furnace of copper boiling, and a multitude of black people of every description chained together, every one of their countenances expressing dejection and sorrow, I no longer doubted of my fate; and, quite overpowered with horror and anguish, I fell motionless on the deck and fainted.

"When I recovered a little, I found some black people about me, who I believed were some of those who had brought me on board and had been receiving their pay; they talked to me in order to cheer me, but all in vain. I asked them if we were not to be eaten by those white men with horrible looks, red faces, and long hair. They told me I was not; and one of the crew brought me a small portion of spirituous liquor in a wine glass, but, being afraid of him, I would not take it out of his hand. One of the blacks, therefore, took it from him and gave it to me, and I took a little down my palate, which, instead of reviving me, as they thought it would, threw me into the greatest consternation at the strange feeling it produced, having never tasted any such liquor before. Soon after this, the blacks who brought me on board went off and left me abandoned to despair.

"I now saw myself deprived of all chance of returning to my native country, or even the least glimpse of hope of gaining the shore, which I now considered as friendly; and I even wished for my former slavery in preference to my present situation, which was filled with horrors of every kind, still heightened by my ignorance of what I was to undergo. I was not long suffered to indulge my grief. I was soon put down under the decks, and there I received such a salutation in my nostrils as I had never experienced in my life; so that, with the loathsomeness of the stench and crying together, I became so sick and low that I was not able to eat, nor had I the least desire to taste anything. I now wished for the last friend, death, to relieve me; but soon, to my grief, two of the white men offered me eatables; and, on my refusing to eat, one of them held me fast by the hands and laid me across, I think, the windlass, and tied my feet, while the other flogged me severely." (*The Annals of America* [1784-1796], p. 576-577)

Gustavus Vassa also recounted in his narrative a chilling episode which took place on another slave ship, when the horrors of the slave trade became more widely known. The slave ship *Zong* left Sao Tome (off West Africa) in August of 1781 with 442 slaves. Disease ravaged the ship, leaving sixty slaves and seven crewmen dead. Many of the surviving slaves were dying.

Knowing that insurance would not pay for sick slaves or slaves killed by illness, but it would pay for slaves who had drowned, the captain ordered fifty-four Africans thrown overboard. The next day he drowned forty-two more, followed by another thirty-six on the third day. When the captain arrived in Liverpool, the *Zong's* owners filed an insurance claim for 132 drowned slaves.

Though Gustavus Vassa attempted to right this terrible wrong, he was unsuccessful, for no one would listen to a black man's pleas for justice. However, later, a British judge ruled against the *Zong*'s owners, claiming that the captain and crew were at fault ("*Zong* Massacre–Wikipedia"). The fictional movie *Belle* which premiered in 2013 was based on this event. Known as the *Zong* massacre, this case was seen to contribute to the abolition of slavery in Britain ("*Belle* 2013 film– Wikipedia").

As America continued to progress in its self-governance and in its expansion to the West, the specter of slavery still haunted its upward spiral. On July 4, 1829, William Lloyd Garrison, at the age of twenty-four, became a militant crusader for "abolition now," when he delivered an address on slavery called "The Dangers of the Nation." Several passages from this speech appear below:

"Fifty-three years ago, the Fourth of July was a proud day for our country. It clearly and accurately defined the rights of man; it made no vulgar alterations in the established usages of society; it presented a revelation adapted to the common sense of mankind; it vindicated the omnipotence of public opinion over the machinery of kingly government; it shook, as with the voice of a great earthquake, thrones which were seemingly propped up with atlantean pillars; it gave an impulse to the heart of the world, which yet thrills to its extremities.

"Sirs, I am not come to tell you that slavery is a curse,

debasing in its effect, cruel in its operation, fatal in its continuance. The day and the occasion require no such revelation. I do not claim the discovery as my own, that 'all men are created equal,' and that among their inalienable rights are 'life, liberty, and the pursuit of happiness.' Were I addressing any other than a free and Christian assembly, the enforcement of this truth might be pertinent. Neither do I intend to analyze the horrors of slavery for your inspection, nor to freeze your blood with authentic recitals of savage cruelty. Nor will time allow me to explore even a furlong of that immense wilderness of suffering which remains unsubdued in our land. I take it for granted that the existence of these evils is acknowledged, if not rightly understood. My object is to define and enforce our duty as Christians and philanthropists...." (*The Annals of America* [1821-1832], p. 303-304)

****

During the early 1800s, patriotic Americans heralded the production of art, architecture, and literature based on American themes and created by Americans. This was likely due to the belief by intellectuals both in the United States and in Europe that the United States lacked its own cultural heritage, that her culture was imitative of European culture. Charles Ingersoll, a Philadelphia lawyer, did not subscribe to this belief. Rather, he felt that America's greatness derived from her political, social, and educational institutions and in her technological inventiveness.

On October 18, 1823, he spoke to the American Philosophical Society at Philadelphia on the topic "A Discourse Concerning the Influence of America on the Mind." It attracted worldwide attention. Below are several excerpts:

"Among the curiosities of American literature, I must mention the itinerant book trade. There are, I understand, more than 200 wagons which travel through the country, loaded with books for sale. Many biographical accounts of distinguished Americans are thus distributed. Fifty thousand copies of Mr. Weems' *Life of Washington* have been published and mostly circulated in this way throughout the interior."

"I may be allowed, however, to say that the cotton gin has been of more profit to the United States than ten times all they ever received by internal taxation; that our grain-mill machinery, applied to the great staples of subsistence, is very superior to that of Europe; that there are in the Patent Office models of more than twenty different power looms, of American invention, operated on and weaving solely by extraneous power – steam, water, wind, animals, and otherwise; and that the English machines for spinning have been so improved here that low-priced cottons can be manufactured cheap enough to undersell the English in England after defraying the charges of transportation. Where American ingenuity has been put to trial, it has never failed. In all the useful arts and in the philosophy of comfort – that word which cannot be translated into any other language, and which, though of English origin, was reserved for maturity in America – we have no superiors. If laborsaving machinery has added the power of a hundred millions of hands to the resources of Great Britain, what must be the effect of it on the population and means of the United States? Steam navigation, destined to have greater influence than any triumph of mind over matter, equal to gunpowder, to printing, and to the compass, worthy to rank in momentum with religious reformation, and civil liberty, belongs to America."

"I shall conclude with some views of the American church.... In estimating the progress and condition of the mind in America...I have neither disposition nor occasion to deny that the condition of religion is one of the best tests of the general intellectual state. Independently of their help in the cure of souls, the clergy have always rendered the most important services to the human understanding. Learning and science were long in their exclusive care. In those periods when the mind was most depressed, the church was the chancery of its preservation. To it, we owe nearly all the best relics of ancient learning; from it, we still receive much of our education; for here, as elsewhere, most of our teachers are ecclesiastics...."

"Still less, however, than national disparagement was national vanity the shrine of my sacrifice. Comparative views are indispensable. I might have compared America now with America forty years ago, which would have presented a striking and enlivening contrast. But I preferred the bolder view of America compared with Europe, disclaiming, however, invidious comparisons, which have been studiously avoided. The cause asserted is of too high respect to be defended by panegyric or avenged by invective. The truth is an ample vindication. Let us strive to refute discredit by constant improvement. Let our intellectual motto be that naught is done while aught remains to be done; and our study, to prove to the world that the best patronage of religion, science, literature, and the arts, of whatever the mind can achieve, is *self-government*." (*The Annals of America* [1821-1832], p. 98-103)

However, in 1829, Thomas Carlyle wrote an article attacking the pernicious influence of technology on the lives of Americans. In his "Signs of the Times," Carlyle deplored the effects that mechanism and technology had on the human mind and soul. He feared that man's never-ending quest for technology would subordinate his spiritual nature to his physical needs.

Feeling that this article needed a strong rebuttal, Timothy Walker, a lawyer and New England scholar, wrote a reply entitled "Defense of Mechanical Philosophy" in July of 1831. In this article, he stated,

"The smaller the number of human beings, and the less the time it requires to supply the physical wants of the whole, the larger will be the number and the more the time left free for nobler things." The final paragraphs of this timely article (which still holds true today!) agree with the premise of this book, i.e. that God's nature is revealed in placing certain people in crucial time periods upon the earth to bring about the advancement of civilization...and his kingdom: "But let us not be misunderstood. The condition we speak of is not one of perfection. This we neither believe in nor hope for. Supposing it possible in the nature of things, it would be anything but desirable; for with nothing left to achieve or gain, existence would become empty and vapid. But if, with this explanation, our views should pass for visionary, we cannot help it. We cannot go back to the origin of mankind and trace them down to the present time without believing it to be a part of the providence of God that His creatures should be perpetually advancing. The first men must have been profoundly ignorant except so far as the supreme Being communicated with them directly. But with them commenced a series of inventions and discoveries which have been going on up to the present moment. Every day has beheld some addition to the general stock of information. When the exigency of the times has required a new truth to be revealed, it has been revealed.

"Men gifted beyond the ordinary lot have been raised up for the purpose: witness Cadmus, Socrates, and the other sages of Greece; Cicero and the other sages of Rome; Columbus, Galileo, Bacon, Newton, and the other giant spirits of modern times. We cannot regard it as an abuse of language to call such men inspired, that is, preeminently endowed beyond all their contemporaries and moved by the invisible agency of God to enlighten the world on subjects which had never, till they spoke, occupied the minds of men. In other words, we believe that the appearance of such men, at the exact times when all things were ready for the disclosures they were to make, was not the result of accident but the work of an overruling Providence. And if such had been the beneficent operation of Providence upon the minds of men in all past times – how can we, without irreverence, adopt any other conclusion than that He, who changes not, will still continue, through all future time, to make known through gifted men, as fast as the world is prepared to receive them, new truths from His exhaustless store?" (*The Annals of America* [1821-1822], p. 452)

On February 28, 1830, Zelotes Fuller, a Philadelphia Universalist, spoke out against what he considered to be an attack on the First Amendment, when he delivered a Washington birthday address. Below are excerpts from this speech:

"No government under heaven affords such encouragement as that of America to genius and enterprise, or promises such rich rewards to talent and industry. Here, if a man rise to eminence, he rises by merit and not by birth, nor yet by mammon. This is as it ought to be – this is perfect justice. By the liberal government of our country, ample provision is made for the encouragement of the honest and ingenious artist, and due support is given to every laudable undertaking. Here, talent is not frowned into silence or trampled in the dust for the want of gold to support its dignity, nor for the want of noble parentage but commands the respectful attentions of all the truly wise and candid, however obscure the corner from whence it emanates, and receives that encouragement and support from a generous government to which it is justly and lawfully entitled."

"Brethren and friends of America! Something more than half a century ago, Washington and his distinguished companions nobly asserted, and more nobly defended, the rights and privileges we have been considering. The names of these men and their unwearied exertions in the cause of freedom are worthy of our highest admiration, and deserve to pass down the current of time to other generations, that they may live forever in the grateful recollections of all the most virtuous of the human race. May we and our children rise up and call them blest – rise up and rally round the institutions they have given us and prove ourselves worthy to be called their sons. May we preserve these rights and privileges, and hand them unimpaired down to the generation that shall come after us as a priceless inheritance, yea, the richest earthly boon to man."

"Proud, happy, thrice happy America! the home of the oppressed, the asylum of the emigrant where the citizens of every clime and the child of every creed roam free and untrammeled as the wild winds of heaven, baptized at the font of liberty in fire and blood; cold must be the heart that thrills not at the mention of thy name! Search creation around, my countrymen, and where do you find a land that presents such a glorious scene for contemplation! Look at our institutions, our seminaries, our agricultural and commercial interests, and above all, and more than all, look at the gigantic strides we are making in all that ennobles humankind! When the old world with its pride, pomp, and circumstance shall be covered with the mantle of oblivion; when thrones shall have crumbled, and dynasties shall have been forgotten; then will our happy America, we trust, stand amid regal ruin and national desolation, towering sublime like the last mountain in the deluge; majestic, immutable, and magnificent, in the midst of blight, ruin, and decay - the last remnant of earth's beauty - the last resting place of liberty and the light of heaven!" (*The Annals of America* [1821-1832], p. 355-361)

Chapter Twenty-Three

To give you, my Reader, an idea of the behavior of people in America during the early 1800s, we have an eyewitness account of President Andrew Jackson's inauguration in March of 1829. Mrs. Samuel Harrison Smith, known as the grande dame of Washington society, wrote a surprising and "horrified" description of that day in a letter to a friend. It is surprisingly insightful about the manners (or lack thereof) of the populace during that time period. Excerpts appear below:

"But I will not anticipate, but will give you an account of the inauguration in mere detail. The whole of the preceding day, immense crowds were coming into the city from all parts, lodgings could not be obtained, and the newcomers had to go to Georgetown, which soon overflowed, and others had to go to Alexandria. I was told the Avenue and adjoining streets were so crowded on Tuesday afternoon that it was difficult to pass.

"A national salute was fired early in the morning, and ushered in March 4. By 10 o'clock, the Avenue was crowded with carriages of every description, from the splendid baronet and coach, down to wagons and carts, filled with women and children, some in finery and some in rags, for it was the people's president, and all would see him; the men all walked.

"The day was...delightful, the scene animating, so we walked backward and forward, at every turn meeting some new acquaintance and stopping to talk and shake hands...We continued promenading here until near three, returned home unable to stand, and threw ourselves on the sofa.

"Someone came and informed us the crowd before the president's house was so far lessened that they thought we might enter. This time we effected our purpose. But what a scene did we witness! The majesty of the people had disappeared, and a rabble, a mob, of boys, Negroes, women, children– scrambling, fighting, romping. What a pity, what a pity! No arrangements had been made, no police officers placed on duty, and the whole house had been inundated by the rabble mob. We came too late.

"The President, after having been *literally* nearly pressed to death and almost suffocated and torn to pieces by the people in their eagerness to shake hands with Old Hickory, had retreated through the back way, or south front, and had escaped to his lodgings at Gadsby's. (Note: Gadsby's Tavern, named for the Englishman, John Gadsby, was a tavern and hotel known for its warm hospitality. It was the center of political, social, and cultural life for nearly a century.) Cut glass and china to the amount of several thousand dollars had been broken in the struggle to get the refreshments. Punch and other articles had been carried out in tubs and buckets, but had it been in hogsheads it would have been insufficient; ice creams and cake and lemonade for 20,000 people, for it is said that number were there, though I think the estimate exaggerated. Ladies fainted, men were seen with bloody noses, and such a scene of confusion took place as is impossible to describe, those who got in could not get out by the door again but had to scramble out of windows.

"At one time, the President, who had retreated and retreated until he was pressed against the wall, could only be secured by a number of gentlemen forming around him and making a kind of barrier of their own bodies; and the pressure was so great that Colonel Bomford, who was one, said that at one time he was afraid they should have been pushed down or on the President. It was then the windows were thrown open and the torrent found an outlet, which otherwise might have proved fatal.

"This concourse had not been anticipated and therefore not provided against. Ladies and gentlemen only had been expected at this levee, not the people en masse. But it was the people's day, and the people's President, and the people would rule. God grant that one day or other the people do not put down all rule and rulers. I fear, enlightened freemen as they are, they will be found, as they have been found in all ages and countries where they get the power in their hands, that of all tyrants, they are the most ferocious, cruel, and despotic. The noisy and disorderly rabble in the president's house brought to my mind descriptions I had read of the mobs in the Tuileries and at Versailles. I expect to hear the carpets and furniture are ruined, the streets were muddy, and these guests all went thither on foot." *(The Annals of America* [1821-1832], p. 288-290)

* * * * * * * * * * * * * *

The Englishman James Smithson (c. 1765-1829) left a bequest to found an institution under his name in Washington, D. C. However, Congress waited until 1846 to set up the Smithsonian Institution, under a board of regents, with Joseph Henry, scholar and physicist, as its first secretary and director. Henry developed and guided the institution for the next thirty-three years under the terms of Smithson's will, which determined "an Establishment for the increase and diffusion of knowledge among men." In 1904, Smithsonian Regent Alexander Graham Bell brought Smithson's remains to the United States to rest at the institution which his bequest created ("James Smithson, Founding Donor/Smithsonian Institution Archives").

The Smithsonian is the world's largest museum and research complex, consisting of nineteen museums and galleries, the National Zoological Park, and nine research facilities. Its mission and vision is, as follows: "Shaping the future by preserving our heritage, discovering new knowledge, and sharing our resources with the world." ("AKA/Strategy–Smithsonian")

Its governance consists of the following: the Chief Justice of the United States, the Vice-President of the United States, three members of the United States Senate, three members of the United States House of Representatives, and nine citizens. The Board of Regents meets at least four times a year and typically convenes in the

Regents Room ("Smithsonian Institution–Government Information Fine Art--LibGuides...").

* * * * * * * * * * * * * * *

As the fledgling United States of America struggled to define itself on the world stage, the prospect of disunity haunted the very fabric of the republic. Some leaders, especially those in the South, such as Robert Haynes of South Carolina, upheld the idea of strict constructionism, asserting that "there is no evil more to be deprecated than the consolidation of this government." This began a debate that featured Daniel Webster of Massachusetts, who delivered one of the most eloquent orations ever delivered in the Senate in January of 1830.

He denied Haynes' belief in the absolute sovereignty of the states and, instead, affirmed the unity of the states and the people under the national government and the final sovereignty of the Constitution. Below are the final paragraphs of Daniel Webster's impassioned oration:

"I profess, sir, in my career hitherto, to have kept steadily in view the prosperity and honor of the whole country, and the preservation of our federal Union. It is to that Union we owe our safety at home, and our consideration and dignity abroad. It is to that Union that we are chiefly indebted for whatever makes us most proud of our country – that Union we reached only by the discipline of our virtues in the severe school of adversity. It had its origin in the necessities of disordered finance, prostrate commerce, and ruined credit. Under its benign influences, these great interests immediately awoke, as from the dead, and sprang forth with newness of life. Every year of its duration has teemed with fresh proofs of its utility and its blessings. And although our territory has stretched out wider and wider, and our population spread father and farther, they have not outrun its protection or its benefits. It has been to us all a copious fountain of national, social, and personal happiness.

"I have not allowed myself, sir, to look beyond the Union, to see what might be hidden in the dark recess behind. I have not cooly weighed the chances of preserving liberty when the bonds that unite us together shall be broken asunder. I have not accustomed myself to hang over the precipice of disunion, to see whether, with my short sight, I can fathom the depth of the abyss below; nor could I regard him as a safe counselor in the affairs in this government whose thoughts should be mainly bent on considering, not how the Union may be best preserved but how tolerable might be the condition of the people when it should be broken up and destroyed. While the Union lasts, we have high, exciting, gratifying prospects spread out before us, for us and our children. Beyond that I seek not to penetrate the veil.

"God grant that in my day, at least, that curtain may not rise! God grant that on my vision never may be opened what lies behind! When my eyes shall be turned to behold for the last time the sun in heaven, may I not see him shining on the broken and dishonored fragments of a once glorious Union; on states dissevered, discordant, belligerent; on a land rent with civil feuds, or drenched, it may be, in fraternal blood! Let their last feeble and lingering glance rather behold the gorgeous ensign of the republic, now known and honored throughout the earth, still full high advanced, its arms and trophies streaming in their original luster, not a stripe erased or polluted, nor a single star obscured, bearing for its motto, no such miserable interrogatory as 'What is all this worth?' nor those other words of delusion and folly, 'Liberty first and Union afterwards'; but everywhere, spread all over in characters of living light, blazing on all its ample folds, as they float over the sea and over the land, and in every wind under the whole heavens, that other sentiment, dear to every true American heart – Liberty and Union, now and forever, one and inseparable!" (*The Annals of America* [1821-1832], p. 354-355)

* * * * * * * * * * * * * *

The young United States had problems with the Barbary pirates which operated off the coast of North Africa as far back as the time of the Crusades. According to legend, these pirates sailed as far as Iceland, plundering merchant ships, attacking ports, and seizing captives as slaves. Most seafaring nations found it easier, and cheaper, to bribe the pirates rather than fight them in a war.

The pirates were largely sponsored by the Arab rulers of Morocco, Algiers, Tunis, and Tripoli.

In the early years of the nineteenth century, Thomas Jefferson decided to halt the payment of tribute. War broke out between the small but determined U. S. Navy and the Barbary Pirates. This, followed by a second war, finally settled the issue. Piracy off the African coast faded from memory, only to resurface in recent years when Somali pirates clashed with the U. S. Navy once again. ("Piracy Attacks surge off Somalia–CNN–CNN.com") However, these early skirmishes of the U. S. Navy in distant lands shaped the perception of the military of the United States as a force to be reckoned with ("Barbary Pirates Battled By U.S. Navy 200 Years Ago–ThoughtCo").

By 1830, American ships were in the forefront of world trading markets. From the stern atmosphere of New England, the ships sailed to the lush islands of the South Pacific for food and water and to Bombay or Canton for cargoes of spices, tea, and silk ("Activities–The Mariners Museum/EXPLORATION through the AGES"). The whaling industry reaped big profits, for Americans needed whale oil for lamps, whalebone for corsets, and spermaceti for candles ("History of Whaling–Wikipedia"). For a sailor drifting a thousand miles from land on a three-year voyage to whaling grounds, scattered from the Indian Ocean to the Bering Straits ("Spatial and Seasonal Distribution of American Whaling and Whales in..."), the sea demanded humility, as suggested by the following quote: "O God, thy sea is so great, and my boat is so small." ("O God, Thy Sea is So Great...–South Fulton Street Church of Christ")

Home ports for whaling were confined to the Atlantic Coast from Long Island to northern Massachusetts. Nantucket, and New Bedford were the most famous whaling towns. Around 329 ships were registered out of the port of New Bedford in the peak year of 1857 ("History of the United States Merchant Marine–Wikipedia").

Whaling was a dangerous business with oar-propelled boats in the midst of a "pod" or herd of monster-size sperm whales. Sometimes a wild chase ensued until the selected whale was harpooned and tons of blubber stripped from its body. The blubber was "tried out" or refined into whale oil in huge kettles on deck. The blubber was cut into blocks called "horse pieces," which were then sliced into "Bible leaves," which were boiled in "try-pots." ("A Whaler's TOIL AT SEA, IN PORT, AND IN MEMORY/Thomas...")

American trade with China was largely conducted by Massachusetts merchants. Until 1842, Canton in south China was the only port where foreign trade was allowed. Chinese merchants built their hongs (monopolistic trading establishments) along the banks of the Pearl River, where tea, silk, and spices were loaded. Opium was also traded, though usually illegally ("Canton: Common and Unusual views by user from Antiques and Fine art..."). The Far East trade led to the design and use of the famed clipper ships that dominated the seas during this time period (*The Annals of America* [1833-1840], p. 522).

* * * * * * * * * * * * * *

During the 1840s, the United States added 1.2 million square miles to its growth, a gain of sixty percent. Though some Americans favored this growth, believing in the "manifest destiny" of America, "from sea to shining sea," many others did not. Some did not want one nation of many states; they preferred for each state to be autonomous ("Manifest Destiny–Weber State University").

As the United States expanded westward, Texas sought to secure its independence from Mexico. A famous battle during this war was fought in 1836 at the Alamo which was built as a Roman Catholic mission in 1718. Hoping to prevent Texas from gaining its independence, General Antonio Lopez de Santa Anna, in command of the Mexican Army, approached San Antonio with an army of over 6,000 soldiers ("Battle of the Alamo–Wikipedia")

The Texans, numbering about 200 men, retreated to the Alamo. Among these brave men were Lieutenant Colonel William Barret Travis and the famous frontiersmen James Bowie and Davy Crockett. The siege of the Alamo lasted thirteen days. All of the Texans who fought died in the battle ("Battle of the Alamo/HistoryNet").

"Remember the Alamo!" became the battle cry that spurred General Sam Houston to gather the army he needed to fight for Texas. He retreated to the east and surprised Santa Anna by turning on the Mexicans and surprising them during their afternoon siesta. In only eighteen minutes, Sam Houston and his army captured or killed most of the Mexican Army of about 1,400 men ("Battle of San Jacinto– United States American History"). The next day, Houston's army captured Santa Anna and forced him to sign a treaty granting Texas its independence. Texas became the 28th state in 1845 ("Mexican American War Timeline– MexicanHistory.org").

However, the United States continued to have border problems with Mexico in regard to Texas. The Mexican War (1846-1848) resulted from decades of disagreements between the United States and Mexico. Also, the U. S. Government claimed that Mexico owed U. S. Citizens about three million dollars, because of lives and property lost in Mexico since Mexico's war for independence ended in 1821. At the end of the war, the United States gained more than 525,000 square miles of territory ("GC3AP16 Whose Side Are You On? [Traditional Cache] in Baja...").

The Mexican War resulted in giving training to many officers who later fought in the Civil War, such as Ulysses S. Grant, William T. Sherman, George B. McClellan, George Gordon Meade, Robert E. Lee, Stonewall Jackson, and Jefferson Davis. Several states and parts of four other states were added to the land size of the United States by the Mexican Cession. However, the war revived the questions and quarrels about slavery. These bitter disagreements became instrumental in events leading up to the Civil War in America ("Mexican War–RootsWeb: Freepages–Ancestry.com").

* * * * * * * * * * * * * *

Though most Americans lived outside the urban centers of the United States, cities increasingly dominated their lives. Most goods made their way slowly to New Orleans on the inland waterways. Towns on the mid-western rivers and the Great Lakes grew into cities. During the 1840s, railroads were built to the Midwest and South, entering Chicago in 1852. Trading cities like St. Louis and

Cincinnati grew rapidly, serving as depots and shipping centers. Lining the railroads were slaughter houses, lumber yards, grain elevators, and cotton warehouses. However, in the absence of public safety standards, epidemics were common, and fires were a constant danger (*The Annals of America* [1841-1849], p. 29-30).

During this time period, S.F.B. Morse had implemented the telegraph, while Louis Daguerre was experimenting with early cameras which produced daguerreotypes. Morse and others were experimenting with cameras made of cigar boxes and spectacle lenses. Soon, most towns had a daguerreotypist at work (*The Annals of America* [1841-1849], p. 40).

From about 1811 - 1840, the Oregon Trail was laid down by traders and fur trappers. It could only be traveled by horseback or on foot. Improvements on the trail in the form of better roads, ferries, bridges and cutoffs made the trip safer and faster each year. Soon, the remote Oregon Territory beckoned to settlers in the Midwest to the extent that the first migration to Oregon occurred in 1843 ("Oregon Trail–Wikipedia"). A party of more than a thousand people converged on Independence, Missouri, with all they could carry of their belongings and with 5,000 cattle to make the overland trip to Oregon. They had 120 wagons, drawn by six ox teams with an average of six yokes to the team and several thousand loose horses and cattle.

Since some pioneers had only a few cattle, they traveled in the light column, whereas those with many cattle joined the heavy or cow column. Under the leadership of Jesse Applegate, he described the journey in an article with the title "A Day with the Cow Column." It gives us an idea of a day spent on the Oregon Trail with the emigrants (*The Annals of America* [1841-1849], p. 89). Selections of this interesting and topical narrative appear below:

"It is 4 A.M.; the sentinels on duty have discharged their rifles – the signal that the hours of sleep are over; and every wagon and tent is pouring forth its night tenants, and slow-kindling smokes begin largely to rise and float away on the morning air. Sixty men start from the corral, spreading as they make through the vast herd of cattle and horses that form a semicircle around the encampment, the most distant perhaps two miles away.

"The herders pass to the extreme verge and carefully examine for trails beyond, to see that none of the animals have strayed or been stolen during the night. This morning no trails lead beyond the outside animals in sight, and by 5 o'clock the herders begin to contract the great moving circle and the well-trained animals move slowly toward camp, clipping here and there a thistle or tempting bunch of grass on the way. In about an hour, 5,000 animals are close up to the encampment, and the teamsters are busy selecting their teams and driving them inside the 'corral' to be yoked. The corral is a circle 100 yards deep, formed with wagons connected strongly with each other, the wagon in the rear being connected with the wagon in front by its tongue and on chains. It is a strong barrier that the most vicious ox cannot break, and in case of an attack of the Sioux would be no contemptible entrenchment.

"From 6 to 7 o'clock is a busy time; breakfast is to be eaten, the tents struck, the wagons loaded, and the teams yoked and brought up in readiness to be attached to their respective wagons. All know when, at 7 o'clock, the signal to march sounds that those not ready to take their proper places in the line of march must fall into the dusty rear for the day."

"It is on the stroke of 7; the rushing to and fro, the cracking of whips, the loud command to oxen, and what seems to be the inextricable confusion of the last ten minutes has ceased. Fortunately everyone has been found, and every teamster is at his post. The clear notes of the trumpet sound in the front; the pilot and his guards mount their horses, the leading division of wagons moves out of the encampment, and takes up the line of march, the rest fall into their places with the precision of clockwork, until the spot so lately full of life sinks back into that solitude that seems to reign over the broad plain and rushing river as the caravan draws its lazy length toward the distant El Dorado."

"But the picture, in its grandeur, its wondrous mingling of colors and distinctness of detail, is forgotten in contemplation of the singular people who give it life and animation. No other race of men with the means at their command would undertake so great a journey; none save these could successfully perform it with no previous preparation, relying only on the fertility of their invention to devise the means to overcome each danger and difficulty as it arose. They have undertaken to perform, with slow-moving oxen, a journey of 2,000 miles."

"It is now 1 o'clock; the bugle has sounded, and the caravan has resumed its westward journey. It is in the same order, but the evening is far less animated than the morning march; a drowsiness has fallen apparently on man and beast; teamsters drop asleep on their perches and even when walking by their teams, and the words of command are now addressed to the slowly creeping oxen in the softened tenor of women or the piping treble of children, while the snores of teamsters make a droning accompaniment.

"But a little incident breaks the monotony of the march. An emigrant's wife, whose state of health has caused Dr. Whitman to travel near the wagon for the day, is now taken with violent illness. The doctor has had the wagon driven out of the line, a tent pitched, and a fire kindled. Many conjectures are hazarded in regard to this mysterious proceeding and as to why this lone wagon is to be left behind. "

"Everyone is busy preparing fires of buffalo chips to cook the evening meal, pitching tents, and otherwise preparing for the night. There are anxious watchers for the absent wagon, for there are many matrons who may be afflicted like its inmate before the journey is over; and they fear the strange and startling practice of this Oregon doctor will be dangerous. But as the sun goes down, the absent wagon rolls into camp, the bright, speaking face and cheery look of the doctor, who rides in advance, declares without words that all is well, and both mother and child are comfortable."

"It is not yet 8 o'clock when the first watch is to be set; the evening meal is just over, and the corral now free from the intrusion of the cattle or horses, groups of children are scattered over it. The larger are taking a game of romps, "the wee toddling things" are being taught that great achievement that distinguishes man from the lower animals. Before a tent near the river a violin makes lively music, and some youths and maidens have improvised a dance upon the green; in another quarter a flute gives its mellow and melancholy notes to the still air, which as they float away over the quiet river seem a lament for the past rather than a hope for the future."

"But time passes; the watch is set for the night; the council of old men has broken up and each has returned to his own quarter. The flute has whispered its last lament to the deepening night, the violin is silent, and the dancers have dispersed. Enamored youth have whispered a tender 'good night' in the ears of blushing maidens or stolen a kiss from the lips of some future bride – for Cupid here as elsewhere has been busy bringing together congenial hearts, and among those simple people he alone is consulted in forming the marriage tie. Even the doctor and the pilot have finished their confidential interview and have separated for the night. All is hushed and repose from the fatigue of the day, save the vigilant guard and the wakeful leader who still has cares upon his mind that forbid sleep." (*The Annals of America* [1841-1849], p. 89-94)

From the 1830s through 1869, an estimated 350,000 pioneers traveled the Oregon Trail. Use of the trail quickly declined, however, when the first railroad was completed. Oregon became the thirty-third state in 1859. Others followed, until Alaska and Hawaii were the last states to enter the union in 1959 ("List of states by date of admission to the Union–Wikipedia")

* * * * * * * * * * * * * *

A blight on the developing character of America was its mistreatment of the indigenous population of Indians, whom the early settlers encountered. When the first Europeans confiscated America's lands as their own, native Indian tribes looked upon the foreigners as encroachers on their land. Some of the Indians were friendly at the outset of the Europeans' arrival, but others resented the white man and his greed in claiming ownership of Indian land ("Native Americans Land*** – Warpaths2Peacepipes").

The United States Constitution, Article 1, Section 8, states that "The Congress shall have power to...regulate commerce with foreign nations, and among the several states, and with the

Indian tribes...." ("Commerce Clause–Wikipedia") Article 3 of the Northwest Ordinance of 1789 stated: "The utmost good faith shall always be observed toward the Indians; their land and property shall never be taken away from them without their consent...but laws founded in justice and humanity shall from time to time be made, for preventing wrongs being done to them..." ("The Utmost Good Faith Clause–America's History in the Making...")

One would think, from reading the lofty and noble words above, that the Indians would have been well treated by the early U. S. Government. However, this was not the case. As the U. S. population expanded to the West, the U. S. Government confiscated more and more Indian lands. Treaties between the U. S. Government and the Indians were made, then repeatedly broken. ("Treaties Made; Treaties broken–Native America/American Indian...")

Though President Andrew Jackson feigned friendship with the unfortunate native Indians, instructing them to call him "Father," and though a Cherokee had saved the president's life during the War of 1812, Andrew Jackson had the southeastern tribes forcibly removed in the 1830s. Known as the five civilized tribes, because of their easier assimilation into the white man's culture, these tribes were the Cherokee, the Creek, the Choctaw, the Chickasaw, and the Seminole. They were relocated in the territory of what is now the State of Oklahoma. The suffering and the hardships during this traumatic exodus became known as the "Trail of Tears." ("Trail of Tears–Wikipedia") As the black man before them had experienced mistreatment by the white man, so did the red man succumb to the white man's cruelty.

Thirteen overland wagon trains, or detachments, of about 1,000 Cherokees each, made the treacherous trip during one of the harshest winters on record. Though some rode horseback or in wagons, many walked the entire journey of over a thousand miles. Even though doctors usually traveled with most of the detachments, some 5,000 or more died from cholera, whooping cough, starvation, dysentery, and typhus. No one knows exactly how many survived nor how many were buried on the trail ("Trail of Tears–Native American History–HISTORY.com").

After the passage of the Indian Removal Act in 1830, an estimated 60,000 Indians, African slaves, white spouses, and Christian missionaries traveled through Arkansas on their way to their allotted lands in the territory of Oklahoma. Of these, around 21,000 were Creek, 16,000 were Cherokee, 12,500 were Choctaw, 6,000 were Chickasaw, 4,200 were Seminole, and an unknown number of Indians from various smaller tribes. The infamous trail was not one distinct road; rather, it was a web of pathways and rivers, usually beginning in the area near Chattanooga, Tennessee, and culminating in the territory of Oklahoma ("Trail of Tears–*Encyclopedia* of Arkansas").

Dear Reader, I did much research about the Cherokee and their roundup for removal when I wrote my novel *In the Lion's Paw*. As I researched and wrote, I often felt the sting of tears in my eyes because of the brutal abuse of the red man. At the same time, missionaries were giving their lives, bringing the knowledge of Christ to these poor people. When I attended a seminar on the American Indian in Rome, Georgia, while doing research for my novel, I asked the speaker about the present-day religion of the Indians now in Oklahoma. I was told that probably 99% were Christian, though she (the speaker who had earned a doctorate) was not a Christian. She informed me that she could not be a Christian because of the mistreatment of her people by those who called themselves Christian.

The fact that 99% of present-day Native Americans are Christians amazed me because of their terrible abuse by Christian people. Obviously, the Word of God was so powerful and the Christian missionaries among them so true to their faith, that the Indians accepted the truth of the Bible and were not deterred by people who did not practice their faith.

Before writing the novel about the Cherokee removal, I made the thousand-mile trip out to Tahlequah, Oklahoma. Of course, I was in an air-conditioned car, but I wanted to see for myself what the Indians encountered in the topography of the land which they were forced to travel. It was mountainous almost all of the way to Indian country, though the steepest ones were in Tennessee. I could only imagine what the Indians went through as they moved dejectedly along the road (then only narrow dirt pathways) and crossed streams and rivers in their wagons or on horseback or on foot. One of the detachments (which I used in the novel) was on the trail over five months.

Today, some 562 federally recognized tribes live in the United States. Around 229 of these diverse tribes, or nations, are located in Alaska; the rest live in thirty-three other states in the U. S. Indian nations are recognized by the U. S. Government as sovereign governments. Treaties and laws have set a basic contract between the United States and Indian nations. Indian nations ceded millions of acres of land that made the U. S. what it is today. From 1887 - 1934, the U. S. Government confiscated more than ninety million acres, nearly two-thirds of reservation lands from the Indian tribes and gave it to settlers, without any compensation to the tribes. However, in return, the tribes obtained the right to self-government on their own lands ("PDF Indian Nations–NCAI").

Sadly, more than a fourth of Indian people today live in poverty. On the reservations, unemployment rates are more than double the population at large. Also, Indian people have the worst health status of any group in our country and the highest rate of homelessness and overcrowding. Indian tribes own more than fifty million acres of land or about two percent of the United States. ("PDF 562 federally recognized tribes–NCAI")

Probably many books could be written about the way Indians have been mistreated since the first Europeans arrived in America. I have briefly addressed this subject because it continues to be a problem which causes Christians to weep and to fear for our country which was settled by Christian emigrants and which has proclaimed Christian values since its inception. I think that most of us, who are Christians, have a gnawing sense of guilt about our country's mishandling of the Native American population, which posed problems for the early European settlers ("The Book of Resolutions of The United Methodist Church 2016").

A number of laws have been passed to protect native cultures and to correct some of past abuses. These include the American

Indian Religious Freedom Act of 1978; the Native American Graves Protection and Repatriation Act of 1990; the Native American Languages Act of 1990; the Tribal Amendments to the National Historic Preservation Act of 1992; as well as Executive Order #13007 on Native American Sacred Sites of 1996; and Executive Order #13175 on Consultation and Coordination with Tribal Governments ("562 federally recognized tribes–NCAI").

The Department of the Interior has terribly mismanaged tribal lands and has lost track of many billions of dollars in logging and mining and other monies that should have gone to American Indian individuals and tribes. A mandate from Congress has charged the Department of the Interior to give an accounting of Indian trust funds. The Department of the Interior also faces a class action lawsuit (Cobell v. Norton) to settle claims from those who are seeking an accurate historical accounting and payment process. In addition to payments to individual plaintiffs, the U.S. Government has paid $900 million to people to buy back about 1.7 million acres, restoring more of the land base of reservations to tribal control ("Cobell v. Salazar–Wikipedia").

* * * * * * * * * * * * * *

In the 1830s, Alexis de Tocqueville (1805-1859), the famous French diplomat, historian and political scientist, traveled to America to discover the reason for the incredible success of our new nation. He was especially impressed by America's religious fervor. Below are some excerpts from his two-volume classic entitled *Democracy in America,* which was written in 1835:

"In the United States, the sovereign authority is religious... there is no country in the world where the Christian religion retains a greater influence over the souls of men than in America, and there can be no greater proof of its utility and of its conformity to human nature than that its influence is powerfully felt over the most enlightened and free nation of the earth."

"I sought for the key to the greatness and genius of America in her harbors...; in her fertile fields and boundless forests; in her rich mines and vast world commerce; in her public school system and institutions of learning. I sought for it in her democratic Congress and in her matchless constitution."

"Not until I went into the churches of America and heard her pulpits flame with righteousness did I understand the secret of her genius and power."

"America is great because America is good, and if America ever ceases to be good, America will cease to be great." ("Alexis de Tocqueville–The Righteous Republic") Note: Some sources dispute Tocqueville's authorship of the last excerpt, but the most reliable one seemed to be the one noted as the source above.

* * * * * * * * * * * * * *

Before the 1830s the Abolition societies in America were small and almost passive. However, William Lloyd Garrison (1805-1879), American journalist, crusader, and editor of the abolitionist newspaper, *The Liberator*, injected a militant tone into the Abolition movement. He demanded that the slave holders immediately, and without any compensation, grant the Negroes freedom and political and social equality within the United States.

The American Anti-Slavery Society convened for the first time in Philadelphia, in early December of 1833, to give doctrinal and administrative strength to the movement. William Lloyd Garrison wrote the first "Declaration" for the Society which adopted it with minor revisions. Within five years the Society had 1,350 local chapters ("Abolitionism–United States History"). Momentum was building toward the ultimate fracture of the union of states over slavery, though some historians inject that states' rights was the real issue that brought about the American War Between the States ("States' Rights/Civil War Trust"). Below are several paragraphs from William Lloyd Garrison's "Declaration":

"More than fifty-seven years have elapsed since a band of patriots convened in this place to devise measures for the deliverance of this country from a foreign yoke. The cornerstone upon which they founded the temple of freedom was broadly this: 'That all men are created equal: and they are endowed by their Creator with certain inalienable rights; that among these are life, liberty, and the pursuit of happiness.' At the sound of their trumpet call 3 million people rose up as from the sleep of death and rushed to the strife of blood, deeming it more glorious to die instantly as freemen than desirable to live one hour as slaves. They were few in number, poor in resources, but the honest conviction that truth, justice, and right were on their side made them invincible."

"Our trust for victory is solely in God. We may be personally defeated, but our principles never. Truth, justice, reason, humanity must and will gloriously triumph. Already a host is coming up to the help of the Lord against the mighty, and the prospect before us is full of encouragement.

"Submitting this declaration to the candid examination of the people of this country, and of the friends of liberty throughout the world, we hereby affix our signatures to it, pledging ourselves that, under the guidance and by the help of Almighty God, we will do all that in us lies, consistently with this declaration of our principles, to overthrow the most execrable system of slavery that has ever been witnessed upon earth; to deliver our land from its deadliest curse; to wipe out the foulest stain which rests upon our national escutcheon; and to secure to the colored population of the United States all the rights and privileges which belong to them as men and as Americans – come what may to our persons, our interests, or our reputations, whether we live to witness the triumph of liberty, justice, and humanity, or perish untimely as martyrs in this great, benevolent, and holy cause." ("Declaration of the National Anti-Slavery Convention (1833. By William...")

****

As the colonies wrestled with the problems of slavery and the growing threat of a major split between the northern and the southern states, specifically over the existence of slavery, people in other countries were lured to the touted land of the free. Immigrants who wanted to be farmers had heard that America was a wonderful land of opportunity, if one could afford to pay $1.25 for an acre of public land. Gjert Hovland emigrated from Norway to the United States before the mid-1830s, settling first in New York, then moving to Illinois. On April 22, 1835, he sent an encouraging letter from the Kendall settlement in New York to one Torjuls Maeland, extracts of which appear below:

"I must take this opportunity to let you know that we are in the best of health, and that both my wife and I are exceedingly well satisfied. Our son attends the English school and talks English as well as the native-born. Nothing has made me more happy and contented than that we left Norway and came to this country. We have gained more since our arrival here than I did during all the time I lived in Norway, and I have every prospect of earning a living here for myself and my family, even if my family becomes larger, so long as God gives me good health."

"We left our home in Norway on June 24, 1831. Sailing from Gothenburg on July 30, we landed in America September 18, and by October 4 we had reached this place in the interior where we now live. The day after my arrival I began to work for an American. In December I bought myself fifty acres of land. I put up a house which we moved into in the month of March 1832. I then set to work with the greatest will and pleasure, for the land was covered with trees. In the fall I planted corn and three bushels of wheat, and in the spring of 1833 we planted about half a bushel of Indian corn and three bushels of potatoes (the latter in May).

"The next fall we harvested fifteen barrels of wheat, six barrels of Indian corn, and fourteen barrels of potatoes. Wheat, which is grown almost everywhere, is used for daily food. It costs from $3 to $4 a barrel, corn costs from $1.50 to $2 a barrel, and potatoes 50 cents a barrel. Oats are $1 a barrel, being used not for human food, but for the cattle and horses. We purchased a cow in April of the first year we were here for $18, from which we milked six cans a day and sometimes more. A pound of butter costs, in the towns, from 8 to 12 skillings, salt pork from 4 to 8 skillings a pound, and meat 4 skillings a pound.

"Land is measured off here with a pole eight ells and six inches long, this being called a rod. An acre measures sixteen rods in length by ten in breadth. One hundred acres, here called a lot, is a piece of land of considerable size. I am certain that from fifty acres here, we harvest many times more than from a gaard in Norway. I believe that an acre is something more than a *tonde saed* in Norway; it takes two bushels of wheat to sow an acre."

"In America you associate with good and kindly people. Everyone has the freedom to practise the teaching and religion he prefers. The only tax a man pays here is on the land he owns, and even that tax is not large. Nor are there other useless expenditures for the support of persons – as in many places in Europe – who are of more harm than benefit to the country. For the fifty acres I sold I paid $1 a year in taxes. On the piece of land we sold there were more trees than I could count of the kind that produces sugar, and these trees were common everywhere. We took no more than we needed for our own use each year. Usually we did this work in March, when the sap begins to rise in the trees. With a small iron we chopped an opening in the bark of the tree, placing under it a piece of hollowed-out wood as a trough. A tree yields from two to three pails of sweet sap a day, and this sap makes sugar, syrup, ale, and vinegar.

"There is much more I could write to you about, but I will close for this time, with hearty greetings from me and my wife and son to you, my relatives, and acquaintances. Let us be happy in heart and consecrated in spirit so that when the race has been run, when the pilgrim's staff has been laid down, we may be worthy of hearing the glorious words: 'Blessed of my Father, come ye and inherit the kingdom and the righteousness prepared for you.' Wherever we may wander in this earthly sphere, let us seek Him who is the true light and life, and follow His voice which calls to our hearts, no matter where we go or stand. Live well in the sight of God: that is my wish as your friend. Greetings to Knud Oppedal and Johannes Hovland and to all who inquire about me." (*The Annals of America* [1833-1840], p. 115-117)

* * * * * * * * * * * * * *

When the lovely English actress, Frances Anne Kemble, married the wealthy Philadelphian, Pierce Mease Butler, in 1824, little did she know that she would join the Abolition Movement in the United States. Her husband having inherited an estate of two islands in Georgia, Fanny Kemble Butler became the mistress of more than seven hundred slaves. Because her husband did not share her scruples about slavery, Fanny poured out her heart in her diary, as she observed the lives of their slaves.

The Butlers later were divorced, and Fanny, as she was called, returned to England. In 1863 she published her diary *Journal of a Residence on a Georgian Plantation* during the years of 1838-1839. Her purpose in publishing the diary was to discourage the British from supporting the Confederacy in the American Civil War and to encourage sympathy for the North. Below are paragraphs taken from her diary, encompassing her candid and compassionate observations of their slaves' lives:

"I must inform you of a curious conversation which took place between my little girl and the woman who performs for us the offices of chambermaid here – of course, one of Mr. _____'s slaves. What suggested it to the child, or whence indeed she gathered her information, I know not; but children are made of eyes and ears, and nothing, however minute, escapes their microscopic observation. She suddenly began addressing this woman.

'Mary some persons are free and some are not (the woman made no reply). I am a free person (of a little more than three years old). I say, I am a free person, Mary – do you know that?'

'Yes, missis.'

'Some persons are free and some are not – do you know that, Mary?'

'Yes, missis, here,' was the reply; 'I know it is so here, in this world.'

"Here my child's white nurse, my dear Margery, who had hitherto been silent, interfered, saying: 'Oh, then you think it will not always be so?'

'Me hope not, missis.'

"I am afraid, E_____, this woman actually imagines that there will be no slaves in heaven; isn't that preposterous, now, when, by the account of most of the Southerners, slavery itself must be heaven, or something uncommonly like it? Oh, if you could imagine how this title 'Missis,' addressed to me and to my children, shocks all my feelings! Several times I have exclaimed: 'For God's sake do not call me that!' And only been awakened by the stupid amazement of the poor creatures I was addressing to the perfect uselessness of my thus expostulating with them; once or twice, indeed, I have done more – I have explained to them, and they appeared to comprehend me well, that I had no ownership over them, for that I held such ownership sinful, and that, though I was the wife of the man who pretends to own them, I was, in truth, no more their mistress than they were mine. Some of them, I know, understood me, more of them did not.

"Our servants – those who have been selected to wait upon us in the house – consist of a man, who is quite a tolerable cook (I believe this is a natural gift with them, as with Frenchmen); a dairywoman, who churns for us; a laundrywoman; her daughter, our housemaid, the aforesaid Mary; and two young lads of from fifteen to twenty, who wait upon us in the capacity of footmen. As, however, the latter are perfectly filthy in their persons and clothes – their faces, hands, and naked feet being literally encrusted with dirt – their attendance at our meals is not, as you may suppose, particularly agreeable to me, and I dispense with it as often as possible. Mary, too, is so intolerably offensive in her person that it is impossible to endure her proximity, and the consequence is that, among Mr. _____'s slaves, I wait upon myself more than I have ever done in my life before. About this same personal offensiveness, the Southerners, you know, insist that it is inherent with the race, and it is one of their most cogent reasons for keeping them as slaves.

"But, as this very disagreeable peculiarity does not prevent Southern women from hanging their infants at the breasts of Negresses, nor almost every planter's wife and daughter from having one or more little pet blacks sleeping like puppy dogs in their very bedchamber, nor almost every planter from admitting one or several of his female slaves to the still closer intimacy of his bed, it seems to me that this objection to doing them right is not very valid. I cannot imagine that they would smell much worse if they were free, or come in much closer contact with the delicate organs of their white fellow countrymen; indeed, inasmuch as good deeds are spoken of as having a sweet savor before God, it might be supposed that the freeing of the blacks might prove rather an odoriferous process than the contrary.

"However this may be, I must tell you that this potent reason for enslaving a whole race of people is no more potent with me than most of the others adduced to support the system, inasmuch as, from observation and some experience, I am strongly inclined to believe that peculiar ignorance of the laws of health and the habits of decent cleanliness are the real and only causes of this disagreeable characteristic of the race, thorough ablutions and change of linen, when tried, have been perfectly successful in removing all such objections; and if ever you have come into anything like the neighborly proximity with a low Irishman or woman, I think you will allow that the same causes produce very nearly the same effects. The stench in an Irish, Scotch, Italian, or French hovel is quite as intolerable as any I ever found in our Negro houses, and the filth and vermin which abound about the clothes and persons of the lower peasantry of any of those countries as abominable as the same conditions in the black population of the United States. A total absence of self-respect begets these hateful physical results, and in proportion as moral influences are remote, physical evils will abound. Well-being, freedom, and industry induce self-respect, self-respect induces cleanliness and personal attention, so that slavery is answerable for all the evils that exhibit themselves where it exists – from lying, thieving, and adultery to dirty houses, ragged clothes, and foul smells."

"Soon after this visit, I was summoned into the wooden porch, or piazza, of the house to see a poor woman who desired to speak to me. This was none other than the tall, emaciated-looking Negress who, on the day of our arrival, had embraced me and my nurse with such irresistible zeal. She appeared very ill today, and presently unfolded to me a most distressing history of bodily afflictions. She was the mother of a very large family, and complained to me that, what with childbearing and hard field labor, her back was almost broken in two.

"With an almost savage vehemence of gesticulation, she suddenly tore up her scanty clothing and exhibited a spectacle with which I was inconceivably shocked and sickened. The facts, without any of her corroborating statements, bore tolerable witness to the hardships of her existence. I promised to attend to her ailments and give her proper remedies, but these are natural results, inevitable and irremediable ones, of improper treatment of the female frame, and, though there may be alleviation, there cannot be any cure when once the beautiful and wonderful structure has been thus made the victim of ignorance, folly, and wickedness.

"After the departure of this poor woman, I walked down the settlement toward the infirmary, or hospital, calling in at one or two of the houses along the row. These cabins consist of one room, about twelve feet by fifteen, with a couple of closets, smaller and closer than the staterooms of a ship, divided off from the main room and each other by rough wooden partitions, in which the inhabitants sleep. They have almost all of them a rude bedstead, with the gray moss of the forests for mattress, and filthy, pestilential-looking blankets for covering.

"Two families (sometimes eight and ten in number) reside in one of these huts, which are mere wooden frames pinned, as it were, to the earth by a brick chimney outside, whose enormous aperture within pours down a flood of air, but little counteracted by the miserable spark of fire which hardly sends an attenuated thread of lingering smoke up its huge throat. A wide ditch runs immediately at the back of these dwellings, which is filled and emptied daily by the tide. Attached to each hovel is a small scrap of ground for a garden, which, however, is for the most part untended and uncultivated."

"In the midst of the floor, or squatting round the cold hearth, would be four or five little children from four to ten years old, the latter all with babies in their arms, the care of the infants being taken from the mothers (who are driven afield as soon as they recover from child labor) and devolved upon these poor little nurses, as they are called, whose business it is to watch the infant, and carry it to its mother whenever it may require nourishment. To these hardly human little beings I addressed my remonstrances about the filth, cold, and unnecessary wretchedness of their room, bidding the older boys and girls kindle up the fire, sweep the floor, and expel the poultry."

"The infirmary is a large two-story building, terminating the broad orange-planted space between the two rows of houses which form the first settlement; it is built of whitewashed wood, and contains four large-sized rooms. But how shall I describe to you the spectacle which was presented to me on entering the first of these: But half the casements, of which there were six, were glazed, and these were obscured with dirt, almost as much as the other windowless ones were darkened by the dingy shutters, which the shivering inmates had fastened to in order to protect themselves from the cold.

"In the enormous chimney glimmered the powerless embers of a few sticks of wood, round which, however, as many of the sick women as could approach were cowering, some on wooden settles, most of them on the ground, excluding those who were too ill to rise; and these last poor wretches lay prostrate on the floor, without bed, mattress, or pillow, buried in tattered and filthy blankets, which, huddled round them as they lay strewn about, left hardly space to move upon the floor. And here, in their hour of sickness and suffering, lay those whose health and strength are spent in unrequited labor for us; those who, perhaps even yesterday, were being urged on to their unpaid task; those whose husbands, fathers, brothers, and sons were even at that hour sweating over the earth; whose produce was to buy for us all the luxuries which health can revel in, all the comforts which can alleviate sickness.

"I stood in the midst of them, perfectly unable to speak, the tears pouring from my eyes at this sad spectacle of their misery, myself and my emotion alike strange and incomprehensible to them. Here lay women expecting every hour the terrors and agonies of childbirth; others who had just brought their doomed offspring into the world; others who were groaning over the anguish and bitter disappointment of miscarriages. Here lay some burning with fever; others chilled with cold and aching with rheumatism, upon the hard cold ground, the drafts and dampness of the atmosphere increasing their sufferings, and dirt, noise, and stench, and every aggravation of which sickness is capable, combined in their condition. Here they lay like brute beasts, absorbed in physical suffering, unvisited by any of those Divine influences which may ennoble the dispensations of pain and illness, forsaken, as it seemed to me, of all good; and yet, O God, Thou surely hadst not forsaken them! Now pray take notice that this is the hospital of an estate where the owners are supposed to be humane, the overseer efficient and kind, and the Negroes remarkably well-cared for and comfortable."

"I forgot to tell you that in the hospital were several sick babies whose mothers were permitted to suspend their field labor in order to nurse them. Upon addressing some remonstrances to one of these, who, besides having a sick child was ill herself, about the horribly dirty condition of her baby, she assured me that it was impossible for them to keep their children clean; that they went out to work at daybreak and did not get their tasks done till evening, and that then they were too tired and worn out to do anything but throw themselves down and sleep. This statement of hers I mentioned on my return from the hospital, and the overseer appeared extremely annoyed by it, and assured me repeatedly that it was not true." (*The Annals of America* [1833-1840], p. 455-463)

Chapter Twenty-Four

This book which has taken unanticipated twists and turns since its inception has become something of an anthology, but the writers of the different periods portrayed the shifts in national character of America and I think they definitely give to the reader interesting ideas about the formation of our great country and God's hand in its exceptionalism. It seems obvious to me that our Lord let the early Americans wrestle with the horrible quandary of slavery, so that great thinkers and writers would lead the people to a Christian solution. The writers about slavery during this time period were, perhaps inadvertently on their parts, leading the country away from the union that had been often touted and toward its Civil War.

The French writer Michel Chevalier believed that the future course of civilization would be marked by the industrial development then discernible in America. Being a keen observer of American economic life, he wrote a series of letters that were published as a book entitled *Lettres sur l'amerique du Nord* (1836). Expanded second and third editions were published in 1837 and 1838. In 1839, the first English edition *Society, Manners, and Politics* appeared. Several excerpts of Chevalier's astute observations in this book are written below:

"In general, the American is little disposed to be contented, his idea of equality is to be inferior to none, but he endeavors to rise in only one direction. His only means, like his only thought, is to subdue the material world, or, in other words, his means is industry in its various branches – business, speculation, work, action. To this sole object everything is subordinate – education, politics, private and public life. Everything in American society, from religion and morals to domestic usages and daily habits of life, is bent in the direction of this aim common to each and every one.

"But American liberty is not a mystical, undefined liberty; it is practical liberty, in harmony with the peculiar genius of the people and its peculiar destiny; it is a liberty of action and motion which the American uses to expand over the vast territory that Providence has given him and to subdue it to his uses. Liberty of movement is nearly absolute, with the exception of some restraints imposed by the observance of the Sabbath...." (*The Annals of America* [1833-1840], p. 482-494)

* * * * * * * * * * * * * * *

In 1836, William H. McGuffey and his brother, Alexander, produced the first of the celebrated *McGuffey Readers* for the school children of America. Believing that education was primarily a moral and only secondarily an educational matter, the authors sought to instill good moral lessons into their young readers' minds.

The McGuffey family emigrated to America from Scotland in 1774 and brought with them religious zeal and a belief in education. William McGuffey taught in many one-teacher schools, primarily in Kentucky, where he often worked eleven hours a day, six days a week. Today, the *McGuffey Readers* are popular among home-schooled children and in some Protestant religious schools.

Henry Ford cited *McGuffey Readers* as one of his most important childhood memories. He republished all six Readers from the 1867 edition and distributed at his own expense complete sets of them to schools across the United States. He called himself a "lifelong devotee of his boyhood alma mater, the *McGuffey Readers*." (*McGuffey Readers*–Wikipedia) Without a doubt, these moralistic readers for the young minds of America helped to mold generations of citizens into people of high moral tone and character. I wish our public schools would use them today in the classrooms of America! I sense the hand of God working in the use of these fine readers.

* * * * * * * * * * * * * * *

The United States Magazine and Democratic Review began publication in 1837. Its editor, John L. O'Sullivan, passionately engaged the native literary talent of Nathaniel Hawthorne, Henry David Thoreau, Walt Whitman, Edgar Allan Poe, Henry Wadsworth Longfellow, John Greenleaf Whittier and others as contributors to his monthly journal. O'Sullivan coined the phrase "manifest destiny," in 1845, in regard to the new nation of the United States of America (*The Annals of America* [1833-1840], p. 502).

His publication was immersed in the ideals of Jacksonian democracy which upheld greater sympathy for the common man. Though his journal was considered "radical," because of its exaggerated nationalism, I found his thoughts and observations in keeping with the thrust of this book in regard to God's interest in the United States and its exceptionalism, another facet in his divine nature.

O'Sullivan believed that all of history is a record of man's march to perfection. This began with the earliest theocracy among the oldest people in the East, such as those in Judea, Persia, and India. This was the earliest departure from barbarism. Next came the aggrandizement of the state with the civilizations of Rome and Greece. The third order of civilization encompassed the feudal system of the Middle Ages with its emphasis on the aristocratic order of rank and class. According to O'Sullivan, the final order of civilization must be the development of democracy which had its seeds in the young United States ("John L. O'Sullivan's Manifest Destiny and Christian...–MDPl"). Several paragraphs, written in 1839, which tout the "manifest destiny" of America appear below:

The Course of Civilization

"The Declaration of Independence was a tremendous act of revolution, founded upon the rights and sanctioned by the natural justice of mankind. The history of the world records nothing like it either for sublimity of purpose or importance of result. It was as peculiar in its design as it has been permanent and extensive in its influence. A nation, poising itself upon the rights of its people, solemnly absolved in political connection and instituted a government for itself; it did more, it instituted a government drawn from popular choice and confessing the equal rights of men. This was the origin of democratic liberty, the source of true civilization. It established the distinct existence of democracy as a social element, and began a reform destined to cease only when every man in the world should be finally and triumphantly redeemed."

"In this ennobling influence, Christianity and democracy are one. What, indeed, is democracy but Christianity in its earthly aspect, Christianity made effective among the political relations of men. Christianity, in which it accords with every design of Providence, begins with individual man, addressing in lofty persuasions to him, and makes his full development in full solicitude and care. The obstacles reared by artificial life it throws aside; the rubbish heaped by centuries of abuse upon the human spirit it removes, the better to unfold man's inward beauty and bring forth man's inward might. A single soul is worth more in its sight than suns or stars. It has a value more enduring than states. The proudest thrones may crumble, the broadest empires contract and become nothing, but the spirit of the meanest man can never perish; for it is the germ of an immortal, ever expanding, ever quickening existence."

The Great Nation of Futurity

"The American people, having derived their origin from many other nations, and the Declaration of National Independence being entirely based on the great principle of human equality, these facts demonstrate at once our disconnected position as regards any other nation; that we have, in reality, but little connection with the past history of any of them, and still less with all antiquity, its glories, or its crimes. On the contrary, our national birth was the beginning of a new history, the formation and progress of an untried political system, which separated us from the past and connects us with the future only; and so far as regards the entire development of the natural rights of man, in moral, political, and national life, we may confidently assume that our country is destined to be *the great nation* of futurity."

"The far-reaching, the boundless future will be the era of American greatness. In its magnificent domain of space and time, the nation of many nations is destined to manifest to mankind the excellence of divine principles; to establish on earth the noblest temple ever dedicated to the worship of the Most High – the Sacred and the True. Its floor shall be a hemisphere; its roof the firmament of the star-studded heavens; and its congregation a union of many republics, comprising hundreds of happy millions, calling, owning no man master, but governed by God's natural and moral law of equality, the law of brotherhood – of 'peace and goodwill among men.'"

"All this will be our future history, to establish on earth the moral dignity and salvation of man – the immutable truth and beneficence of God. For this blessed mission to the nations of the world which are shut out from the life-giving light of truth has America been chosen; and her high example shall smite unto death the tyranny of kings, hierarchs, and oligarchs, and carry the glad tidings of peace and goodwill where myriads now endure an existence scarcely more enviable than that of beasts of the field. Who, then, can doubt that our country is destined to be the great nation of futurity?" (*The Annals of America* [1833-1840], p. 333 and p. 502-511)

* * * * ** * * * * * * * *

To gain insight into the lives of early Americans and to inject some levity into this writing, one should read *A Diary in America* by Frederick Marryat, published in 1839. Frederick Marryat was an English sailor and popular novelist who began an eighteen-month tour of the United States in the spring of 1837. Earning the hostility of the press, he wanted to discover the effects of egalitarian democracy on a people who were still essentially English. He had obvious distaste for the way the early Americans talked. Though probably not intended to be funny, the excerpts I read made me laugh out loud. Below are some passages from "A Diary in America." I believe they will tickle your funny bone, also.

"Now in America they have a dictionary containing many thousands of words which, with us, are either obsolete or are provincialisms, or are words necessarily invented by the Americans. When the people of England emigrated to the States, they came from every county in England, and each county brought its provincialisms with it. These were admitted into the general stock, and were since all collected and bound up by one Mr. Webster. With the exception of a few words coined for local uses (such as 'snags' and 'sawyers,' on the Mississippi, I do not recollect a word which I have not traced to be either a provincialism of some English county, or else to be obsolete English. There are a few from the Dutch, such as 'stoup,' for the porch of a door, etc. I was once talking with an American about Webster's dictionary, and he observed, "Well, now, sir, I understand it's the only one used in the court of St. James, by the king, queen, and princesses, and that by royal order."

"I recollect once talking with one of the first men in America, who was narrating to me the advantages which might have accrued to him if he had followed up a certain speculation, when he said, 'Sir, if I had done so, I should not only have doubled and trebled, but I should have fourbled and fivebled my money.'

"One of the members of Congress once said, 'What the honorable gentleman has just asserted I consider as catamount to denial' (catamount is the term given to a panther or lynx).

"I presume," replied his opponent, "that the honorable gentleman means *tantamount*."

"No, sir. I do not mean *tantamount*; I am not so ignorant of our language not to be aware that *catamount* and *tantamount* are anonymous."

"The Americans dwell upon their words when they speak – a custom arising, I presume, from their cautious, calculating habits; and they have always more or less of a nasal twang. I once said to a lady, 'Why do you drawl out your words in that way?'

"'Well,' replied she, 'I'd drawl all the way from Maine to Georgia rather than dip my words as you English people do.'"

"A specimen of Yankee dialect and conversation: "Well, now, I'll tell you – you know Marble Head?"

"Guess I do."

"Well, then, you know Sally Hackett."

"No, indeed."

"Not know Sally Hackett? Why she lives at Marble Head."

"Guess I don't."

"You don't mean to say that?"

"Yes, indeed."

"And you really don't know Sally Hackett?"

"No, indeed."

"I guess you've heard talk of her?"

"No, indeed."

"Well, that's considerable odd. Now, I'll tell you – Ephrim Bagg, he that has the farm three miles from Marble Head – just as – but now, are you sure you don't know Sally Hackett?"

"No, indeed."

"Well, he's a pretty substantial man, and no mistake. He has got a heart as big as an ox, and everything else in proportion. I've a notion. He loves Sal the worst kind; and if she gets up there, she'll think she has got to Palestine (Paradise); arn't she a screamer? I were thinking of Sal myself, for I feel lonesome, and when I am thrown into my store promiscuous alone, I can tell you I have the blues, the worst kind, no mistake – I can tell you that I always feel a kind o' queer when I sees Sal, but when I meet any of the other gals I am as calm and cool as the Milky Way," etc.

"The verb 'to fix' is universal. It means to do anything."

"There are two syllables – 'um,' 'hu,' – which are very generally used by the Americans as a sort of reply, intimating that they are attentive, and that the party may proceed with his narrative; but, by inflection and intonation, these two syllables are made to express dissent or assent, surprise, disdain, and . . . a great deal more. The reason why these two syllables have been selected is that they can be pronounced without the trouble of opening your mouth, and you may be in a state of listlessness and repose while others talk. I myself found them very convenient at times, and gradually got into the habit of using them."

"They object to everything nude in statuary. When I was at the house of Governor Everett, at Boston, I observed a fine cast of the *Apollo Belvedere,* but in compliance with general opinion it was hung with drapery, although Governor Everett himself is a gentleman of refined mind and high classical attainments, and quite above such ridiculous sensitiveness. In language it is the same thing; there are certain words which are never used in America, but an absurd substitute is employed. I cannot particularize them . . . lest I should be accused of indelicacy myself. I may, however, state one little circumstance which will fully prove the correctness of what I say.

"When at Niagara Falls, I was escorting a young lady with whom I was on friendly terms. She had been standing on a piece of rock, the better to view the scene, when she slipped down, and was evidently hurt by the fall; she had, in fact, grazed her shin. As she limped a little in walking home, I said, 'Did you hurt your leg much.' She turned from me, evidently much shocked, or much offended; and not being aware I had committed any very heinous offense, I begged to know what was the reason of her displeasure. After some hesitation, she said that as she knew me well, she would tell me that the word 'leg' was never mentioned before ladies.

"I apologized for my want of refinement, which was attributable only to English society, and added that as such articles must occasionally be referred to, even in the most polite circles of America, perhaps she would inform me by what name I might mention them without shocking the company. Her reply was, that the word 'limb' was used. 'Nay,' continued she, 'I am not so particular as some people are, for I know those who always say limb of a table, or limb of a pianoforte.'

"There the conversation dropped; but a few months afterward I was obliged to acknowledge that the young lady was correct when she asserted that some people were more particular than even she was.

"I was requested by a lady to escort her to a seminary for young ladies, and, on being ushered into the reception room, conceive my astonishment at beholding a square pianoforte with four *limbs*. However, that the ladies who visited their daughters, might feel in its full force the extreme delicacy of the mistress of the establishment, and her care to preserve in their utmost purity the ideas of the young ladies under her charge, she had dressed all these four limbs in modest little trousers, with frills at the bottom of them!" (*The Annals of America* [1833-1840], p. 495-501)

* * * * * * * * * * * * * *

By the 1840s, America had reached a level of industrial development unforeseen by its forefathers. Though some of its progress relied on foreign, especially British, capital, much of it was attributable to American inventiveness, known as American or "Yankee ingenuity." I believe, dear Reader, that American exceptionalism, as noted often in this book, came directly from God and is reflective of the nature of God.

The sewing machine, the reaper, agricultural equipment, the experimentations with rubber by Charles Goodyear, and so many other discoveries and innovations made the rest of the world sit up and take notice of the young democracy across the ocean from them (*The Annals of America* [1841-1849], p. 133-142). Though many Americans scoffed at the idea of America's expansion from coast to coast, convinced that the bond among the states would soon be broken, the invention of the steamboat changed many minds.

During the 1840s, steamboats and railroads were making travel from shore to shore possible. Many Americans felt that our nation had the "manifest destiny" to dominate the continent and to become a global empire. In 1844, the telegraph ushered in a modern age of long distance communication. However, because of the bitter conflict over slavery, many Americans rejected the idea of manifest destiny, and the expansionist movement faded from the national agenda prior to the Civil War ("New York Teachers' Monographs, p. 182").

* * * * * * * * * * * * * *

Horace Mann, secretary of the Massachusetts Board of Education for twelve years, increased the length of the school year, established fifty new common schools, and founded three normal schools (the first in America). In 1848, he resigned his post to take the late John Quincy Adams' seat in Congress (*The Annals of America* [1841-1849], p. 460). Many of his ideas were later adopted and developed by Abraham Lincoln in his debates with Stephen A. Douglas (*The Annals of America* [1850-1857], p. 7). In 1850, Mann submitted his annual report of the Board of Education of Massachusetts to the state legislature. A paragraph from this report appears below:

"But to all doubters, disbelievers, or despairers in human progress, it may still be said, there is one experiment which has never yet been tried. It is an experiment, which, even before its inception, offers the highest authority for its ultimate success. Its formula is intelligible to all; and it is as legible as though written in starry letters on an azure sky. It is expressed in these few and simple words:'Train up a child in the way he should go; and, when he is old, he will not depart from it.' This declaration is positive. If the conditions are complied with, it makes no provision for a failure. Though pertaining to morals, yet, if the terms of the direction are observed, there is no more reason to doubt the result than there would be in an optical or a chemical experiment." (*The Annals of America* [1841-1849], p. 468-469)

* * * * * * * * * * * * * *

Gold was discovered in 1848 in the Sacramento Valley in California. People from all parts of the world rushed to California to make their fortunes. European ships made their way nonstop to the American West Coast. Their expeditions were fueled in part by letters, such as one by an anonymous writer, excerpts of which appear below:

"You will recall that I told you that I had decided to go on to California. As a result of this decision, I left New York on February 1, and, after a very pleasant voyage of eight days on board the steamship *Falcon*, I arrived with 300 other passengers at Havana, where we stayed one day. From there we sailed to Chagres, a four days' voyage. Here we left the *Falcon* and took another steamboat up the lovely River Chagres, which is from 60 – 100 feet wide but very shallow.

"As the steamboat could not go up more than about twenty-five miles, we had to continue our journey in canoes. These are from 20 – 80 feet long and in proportion to their length are paddled by from one to eight naked Negroes. I was in one of the smallest canoes with only one Negro. These Negroes are extremely good-natured, honest people. They excel in particular in the exceptional endurance and strength, with which they paddle the canoes up against the strong current all day long without resting except when they eat their simple meals."

"After four days in San Francisco, I once more boarded a small vessel and went about 120 miles up the Sacramento River. Here we took three wagons drawn by oxen to carry our baggage to the mountains, where we hoped to make our fortune by washing and digging for gold. After four days' troublesome journey on foot, we arrived at our destination; but for two reasons we discovered that we could not make our fortune right away. In the first place, the water in the river where we hoped to find gold was too high and, besides, the hostility of the Indians presented a serious obstacle."

"Every man here is armed with a gun, pistols, and knives. My six-barreled pistols which I bought in New York for $12 I have sold for $100. To give you an idea of the prices of various things here and of the cost of living in this place, I shall give you a list of the current prices of the most necessary and common articles. A horse costs from $200 to $500; an ox, $100; and a sheep, $16. Hard bread (for there is no soft bread here), $1.25; flour, 75 cents, dried apples, $1.25; ham, $1.25 – all a pound – molasses, $4 a bottle; sugar, 80 cents a pound; tea, $5 a pound, etc. Boards cost $700 for 1,000 cubic feet, and three small boxes of matches are $1. Potatoes are $1.25 a pound. A pair of boots that cost $2.50 in New York are $20 here. A pair of shoes that were 75 cents in New York are $8 here, and so on. These are high prices, to be sure, but if you work hard you can still make money. In May, I saved $223; in June, $295. Yesterday alone I made $35. All my earnings from May 1 to July 14 amount to $750, which is $120 more than the cost of the journey here."

"Here it must be enough to say that the gold we find is almost completely pure. The size of the nuggets varies. In some places pieces have been found that weighed up to seven pounds. Here, at the river where I am staying, it is found almost like fish scales, very thin and in all kinds of forms. You obtain it by washing out the dirt in a machine which looks like a roller, and that is what it is called. You throw the dirt in one end of the machine, which is somewhat higher than the other, and start the machine, all the time adding a certain quantity of water. By the process, lighter particles, like dirt and pebbles, are washed away, and the gold is left behind, together with a sort of fine black sand which consists mainly of iron particles. This is taken out of the machine and carefully washed out in a pan." (*The Annals of America* [1841-1849], p. 488-490)

San Francisco rapidly grew from a small village of gold seekers in 1849 to a city of over 20,000 people in only a short time. In a volume written in 1855, called *The Annals of San Francisco*, by Frank Soule et al, the city's growth and description were depicted as "San Francisco During and After the Gold Rush." Society was in a state of utter disorganization and chaos.

Few regular houses were built, since building materials and labor were almost nonexistent. Canvas tents, small, rough-board shanties, and frame houses dotted the landscape. Altogether, nearly 40,000 immigrants landed at San Francisco during 1849.

Crimes of thefts, robberies, and murders were occurring every day, but there were no proper officials – noone in authority to bring the offenders to justice. Gambling was the amusement and the major occupation of many classes of people. Hundreds of gambling saloons sprang up in the town. The games played were monte, faro, roulette, rondo, rouge et noir and vingt-[et-] un. Beautiful, well-dressed women dealt the cards and turned the roulette wheel. Many blazing lamps added to the card-dealing festivities of the night.

Only a few years before, San Franciscans were careless about their personal appearance and were rude and crude in their manners. However, they soon began to dress richly and extravagantly and acted with the polished airs of gentlemen.

In 1852, 66,988 immigrants arrived in San Francisco.

Germans, French, English, Scottish, Irish, and Spaniards traveled across the ocean to find their fortunes in the gold rush. Over 20,000 Chinese were included in the number above. People of color, along with Mexicans, Peruvians, and Chileans were continually going and coming. Finally, more churches began to make inroads into the vice, debauchery, and folly of the gold-mining town.

In one of the final paragraphs of Soule's description of San Francisco, he writes as follows below:

"There is a fascination in even the loose, unsettled kind of life at San Francisco. Of many who have left the city after a residence of years, and when they have accumulated a handsome fortune, a considerable number have gladly returned. For many months, perhaps for even a year or two, the immigrant thinks he can never worthily or rationally enjoy existence in such a place; so he determines to make a fortune as soon as possible and decamp forever. But fortunes are now made more slowly, and the old citizen – a few years here make one old in sensation, thought, and experience – changes his sentiments, and he begins to like the town and people for their own sake. The vices and follies, the general mode of living that frightened and shocked him at first, seem natural to the climate and, after all, are by no means so very disagreeable. If he returned to settle in ultra-or pseudo-civilized and quiet states, he would surely feel himself but a 'used-up' man; so he continues where he made his money still to feel, speculate, and enjoy, to work and contend with real men in their keenest and strongest characters." (*The Annals of America* [1841-1849], p. 492-500)

* * * * * * * * * * * * * * *

Walden, arguably one of a half dozen most famous American books, is the record of two years (1845-1847) spent by Henry David Thoreau in contemplative solitude at *Walden* Pond, on the outskirts of Concord, Massachusetts. Thoreau planned to live deliberately and simply on a tract of land owned by another writer, Ralph Waldo Emerson. Thoreau built a log cabin where he lived and frequently entertained family and friends. However, it was a life apart from the usual grind of life, with opportunities for study, meditation, and spiritual growth. Below is an excerpt from the important second chapter of *Walden* which was published in 1854:

"I went to the woods because I wished to live deliberately, to front only the essential facts of life, and see if I could not learn what it had to teach, and not, when I came to die, discover that I had not lived. I did not wish to live what was not life, living is so dear; nor did I wish to practise resignation, unless it was quite necessary. I wanted to live deep and suck out all the marrow of life, to live so sturdily and Spartan-like as to put to rout all that was not life, to cut a broad swath and shave close, to drive life into a corner, and reduce it to its lowest terms, and, if it proved to be mean, why then to get the whole and genuine meanness of it, and publish its meanness to the world; or if it were sublime, to know it by experience and be able to give a true account of it in my next excursion. For most men, it appears to me, are in a strange uncertainty about it, whether it is of the devil or of God, and have somewhat hastily concluded that it is the chief end of man here to 'glorify God and enjoy Him forever.'

"Still we live meanly, like ants; though the fable tells us that we were long ago changed into men; like pygmies we fight with cranes; it is error upon error, and clout upon clout, and our best virtue has for its occasion a superfluous and evitable wretchedness. Our life is frittered away by detail. An honest man has hardly need to count more than his ten fingers, or in extreme cases he may add his ten toes, and lump the rest. Simplicity, simplicity, simplicity! I say, let your affairs be as two or three, and not a hundred or a thousand; instead of a million count half a dozen, and keep your accounts on your thumbnail. In the midst of this chopping sea of civilized life, such are the clouds and storms and quicksands and thousand-and-one items to be allowed for that a man has to live, if he would not founder and go to the bottom and not make his port at all, by dead reckoning, and he must be a great calculator indeed who succeeds. Simplify, simplify.

"Instead of three meals a day, if it be necessary eat but one; instead of a hundred dishes, five; and reduce other things in proportion. Our life is like a German confederacy, made up of petty states, with its boundary forever fluctuating, so that even a German cannot tell you how it is bounded at any moment. The nation itself, with all its so-called internal improvements, which, by the way are all external and superficial, is just such an unwieldy and overgrown establishment, cluttered with furniture and tripped up by its own traps, ruined by luxury and heedless expense, by want of calculation and a worthy aim, as the million households in the land; and the only cure for it as for them is in a rigid economy, a stern and more than Spartan simplicity of life and elevation of purpose. It lives too fast." (*The Annals of America* [1850-1857], p. 313)

* * * * * * * * * * * * * *

Perhaps the final blow to the institution of slavery appeared in a book by Harriet Beecher Stowe in 1852, called *Uncle Tom's Cabin*. During its first year, 300,000 copies were sold, and nearly 3,000,000 since. The character of Uncle Tom elicited much sympathy for the plight of the slave.

An excerpt from the book tells of Tom's basket of cotton being weighed, along with the basket of a poor, feeble woman named Lucy, whom Tom had tried to help:

"Dat ar Tom's gwine to make a powerful deal o' trouble; kept a puttin' into Lucy's basket. One o' these yer dat will get all der niggers to feelin' 'bused if Mas'r don't watch him!" said Sambo.

"Hey-dey The black cuss!" said Legree. "He'll have to get a breakin' in, won't he, boys?"

Both Negroes grinned a horrid grin at this intimation. "Ay, ay! Let Mas'r Legree alone, for breakin' in! De debil heself couldn't beat Mas'r at dat!' said Quimbo.

"Wal, boys, the best way is to give him the flogging to do, till he gets over his notions. Break him in!"

"Lord, Mas'r'll have hard work to get dat out o' him!'

"It'll have to come out of him, though!' said Legree, as he rolled his tobacco in his mouth.

"Now, dar's Lucy – de aggravatinest, ugliest wench on de place!' pursued Sambo.

'Take care, Sam; I shall begin to think what's the reason for your spite agin Lucy.'

'Well, Mas'r knows she sot herself up agin Mas'r, and wouldn't have me, when he telled her to.'

'I'd a flogged her into 't,' said Legree, spitting, 'only there's such a press o' work, it don't seem wuth a while to upset her jist now. She's slender; but these yer slender gals will bear half killin' to get their own way!'

'Wal, Lucy was real aggravatin' and lazy, sulkin' round; wouldn't do nothin' – and Tom he tuck up for her.'

'He did, eh! Wal, then Tom shall have the pleasure of flogging her. It'll be a good practice for him, and he won't put it on to the gal like you devils, neither.'

'Ho, ho! Haw! Haw! Haw!' laughed both the sooty wretches; and the diabolical sounds seemed, in truth, a not unapt expression of the fiendish character which Legree gave them.

'And now, said Legree, 'come here, you Tom. You see I telled ye I didn't buy ye jest for the common work; I mean to promote ye and make a driver of ye; and tonight ye may jest as well begin to get yer hand in. Now, ye jest take this yer gal and flog her; ye've seen enough on't to know how.'

'I beg Mas'r's pardon,' said Tom, 'hopes Mas'r won't set me at that. It's what I ain't used to – never did – and can't do, no way possible.'

''Ye'll larn a pretty smart chance of things ye never did know before I've done with ye!' said Legree, taking up a cowhide and striking Tom a heavy blow across the cheek, and following up the infliction by a shower of blows.

'There!' He said, as he stopped to rest, 'now will ye tell me ye can't do it?'

'Yes, Mas'r,' said Tom, putting up his hand to wipe the blood that trickled down his face. 'I'm willin' to work night and day, and work while there's life and breath in me, but this yer thing I can't feel it right to do; and, Mas'r, I never shall do it – never!'

'Well, here's a pious dog, at last, let down among us sinners! – a saint, a gentleman, and no less, to talk to us sinners about our sins! Powerful, holy critur, he must be! Here, you rascal, you make believe to be so pious – didn't you never hear out of yer Bible,

"Servants, obey yer masters?" 'An't I yer master? Didn't I pay down $1,200 cash for all there is inside ye old cussed black shell? An't yer mine, now body and soul?' he said, giving Tom a violent kick with his heavy boot. Tell me!'

'No! No! No! My soul an't yours, Mas'r! You haven't bought it – ye can't buy it! It's been bought and paid for by one that is able to keep it – no matter, no matter, you can't harm me!'

'I can't!' said Legree, with a sneer, 'we'll see – we'll see! Here, Sambo, Quimbo, give this dog such a breakin' in as he won't get over this month!'

"The two gigantic Negroes that now laid hold of Tom, with fiendish exultation in their faces, might have formed no unapt personification of the powers of darkness. The poor woman screamed with apprehension and all arose as by a general impulse while they dragged him unresisting from the place." (*The Annals of America* [1850-1857], p. 200-202)

Jane H. Walker

Chapter Twenty-Five

The Civil War in America began on April 12, 1861, and lasted until April 9, 1865. Eleven states fought for the South, or the Confederacy, whereas 23 states fought for the North, or the Union. From the beginning, the South was outnumbered and its economy strained to the breaking point. However, the northern economy boomed during the war, because of government purchases for military needs, which stimulated manufacturing and agriculture.

A draftee in the North could pay the government $300 to avoid military service, which caused soldiers to grumble that they were involved in "a rich man's war and a poor man's fight."

Around 620,000 soldiers died during the Civil War, with more than half the deaths caused by disease. These were almost as many as the total American deaths from all other wars from the Revolutionary War (1775-1783) through the Vietnam War (1957-1975) (*The World Book* "CI-CZ," 1997, p. 614-634). Oftentimes, epochs of history can best be described by the songs of those eras. The favorite song of the South, as it fought for its way of life was the catchy music and words of "Dixie." Though the song originated in the blackface minstrel shows of the 1850s, Daniel Decatur Emmett is generally credited with adapting it into the version recognized today. Other versions of the song exist, but probably the best known is as follows below ("Dixie's Land–Wikipedia"):

"Oh, I wish I was in the land of cotton,
Old times there are not forgotten;

Look away! Look away! Look away, Dixie Land!
In Dixie Land where I was born in,
Early on one frosty morning,
Look away! Look away! Look away, Dixie Land!

(Chorus)
Then I wish I was in Dixie! Hooray! Hooray!
In Dixie Land I'll take my stand, to live and die in Dixie!
Away! Away! Away down South in Dixie!
Away! Away! Away down South in Dixie!"

Though many associate the lyrics of the song with the ideology of the Old South, they probably do not know that "Dixie" was a favorite of President Abraham Lincoln; it was played at some of his political rallies, and he also wanted it played at the announcement of General Robert E. Lee's surrender ("Dixie [song] Wikipedia"). The favorite war song of the North, and another favorite of its president, Abraham Lincoln, was "The Battle Hymn of the Republic" which is now included in many hymnals and sung by people of the North and also the South.

The background of the hymn began when its creator, Julia Ward Howe, visited an army camp near Washington, D.C., with her minister and a band of soldiers, where they all sang the refrain of "John Brown's Body." Her minister asked her to write "some good words for that stirring tune," which she did. Her poem was published in the *Atlantic Monthly* in February of 1862, for which she received a fee of $4 ("The Battle Hymn of the Republic"/Julia Ward Howe/1st Edition). Its words never fail to bring a sense of love and pride for citizenship in the greatest country the world has ever known. Two of the stanzas ("Battle Hymn of the Republic-Wikipedia") appear below:

"Mine eyes have seen the glory of the coming of the Lord;
He is trampling out the vintage where the grapes of wrath are stored;
He hath loosed the fateful lightning of His terrible swift

sword:
His truth is marching on.

(Chorus)
Glory, glory, hallelujah!
Glory, glory, hallelujah!
Glory, glory, hallelujah!
His truth is marching on.
In the beauty of the lilies Christ was born across the sea,
With a glory in His bosom that transfigures you and me.
As he died to make men holy, let us die to make men free,
While God is marching on."

* * * * * * * * * * * * * *

Below are some poignant words of President Abraham Lincoln. For the first time I have ever thought about Lincoln's first name, it comes to me that he has the same name of the earliest patriarch of Israel, Abraham, whom God called from his home in Ur to come to the land that he would give to him and his descendants. This was the beginning of the nation of Israel. I find a divine symbolism in this, as I sit at my computer and type these thoughts. Below are the words of Lincoln during this most trying time of his life:

"We on our side, are praying to Him to give us victory, because we believe we are right; but those on the other side pray to Him, look for victory, believing they are right. What must He think of us?" Abraham Lincoln (*The Annals of America* [1858-1865], p. 325)

"If there is a worse place than Hell, I am in it." Abraham Lincoln ("Talk: Abraham Lincoln–Wikiquote")

"This war is eating my life out. I have a strong impression that I shall not live to see the end." Abraham Lincoln ("Abraham Lincoln: The Prairie Years and the War Years")

* * * * * * * * * * * * * *

We have all seen pictures and statues of Abraham Lincoln, but we are probably unable to derive a more comprehensive view of the great man who managed to save the weak union of states from dissolution. However, in 1862 the author Nathaniel Hawthorne met with the president and wrote a description which gives us a flesh-and-blood semblance of him in an article entitled "Tales, Sketches and Other Papers" for the *Atlantic Monthly*. Lincoln's qualities of humility and humanity were what the author admired most about him. Hawthorne was a member of a Massachusetts delegation that presented a gift of a splendid whip from a Massachusetts whip factory to President Lincoln.

The article described the whip as an exceedingly long one, its handle wrought in ivory. It was ornamented with a medallion, suggestive of how the President would use such an instrument in dealing with the rebels. Along its entire length was a succession of gold beads and ferrules. It was this occasion that prompted the article about Lincoln, several paragraphs of which appear below:

"By and by there was a little stir on the staircase and in the passageway, and in lounged a tall, loose-jointed figure, as of an exaggerated Yankee port and demeanor, whom as being about the homeliest man I ever saw, yet by no means repulsive or disagreeable, it was impossible not to recognize as Uncle Abe.

"Unquestionably, Western man though he be, and Kentuckian by birth, President Lincoln is the essential representative of all Yankees, and the veritable specimen, physically, of what the world seems determined to regard as our characteristic qualities. It is the strangest and yet the fittest thing in the jumble of human vicissitudes that he, out of so many millions, unlooked for, unselected by any intelligible process that could be based upon his genuine qualities, unknown to those who chose him, and unsuspected of what endowments may adapt him for his tremendous responsibility, should have found the way open for him to fling his lank personality into the chair of state – where, I presume, it was his first impulse to throw his legs on the council table and tell the cabinet ministers a story.

"There is no describing his lengthy awkwardness, nor the uncouthness of his movement; and yet it seemed as if I had been in the habit of seeing him daily and had shaken hands with him a thousand times in some village street; so true was he to the aspect of the pattern American, though with a certain extravagance which, possibly, I exaggerated still further by the delighted eagerness with which I took it in. If put to guess his calling and livelihood, I should have taken him for a country schoolmaster as soon as anything else. He was dressed in a rusty black frock coat and pantaloons, unbrushed, and worn so faithfully that the suit had adapted itself to the curves and angularities of his figure and had grown to be an outer skin of the man. He had shabby slippers on his feet. His hair was black, still unmixed with gray, stiff, somewhat bushy, and had apparently been acquainted with neither brush nor comb that morning, after the disarrangement of the pillow; and as to a nightcap, Uncle Abe probably knew nothing of such effeminacies. His complexion is dark and sallow, betokening, I fear, an insalubrious atmosphere around the White House; he has thick black eyebrows and an impending brow; his nose is large, and the lines about his mouth are very strongly defined.

"The whole physiognomy is as coarse a one as you would meet anywhere in the length and breadth of the states; but, withal, it is redeemed, illuminated, softened, and brightened by a kindly though serious look out of his eyes and an expression of homely sagacity that seems weighed with rich results of village experience. A great deal of native sense; no bookish cultivation, no refinement; honest at heart, and thoroughly so, and yet, in some sort, sly – at least endowed with a sort of tact and wisdom that are akin to craft, and would impel him I think, to take an antagonist in flank, rather than to make a bull-run at him right in front. But, on the whole, I like the sallow, queer, sagacious visage, with the homely human sympathies that warmed it, and, for my small share in the matter, would as lief have Uncle Abe for a ruler as any man whom it would have been practicable to put in his place."

"Good heavens! What liberties have I been taking with one of the potentates of the earth, and the man on whose conduct more important consequences depend than on that of any other historical personage of the century! But with whom is an American citizen entitled to take a liberty if not with his own chief magistrate? However, lest the above allusions to President Lincoln's little peculiarities (already well known to the country and to the world) should be misinterpreted, I deem it proper to say a word or two in regard to him of unfeigned respect and measurable confidence. He is evidently a man of keen faculties, and, what is still more to the purpose, of powerful character. As to his integrity, the people have that intuition of it which is never deceived." (*The Annals of America* [1858-1865], p. 395-397)

* * * * * * * * * * * * * *

It has been said by historians that the South's defeat at Gettysburg, Pennsylvania, on July 1-3, 1863, was the turning point of the Civil War. The Union army numbered 94,000 men, while the Confederate army numbered 72,000 troops. Union losses numbered over 23,186; the Confederacy lost 31,621 men. On the final day of the Battle of Gettysburg, General George Pickett led 13,000 Confederate troops against the Union soldiers in a battle that became immortalized as "Pickett's Charge." The attack was disastrous, leaving three-fourths of the Confederates dead ("Battle of Gettysburg: 30 Facts for Kids***–The Civil War").

On July 6, three days later, Pickett wrote the following heart-wrenching letter about that fateful battle to the woman who later became his wife:

"On the Fourth – far from a glorious Fourth to us or to any with love for his fellowmen – I wrote you just a line of heartbreak. The sacrifice of life on that bloodsoaked field on the fatal 3rd was too awful for the heralding of victory, even for our victorious foe, who, I think, believe as we do, that it decided the fate of our cause. No words can picture the anguish of that roll call – the breathless waits between the responses. The 'Here' of those who, by God's mercy, had miraculously escaped the awful rain of shot and shell was a sob – a gasp – a knell – for the unanswered name of his comrade called before his. There was no tone of thankfulness for having been spared to answer to their names, but rather a toll and an unvoiced wish that they, too, had been among the missing.

"But for the blight to your sweet young life, but for you, only you, my darling, your soldier would rather by far be out there, too, with his brave Virginians – dead.

"Even now I can hear them cheering as I gave the order, 'Forward!' I can feel their faith and trust in me and their love for our cause. I can feel the thrill of their joyous voices as they called out all along the line, 'We'll follow you, Marse George. We'll follow you, we'll follow you.' Oh, how faithfully they kept their word, following me on, on to their death, and I, believing in the promised support, led them on, on, on. Oh, God!

"I can't write you a love letter today, my Sallie, for, with my great love for you and my gratitude to God for sparing my life to devote to you, comes the overpowering thought of those whose lives were sacrificed – of the brokenhearted widows and mothers and orphans. The moans of my wounded boys, the sight of the dead, upturned faces flood my soul with grief, and here am I, whom they trusted, whom they followed, leaving them on that field of carnage, leaving them to the mercy of ---- and guarding 4,000 prisoners across the river back to Winchester. Such a duty for men who a few hours ago covered themselves with glory eternal.

"Well, my darling, I put the prisoners all on their honor and gave them equal liberties with my own soldier boys. My first command to them was to go and enjoy themselves the best they could, and they have obeyed my order. Today, a Dutchman and two of his comrades came up and told me that they were lost and besought me to help them find their commands. They had been with my men and had gotten separated from their own comrades. So I sent old Floyd off on St. Paul to find out where they belonged and deliver them. This is too gloomy and too poor a letter for so beautiful a sweetheart, but it seems sacrilegious, almost, to say I love you, with the hearts that are stilled to love on the field of battle." (*The Annals of America* [1858-1865], p. 429-430)

In memory of the thousands of soldiers of both sides, who died in the Battle of Gettysburg, the National Soldiers' Cemetery was established at Gettysburg. For the dedication ceremony on November 19, 1863, Lincoln was invited to make "a few appropriate remarks." Lincoln left Washington for Gettysburg on November 18, while his son Tad lay sick in bed. Traveling by train he wrote the final draft of the words he would speak at the cemetery dedication. When

Lincoln arrived for the ceremony, some 15,000 people awaited him on Cemetery Hill. Though some of the speakers had orations which lasted several hours, Lincoln delivered the now famous Gettysburg Address in three minutes, as follows below:

"Four score and seven years ago our fathers brought forth on this continent a new nation, conceived in liberty and dedicated to the proposition that all men are created equal.

"Now we are engaged in a great civil war, testing whether that nation or any nation so conceived and so dedicated can long endure. We are met on a great battlefield of that war. We have come to dedicate a portion of that field as a final resting place for those who here gave their lives that that nataion might live. It is altogether fitting and proper that we should do this.

"But, in a larger sense, we cannot dedicate – we cannot hallow – this ground. The brave men, living and dead, who struggled here have consecrated it far above our poor power to add or detract. The world will little note nor long remember what we say here, but it can never forget what they did here. It is for us, the living, rather to be dedicated here to the unfinished work which they who fought here have thus far so nobly advanced.

"It is rather for us to be here dedicated to the great task remaining before us – that from these honored dead we take increased devotion to that cause for which they gave the last full measure of devotion, that we here highly resolve that these dead shall not have died in vain; that this nation, under God, shall have a new birth of freedom; and that government of the people, by the people, for the people shall not perish from the earth." (*The Annals of America* [1858-1865], p. 462-463)

The North counted nearly 360,000 dead, the South nearly 260,000, though death by disease was more common than in battle ("Civil War Medical Care, Battle Wounds, and Disease–Civil War Home"). The will of the South was completely broken when General William Tecumseh Sherman, leading 62,000 men, attacked Atlanta in July of 1864, in a siege which lasted several months, leaving it in smoking ruins, and began his infamous 300-mile march through Georgia to Savannah and the sea ("Battle of Atlanta–Wikipedia").

Occupying Savannah on December 21, Sherman sent a message to Lincoln, stating, "I beg to present to you as a Christmas gift the city of Savannah with 150 heavy guns and plenty of ammunition and also about 25,000 bales of cotton." ("Sherman's March to the Sea–Wikipedia")

If the Battle of Gettysburg was the turning point of the Civil War, certainly the Battle of Vicksburg sealed the South's fate. Lincoln said, "Vicksburg is the key; the war can never be brought to a close until that key is in our pocket." ("The Key in Lincoln's Pocket/Civil War Trust") I had always envisioned the Civil War as mainly being fought by the Eastern Seaboard states, but little did I know differently, until I did some research about the battle for Vicksburg on the Mississippi River by the Union forces.

Vicksburg is situated on a 200-foot cliff on the Mississippi River. Ladders were used by Union soldiers in an attempt to scale the bluffs in places where they were not so steep. Over 500 caves, known locally as "bombproofs," were dug into the yellow clay hills of Vicksburg. Union soldiers called the town "Prairie Dog Village." As General Ulysses Grant and his northern army made their way down the Mississippi River to Vicksburg, the residents of the town prepared as best they could for the attack ("Siege of Vicksburg–Wikipedia"). A Southern woman who survived the furious onslaught kept a daily journal which has left for us her vivid descriptions of all that she and her family suffered during the siege. It gives us another frightening perspective of our internecine war.

First published in 1864, the small journal with the title "My Cave Life in Vicksburg" describes how the residents of Vicksburg dug caves into the hills of the town, where they lived for many weeks during the battle. Their black servants lived with them in the damp caves. Some families even hung pictures on the walls of the caves and put rugs on the dirt floors to simulate their homes.

As the battle raged on, starvation weakened the Confederate soldiers, as well as the populace of the city. People were reduced to eating horses, mules, dogs, cats, rats, and even shoe leather. The Union Army survived on hardtack, beans and coffee. A member of the Confederate Ransom's Brigade wrote the following about the

Battle of Vicksburg:

"As our line of battle started and before our yell had died upon the air the confederate fortifications in our front were completely crowded with the enemy, who with an answering cry of defiance, poured into our ranks, one continuous fire of musketry, and the forts and batteries in our front and both sides, were pouring in to our line, an unceasing fire of shot and shell, with fearful results, as this storm of fire sent us, intermixed with the bursting shells and that devilish rebel yell, I could compare to nothing but one of Dante's pictures of Hell, a something too fearful to describe." ("Battle of Vicksburg Civil War Vicksburg Battle Mississippi")

An interesting aside is that the little journal, mentioned several paragraphs above, was said to be written "by a lady," whose name was not given, as it was thought improper for a woman to have her name in print. It is known now, however, that the brave woman was Mary Ann Webster Loughborough. Another interesting aspect of the Battle of Vicksburg was that an unusual problem arose for the Confederates, in that the dead and wounded of Grant's army lay in the heat of Mississippi summer. With the odor of deceased men and horses filling the air and the wounded crying for medical help, the Confederates requested a truce, so the Union could recover the wounded and dead.

Though at first, Grant refused, thinking it would show weakness, he finally agreed, and the Confederates held their fire while the Union recovered their dead and wounded. Amazingly, soldiers on both sides mingled and traded as if no hostilities existed, if only for the moment ("My Cave Life in Vicksburg: With Letters of Trial and Travel" by Mary Ann Webster Loughborough). At the end of the battle, when Lincoln was informed of Union victory, he stated, "The Father of Waters again goes unvexed to the sea." ("Siege of Vicksburg–Wikipedia")

* * * * * * * * * * * * *

On April 9, 1865, the two great generals of the North and the South, Ulysses Grant and Robert E. Lee, met in the little rural settlement of Appomattox Court House, Virginia, to end the war.

They met in the home of a farmer named Wilmer McLean. General Lee's army, having retreated from Richmond and Petersburg, had bivouacked near Appomattox Court House the day before. When Lee found the road to Lynchburg blocked by Union troops and his situation hopeless, he accepted Grant's proposal for the surrender of his army ("Appomattox Campaign–*Encyclopedia Virginia*"). Grant described in his *Personal Memoirs* (1885) his meeting with Lee:

"What General Lee's feelings were I do not know. As he was a man of much dignity, with an impassable face, it was impossible to say whether he felt inwardly glad that the end had finally come, or felt sad over the result, and was too manly to show it...But my own feelings, which had been quite jubilant...were sad and depressed. I felt like anything rather than rejoicing at the downfall of a foe who fought so long and valiantly, and had suffered so much for a cause." ("Meeting of Grant and Lee April 9, 1865 first step to war's end...")

Below is an account of the meeting of the two generals by Brigadier General Horace Porter, Grant's aide-de-camp, as published in 1887 in *Battles and Leaders of the Civil War:*

"The contrast between the two commanders was striking and could not fail to attract marked attention as they sat ten feet apart facing each other. General Grant, then nearly forty-three years of age, was five feet eight inches in height, with shoulders slightly stooped. His hair and full beard were a nutbrown, without a trace of gray in them. He had on a single-breasted blouse, made of dark-blue flannel, unbuttoned in front, and showing a waistcoat underneath. He wore an ordinary pair of top boots, with his trousers inside, and was without spurs. The boots and portions of his clothes were spattered with mud. He had on a pair of thread gloves, of a dark-yellow color, which he had taken off on entering the room. His felt, 'sugarloaf,' stiff-brimmed hat was thrown on the table beside him. He had no sword, and a pair of shoulder straps was all there was about him to designate his rank. In fact, aside from these, his uniform was that of a private soldier.

"Lee, on the other hand, was fully six feet in height and quite erect for one of his age, for he was Grant's senior by sixteen years.

His hair and full beard were a silver-gray, and quite thick, except that the hair had become a little thin in front. He wore a new uniform of Confederate gray, buttoned up to the throat, and at his side he carried a long sword of exceedingly fine workmanship, the hilt studded with jewels. It was said to be the sword that had been presented to him by the State of Virginia. His top boots were comparatively new and seemed to have on them some ornamental stitching of red silk. Like his uniform, they were singularly clean and but little travel stained. On the boots were handsome spurs, with large rowels. A felt hat, which in color matched pretty closely that of his uniform, and a pair of long buckskin gauntlets lay beside him on the table. We asked Colonel Marshall afterward how it was that both he and his chief wore such fine toggery and looked so much as if they had turned out to go to church, while with us our outward garb scarcely rose to the dignity even of the "shabby genteel."

"General Grant began the conversation by saying: 'I met you once before, General Lee, while we were serving in Mexico, when you came over from General Scott's headquarters to visit Garland's brigade, to which I then belonged. I have always remembered your appearance, and I think I should have recognized you anywhere.' 'Yes,' replied General Lee, 'I know I met you on that occasion, and I have often thought of it and tried to recollect how you looked, but I have never been able to recall a single feature.'"

"The hour of noon had now arrived, and General Grant, after shaking hands with all present who were not to accompany him, mounted his horse, and started with his staff for Washington without having entered the enemy's lines. Lee set out for Richmond, and it was felt by all that peace had at last dawned upon the land. The charges were now withdrawn from the guns, the campfires were left to smolder in their ashes, the flags were tenderly furled – those historic banners, battle-stained, bullet-riddled, many of them but remnants of their former selves, with scarcely enough left of them on which to imprint the names of the battles they had seen – and the Army of the Union and the Army of Northern Virginia turned their backs upon each other for the first time in four long, bloody years."
('General Horace Porter–Dictionary definition of General Horace

Porter")

Lee's surrender of the Army of Northern Virginia was marked with dignity and goodwill. The southern general's farewell to his army was read by Colonel Charles Marshall one day after his surrender on April 10, 1865. It follows below:

"After four years of arduous service, marked by unsurpassed courage and fortitude, the Army of Northern Virginia has been compelled to yield to overwhelming numbers and resources. I need not tell the survivors of so many hard-fought battles, who have remained steadfast to the last, that I have consented to this result from no distrust of them; but, feeling that valor and devotion could accomplish nothing that could compensate for the loss that would have attended the continuation of the contest, I have determined to avoid the useless sacrifice of those whose past services have endeared them to their countrymen.

"By the terms of the agreement, officers and men can return to their homes and remain there until exchanged. You will take with you the satisfaction that proceeds from the consciousness of duty faithfully performed; and I earnestly pray that a merciful God will extend to you His blessing and protection.

"With an increasing admiration of your constancy and devotion to your country, and a grateful remembrance of your kind and generous consideration of myself, I bid you an affectionate farewell." ("Lee's Farewell Address–Wikipedia")

I am almost certain, dear Reader, that you noted that both Lincoln and Lee called upon God in their remarks after the terrible war. God was very much in the minds of great leaders of the North and the South, as they fought one of the great battles that have beleaguered our nation.

Though the union of states was preserved after the war, in what form would the nation proceed? Would the Confederate states be received back into the Union with full political rights? What about the Confederate leaders? Would they retain their full political rights? Should the federal government bear responsibility for former Negro slaves?

The most pressing need of the vanquished Southerners was

sheer physical survival. Transportation was impossible, for railroads had been demolished. Savings had been wiped out, for Confederate currency or bonds would never be repaid ("PDF Reconstruction"). Though Southerners for the most part still had their land, the workers who had labored in the fields had been freed ("The Civil War Veteran: A Historical Reader").

Confederate soldiers were released on parole and given three days' rations. They were also allowed to keep their horses and mules to take home to plant spring crops. Officers had permission to keep their sidearms ("The Routledge Companion to the American Civil War Era").

Two days after the surrender of Lee's army, Lincoln spoke from the balcony of the White House about his plans for reconstruction. The large and boisterous crowd that heard him wanted to celebrate the victory and vent their dissatisfaction in regard to the rebels, but Lincoln instead spoke without vindictiveness or eloquence, excerpts of which are below:

"We meet this evening not in sorrow but in gladness of heart. The evacuation of Petersburg and Richmond and the surrender of the principal insurgent army give hope of a righteous and speedy peace, whose joyous expression cannot be restrained. In the midst of this, however, He from whom all blessings flow must not be forgotten.

"A call for a national thanksgiving is being prepared and will be duly promulgated. Nor must those whose harder part give us the cause of rejoicing be overlooked. Their honors must not be parceled out with others. I myself was near the front and had the high pleasure of transmitting much or the good news to you; but no part of the honor for plan or execution is mine. To General Grant, his skillful officers and brave men, all belongs. The gallant Navy stood ready but was not in reach to take active part.

"By these recent successes, the reinauguration of the national authority – reconstruction – which has had a large share of thought from the first, is pressed much more closely upon our attention. It is fraught with great difficulty. Unlike a case of war between independent nations, there is no authorized organ for us to treat with – no one man has authority to give up the rebellion for any other man. We simply must begin with and mold from disorganized and discordant elements. Nor is it a small additional embarrassment that we, the loyal people, differ among ourselves as to the mode, manner, and measure of reconstruction." (*The Annals of America* [1858-1865], p. 573)

Three nights later, Lincoln was killed. His plans for the postwar reconstruction had not yet begun. Let's look back during that sad and chaotic time during our nation's history, and it may make us appreciate our country even more. On the evening of Good Friday, April 14, 1865, President Lincoln was seated in a box at Ford's Theatre in Washington, when he was assassinated by the actor John Wilkes Booth. Nine other persons were also implicated in the murder. Booth was captured in a barn near Bowling Green, Virginia, on April 26, where he was shot, likely killing himself. Four of the other conspirators were hanged, four were imprisoned, and the ninth was acquitted.

Gideon Welles, Lincoln's secretary of the navy, was present when Lincoln lay dying at a house near the theatre, where he was carried after being shot. Welles kept a diary of the events as they transpired from April 15 to May 12. The diary was published in Boston in 1911. Below are several paragraphs from the diary which document the agony and grief of our country during those days and the intense suffering of the great man who managed to hold together and preserve these United States:

"April 15. A door which opened upon a porch or gallery and also the windows, were kept open for fresh air. The night was dark, cloudy, and damp, and about six it began to rain. I remained in the room until then without sitting or leaving it, when, there being a vacant chair which someone left at the foot of the bed, I occupied it for nearly two hours, listening to the heavy groans and witnessing the wasting life of the good and great man who was expiring before me.

"About 6 A.M. I experienced a feeling of faintness and, for the first time after entering the room, a little past eleven, I left it and the house, and took a short walk in the open air. It was a dark and gloomy morning, and rain set in before I returned to the house, some fifteen minutes later. Large groups of people were gathered every few rods, all anxious and solicitous. Some one or more from each group stepped forward as I passed to inquire into the condition of the president and to ask if there was no hope. Intense grief was on every countenance when I replied that the President could survive but a short time. The colored people especially – and there were at this time more of them, perhaps, than of whites – were overwhelmed with grief."

"A little before seven, I went into the room where the dying President was rapidly drawing near the closing moments. His wife soon after made her last visit to him. The death struggle had begun. Robert, his son, stood with several others at the head of the bed. He bore himself well, but on two occasions gave way to overpowering grief and sobbed aloud, turning his head and leaning on the shoulder of Senator Sumner. The respiration of the President became suspended at intervals and at last entirely ceased at twenty-two minutes past seven."

"I went after breakfast to the Executive Mansion. There was a cheerless cold rain and everything seemed gloomy. On the Avenue in front of the White House were several hundred colored people, mostly women and children, weeping and wailing their loss. This crowd did not appear to diminish through the whole of that cold, wet day; they seemed not to know what was to be their fate once their great benefactor was dead, and their hopeless grief affected me more than almost anything else, though strong and brave men wept when I met them.

"At the White House all was silent and sad. Mrs. W. (Welles) was with Mrs. L. (Lincoln) and came to meet me in the library. Speed (Attorney General) came in, and we soon left together. As we were descending the stairs, "Tad," who was looking from the window at the foot, turned and, seeing us, cried aloud in his tears, 'Oh, Mr. Welles, who killed my father?' Neither Speed nor myself could restrain our tears nor give the poor boy any satisfactory answer."

"April 18, Tuesday. Details in regard to the funeral, which takes place on the 19th, occupied general attention and little else than preliminary arrangements and conversation was done at the cabinet meeting. From every part of the country comes lamentation. Every house, almost, has some drapery, especially the homes of the poor. Profuse exhibition is displayed on the public buildings and the dwellings of the wealthy, but the little black ribbon or strip of black cloth from the hovel of the poor Negro or the impoverished white is more touching.

"I have tried to write something consecutively since the horrid transactions of Friday night, but I have no heart for it, and the jottings down are mere mementos of a period, which I will try to fill up when more composed and I have leisure or time for the task.

"Sad and painful, wearied and irksome, the few preceding incoherent pages have been written for future use, for the incidents are fresh in my mind and may pass away with me but cannot ever be by me forgotten.

"April 19. The funeral on Wednesday, the 19th, was imposing, sad, and sorrowful. All felt the solemnity and sorrowed as if they had lost one of their own household. By voluntary action, business was everywhere suspended, and the people crowded the streets."

"There were no truer mourners, when all were sad, than the poor colored people who crowded the streets, joined the procession, and exhibited their woe, bewailing the loss of him whom they regarded as a benefactor and father. Women, as well as men, with their little children, thronged the streets; sorrow, trouble, and distress depicted on their countenances and in their bearing." (*The Annals of America* [1858-1865], p. 576-580)

Another source I read rendered the following message: "Now he belongs to the ages," said Secretary of War Edwin Stanton ("This Day in Quotes: 'Now he belongs to the ages'–or maybe to the...).

"All over the capital, black mourning crape appeared around columns and pillars of government buildings and draped from roofs and windows. It was stretched in folds across the facade of the White House and other homes, offices, hotels, shops, and places of business. It bordered oversize mirrors in the East Room of the White House in readiness for the funeral service of the president.

"The spacious East Room of the White House was crammed with dignitaries for the president's funeral service four days after his death. Unresponsive to the solicitude of others and weakened by lack of sleep and loss of appetite, Mrs. Lincoln remained upstairs, alone in her trauma and sorrow. President Andrew Johnson stood near the coffin which rested above a raised catafalque under an ornately domed canopy. General Ulysses S. Grant, no stranger to the carnage of the battlefield dead, wept openly near the coffin.

"The mile-long funeral procession from the White House to the Capitol included many delegations and individuals. Those in the lead reached the end before the last had even left the White House. As Lincoln's casket lay in the rotunda of the Capitol during fourteen hours of viewing, forty thousand mourners filed by it. Again, the dignitaries were present at the train depot the next day for a final farewell, when Lincoln's remains were taken back to Springfield, Illinois ("The White House and Lincoln's Assassination–White House Historical...").

* * * * * * * * * * * * * *

Apparently, relations between the United States and England had mellowed since their last confrontation in the War of 1812, for Queen Victoria of England sent the following poignant letter to Mary Todd Lincoln, dated April 29, 1865:

"Dear Madam,

"Though a Stranger to you, I cannot remain silent when so terrible a calamity has fallen upon you & your Country & must personally express my deep & heartfelt sympathy with you under the shocking circumstances of your present dreadful misfortune –

"No one can better appreciate than I can, who am myself utterly broken-hearted by the loss of my own beloved Husband, who was the Light of my Life, – my Stay – my all, – what your sufferings must be; and I earnestly pray that you may be supported by Him to whom Alone the sorely stricken can look for comfort, in this hour of heavy affliction. With the renewed Expression of true sympathy, I remain,dear Madam,

"Your Sincere friend
Victoria Rg" ("Letters of Note: I cannot remain silent")

I found Mary Todd Lincoln's response in an article on the internet. It had no greeting, only the following words:

"I have received the letter which Your Majesty has had the kindness to write and am deeply grateful for its expressions of tender sympathy, coming as they do from a heart which from its own Sorrow, can appreciate the intense grief I now endure. Accept, madam, the assurances of my heartfelt thanks and believe me in the deepest sorrow, Your Majesty's Sincere and grateful friend, MARY LINCOLN" ("Mary Lincoln's response to Queen Victoria–White House Historical...")

* * * * * * * * * * * * * *

The sheer greatness of the man, Abraham Lincoln, manifested itself during his life but especially after his death, for his untimely and tragic demise brought about a groundswell of grief. Much has been written about his assassination and the days and months and years which followed. Many well-known writers of the era channeled their thoughts and grief into written words.

Walt Whitman composed one of the most beautiful elegies ever written, considered his best poem, after Lincoln's death. He gave it the title "When Lilacs Last in the Dooryard Bloomed." Whitman also wrote in *Specimen Days:*

"Of all the days of the war, there are two especially I can never forget. These were the day following the news, in New York and Brooklyn, of that first Bull Run defeat, and the day of Abraham Lincoln's death. I was home in Brooklyn on both occasions.

"The day of the murder we heard the news very early in the morning. Mother prepared breakfast – and other meals afterward – as usual, but not a mouthful was eaten all day by either of us. We each drank half a cup of coffee; that was all. Little was said. We got every newspaper morning and evening, and the frequent extras of that period, and passed them silently to each other." Soon after Lincoln's assassination, Whitman began working on his poem "When Lilacs Last in the Dooryard bloomed." It is written in sixteen parts. His grief over the president's death is almost palpable in the words of his poetry. The poem is so long, I didn't include it, but it may be found in *The Annals of America,* 1866-1883, p. 44-50.

* * * * * * * * * * * * * *

Three U. S. presidents - Abraham Lincoln, Andrew Johnson, and Ulysses Grant - were the architects of Reconstruction policies, from the middle of the war until 1876. Assuming the presidency after Lincoln's assassination, Andrew Johnson envisioned a rapid, lenient type of Reconstruction. This involved a complete reentry of the seceded states into full statehood, a renunciation of secession policies, and acceptance of the end of slavery, but this included no advancement in the civil and political rights of the freedmen.

However, Radical Republicans dominated early Reconstruction efforts from 1866-1868. They promoted the revolutionary emphasis on racial equality embodied in the Civil Rights Act of 1866 and the Fourteenth and Fifteenth Amendments. These men of the first Republican Party believed in government, especially as it enacted measures during the Civil War to defeat the Confederacy.

Because President Andrew Johnson wanted to enforce Lincoln's ideas of conciliation with the embattled Confederacy, he became the first and only president of the United States at that time to be impeached. Only one vote decided his acquittal ("Reconstruction Era–Wikipedia").

Ways of fighting all-out war included the first federal income tax, the Homestead Act, military conscription, subsidies to construct transcontinental railroads, U. S. Bonds and the greenback dollar. The Quartermaster Corps employed more than 100,000 people by 1864 and became the agency of the North, which produced the materiel to defeat the South. It also brought about the emancipation of four million slaves and, by executive order and military force, the confiscation of $3.5 billion in property. They paid for and armed Grant's and Sherman's armies which crushed the Confederacy, freed the slaves, and saved the United States from dissolution and extinction.

Of all the elements of Reconstruction, the Fourteenth Amendment should be embraced as a holy writ that binds our states into a national community. It is based, in part, on words proposed by John Bingham of Ohio, an evangelical Christian and former abolitionist. Section one follows: "All persons born or naturalized in the United States, and subject to the jurisdiction thereof, are citizens of the United States and of the states wherein they reside. No state shall make or enforce any law which shall abridge the privileges or immunities of citizens of the United States; nor without due process of law; nor deny to any person within its jurisdiction the equal protection of the laws."

In 1869, Frederick Douglass addressed one of the last annual meetings of the American Antislavery Society which at that time celebrated the passage of the Fifteenth Amendment. This amendment guaranteed black men the right to vote. This was seen by many as the last act of Reconstruction. Douglass' words then still apply to the current racial and constitutional strife. His words are below:

"But slavery is not honestly dead...it did not die honestly," he said. "Had [slavery's] death come of moral conviction instead of political and military necessity; had it come in obedience to the enlightenment of the American people; had it come at the call of the humanity...of the slaveholder, as well as the rest of our fellow citizens, slavery might be looked upon as honestly dead."

As a former slave, he was reminding his country that slavery was crushed by military might in an all-out war which had changed the minds of some, but not of many others (Slavery Did Not Die Honestly–*The Atlantic*). Today, we are still witnessing racial strife, such as we have seen in Ferguson, Missouri, and Baltimore, Maryland. The 150th anniversary of the passage of the Fourteenth Amendment arrived in June of 2016 ("14th Amendment 150th Anniversary/OneTubeRadio.com"). We would do well to remember the wisdom of leaders such as Frederick Douglass who could foresee the racial strife that could likely plague the United States forever.

After the end of the war, as the South lay in ruins, a group of Confederate veterans met to form a social club ostensibly to shield white people from harassment by Negroes. On Christmas Eve in 1865, the Ku Klux Klan was organized in Pulaski, Tennessee. From the Greek word, "kyklos," meaning "circle," and the Scottish-Gaelic word, "clan," the group called their organization the Ku Klux Klan, or the K.K.K. Nathan Bedford Forrest, a former Confederate general, was the Klan's first leader or grand wizard. However, in 1869, he tried unsuccessfully to disband it as he became critical of the Klan's excessive violence ("KKK founded–Dec. 24, 1865–HISTORY.com")

The Klan was active during four periods after its founding: 1) the mid-1860s to the early 1870s; 2) 1915 to 1944; 3) the late 1940s to the early 1970s, and 4) since the mid-1970s. In 1871, Congress passed the Force bill which gave the President authority to use federal troops against the Klan. It soon disappeared, only to resurface again in the next century.

Klan members believed in the superiority of the white race and terrorized blacks to keep them from voting or embracing other rights they had gained during Reconstruction. Black people were threatened, beaten, and murdered by Klansmen who wore robes and hoods and burned crosses to frighten black people, Jews, and other minorities. They often dressed in full regalia and draped white sheets over their horses when they rode through the towns at night. Though the Klan continued to reemerge, even boasting more than two million members throughout the nation in the mid-1920s, it soon lost any degree of respectability and now has about 6,000 members. Most of these live in the South (*The World Book* "J-K," 1997, p. 389-390).

The Civil War has been called the first modern war, for it changed the way of waging war. Its soldiers used repeating arms which could fire several shots without reloading and breech-loading weapons, which were loaded from behind the barrel instead of at the muzzle. Observation balloons, ironclad ships, mines, and submarines, along with railroads and telegraphy were used for the first time in warfare ("AE Aeragon–First Modern War").

Newspapers and magazines of the North sent over 150 correspondents to the field to record the war. The telegraph, the recently established news agency in New York, and the new art of photography made extensive news coverage of the war possible. Mathew Brady organized photography teams that recorded the scenes of war in more than 7,000 photographs, which ushered in a new direction in popular journalism (*The Annals of America*

[1858-1865], p. 358).

After the war, Americans ratified, or approved, the Thirteenth Amendment to the Constitution, which officially abolished slavery throughout the United States. Democracy in the United States had survived its "fiery trial" and remained one nation, rather than a split country. The outcome of the war resulted in the rise of the United States to a major world power (*The World Book* "Ci-Cz," 1997, p. 634).

* * * * * * * * * * * * * *

As the United States wrestled with the obstacles of Reconstruction, American Indian problems resurfaced in 1870. Chief Red Cloud, leader of the largest tribe of the Teton Sioux Nation, visited the East and gave a speech at a reception in his honor at Cooper Union in New York. Though he was a persistent critic of the government and its Indian agents, whom he charged with graft and corruption, he openly opposed further wars that would only hurt his people. He longed for peace and fairness in dealings with the U. S. Government. Below are excerpts from his speech which was both genuine and heart-breaking:

"My brethren and my friends who are here before me this day, God Almighty has made us all, and He is here to bless what I have to say to you today. The Good Spirit made us both. He gave you lands and He gave us lands. He gave us these lands; you came in here, and we respected you as brothers. God Almighty made you but made you all white and clothed you, when He made us He made us with red skins and poor; now you have come.

"When you first came we were very many and you were few; now you are many, and we are getting very few, and we are poor. You do not know who appears before you today to speak. I am a representative of the original American race, the first people of this continent. We are good and not bad. The reports that you hear concerning us are all on one side. We are always well disposed to them. You are here told that we are traders and thieves, and it is not so. We have given you nearly all our lands, and if we had any more land to give we would be very glad to give it. We have nothing now. We are driven into a very little land, and we want you now, as our dear friends, to help us with the government of the United States.

"The Great Father made us poor and ignorant – made you rich and wise and more skillful in these things that we know nothing about. The Great Father, the Good Father in Heaven, made you all to eat tame food – made us to eat wild food – gives us the wild food. You ask anybody who has gone through our country to California; ask those who have settled there and in Utah, and you will find that we have treated them always well. You have children; we have children. You want to raise your children and make them happy and prosperous; we want to raise and make them happy and prosperous. We ask you to help us to do it."

"Look at me. I am poor and naked, but I am the Chief of the Nation. We do not want riches, we do not ask for riches, but we want our children properly trained and brought up. We look to you for your sympathy. Our riches will...do us no good; we cannot take away into the other world anything we have – we want to have love and peace...We would like to know why commissioners are sent out there to do nothing but rob [us] and get the riches of this world away from us?"

"And I am going to leave you today, and I am going back to my home. I want to tell the people that we cannot trust his agents and superintendents. I don't want strange people that we know nothing about. I am very glad that you belong to us. I am very glad that we have come here and found you and that we can understand one another. I don't want any more such men sent out there, who are so poor that when they come out there their first thoughts are how they can fill their own pockets.

"We want preserves in our reserves. We want honest men, and we want you to help to keep us in the lands that belong to us so that we may not be a prey to those who are viciously disposed. I am going back home. I am very glad that you have listened to me, and I wish you good-bye and give you an affectionate farewell." (*The Annals of America* [1866-1883], p. 242-244)

It appears, from several references to the Great Father and the Good Father in Heaven, that Chief Red Cloud was a Christian or certainly a believer in the Christian's God. The nature of God is revealed in the words of Chief Red Cloud who obviously had been introduced to the true God. He spoke as well as any educated white man.

* * * * * * * * * * * * * *

In 1871, Count von Hubner, an Austrian career diplomat, took a leisurely trip around the world, including in his itinerary several American cities. A book which included his impression of American cities was published in Paris in 1873. Below are interesting excerpts from the translation of this book:

"If we, children of old Europe, who cling to the present as the logical natural continuation of the past, who cherish old recollections, traditions, and habits, if we do homage to your success, obtained under institutions which, on all essential points, are contrary to ours, this is a proof of our impartiality. For let us not deceive ourselves. America is the born antagonist of Europe. The first arrivals, the precursors of your actual greatness, those who sowed the seed, were discontented men. Intestine divisions and religious persecutions tore them from their homes and threw them on America's shores.

"They brought with them and planted in the soil of their new country the principle for which they had suffered and fought – the authority of the individual. He who possesses it is free in the fullest sense of the term. And, as in that sense you are all free, each of you is the equal of every other. Your country then is the classic soil of liberty and equality and it has become so from the fact that it was peopled by the men whom Europe expelled from its bosom. That is why you, in conformity with your origin, and we, by a totally different genesis, are antagonistic.

"You offer liberty and equality to everyone. It is to the magic charm of these two words, more than to your gold fields, that you owe the influx of your immigrants and the enormous and ever growing increase of your population. Russia and Hungary still have miles of uncultivated lands; Algeria needs and clamors for hands; but no one goes there. The great mass of emigrants turn their steps to North America. Why? First to find bread, an article which in our overpopulated Europe it is no longer easy to procure; next, to obtain liberty and equality. The emigrants go to you for bread, individual liberty, and social equality, and they find space; that is liberty to work and equality of success if they bring with them the necessary qualifications."

"Compared to Europe, your country is as a sheet of white paper. Everything has to be begun; everything is new. In Europe one rebuilds or restores or modifies or adds (if one has space, which is more and more rare) a wing to one's house. But unless you demolish what exists, you don't rebuild the foundations; for what abounds in America is what we lack most – space. To become American would be to presuppose the entire destruction of Europe.

"There is another reason why you cannot serve as a model in spite of the admiration you excite. How choose as a model a thing which is incomplete? You are at the growing age; you are not yet fully formed. What will you be when you have come to maturity? You do not know and no one can predict, for history offers no example of such a genesis. What new race will spring from this mixture of Celts, Germans, and Mongols? We cannot tell, no one can; we only know that a great change will result.

"There remains also the unsolved problem as to liberty of conscience, the right of each one to worship the Supreme Being according to his own fashion. Until now, this system has worked well. Life is easy here for everybody, for everyone has space. To prevent a disagreeable meeting, one has only to cross to the other side of the street; it is wide enough for all. But the day will come, although it is now far-off, when this illimitable space will be narrowed and when it will be difficult by flight to escape those who do not share your religious convictions. Even in your country the question of liberty of conscience has not yet been definitively settled." (*The Annals of America* [1866-1883], p. 287-288)

* * * * * * * * * * * * * *

From 1873-1874, at the request of *Scribner's Monthly* magazine, Edward King traveled through the South to report on the economic status of the area, after the devastation of the war. King was a skilled journalist and social observer who had worked for the

Springfield (Massachusetts) *Daily Union* and *Springfield Republican*. He wrote a number of articles after the war which became the best accounts of the postwar South. These articles formed a collection called "The Great South." Below are excerpts from this work:

"During my stay in Natchez, one of the many gentlemen interested in cotton planting on the west, or Louisiana, side of the river invited me to accompany him on a tour of inspection. The rapidly rising river threatened to inundate the lands on which hundreds of Negroes had been expending weeks of patient care, and the planter felt it his duty to take a horseback ride over the trio of plantations under his charge; so we crossed the Mississippi and rode twelve miles into the interior of Louisiana.

"On the road, which led along the lovely banks of Lake Concordia, the planter chatted of some of the vexations by which he is daily beset, and spoke rather hopelessly of the labor problem. The conditions of society, too, he thought very bad, and that it was an actual hindrance to the development of the section.

'Are the Negroes,' I asked him, 'aggressive and insolent toward the white people?'

"But as the planter was about to answer this question, we approached a ferryboat, or barge, in which we were to cross the arm of the lake to the island on which my friend's plantations were situated. An old Negro man, much the worse for liquor, was preparing to monopolize the boat with his mule team, but held back the mules and touched his hat with drunken courtesy as we came up.

'Stand aside, uncle,' said the planter firmly, but very politely; 'we wish to cross at once, and there is not room for us all.'

'Yas, sah; yas, Colonel,' said the old man. 'I's willin' to waid on you gemmen 'cause you is gemmen; but ef yer was no count folks, I'd go for yer. Ride in, Colonel.'

"We crossed the field, bordered by noble cypresses and oaks, stopping now and then to watch the Negroes as they carefully prepared the ground which an inundation might, in less than a day, reduce to a hopeless wilderness of mud. Entering the house of the overseer, we found that functionary smoking his pipe and reposing after a long ride over the plantation. He was a rough, hearty, good-natured man, accustomed to living alone and faring rudely. I asked him what he thought of the Negro as a free laborer.

'He works well, mostly, sir. These yer Alabama niggers that's workin' on our plantations now do well on wages. They make some little improvements around their cabins, but mighty little, sir. Ef politics would only let 'em alone, they'd get along well enough, I reckon.'

'Do the Negroes on this plantation vote?'

'I reckon not (laughing). I don't want my niggers to have anything to do with politics. They can't vote as long as they stay with us, and these Alabama boys don't take no interest in the elections here.'

'What do they receive as monthly wages?'

'From $10 to $16. It costs us about $15 per head to bring 'em from Alabama. These niggers likes wages better than shares. We keep a store here, and Saturday nights, most of the money they have earned comes back to us in trade. They're fond o' whiskey and good things to eat.'"

"The laborers were coming in from the field in a long picturesque procession. As it was springtime, many of them had been plowing and were mounted upon the backs of the stout mules which had been their companions all day. Some of the men were singing rude songs; others were shouting boisterously and scuffling as they went their way along the broad pathway, bordered by giant cypresses and noble oaks. The boys tumbling and wriggling in the grass perpetually exploded into guffaws of contagious laughter. Many of the men were tall and finely formed. They had an intelligent look and were evidently not so degraded as those born on the Louisiana lowlands. The overseer sat on the veranda of his home, now and then calling out a sharp command or a caution, the Negroes looking up obsequiously and touching their hats as they heard his voice.

"When the mules were stabled, the men came lounging back to the cabins, where the women were preparing their homely supper; and an hour afterward we heard the tinkle of banjos, the pattering of feet, and uproarious laughter. The interiors of the Negro cabins were of the ruder description. The wretched huts in which the workmen live seem to them quite comfortable, however. I saw no one who appeared discontented with his surroundings. Few of these laborers could read at all. Even those who had some knowledge of the alphabet did not seem to be improving it."

"I ventured to suggest that on the plantation he had every facility for a superb garden, and to wonder that the overseers did not employ some of the Negroes to cultivate a plot of ground that its fruits might appear on the table.

'Oh, oh,' laughed the overseer.'Make a garden here; reckon it would have to have a mighty high wall; the niggers would steal everything in it as fast as it was ripe.'

"But I suggested that if each of the Negroes had a small garden, which he seemed to have ample time after hours to cultivate, he would not desire to steal.

"The Colonel smiled gravely, and the overseer shook his head incredulously, adding:'These is good niggers, but stealing is as natural as eating to them'; and with this remark, we were ushered into the supper room, where two black servant girls ran nimbly about bringing in plain but substantial fare, which our hard riding made thoroughly palatable."

"There is still much on one of these remote and isolated plantations to recall the romance which surrounded them during the days of slavery. The tall and stalwart women, with their luxuriant wool carefully wrapped in gaily colored handkerchiefs, the picturesque and tattered children, who have not the slightest particle of education and who have not been reached, even since the era of Reconstruction, by the influences of schools and teachers; the groups of venerable darkies, with their gray slouch hats and impossible garments, who chatter for hours together on the sunny side of some outbuildings; and the merrymakings at night, all recall a period which the planter will tell you with a mournful look, comprised the halcyon days of Louisiana.

"The thing which struck me as most astonishing here, in the cotton lands, as on the rice plantations of South Carolina, was the absolute subjection of the Negro. Those with whom I talked would not directly express any idea. They gave a shuffling and grimacing assent to whatever was suggested; or, if they dissented, would beg to be excused from differing verbally and seemed to be much distressed at being required to express their opinions openly. Of course, having the most absolute political liberty, because in that section they were so largely in the majority numerically, that no intimidation could have been practised, it seemed astonishing that they should be willing to forgo the right to vote and to willingly isolate themselves from their fellows.

"I could not discover that any of the Negroes were making a definite progress, either manifested by a subscription to some newspaper or by a tendency to discussion; and while the planter gave me the fullest and freest account of the social status of the Negroes employed by him, he failed to mention any sign of a definite and intellectual growth. The only really encouraging sign in their social life was the tendency to create for themselves homes and now and then to cultivate the land about them." (*The Annals of America* [1866-1883], p. 334-339)

* * * * * * * * * * * * * *

Between 1860 and 1890, the population of the United States doubled to 63,000,000; of these, 10,000,000 were immigrants. Many of these new Americans never got over their homesickness for their native countries. In 1876, Thomas Westendorf, a public school music teacher in Plainfield, Indiana, wrote the poignant song "I'll Take You Home Again, Kathleen," while his wife was away on a short trip. The song expresses his loneliness while she is away and his promise to take her back to the old country where she longed to go. I am certain that the words of the song strike the chords of homesickness in emigrants from every land in the new and faraway countries where they settle.

The song was a favorite of Thomas Alva Edison and also of Henry Ford who liked it so much, he placed an autographed copy in his Denver museum. When I hear the song or think about its words, I always feel tears well in my eyes. Read the words below, dear Reader, and see whether you, too, feel the loneliness of a person (especially a woman) in a new land across a vast ocean:

"I'll take you home again, Kathleen,
Across the ocean, wild and wide.
To where your heart has ever been
Since first you were my bonny bride.
The roses all have left your cheek –
I've watched them fade away and die.
Your voice is sad whene'er you speak,
And tears bedim your loving eyes.
I know you love me, Kathleen dear,
Your heart was ever fond and true;
I always feel when you are near
That life holds nothing, dear, but you.
The smiles that once you gave to me
I scarcely ever see them now,
Though many many times I see
A darkening shadow on your brow.
To that dear home beyond the sea
My Kathleen shall again return,
And when thy old friends welcome thee
Thy loving heart will cease to yearn.
Where laughs the little silver stream
Beside your mother's humble cot
And brightest rays of sunshine gleam –
There all your grief will be forgot.

(Chorus)
Oh I will take you back, Kathleen,
To where your heart will feel no pain,
And when the fields are fresh and green
I'll take you to your home again."
(*The Annals of America* [1866-1883], p. 345-346)

Jane H. Walker

Chapter Twenty-Six

In 1876, America celebrated its centennial at the Philadelphia International Exhibition. Only the upheld hand and torch of the Statue of Liberty (which was being constructed in France as a gift from that country to the United States) was on display, hinting at the majesty and beauty of the entire statue which would be completed and dedicated some ten years later.

Featured at the centennial exhibition were the new inventions of the typewriter, the telephone, and the Westinghouse air brake. This celebration of one hundred years of independence heralded the greatest period of expansion and innovation our country had yet known. Huge, efficient corporations and trusts resulted from American industry. The manifest destiny and exceptionalism of the United states were on the cusp of American know-how. Surely, God's hand guided our young nation.

The oil and steel industries and the railroads presaged the advancement of America on the world stage. In 1874, Joseph Glidden invented barbed wire, and the West began to fence itself in. The Philadelphia celebration was only a bare hint of remarkable things on the horizon for the United States of America (*The Annals of America* [1866-1883], p. 355).

* * * * * * * * * * * * *

As a symbol of great friendship between two countries, France gave the Statue of Liberty to the United States in 1884. It was dedicated in 1886. The idea for the statue came from Edouard-

Rene Lefebrure de Laboulaye, a prominent French politician and historian who greatly admired the United States.

In 1871, Frederic Auguste Bartholdi, friend of Laboulaye and noted French sculptor, sailed to the United States to seek support for the project. He selected Bedloe's Island (now called Liberty Island) in Upper New York Bay as the site for the monument. French engineer Alexander Gustave Eiffel designed a framework to support the statue. He later built the famous Eiffel Tower in Paris. The statue stands 151 feet-1 inch high and is covered with 300 sheets of copper fastened together with rivets (threadless bolts). The copper is only 3/32 inch thick.

Liberty is depicted as a proud and majestic woman draped in a flowing robe. Bartholdi used his mother's face as a likeness for the statue. In her right hand she holds a glowing torch. Her crown has seven spikes that stand for the light of liberty shining on the seven seas and the seven continents. In her left arm she cradles a tablet bearing the date of the Declaration of Independence. A chain that represents tyranny or despotic rule lies broken at her feet.

In 1883, Emma Lazarus wrote a poem called "The New Colossus" which was placed on the interior wall of the pedestal in 1903. I had never thought about Lazarus' surname being the same as that of Jesus' friend whom he raised from the dead, until this writing. Is there a Christian symbolism and meaning here? The poem reads as follows:

> "Not like the brazen giant of Greek fame,
> With conquering limbs astride from land to land;
> Here at our sea-washed, sunset gates shall stand
> A mighty woman with a torch, whose flame
> Is the imprisoned lightning, and her name
> Mother of Exiles. From her beacon-hand
> Glows world-wide welcome; her mild eyes command
> The air-bridged harbor that twin cities frame.
> 'Keep, ancient lands, your storied pomp!' cries she
> With silent lips. 'Give me your tired, your poor,
> Your huddled masses yearning to breathe free,

CAN WE FATHOM THE NATURE OF GOD?

The wretched refuse of your teeming shore.
Send these, the homeless, tempest-tost to me.
I lift my lamp beside the golden door!'"

The statue was disassembled in Paris before sending it to the United States. It was packed in 214 wooden crates for shipment to the U. S. The French ship *Isere* brought the statue across the Atlantic and landed in the United States on June 17, 1885,

"Liberty Enlightening the World," as it was called, was dedicated on October 28, 1886 in Upper New York Bay. New York City featured a grand parade and the harbor was filled with boats. President Grover Cleveland and members of his Cabinet were present at the ceremonies. Bartholdi and representatives of the French government also participated. From the 1880s to the 1890s, millions of immigrants passed the Statue of Liberty as they entered the United States at nearby Ellis Island. Why could these immigrants assimilate, but present-day ones sometimes cannot? Maybe it is the legitimacy of those who came before.

The Statue of Liberty required major repairs by the early 1980s, and a $30-million restoration project was planned. Official celebrations marked the opening of the newly restored Statue of Liberty on July 4, 1986. A grand ceremony was also held on October 28, 1986, 100 years after the original dedication of the grand statue (*The World Book* "So-Sz," 1997, p. 872-879).

Dear Reader, what a beautiful symbol of freedom and friendship and democracy and hope stands in New York harbor. I believe the Statue of Liberty was inspired by God himself. The Statue of Liberty is a beacon of enlightenment to all who enter our country, and it is the gateway to the nation that is "set upon a hill," cherished not only by its inhabitants but also by the rest of the world. I believe it is symbolic of God's nature.

* * * * * * * * * * * * *

Perhaps the leaders of our nation felt they had dealt well with the black slave issue at the end of the Civil War, even giving to the freed slaves the right to vote. However, the American Indian problem continued to nettle the conscience of the country, founded in the most part by Christians. The Indians by the 1880s were confined on reservations, but their problems would not go away.

Carl Schurz was Secretary of the Interior from 1877-1881; his department included the Bureau of Indian Affairs. Schurz wrote an article entitled "Present Aspects of the Indian Problem," which was published in *North American Review* in July of 1881. Below are several paragraphs of his lengthy article which reveals his compassion for the dispossessed red man:

"That the history of our Indian relations presents, in great part, a record of broken treaties, of unjust wars, and of cruel spoliation is a fact too well known to require proof or to suffer denial. But it is only just to the government of the United States to say that its treaties with Indian tribes were, as a rule, made in good faith, and that most of our Indian wars were brought on by circumstances for which the government itself could not fairly be held responsible. Of the treaties, those were the most important by which the government guaranteed to Indian tribes certain tracts of land as reservations to be held and occupied by them forever under the protection of the United States, in the place of other lands ceded by the Indians. There is no reason to doubt that in most, if not all, of such cases those who conducted Indian affairs on the part of the government, not anticipating the rapid advance of settlement, sincerely believed in the possibility of maintaining those reservations intact for the Indians, and that, in this respect, while their intentions were honest, their foresight was at fault.

"There are men still living who spent their younger days near the borders of 'Indian country' in Ohio and Indiana; and it is a well-known fact that, when the Indian Territory was established west of the Mississippi, it was generally thought that the settlements of white men would never crowd into that region, at least not for many generations. Thus were such reservations guaranteed by the government with the honest belief that the Indians would be secure in their possession, which, as subsequent events proved, was a gross error of judgment."

"But will those who are hungry for the Indian lands sit still? It will be easy for the rough and reckless frontiersmen to pick quarrels with the Indians. The speculators, who have their eyes upon every opportunity for gain, will urge them on. The watchfulness of the government will, in the long run, be unavailing to prevent collisions. The Indians will retaliate. Settlers' cabins will be burned and blood will flow. The conflict once brought on, the white man and the red man will stand against one another, and, in spite of all its good intentions and its sense of justice, the forces of the government will find themselves engaged on the side of the white man. The Indians will be hunted down at whatever cost. It will simply be a repetition of the old story, and that old story will be eventually repeated whenever there is a large and valuable Indian reservation surrounded by white settlements. Unjust, disgraceful as this may be, it is not only probable but almost inevitable. The extension of our railroad system will only accelerate the catastrophe." *(The Annals of America* [1866-1883], p. 495-498)

* * * * * * * * * * * * * *

The Great American Desert had long held back the settlement of lands beyond the Rocky Mountains. When the Civil War began in 1860, westward settlement had only reached Kansas. From there to the Rockies was the domain of the Indian and largely unknown to the white man. Of course, beyond the Rockies, almost isolated, lay the rich mines of rapidly developing California.

After the war, in 1869, the Union Pacific-Central Pacific rail line was completed. By 1884, three other lines had reached the west coast. In 1893, the Great Northern opened up the wheat regions of the Dakotas and reached the Pacific. Population and development rapidly followed.

With less than 100 miles of railroad in 1865, post-war Kansas had 3,000 miles by 1880. With the railroads came the cowtowns of America's best-loved folklore towns, such as Abilene, Wichita, and Dodge City. The cowboys, the bad men and the gun fights provided fodder for books and movies of the time period (*The Annals of America* [1866-1883], p. 519-523).

* * * * * * * * * * * * * *

From 1867-1880, the gorgeous national parks of our great nation were discovered and created. John Muir led the way to the founding of Yosemite National Park in 1867. Ferdinand Hayden explored the Great Plains and the Rocky Mountains for thirty years, which led to the creation of Yellowstone National Park in 1869. Clarence King worked for the creation of Sequoia National Park between 1870 and 1880. These parks of heavenly beauty showcase the loveliness and the pristine quality of our great country for future generations to enjoy (*The Annals of America* [1866-1883], p. 527).

* * * * * * * * * * * * * * *

The invention of the telegraph by Samuel F. B. Morse (1791-1872), during the mid-1800s, and his first message, "What hath God wrought?," heralded an explosion of later inventions in America. Long before Morse's message which was sent from Washington to Baltimore on May 24, 1844, signaling systems that enabled people to communicate over distances were very primitive. Sometimes, flags, bells, lights, or smoke were sent from a high tower or a distant hill. This was not a reliable way to convey messages.

The young republic offered a prize of $30,000 to anyone who could invent a way of communicating over long distances. The legislators had no way of knowing that this invention would involve the use of electricity. Also, the first message, "What hath God wrought?" indicated the hand of God in the creation not only of the telegraph but also of the early exceptionalism of America.

With President Tyler's signature, Morse received the $30,000 and was given the go-ahead to invent an underground telegraph line between Washington and Baltimore. This caused some delay, however, because unbeknownst to Morse, the wire had defective insulation which made the project impossible. Because a deadline for the invention was rapidly approaching, Morse was desperate to fulfill his mission.

Morse had hired the ingenious construction engineer, Ezra Cornell, who suggested that the wires be strung overhead on lines and poles. Morse agreed to this, and it was successful in linking the Supreme Court Chamber of the Capitol building with the railroad station in Baltimore. Within Morse's lifetime, the telegraph lines extended westward and even connected the continents of Europe and America ("Invention of the Telegraph–Samuel F. B. Morse Papers at the Library...").

Morse developed a code of dots and dashes as a system to send messages over the telegraph wires. A short sound was called a "dit," whereas a long sound was called a "dah." Written code used dots and dashes to stand for dits and dahs. Morse patented the code, named after him, in 1840 ("June 20, 1840: A Simple Matter of Dots and Dashes/WIRED").

No recount of the exceptionalism of America would be complete without including the life and inventions of Thomas Alva Edison (1847-1931). The United States became an industrial world power because of the work of Edison and other manufacturing pioneers in the late 1800s. Though some scientists and historians consider his development of the research lab as his finest achievement, he also invented practical electric lighting, the phonograph, and improvements to the telephone, the telegraph, and motion pictures. Edison received 1,093 U. S. Patents, the most ever issued from that office to one person (*The World Book* "E", 1997, p. 77).

Edison was born in Ohio but moved with his family to Port Huron, Michigan, when he was seven years old. Due to illness, he did not attend school until he was eight years old. Though the schoolmaster thought Edison was a stupid boy, his mother thought otherwise and took him out of school, determined to teach him at home ("Thomas Alva Edison"). This was all that Edison ever received of formal schooling. However, his mother encouraged him to read such books as Gibbon's *Decline and Fall of the Roman Empire* and Hume's *History of England,* as well as other great literary works ("Thomas Edison: Inventor of the Age of Electricity").

Edison was left permanently deaf around the age of twelve, when he began selling newspapers on the newly established Grand Trunk Railway which made daily runs between Port Huron and Detroit. One morning when he was delayed in boarding the train, which was already pulling away, he tried to clamber aboard the freight car with both arms full of newspapers. When he could not keep his balance, a trainman grabbed him by the ears and pulled him up ("Thomas Alva Edison").

This caused his deafness about which he remarked, "I haven't heard a bird sing since I was twelve years old." However, he never indulged in self-pity and even had a detached sense of humor throughout his many successes and failures ("Edison, Thomas Alva 2"). When he was fifteen, he rescued the son of a telegraph operator from an oncoming railroad car. As a reward, the operator gave Edison telegraph lessons, and he became a telegraph operator for the Western Union Telegraph Company in Port Huron. Working as a telegrapher in a number of midwestern cities, Edison studied the mechanical, electrical, and chemical elements of telegraphy and experimented with telegraph equipment. Though he had a hearing impairment, he became proficient in receiving news reports by telegraph (*The World Book* "E", 1997, p. 78).

Edison later moved to Boston and New York City, then in 1870 to Newark, New Jersey. In 1876, he built a laboratory in Menlo Park, about 25 miles south of Newark. Receiving financial support from Western Union, Edison and his assistants did research that transformed the world. Because of his many inventions, he became known as the Wizard of Menlo Park.

He was fascinated by the recently invented telegraph and by the mysteries of electricity. He learned the Morse Code and was soon an expert telegrapher. It was Edison who described genius as being "1 percent inspiration and 99 percent perspiration (same source as above, p. 81). His power of concentration and mental acuity were extraordinary, as Matthew Josephson, a biographer, wrote:

"Like one possessed, he would carry in his head the entire plan of some new and elaborate invention, in all its complex details, for days on end. He had the gift of total recall. His memory was so extensive that he would work out many aspects of a difficult problem in his mind, oblivious to his surroundings, forgetting the time, the place, and even his own identity." ("Thomas Edison's Light Bulb–Heart of Wisdom")

In 1878, he began research on electrical lighting. This was only a novelty at first, because few homes and businesses had electricity.

He then began concentrating on producing electricity in central power plants which would distribute it over wires to businesses and homes.

To promote the construction of electric power plants in cities, Edison and his associates moved to New York City in 1881. There he built the Pearl Street Station, a steam electric power plant near Wall Street. After 1890, hundreds of communities throughout the world had Edison power stations.

Other equipment had to be readily available to make the electric lighting system commercially successful, such as generators, power cables, electric lamps, and lighting fixtures. Edison and others invested in companies that manufactured this equipment. The General Electric Company was formed in 1892, when these companies combined with others.

In 1886, Edison moved to a residential area of West Orange, New Jersey, called Llewellyn Park. There he built a laboratory which was ten times the size of the one in Menlo Park. This lab was Edison's true home for the rest of his life (*The World Book* "E," p. 79-81).

Oh, Reader, I see the hand of God in the life of Thomas Edison who contributed so much to the exceptionalism of America. He could have been born and lived in another country, but God placed him in America. His inventions gave the United States industrial superiority over other nations.

Edison married Mary Stilwell in 1871, and they had three children. Edison nicknamed the first two "Dot" and "Dash" after the telegraph code. Mary died in 1884. In 1886, he married Mina Miller and they had three children. Their son Charles served as secretary of the U. S. Navy in 1940 and as Governor of New Jersey from 1941-1944.

Edison and Henry Ford became close friends after Edison encouraged Ford to use the gasoline engine in the automobile (same *World Book* source above, p. 79-81). Ford arranged the elaborate fiftieth anniversary of the invention of the light bulb ("Lights Golden Jubilee–The Henry Ford"). At the event, a radio announcer solemnly intoned, "And Edison said, 'Let there be light.'" ("PDF

Light's Golden Jubilee–Library of Congress") When Edison's West Orange laboratory was destroyed by fire in December 1914, he said, "I am 67, but I'm not too old to make a fresh start. I've been through a lot of things like this. It prevents a man from being afflicted with ennui." ("Thomas Edison Quotes/Quote Catalog") Henry Ford assisted in financing the rebuilding of the plant ("Thomas Edison's Reaction to His Factory Burning...–Business Insider").

* * * * * * * * * * * * *

When I have discussed the people who contributed so much to America's exceptionalism, I am often asked the question, "Was he (or she) a Christian?" My young granddaughter asked me this question about several of the great thinkers whom I have included in this book, and I had to say, "no, they were not Christians." Why, if they were so enlightened, did they not know the truth that can only be found in the Bible? I wish I had a better answer, but all I know to reply is that these people probably never had anyone to carry them to church and to teach them the Bible. This is the only explanation I have. However, I did tell my granddaughter that Sir Isaac Newton was a Christian, and he was one of the foremost scientists who ever lived, as I mentioned before in this book.

The great spiritual leader, Dr. Norman Vincent Peale, mentioned Thomas Edison in remarks he made some years ago. Below is what he said:

"Some years ago a famous industrialist asked me to come and see him. His wife had died, leaving him with a terrible sense of grief and loss. He wanted assurance that he would be reunited with her some day. 'Do you truly believe?' he asked me, 'that after we die another life is waiting for us?'

"I told him that I was absolutely convinced. I said we had the promises of the Bible, the Resurrection of Jesus Christ, the deepest instincts of countless people throughout history. I said I had no doubts about it whatsoever.

"But what about scientific proof? He wanted to know. I said, "Let me tell you something about the greatest scientist our nation ever produced: Thomas A Edison. I knew his widow, and one day when I was in her home I said to her, 'Tell me about your husband.

What sort of mind did he really have?'

"She said, 'Exactitude was the mark of my husband's mind. He was not sentimental. He had to know something for sure before he would say it or record it. It had to be proven.' Then she told me that when her husband was dying, he could barely speak. His doctor, who was also a family friend, noticed that the great inventor was trying to say something. He leaned close and heard Edison whisper, 'It's very beautiful over there.' Those were his last words.

"I said to the industrialist, Edison would not lie. He would not fabricate anything. He would report only what he saw. Is that scientific proof enough for you?"

'Yes,' he said, 'I think he glimpsed the land where my wife is waiting for me.'

"I think so, too."

"Dear Jesus, thank You for Your promise that some day we will be with You in 'the Land that is fairer than day.'" ("Thomas Edison's Glimpse of Heaven/*Guideposts*")

Jane H. Walker

Chapter Twenty-Seven

After the American Civil War, the United States became an economic powerhouse. Factories built by the North to defeat the Confederacy were not shut down at the war's end. Rather, they were converted to peacetime usefulness. Small businesses began to grow, beginning with the railroads.

By the end of the nineteenth century, the nation's economy was dominated by a few, very powerful individuals. In 1850, most Americans were self-employed; by 1900, most Americans worked for someone else. These employers included the heads of industry who became household names, such as John D. Rockefeller of Standard Oil, Andrew Carnegie of Carnegie steel, and J. Pierpont Morgan, the great banker who controlled many industries.

The growth of American economy was astounding. From the end of Reconstruction in 1877 to the end of the century, the U. S. economy nearly doubled in size. New technologies and new business practices created an elite pool of American industrialists. In addition to several already named, others included Cornelius Vanderbilt, John Jacob Astor, and Andrew W. Mellon ("Meet the 24 Robber Barons Who Once Ruled America").

The competition was ruthless and the tactics of some of the powerful industrialists were not always fair. However, there were few laws regulating business conduct at that time. Business men who could not provide the best product at the lowest price were either driven into bankruptcy or were bought up by successful industrialists.

In less than 25 years, America's new millionaires changed New York's Fifth Avenue from a dirt, rutted road into a magnificent street, bordered with palatial homes. The American economy continued to grow. By 1914, the small, struggling nation had become the largest industrialized country in the world.

However, amid the great wealth of the economic elite was terrible poverty. How could some become so successful while others struggled just to survive? This poignant question caused Americans to develop new attitudes toward wealth.

They wondered what role their government should have in this trend. Congress, the president, and the courts seemed to favor the rampant industrialization of America. Yet, leadership on the political level was lacking. Corruption spread throughout city, state, and national governments. For better or for worse, true leadership remained among the economic magnates who ruled the Gilded Age of the American economy ("The Gilded Age[ushistory.org]").

Though some of the wealthy tycoons were called "robber barons," some of the same people became known for the contributions they made to our country and to philanthropies ("Captain of Industry–Wikipedia"). One such man was Andrew Carnegie. Andrew Carnegie (1835-1919) was born in Dunfermline, Fife, Scotland, in a typical weaver's cottage with only one room which was shared with a neighboring weaver's family. When Carnegie was thirteen, his family faced hard times and actual starvation. Carnegie's father was a handloom weaver and his mother sold potted meats at her "sweetie shop."

In 1848, the Carnegie family moved to Allegheny, Pennsylvania, in the United States, hoping to have a better life. Andrew's first job at the age of thirteen in 1848 was as a bobbin boy, changing spools of thread in a cotton mill twelve hours a day, six days a week, in a Pittsburgh cotton factory. His beginning wage was $1.20 a week ($36.36 in 2017 dollars).

On Saturday nights in the city of Pittsburgh, Colonel James Anderson opened his personal library of 400 volumes to working boys in the city. Carnegie was a regular borrower who became a "self-made man" from such wide reading opportunities. He was so grateful to Colonel Anderson for the use of his library that he "resolved, if ever wealth came to me, [to see to it] that other poor boys might receive opportunities similar to those for which we were indebted to the noble man."

Amassing a fortune in the steel industry, Carnegie controlled the most extensive integrated iron and steel businesses ever owned by an individual in the United States. He also became a well-regarded writer and was a powerful supporter of the movement for spelling reform as a way to promote the spread of the English language. He used his money in many philanthropic enterprises, including the establishment of public libraries throughout the United States, Britain, Canada, and other English-speaking countries. During the last years of the nineteenth century, the idea that free libraries should be available to the American public gained acceptance.

His interest in music brought about the construction of 7,000 church organs. He also built and owned Carnegie Hall in New York City. The list of his philanthropic ventures is extensive. During the last eighteen years of his life, he gave to foundations, charities, and universities about $350 million ("Andrew Carnegie–Wikipedia").

In his 1889 article, entitled "The Gospel of Wealth," he urged wealthy people to use their riches to improve the quality of life of other people. This stimulated a wave of philanthropy from other wealthy industrialists. Andrew Carnegie wrote the following words in a letter to himself in 1868, at the age of 33, which appear to be his philosophy concerning his great wealth:

"I propose to take an income no greater than $50,000 per annum! Beyond this I need ever earn, make no effort to increase my fortune, but spend the surplus each year for benevolent purposes! Let us cast aside business forever, except for others. Let us settle in Oxford and I shall get a thorough education, making the acquaintance of literary men. I figure that this will take three years active work. I shall pay especial attention to speaking in public. We can settle in London and I can purchase a controlling interest in some newspaper or live review and give the general management of it attention, taking part in public matters, especially those connected with education and improvement of the poorer classes. Man must have no idol and the amassing of wealth is one of the worst species of idolatry! No idol is more debasing than the worship of money! Whatever I engage in I must push inordinately; therefore should I be careful to choose that life which will be the most elevating in its character. To continue much longer overwhelmed by business cares and with most of my thoughts wholly upon the way to make more money in the shortest time, must degrade me beyond hope of permanent recovery. I will resign business at thirty-five, but during these ensuing two years I wish to spend the afternoons in receiving instruction and in reading systematically!"

In 1889, Carnegie published "Wealth" in the June issue of the *North American Review*. In it, he proclaimed that the life of a wealthy industrialist should encompass two parts – the accumulation of wealth and the subsequent distribution of this wealth to noble causes. He urged wealthy people to use their riches to improve the quality of life of other people. Philanthropy, he felt, made life worthwhile. He claimed that a "man who dies rich dies disgraced." ("Andrew Carnegie–*New World Encyclopedia*")

* * * * * * * * * * * * *

In 1898, the U.S. *Maine* battleship was mysteriously sunk in Havana harbor. This led to American intervention in the Cuban War of Independence from Spain. The Spanish-American War was fought for ten weeks in both the Caribbean and the Pacific, as the United States fought to free Cuba from Spanish rule ("Spanish-American War–Wikipedia"). For nearly 400 years, Cuba had been an integral part of the Spanish nation ("A Brief History of Cuba–Captivating Cuba").

As the U. S. rapidly built a powerful navy in the 1890s, Theodore Roosevelt served as Assistant Secretary of the Navy from 1897-1898. He was an aggressive supporter of Cuba in its war with Spain. He wanted to help the Cuban people and also to promote the Monroe Doctrine. The Monroe Doctrine, as articulated by President James Monroe in an address to Congress in 1823, stated: "The American continents...are henceforth not to be considered as subjects for future colonization by any European powers." ("The Monroe Doctrine–USHistory.org") The independent territory of the Western Hemisphere was to be solely the United States' domain, and in exchange, the United States pledged to avoid involvement in European political affairs.

About 15,000 American troops attacked 1270 entrenched Spaniards in Cuba. More than 200 U. S. soldiers were killed and around 1200 wounded in the fighting. The invasion of Guantanamo Bay occurred between June 6 and 10, 1898.

When the Spanish squadron attempted to leave the harbor on July 3, American forces either destroyed or grounded five of its six ships. However, the American occupation force became crippled with yellow fever. Theodore Roosevelt was chosen by concerned officers to draft a request to Washington that it withdraw the Army, described by a general as an "army of convalescents."

On December 10, 1898, the Treaty of Paris was signed in Paris and ratified by the U. S. Senate on February 6, 1899. The U. S. took possession of all of Spain's colonies outside of Africa in the treaty, including the Philippines, Guam, and Puerto Rico. Cuba became a U. S. protectorate.

Though formerly under the jurisdiction of the U. S. Military Government, Cuba formed its own civil government and gained its independence on May 20, 1902. This was the end of the U.S.M.G. over the island. However, the United States did establish a perpetual lease of Guantanamo Bay.

The Spanish-American War actually served to repair relations between the American North and South. For the first time since the Civil War, both sides fought a common enemy together. Many friendships were formed between soldiers of northern and southern states during their tours of duty ("Spanish-American War–Wikipedia").

* * * * * * * * * * * * * *

As America moved into the industrial age, near the end of the nineteenth century, the size of buildings began expanding vertically, rather than outwardly. Skyscrapers appeared first in Chicago, then in New York. Skyscrapers necessarily depended upon the invention of the safety elevator by Elisha Otis in 1852 or 1857 (Note: I've seen both dates in different sources.).

Skyscrapers also relied on the use of steel by 1895, which was refined from iron in the middle of the nineteenth century. Steel was strong and light, unlike former building materials. Major cities, especially in America, strived for the tallest buildings in the world. The Empire State Building in New York was the world's highest building for four decades. Today, buildings in other countries have surpassed it in height. In 2009 the Burj Khalifa in Dubai (United Arab Emirates) became the tallest building in the world with a height of 2,722 feet ("Skyscraper–Wikipedia").

Before the building of skyscrapers, a high floor required a lot of climbing stairs, so rent was less for these spaces. However, the invention of the safety elevator changed that. Now, it's the penthouse that costs the most ("The First Elevator–The Architecture and Development of New York").

The men who actually built the first skyscrapers became almost legendary heroes. Workers called "roughnecks" labored hundreds of feet above the ground without harnesses or safety ropes or even hard hats. Seasoned workers were called "fixers," while new men on the job were called "snakes." These snakes were deadly to be around, because a falling man would grab anything, or anybody, on the way down.

Skyscraper workers had eight-hour working days, ate when they could, oftentimes sitting on beams hundreds of feet above the street below, and had no toilet breaks. One slip...and one was dead. A building foreman named William Starrett was quoted as saying, "Building skyscrapers is the nearest peace-time equivalent of war. In fact, the analogy is startling, even to the occasional grim reality of a building accident where maimed bodies, and even death, remind us that we are fighting a war of construction against the forces of nature." ("Building New York City/HistoryTV")

Native American Mohawks, called skywalkers, often worked on the skyscrapers, lured by the extra pay of $4.00 a day, *twice* the going rate for manual labor. Though it was thought that they did not fear great heights, in actuality they did, but they never showed it. Two out of five workers either fell to their deaths or became disabled ("Building New York City/History TV–History.co.uk").

On September 11, 2001, Mohawk ironworkers were setting steel on another building, when a jet roared overhead, barely fifty feet from the crane they were using to set steel girders in place. The crew's leader, Dick Oddo, said, "I looked up and I could see the rivets on the plane. I could read the serial numbers it was so low, and I thought 'What is he doing going down Broadway?'" Other ironworkers watched in disbelief as the plane flew down Broadway and into one of the towers of the 110-story World Trade Center, only ten blocks away.

Iddo said that at first he thought it was pilot error, but then another jet flew by. "When the plane hit the second tower, I knew it was all planned," he said. Many of the Mohawks had worked on the Twin Towers some three decades before. Because they were familiar with the layouts of the buildings, they raced to the site, hoping to help people escape the erupting inferno.

After helping survivors escape from the buildings, which finally came crashing down, the Indians joined in the search for victims, hidden under the rubble. Many Mohawk ironworkers also volunteered to help with the cleanup during the many months that followed. Hundreds of Mohawks had worked on erecting the World Trade Center from 1966-1974. In keeping with ironworking tradition, the last girder was signed by Mohawk ironworkers. The Mohawk Indians were truly the unsung heroes of the tragedy of September 11, 2001 ("The Mohawks Who Built Manhattan–Native Village.org").

* * * * * * * * * * * * *

It has been said that the automobile affected American everyday life in the early 1900s more than anything else. Though automobile technology existed in the nineteenth century, Henry Ford later made the car accessible to the American people. Using the assembly line to make cars, he paid his workers more than double what other laborers were being paid. In 1914, the Model T sold for $490. By 1920, over eight million registrations had occurred. By the end of the decade, auto ownership nearly tripled to 23 million.

Many spin-off businesses developed along with the growth of the automobile industry. The demand for vulcanized rubber soared as road construction brought about thousands of new jobs. State and local governments began funding highways. The highway laws of 1916 and 1921 were the first federal interventions into road financing in the United States. These laws established the Federal Bureau of Public Roads.

As gas stations sprang up, mechanics found work, repairing the problems that inevitably arose with automobile usage. Oil and steel industries flourished, and rest stops called motels dotted the major long-distance routes. Diners were built for hungry travelers who wanted cheap, fast food to eat on the run.

However, as new businesses prospered, old ones decayed. As Americans opted for cars to reach their destinations, the nation's rails were neglected. European nations strengthened their mass transit systems, while Americans elected to drive their cars, rather than use the railways.

The automobile changed the lives of people in America – for the good in some ways and not so good in others. Families could travel to places which were previously off limits. Rural dwellers could easily travel to towns and cities to shop.

Though young people gained more independence with driving cars, this freedom helped to form relaxed sexual conduct. Traffic jams and car accidents brought new worries and new legislative action to the forefront. However, without question, the automobile changed the world outlook of Americans ("The Age of the Automobile [ushistory.org]").

* * * * * * * * * * * * * *

Leaving the earth and flying through the air became the dream of mankind throughout the ages. Though scientists and engineers designed primitive airplanes, actually types of balloons, beginning in 1783 in France and elsewhere, the Wright brothers in America made the first powered, controlled, and sustained flights on December 17, 1903, at Kitty Hawk, North Carolina. Immediately after their first powered flights, they worked to develop a marketable product ("Early flying machines–Wikipedia").

The airplane figured largely in the victory of America and

the Allied forces in World War I. In only a few short years, from 1903 to the beginning of World War I in 1914, the airplane became perfected to the extent that it could be piloted over oceans to engage in combat. Can you not, oh Reader, see the hand of God in this feat ("Aviation in World War 1–Wikipedia")?

The First World War (1914-1918) pitted the United States and its Allies, which included Great Britain, France, Russia, Italy, and Japan, against the Central Powers, which included Germany, Bulgaria, Hungary, and Turkey. Though each side expected quick victory, the war lasted four years and killed ten million troops. It was originally called the Great War.

Though the assassination of Archduke Francis Ferdinand of Austria-Hungary triggered the war, the chief causes were the rise of nationalism; the building of military power; the competition for colonies; and the system of military alliances. The defeat of the Central Powers led to the fall of four great dynasties in Germany, Russia, Austria-Hungary, and Turkey. The war also resulted in the Bolshevik Revolution in Russia and the destabilization of Europe. Conditions following the war led to the Second World War which began in 1939 (*The World Book* "WXYZ" 1997, p. 454-469).

* * * * * * * * * * * * * *

Along with the outbreak of World War I in 1914, the terrible Flu Pandemic also erupted during the war in 1918. Recent studies have estimated that between 50 and 100 million people (or 3-5 % of the world's population) perished, making it one of the deadliest disasters in human history. Though the flu usually was a killer of the elderly and young children, it was most deadly then for young adults, ages twenty to forty.

The flu infected 28% of all Americans, and an estimated 675,000 Americans died during the pandemic, ten times as many as in the World War. Half of the U. S. soldiers who died in Europe were victims of the influenza virus and not the enemy. On December 28, 1918, the *Journal of the American Medical Association* included an article, an excerpt of which appears below:

"... 1918 has gone: a year momentous as the termination of the most cruel war in the annals of the human race; a year which marked the end at least for a time, of man's destruction of man; unfortunately a year in which developed a most fatal infectious disease causing the death of hundreds of thousands of human beings. Medical science for four and one-half years devoted itself to putting men on the firing line and keeping them there. Now it must turn with its whole might to combating the greatest enemy of all – infectious disease." ("Introduction: The Great enemy–Infectious Disease–NCBI–NIH")

The flu strain was so virulent that people were struck with illness on the street and died rapid deaths. An anecdote of 1918 told of four women playing bridge together late into the night. Overnight, three of the women succumbed to the flu. People on their way to work suddenly developed the flu and died within hours. One doctor wrote that patients with ordinary influenza would "develop the most viscous type of pneumonia that has ever been seen" and another physician said his patients "died struggling to clear their airway of a blood-tinged froth that sometimes gushed from their nose and mouth." In 1918 children would skip rope and sing to the rhyme:

"I had a little bird,
Its name was Enza.
I opened the window,
And in-flu-enza."

Everyone was affected by the pandemic. One quarter of the United States and one-fifth of the world were infected with the influenza. In early 1919, even President Woodrow Wilson suffered from the flu while negotiating the treaty of Versailles to end World War I. Gauze masks were distributed by the public health departments to be worn in public. Sales could not be held in stores, and funerals were limited to fifteen minutes. In a single year, more people died of influenza than in four years of the Black Death Bubonic Plague from 1347-1351 ("The 1918 Influenza Pandemic–virus").

Different strains of influenza and the years of their pandemics are as follows:
1889-1890: Asiatic or Russia Flu – one million deaths
1918-1920: Spanish Flu – 20-100 million deaths

1957-1958: Asian Flu – one to 1.5 million deaths
1968-1989: Hong Kong Flu – 0.75-one million deaths
1977-1978: Russian Flu – no accurate count of deaths
2009: Swine Flu – 18,000 deaths
("Influenza pandemic–Wikipedia")

According to an article I read in Wikipedia, regarding the global Spanish flu pandemic of 1918, "Physicians tried everything they knew, everything they had ever heard of, from the ancient art of bleeding patients, to administering oxygen, to developing new vaccines and sera (chiefly against what we now call Hemophilus influenzae – a name derived from the fact that it was originally considered the etiological agent – and several types of pneumococci). Only one therapeutic measure, transfusing blood from recovered patients to new victims, showed any hint of success." ("Spanish flu research–Wikipedia")

In 1931, viral growth in embryonated hens' eggs was reported by several colleagues at Vanderbilt University. The research was continued by several pioneers in the field, including Jonas Salk, which led to the first experimental influenza vaccines. The U. S. military developed the first approved inactivated vaccines for influenza in the 1940s, which were used in the Second World War ("Influenza Vaccine–Wikipedia").

For decades a "universal vaccine" has been researched, one that would not have to be made for each flu season in each hemisphere. Upon speaking with those who have studied the terrible toll of influenza outbreaks on lives and businesses, it's not a question of whether or not we will have another terrible worldwide pandemic. It's not a question of "if," but "when." ("Experts say: Not 'If' But 'When' for Global Flu Pandemic")

* * * * * * * * * * * * * *

Though the United States experienced economic depressions from the time of its inception, the cycles would only last a year or two, before business activity would begin to pick up again. However, the Great Depression was different. It lasted ten years, beginning with the stock market collapse on October 29, 1929, and ending with the onset of World War II in 1939. It was a devastating time for America

("Great Depression–Wikipedia").

By 1933, some 15 million Americans were unemployed, and almost half of the country's banks had closed. Soup kitchens, bread lines, and thousands of homeless people were tragic scenes of the times. Farmers could not afford to harvest their crops and were forced to leave them rotting in the fields while people were starving. Herbert Hoover was President when the depression began, and he received criticism for the federal government's non-intervention into the swirling financial chaos of the worsening depression. Local and state governments could not afford to help ("The Great Depression–Facts and Summary–HISTORY.com").

Many people who lost their homes clustered together in makeshift, shabby shacks, built from flattened tin cans and old crates. These group shelters were called "Hoovervilles" in angered reference to President Hoover's failure to end the depression. According to an article I read in *World Book* about the Great Depression, a person who grew up in Oklahoma during the depression described a visit to a "Hooverville" in Oklahoma City: "Here were all these people living in old rusted out car bodies... One family . . . [was] living in a piano box. This wasn't just a little section, this was maybe 10 miles wide and 10 miles long. People living in whatever they could junk together...."

In 1932, Franklin D. Roosevelt was elected President. He thought the federal government had the main responsibility of overcoming the depression. He called Congress into a special session, known as the "Hundred Days," to pass laws to ease the depression. He referred to his program as the "New Deal."

The new laws put into place to deal with the depression had three main purposes. They were to help the needy, provide jobs, and encourage business. The Civilian Conservation Corps (CCC); The Federal Emergency Relief Administration (FERA); and the Works Progress Administration (WPA) were put into effect. In 1935, Congress passed the Social Security Act which is still in effect in 2018. For the first time, it provided Americans with relief from unemployment and disability and established pensions for old age.

The Great Depression was worldwide and caused the rise

of extremist political movements in European countries. The Nazi regime in Germany, led by Adolph Hitler, was responsible for the Jewish Holocaust during World War II. When America entered the war in 1941, the nation's factories began producing again and creating jobs. The unemployment rate was reduced to its pre-Depression level.

Many new laws were enacted during the Great Depression that gave the government much more power than at any time during our nation's history. Whereas people had relied on themselves and their hard work to better their lives, the Depression brought about their loss of jobs and homes and forced them to rely on the government rather than themselves for their livelihood (*The World Book* "G," 1997, p. 338-343).

Those who lived through the Great Depression are often referred to as the "Greatest Generation," because of their courage and ingenuity in providing food and shelter for their families when everything was suddenly taken away from them ("The Greatest Generation–Investopedia").

Jane H. Walker

Chapter Twenty-Eight

Space exploration began with designs of rocket engines in the early 20th century by key scientists in three countries, i.e. Robert Goddard in the United States; Konstatin Tsiolkovski in Russia; and Hermann Oberth in Germany. However, only in the latter half of the 20th century were rockets created that were powerful enough to open space to human exploration. During the middle part of the 20th century, World War II became the proving ground of rocket engineers in Germany ("Rocket History–20th Century and Beyond–Glenn Research Center").

In Adolph Hitler's quest to rule the world, he saw the possibilities of winning the war in the work of brilliant German scientists and engineers who led the world in their rocket research. The plan was for the Third Reich to rule for a thousand years. In doing research for this book, I found a book entitled *Operation Paperclip* by Annie Jacobsen, which outlined the secretive work of these accomplished Germans. The book also documents the efforts of the United States to bring many of these German scientists and engineers to America to initiate the United States space program (*Operation Paperclip*, p. 1-5).

As World War II progressed, Hitler needed a weapon that would bring victory to Germany. He was fortunate to have a cadre of scientists and engineers who had been working on rockets, supposedly for space exploration, for years. One of these scientists, Werhner Von Braun, developed the V-2 rocket which could be (and was) used as a weapon by the Third Reich (p. 9).

Nothing in the world of rocketry could compare with the giant V-2 rocket. The "V" stood for *Vergeltungswaffe* (vengeance weapon). The technology of German scientists and engineers had far surpassed that of America and our allies. The V-2 was 46 feet long and carried up to 2,000 pounds of explosives in its nose cone. It could travel 190 miles at speeds up to five times the speed of sound. More V-2 rockets were fired at Belgium than England. The single most destructive attack occurred when a V-2 fell on a cinema in Antwerp, killing 567 moviegoers (p. 11).

In Jacobsen's book, *Operation Paperclip*, she tells about a party in December of 1944 at a magnificent, moated 800-year-old stone castle called Varlar in the pine forests of Coesfeld, Germany. The castle had turrets, balustrades, and lookout towers. The banquet hall was decorated in full Nazi regalia. On the walls, flags featuring Germany's national eagle-and-swastika emblem hung from the walls. Here, guests of the Third Reich dined on china which repeated the flags' motif of eagle and swastika.

Outside, the snow-covered grounds of Varlar Castle were the wartime scenes of metal platforms of portable rocket-launch pads. A V-2 missile sat on each pad. Since the beginning of the war, Hitler had boasted about "hitherto unknown, unique weapons" that could not be shot down from the sky and that could defeat his enemies. The V-2 was his pride and joy.

The castle party of the Third Reich elite was a celebration of pomp and power. In between courses of the meal, the castle lights were extinguished and the grand banquet hall became dark and silent. Suddenly, the tall curtain at the end of the long hall opened, and guests looked out upon the dark, snow-white lawns. A guest described the next moment: "The room suddenly lit [up] with the flickering light of the rocket's exhaust and [was] shaken by the reverberations of its engines."

The spectacle began when the inferno of rocket fuel lifted the massive V-2 rocket into flight, on a trajectory to Belgium. One of Hitler's generals said he had "unbelievable" feelings of pride, and during a prior launch he actually had wept with joy. After each rocket launch, the celebratory crowd would clap and cheer and sip champagne, until the next rocket blasted away (p. 7-11).

Of course, the focus of this book is not to rehash World War II and the atrocities of the Third Reich. However, in reading *Operation Paperclip*, I was stunned and shaken by the evil that was prevalent in a country that gave us fine music and other features of a civilized and resourceful society. The Nazi regime systematically worked to death and murdered 6,000,000 Jews ("The Holocaust–Wikipedia").

Believing that Germans were "racially superior" and that Jews and other ethnic groups were "inferior," (p. 122) the Nazis forced these people to work around the clock in an underground factory called Mittelwerk near the Buchenwald Concentration Camp in central Germany. Dear Reader, many prisoners were Jews, God's chosen people. Nazi prisoners worked at making the V-2 bomb in appalling conditions, with no daylight and little food, sleep, or proper sanitation. Though digging tunnels was hard labor, the S.S. (*Schutzstaffel* - "protection squadron, p. x") feared the prisoners might revolt, if they had mining tools, so they dug with their bare hands. The S.S. was foremost an agency of surveillance and terror in the Nazi regime (p. 13-14).

From August 1943 until April 1945, a complex of factories, storage depots, facilities, and prison camps, some underground, operated under the name Mittelbau. These all existed to build and test the V-2 rocket near Nordhausen in central Germany. More than 60,000 prisoners died in the manufacture of the V-2 rocket ("V2ROCKET.COM–Mittelwerk/DORA").

At the end of World War II, the United States, England, and Russia wanted not only the design, and parts, of the V-2 rocket but also the German scientists and engineers who were the masterminds of Hitler's wonder weapons. The Allies were obsessed with the Nazis' war weapons. General Dwight D. Eisenhower, Supreme Allied Commander in Europe, said, "It seemed likely that, if the German had succeeded in perfecting and using these new weapons six months earlier than he did, our invasion of Europe would have proved exceedingly difficult, perhaps impossible." Oh, Reader, when I read those words, a chill went up my spine, for Germany and the evil Axis powers could have won the war. I believe that God intervened on behalf of America and its Allies.

When Germany surrendered, the United States, England, and Russia rushed to confiscate the weapons and also the masterminds who had created the weapons, especially the V-2 rocket. In Washington, D.C., inside the Pentagon, a secret U. S. rocket intelligence group was formed, headed by Colonel Gervais William Trichel. Since the United States was twenty years behind Germany in rocket development, Trichel saw an opportunity to close the gap and also save the U. S. military money in research and development costs (p. 11-12).

Trichel ordered that 100 V-2 rockets be shipped to the White Sands Proving Ground in New Mexico for the Americans to study. Trichel also coordinated the effort to find and interrogate the German rocket specialists who had built the V-2. The mission began when the U. S. Army arrived in the town of Naudhausen, Germany in 1944 ("Special Mission V-2/Defense Media Network").

As a last stand of Nazism, while Hitler allegedly hid in his 50-feet deep Reich Chancellery Bunker in Berlin ("Adolf Hitler's Bunker: Nazi Leader Retreats Underground, Jan. 16..."), these rocket specialists were rounded up by the S.S. and sent 400 miles south to a redoubt in the Bavarian Alps. Among these key scientists and engineers were Werhner Von Braun and his brother, Magnus. Most of these specialists knew that the war was over and that they must choose between being captured by the Americans or the Russians ("PDF Untitled" p. 112).

As the liberation of Germany began in April of 1945, an American photographer and sharpshooter named John Risen Jones, Jr., arrived at the slave tunnels at Nordhausen. Though he had been on the continent for 195 days, engaged in fierce combat and slogging through snow, sleet, and mud, nothing had prepared him for the death tunnels at Naudhausen, where the V-2 rockets had been manufactured. The photographs he took of the tragedy that had befallen thousands of V-2 rocket laborers in Hitler's tunnels of death were grim proof of all that had occurred there. It was said that the young photographer and Army private would not speak of it for 51 years (*Operation Paperclip*, p. 46-47).

As Wernher Von Braun and other scientists hid out in their snow-capped redoubt in the Bavarian Alps at the end of the war, they were listening to the national radio as it played Bruckner's *Symphony No. 7*. The lovely music was interrupted by a long military drum roll, followed by the words of the radio announcer: "Our Fuhrer Adolph Hitler, fighting to the last breath against Bolshevism, fell for Germany this afternoon in his operational headquarters in the Reich Chancellery." Though the fight was a fabrication, Hitler was indeed dead and the war was over.

Realizing their precarious situation, Wernher Von Braun approached several other rocket specialists about moving quickly and making a deal with the American Army. Von Braun's brother, Magnus, climbed on his bike and pedaled down the steep mountain, continuing on until he came upon American liberators. Explaining in broken English that his brother had invented the V-2 weapon and wanted to surrender and make a deal with the Americans in regard to the V-2 rocket, Magnus was told to go back and tell his brother to come and surrender himself (p. 66-67).

A small group of the rocket specialists made the trip down the mountain and were warmly welcomed by the Americans. Years later, Von Braun said, "I did not expect to be kicked in the teeth... the V-2 was something we had and you didn't have. Naturally, you wanted to know all about it." So confident were Von Braun and other rocket specialists about their value to the U. S. Army, they insisted on seeing General Eisenhower, whom they called, "Ike"(p. 68-69). After their surrender, Wernher von Braun spoke the following words to the press:

"We knew that we had created a new means of warfare, and the question as to what nation, to what victorious nation we were willing to entrust this brainchild of ours was a moral decision more than anything else. We wanted to see the world spared another conflict such as Germany had just been through, and we felt that only by surrendering such a weapon to people who are guided by the Bible could such an assurance to the world be best secured." ("Wernher von Braun–Wikiquotes")

Sixteen American ships, containing the parts for 100 V-2 rockets, sailed from Antwerp, Belgium, bound for New Orleans and White Sands Proving Ground in New Mexico. However, the V-2 technology documentation, hidden by Von Braun's staff, was still unaccounted for. Finally, these important papers were confiscated by the Americans. Without them, the U. S. would have had a difficult time assembling V-2s from their scattered parts.

Oh, Reader, this is ... amazingly... the way that the United States missile and space program began...by Nazi scientists and engineers! Around 1600 German rocket specialists were given clearance to come and live and work on the rocket program for the United States. Many of these men had committed heinous crimes in the defense of Germany, including Werhner Von Braun. Some had even been involved in the Nuremberg Trials (p. 1x-xii). The Nuremberg Trials were thirteen trials which judged leaders of Germany for their actions during World War II , 1939-1945). This mission was called *Operation Paperclip,* because U. S. personnel who oversaw this project would attach a paperclip to the files of those Germans whose loyalty to the United States was questionable (*Operation Paperclip,* p. 227).

Annie Jacobsen's book documents the Nazi intelligence which the U. S. used after the top Nazi rocket specialists were brought to America. It was Nazi rocket scientists who suggested placing nuclear bombs on rockets and who began developing the intercontinental ballistic missiles (p. 378). Nazi engineers who had designed Hitler's bunker beneath Berlin then designed underground fortresses for the U. S. Government in the Catoctin and Blue Ridge mountains ("Operation Nazification–Let's Try Democracy").

Nazi scientists brought over their knowledge of biological weapons, such as sarin and tabun (p. 149). A new agency called NASA (National Aeronautics and Space Administration) was created to visit and to weaponize outer space (p. 397). In 1947, when Operation Paperclip was in danger of being terminated, President Harry S. Truman transformed the military with the National Security Act and created the CIA (Central Intelligence Agency, p. 287).

Dear Reader, I don't know how to assess our nation's

cultivation of German war criminals, brilliant and accomplished though they were, but they certainly gave the United States the edge it needed in war preparedness and space exploration. The United States, England, and Russia rushed in to Germany at the war's end, hoping to find the advanced weapons and designs of Hitler's rocketry. Only by a few days' time was the United States able to secure the weapons and technology and the main scientists and engineers to assist our country. I believe that God brought this about!

Though it would be interesting to delve into the lives of all of the hundreds of the German scientists and engineers who came to the United States after World War II and who took top positions in the U. S. space program, I will enlarge upon the life of Wernher Von Braun only. In 1955, Von Braun and many of his fellow rocket specialists became U. S. Citizens in a public ceremony held in the Huntsville High School auditorium in Huntsville, Alabama ("Wernher von Braun/Biography, Quotes, & Facts/*Britannica. com*").

Wernher Von Braun's friends knew him as a "merry heathen" before the 1950s. He showed no interest in the church or biblical teachings during his younger years. However, during the 1960s and 1970s, he began to sort out his thinking about religious matters, eventually becoming a devout Lutheran. Later in life, he joined an Episcopal congregation. As his fame increased, he was often asked the question: "Dr. von Braun, do you believe in God? His answer was always quick and to the point: "Yes, absolutely!" Below are excerpts from some of his sayings and writings:

"It is so obvious that we live in a world in which a fantastic amount of logic, of rational lawfulness, is at work. We are aware of a large number of laws of physics and chemistry and biology which, by their mutual interdependence, make nature work as if it were following a grandiose plan from its earliest beginnings to the farthest reaches of its future destiny. To me, it would be incomprehensible that there should be such a gigantic master plan without a master planner behind it. This master planner is He whom we call the Creator of the Universe...One cannot be exposed to the law and order of the universe without concluding that there must be a Divine intent behind it all."

"For me, there is no real contradiction between the world of science and the world of religion. The two are dealing with two different things, but they are not in conflict with each other. Theologians are trying to describe the Creator; scientists are trying to describe His creation. Science and religion are not antagonists; on the contrary, they are sisters...While, through science, man tries to harness the forces of nature around him, through religion he tries to harness the forces of nature within him..."

Erik Bergaust - author, science writer, and outdoorsman - met Von Braun in 1950, and the two became close friends. He wrote of a campfire evening in the Virginia mountains during a fishing trip with Von Braun in the summer of 1970. "The last fishing story of the evening had been told," he wrote. "The men were sitting around the flaming logs, each submerged in his own deep thoughts under an endless sky with myriads of stars. Finally, I broke the silence. 'Wernher, what do you think of the hereafter?' I asked. Von Braun replied, 'I believe in an immortal soul that can cherish the rewards or suffer the penalty decreed in the Last Judgment.'" Below are more excerpts of Wernher Von Braun's thoughts from the campfire evening in 1970:

"Our life does not have materialistic and intellectual aspects alone. This is as true today as it was centuries ago. We cannot live without ethical laws and some belief in a Last Judgment, where every one of us has to account for what he did with God's precious gift of life on Earth...More than ever, mankind's survival depends on adherence to some basic ethical principles. Our adherence to such principles alone will decide whether our new inventions in the field of atomic energy will provide mankind with an inexhaustible supply of energy and wealth, or whether mankind will perish by its abuse..."

"Our knowledge and use of the laws of nature that enable us to fly to the Moon also enable us to destroy our home planet with the atom bomb. Science itself does not address the question whether we should use the power at our disposal for good or for evil. The guidelines of what we ought to do are furnished in the moral law of God. It is no longer enough that we pray that God may be with us on our side; we must learn again to pray that we may be on God's side."Paraphrasing Abraham Lincoln's words, spoken more than a hundred years before, Von Braun said, 'I am not concerned that the Lord be on my side. I am concerned that I be on the Lord's side!'"

James Fletcher, one of Wernher Von Braun's colleagues who gave a eulogy of Von Braun at his funeral which was filled with the somber yet powerful organ notes of Brahms and Bach, said of the brilliant scientist:

"In the words of the prophet Joel, '**your young men shall see visions, and your old men shall see dreams.**' Fortunately for the human race, a few men arise in each century who '**see visions and dream dreams**' that give hope and spiritual nourishment to us all...Werhner von Braun was such a man...He clung to what seemed an impossible dream for his entire life, despite pressures of politics, bureaucratic entanglements, war, loss of fortune, and even, especially personal criticism. Nearly all of our major technical accomplishments today, on Earth as well as in space, were foreseen by him at one time or another during his lifetime. The manned voyage to the Moon, the unmanned exploration of the solar system, and, by observing platforms, the entire universe were all part of his vision.

"They are now reality, and an integral part of our consciousness. Television satellites, weather satellites, Earth resources satellites, and many more 'down-to-Earth' programs were not only predicted by him, but he and his associates – many of whom are here today – brought many of these projects to fruition. And his dreams carried well into the future.... Those of us who remain must transform those dreams of the future into reality, and pass on to the next generation what can be and should be their own dreams... I sincerely hope that Wernher von Braun's passing shall be a reminder for all of us of what one person can do to show the world the magnificent future which is in store for it, and the wonders that man is capable of performing."

Another eulogist at Von Braun's funeral, named Ernst Stuhlinger, said of his longtime boss and friend: "Wernher has always felt deeply grateful to this country which became his second home. More than thirty years ago, it was his 'haven of promise';

later, he often remarked how wonderful America had been to him and his family, and to all his friends who immigrated with him. However, he never failed to add that his team really consisted of all the thousands and thousands of men and women in government, industry, universities, and the armed forces who gave him their talents and their confidence, and who all share credit for the success of the space adventure.

"With a deep-rooted interest in philosophy and religion, he saw no conflict between scientific knowledge and religious faith.'The natural sciences,' he said, 'deal with creation; religion deals with the creator. The two are really complementing each other perfectly....'

'When my journey comes to an end,' he once remarked, 'I hope that I can retain my clear mind and perceive not only those precious last moments of my life, but also the transition to whatever will come then. A human being is so much more than a physical body that withers and vanishes after it has been around for a number of years. It is inconceivable to me that there should not be something else for us after we have finished our earthly voyage. I hope that I can observe and learn, and finally know what comes after all those beautiful things we experience during our lives on Earth.'" ("The religion of Wernher von Braun, rocket engineer, inventor")

In 1960, Wernher von Braun was made director of the newly established National Aeronautics and Space Administration, or NASA, with a commission to build the Saturn rockets that would take man to the moon. The launch complex and hangar for the Saturn V rocket were established at Cape Canaveral on Florida's east coast. Another Nazi, Kurt Debus, was chosen as director of this endeavor (*Operation Paperclip*, p. 397). As I read Annie Jacobsen's fascinating and well-researched book *Operation Paperclip*, I knew that she questioned the United States' bringing to our country high-ranking Nazis who had only recently waged war against us. However, I felt that God brought this about. Otherwise, America's enemies would have benefitted from their expertise and would have posed a danger to our country. Yes, God is the reason for America's exceptionalism. He gave our country the tools it needed to excel and prevail and, especially...to protect Israel.

Chapter Twenty-Nine

A listing of notable people and events of the twentieth century would not be complete without including the birth and accomplishments of Albert Einstein. Though he was born in 1879, some of his major work was done during the twentieth century. Also, though he was born in Ulm, Wurttemberg, Germany, he lived in several other countries in Europe, including Italy, Switzerland, and England, eventually becoming an American citizen in 1940 ("Albert Einstein–Wikipedia").

In 1905, while living in Switzerland, Einstein published four groundbreaking papers on the photoelectric effect, Brownian motion, special relativity, and the equivalence of mass and energy. These brought him to the acclaim of the academic world, at the age of 26. The year 1905 was called Einstein's *annus mirabilis* (miracle year). These four works became the foundation of modern physics and altered understanding of space, time, and matter. He published more than 300 scientific papers along with over 150 non-scientific works (*Annus Mirabilis* papers–Wikipedia). In 2014, more than 30,000 of Einstein's papers were released by universities and archives ("Albert Einstein–Wikipedia").

Before becoming a United States citizen, after visiting in America, Einstein published an essay in 1921, entitled "My First Impression of the U.S.A.," in which he characterized Americans. He wrote, "What strikes a visitor is the joyous, positive attitude to life... The American is friendly, self-confident, optimistic, and without envy." ("Bulletin of the Atomic Scientists")

Having a great appreciation for music at an early age, Einstein later wrote, "If I were not a physicist, I would probably be a musician. I often think in music. I live my daydreams in music. I see my life in terms of music...I get most joy in life out of music." Einstein played the piano and also the violin. It was said that he "fell in love" with Mozart's violin sonatas, at the age of 13 ("Albert Einstein–Wikipedia").

From 1933-1955, Einstein was a professor at the Institute for Advanced Study in Princeton, New Jersey, where he continued to work in that capacity until his death in 1955. Time named him "Person of the Century" in 1999 ("Man of the Century–American Physical Society"). Einstein's aversion to war led him to befriend author Upton Sinclair and film star Charlie Chaplin who were also pacifists. Chaplin recalled that while Einstein's outward appearance was calm and gentle, it seemed to conceal "a highly emotional temperament" and "extraordinary intellectual energy." ("Albert Einstein–Wikipedia")

Chaplin also recounted that Einstein's wife, Elsa, told him about the time Einstein conceived his theory of relativity. As he sat at his breakfast one morning, he ignored his food and appeared to be lost in thought. Finally, he sat at his piano and began playing. He continued to play, stopping at intervals to write notes. Then, he went to his study upstairs, where he remained two weeks, with Elsa bringing up his food. At the end of two weeks, he came downstairs, holding his theory on two sheets of paper ("Albert Einstein and Charlie Chaplin were close friends.").

The German Student Union targeted Einstein's work for their infamous Nazi book burnings. Nazi propaganda minister Joseph Goebbels proclaimed, "Jewish intellectualism is dead." A German magazine listed Einstein as an enemy of the German regime, stating he was "not yet hanged," and offered a $5,000 bounty on his head ("The Pandora Society>>October 17th, 1933–Einstein Evades the Nazis").

Though Einstein was Jewish, he was not an orthodox Jew. However, he espoused many Jewish causes. Upon meeting Winston

Churchill, Austen Chamberlain, and Lloyd George, Einstein requested their help in bringing Jewish scientists out of Germany during the war. Churchill immediately responded and later observed that as a result of Germany having driven out the Jews, they had lowered their "technical standards" and had enriched the Allies' technology ahead of their own ("Refugee Status/Albert Einstein/Nazi Germany–scribd"). Dear Reader, I see the hand of God in the placement of Einstein and other brilliant scientists in America before and after the Second World War. Also, Einstein's Jewish ancestry and his help with Semitic causes were surely what God wanted and inspired.

Einstein was offered the position of President of Israel in 1952, only a few years after Israel once again became a nation. Israel's ambassador to Washington, Abba Eban, explained that the offer "embodies the deepest respect which the Jewish people can repose in any of its sons." Einstein, however, declined, writing in his response that he was "deeply moved" and "at once saddened and ashamed" that he could not accept it ("Offering the Presidency of Israel to Albert Einstein").

He became an American citizen just before America entered the Second World War in 1941. Though he was a pacifist, he greatly helped America and its Allies to win the war. He endorsed a letter to President Franklin Roosevelt, alerting him to the likely development of "extremely powerful bombs of a new type" by Germany and recommending that the United States pursue a similar course. This led to what became known as the Manhattan Project ("Einstein–Szilard letter–Wikipedia").

Einstein is best known in American culture for his mass=energy equivalent formula: $E=mc^2$ (which is known as "the world's most famous equation."). In 1921, he was awarded the Nobel Prize in Physics for his "services to theoretical physics," especially his discovery of the law of the photoelectric effect ("Albert Einstein biography–Biography"). The name "Einstein" is now considered synonymous with the word "genius." ("Einstein synonyms")

Though Einstein denounced using the newly discovered

nuclear fission as a weapon, he did support defending America during the war, realizing that the bombs created from this knowledge would be dropped on Hiroshima and Nagasaki. By signing the letter to Roosevelt, he went against his pacifist principles. However, in 1954, a year before his death, he said to his old friend, Linus Pauling, "I made one great mistake in my life – when I signed the letter to President Roosevelt recommending that atom bombs be made; but there was some justification– the danger that the Germans would make them...." ("Einstein and Oppenheimer: The Meaning of Genius")

Einstein's death was caused by the rupture of an abdominal aortic aneurysm. Enroute to the hospital, he took the draft of the speech he was writing for a television appearance, commemorating the seventh anniversary of the rebirth of the State of Israel, but he didn't live to complete it. Dear Reader, I think it is remarkable that he had Israel on his mind when he was at death's door.

Refusing surgery, he said, "I want to go when I want. It is tasteless to prolong life artificially. I have done my share, it is time to go. I will do it elegantly." Early the next morning, he was dead in Princeton Hospital at the age of 76, having worked until near the end of his life. Though his body was cremated, his brain was removed by the pathologist of Princeton Hospital without the permission of his family, in the hope that future neuroscience might discover the origin of his great intelligence. At Einstein's memorial service, nuclear physicist Robert Oppenheimer described him as a person: "He was almost wholly without sophistication and wholly without worldliness...There was always with him a wonderful purity at once childlike and profoundly stubborn." ("Albert Einstein–Wikipedia")

* * * * * * * * * * * * * *

America has fought two world wars, and events are shaping up in such a way that a third world war may be imminent. During the Second World War, the United States allied itself with its mother country, England, and other allies against the evils of the Third Reich of Germany, led by the madman, Adolph Hitler. Though many heroes surfaced in the many theaters of the war, one man with the gift of splendid oratory galvanized not only his own country but also the United States and its allies into the war effort and, ultimately, victory.

Edward R. Murrow said of Winston Churchill, "He mobilized the English language and sent it into battle." Thomas Sowell said of Winston Churchill, "It is enough of a claim to historic greatness for a man to have saved his own country. Winston Churchill may have saved civilization." ("The Wit and Wisdom of Winston Churchill: A Treasury of more than...").

Churchill himself said, "It is the English-speaking nations who, almost alone, keep alight the torch of freedom." ("Summer 1938 [Age 63]–The International Churchill Society") We can see God's nature unfolding in the eloquent and powerful oratory of a man who aroused the good in man to be victorious in the face of great evil. Also, we perceive that America's exceptionalism, brought about by God, helped greatly in the defeat of evil.

At the end of World War II, in 1945, the United Nations was established, with its headquarters in New York City. Today, around 185 nations are members of the U.N. which promises to work for world peace, security, and the betterment of humanity. Though this organization has been successful to a degree, it has also had its failures. Its critics decry the fact that the United States bears most of the financial burden of its existence. Also, American critics of the U. N. vow to ensure that its policies never override the laws and policies of the United States ("Modernizing the United Nations System: Civil Society's Role in... p. 195"). Since rogue nations have been admitted as members of the U. N., some of which have pledged death to Israel and America, many Americans feel betrayed by the organization and would like to withdraw our membership.

* * * * * * * * * * * * * *

Though the United States and Russia (then known as U.S.S.R, or Union of Soviet Socialist Republics) fought together as allies during World War II, their relationship after the war morphed into mutual distrust and dislike, known as the Cold War. The Cold War lasted from 1945 to 1980. Capitalism versus communism struggled on a world stage for supremacy, with major crises occurring, such as the Cuban Missile Crisis, Vietnam, and the Berlin Wall. During that time, as even now, the growth of weapons of mass destruction was the most frightening issue ("Cold War/Essential Humanities").

During the decades of the Cold War, the United States practiced policies of containment and detente. The goal of containment was to stop the Soviet Union from forcibly injecting communism beyond the countries which it already ruled or occupied. During the 1970s, Presidents Richard Nixon, Gerald Ford, and Jimmy Carter espoused detente, or the lessening of Cold War tensions and the achievement of peaceful coexistence with the Soviet Union ("Cold War History Richard Nixon, Gerald Ford, Jimmy Carter"). President Ronald Reagan immensely disliked detente. At a 1981 news conference, he said,

"So far detente's been a one-way street that the Soviet Union has used to pursue its own aims. Their goal must be the promotion of world revolution and a one world communist or socialist state." President Reagan felt that the Soviets considered the American detente as a sign of weakness and vulnerability." He said, "Our strategy is defensive; our aim is to protect the peace by ensuring that no adversaries ever conclude they could beat us in a war of their own choosing."

Reagan predicted the collapse of the Soviet Union because its economy and military strength were inferior to those of the West, including the United States and the British Empire. As America began building up its military in an "arms race," Reagan introduced another policy which would promote freedom and democracy throughout the world. This policy, called the "Reagan Doctrine" was expressed in a speech which Reagan gave in London to the British Parliament in 1982. Excerpts of that speech are below:

"History teaches the dangers of government that overreaches–political control taking precedence over free economic growth, secret police, mindless bureaucracy, all combining to stifle individual excellence and personal freedom..."

"It is the Soviet Union that runs against the tide of history by denying human freedom and human dignity to its citizens."

"What I am describing now is a plan and a hope for the long term–the march of freedom and democracy which will leave Marxism-Leninism on the ash-heap of history, as it has left other tyrannies which stifle the freedom and muzzle the self-expression of the people."

"Our military strength is a prerequisite to peace, but let it be clear we maintain this strength in the hope it will never be used, for the ultimate determinant in the struggle that's now going on in the world will not be bombs and rockets, but a test of wills and ideas, a trial of spiritual resolve, the values we hold, the beliefs we cherish, the ideals to which we are dedicated." ("Ronald Reagan and Executive Power/Presidential Leadership in the...")

The collapse of communism throughout Eastern and Central Europe brought freedom, democracy, and the end of Soviet domination of this region. On June 12, 1987, President and Mrs. Reagan arrived in Berlin, where they were taken to the Reichstag. There, they viewed the wall that separated East and West Berlin from the balcony. Then, at Brandenburg Gate, in front of two panes of bulletproof glass, Reagan made the speech that has thrilled freedom-loving people everywhere. The part of it about the Berlin Wall appears below:

"We welcome change and openness; for we believe that freedom and security go together, that the advance of human liberty can only strengthen the cause of world peace. There is one sign the Soviets can make that would be unmistakable, that would advance dramatically the cause of freedom and peace. General Secretary Gorbachev, if you seek peace, if you seek prosperity for the Soviet union and Eastern Europe, if you seek liberalization, come here to this gate. Mr. Govbachev, open this gate. Mr. Gorbachev, tear down this wall!" ("Tear down this wall!–Wikipedia")

In 1988, the people of Afghanistan, with American assistance, forced the Soviet military from their country. In 1989, the Berlin Wall that divided East and West Berlin for nearly three decades was torn down by the German people. This led to Germany's reunification in 1990 and the end of Communism in Eastern and Central Europe.

The Cold War ended in 1991 when the Soviet Union was dissolved, two years after President Reagan left office. Reagan's policies of preserving peace through strength significantly brought this about. America and its allies won and ended the Cold War ("The Cold War Timeline–History").

Chapter Thirty

On May 14, 1948, the entire world witnessed the rebirth of the State of Israel nearly 2000 years after it was conquered by the Roman army in 70 A.D ("Declaring the State of Israel on May 14, 1948–Newsweek"). This was unprecedented in history. The fact that the Jews had lived in other countries for 2000 years, and then had become a nation again - with laws and mores and language intact during two millennia - was a miracle that only God could accomplish. God's will and nature brought this about.

The prophet Amos lived around 2700 years ago, when the Israelites were being forced out of their homeland by continuing foreign invasions. However, in Amos 9:14-15, he prophesied that the Jewish exiles would return to the land that God gave them and would never be uprooted again. When the Jews declared their independence in 1948, armies from surrounding, hostile countries invaded the tiny nation ("10 Prophecies Fulfilled in 1948–Watchman Bible Study").

Azzam Pasha, Secretary General of the Arab League, said, "This will be a war of extermination and a momentous massacre which will be spoken of like the Mongolian massacres and the Crusades." Despite its tiny size, however, Israel prevailed and continues to exist today ("Azzam Pasha quotation–Wikipedia").

Doesn't this reflect the nature of God, dear Reader? The words of his prophet Amos (Amos 9:14-15) appear below:

"And I will bring again the captivity of my people of Israel, and they shall build the waste cities, and inhabit them; and they

shall plant vineyards, and drink the wine thereof; they shall also make gardens, and eat the fruit of them.

And I will plant them upon their land, and they shall no more be pulled up out of their land which I have given them; saith the Lord thy God."

Many prophecies were fulfilled when Israel became a nation again in 1948. This was only three years after the end of the Holocaust, when the Nazis killed about two-thirds of the population of Europe. One prophecy, of course, was the passage from Ezekiel, mentioned earlier in this tract, about the dried bones which were symbolic of Israel. As you may recall, they became alive again and provided a great army for Israel. This was prophesied about 2600 years ago. (Ezekiel 37)

The prophet Isaiah wrote around 701-681 B.C. that Israel would be reborn in one day. This became true when Israel claimed independence as a nation on May 14, 1948, around 2000 years after being conquered by the Roman Empire. The words of Isaiah 66:7-8, predicting this miraculous event, are below:

"Before she travailed, she brought forth; before her pain came, she was delivered of a man child. Who hath heard such a thing? Who hath seen such things? Shall the earth be made to bring forth in one day? Or shall a nation be born at once? for as soon as Zion travailed, she brought forth her children:

"Shall I bring to the birth, and not cause to bring forth? saith the Lord: shall I cause to bring forth, and shut the womb? saith thy God."

Another prophecy in regard to Israel's rebirth as a nation was that Israel would be reestablished as a united country. The prophet Ezekiel predicted that God would bring back the Israelites as a united nation. During Ezekiel's time, Israel was divided into two kingdoms which experienced two separate captivities. God reunited his people and brought them back to Israel as one nation ("10 Prophecies Fulfilled in 1948–Watchman Bible Study").

God told Jeremiah that the second Israel would be more impressive than the first. The first country of Israel was created when Moses led the descendants of Jacob (known as the Jews) out of Egypt where they had lived and been enslaved for 400 years. They went back to Canaan, where they conquered the tribes who lived there and established their country about 3400 years ago ("Bible history timeline–Fulfilled Bible prophecy").

When Israel was reborn in 1948, after being scattered over the face of the earth for several thousand years, its people returned to their promised land from the United States, China, Russia, South Africa and other places. This is a continuing miracle, as Jews are still leaving their homes in other lands and returning home to Israel ("10 Prophecies Fulfilled in 1948").

Jeremiah 16:14-15 reads as follows: **"Therefore, behold, the days come, saith the Lord, that it shall no more be said, The Lord liveth, that brought up the children of Israel out of the land of Egypt;**

"But, the Lord liveth that brought up the children of Israel from the land of the north, and from all the lands whither he had driven them; and I will bring them again into their land that I gave unto their fathers."

Eastern European and Russian Jews began to immigrate to Palestine after the failed Russian Revolution of 1905. Though surrounding Arab nations fought the Jews, beginning in 1929, at the end of World War II, in 1945, the United States embraced the Zionist movement of Jews returning to their original homeland. In 1949, the U. N.-brokered cease-fires left Israel in permanent control of the land that God originally had given them ("State of Israel proclaimed–May 14, 1948. HISTORY.com").

Fearing an immediate threat from neighboring countries, Israel began a surprise air strike against Egypt in 1967, which was called the Six-Day War. The Arab nations of Syria, Jordan, and Iraq, which had signed peace treaties with Egypt, joined in the fighting within one day. Miraculously, Israeli planes and ground forces destroyed the Arab coalition. Though the Six-Day War proved the superiority of Israel's military might, it exacerbated the problems that exist today between tiny Israel and the large Arab nations that surround it ("Six-Day war ends–June 11, 1967–HISTORY.com").

Israel again greatly increased its borders in 1967, taking back from Jordan, Egypt, and Syria the Old City of Jerusalem, the Sinai Peninsula, the Gaza Strip, the West Bank, and the Golan Heights. In 1979, Israel and Egypt signed a peace agreement in which Israel returned the Sinai in exchange for Egyptian peace and recognition. In 1993, Israel and the Palestine Liberation Organization (P.L.O.) signed a major peace accord which laid out the gradual implementation of Palestinian self-government in the West Bank and Gaza Strip ("Camp David Accords/Egyptian–Israeli history/ *Britannica*.com"). However, in 2000, major fighting between Israelis and Palestinians resumed, and it still continues today in 2018 ("Israeli–Palestinian peace process–Wikipedia").

* * * * * * * * * * * * * *

The North Atlantic Treaty Organization was created in 1949, after World War II, to counter Russia's invasion over Europe. Only twelve countries, including Canada and the United States, were members at its formation. Now, it is a political and military alliance of twenty-nine countries from Europe and North America. English and French are the official languages of NATO ("NATO–Wikipedia").

Though all of NATO members are supposed to contribute at least 2% of their respective GDPs to defense spending, only the U. S. and the U.K. and a few others do this. NATO's policy is to protect and defend the territories and populations of its members. For 365 days of the year, on a 24/7 basis, NATO defends airspace over Albania, Estonia, Latvia, Lithuania, and Slovenia ("NATO fact sheet: 10 things to know–*USA Today*").

Soviet Russia wanted to join NATO in 1954, citing that its joining would help to preserve peace. However, the U.S. and the U.K. prevented this ("That time when the Soviet Union tried to join NATO in 1954"). Since then, Russia has encroached on the Ukraine and Crimea. Russia annexed the Crimean peninsular in 2014. This has brought about the most serious crisis since the Cold War in relations with the United States and the European Union ("Annexation of Crimea by the Russian Federation–Wikipedia").

Can We Fathom the Nature of God?

* * * * * * * * * * * * * *

Perhaps the beginning of the United States space program occurred near the end of World War II, when Germany attacked London with 200-mile range V-2 missiles. These flew sixty miles high over the English Channel at greater than 2,500 miles per hour. During the 1930s and 1940s, Nazi Germany saw the value of using long-distance rockets as weapons. As mentioned earlier in this treatise, some of the brilliant German scientists defected to the United States during, and after, World War II. This had to be the will and nature of God.

After the war, the United States and the Soviet Union began developing their own missile programs. In 1957, the Soviet Union launched the unmanned Sputnik 1 into space. In 1961, Russian Lt. Yuri Gagarin was the first human to orbit the earth.

In 1958, the first United States satellite Explorer 1 was shot into orbit. Alan Shepard became the first American to fly into space. John Glynn was the first American to orbit the earth in 1962 ("Space Race–Wikipedia"). The U. S. definition of space was 80.5 kilometers or 50 miles above Earth ("10 Horrific Disasters of the Space Program–Listverse").

President John F. Kennedy stated the national goal of America in 1961 when he said: "I believe this nation should commit itself to achieving the goal, before this decade is out, of landing a man on the moon and returning him safely to Earth." This goal was accomplished in 1969, when astronaut Neil Armstrong stepped from the lunar module on the moon and spoke the following immortal words: "That's one small step for man; one giant leap for mankind." Armstrong was the first human to walk on the moon. From 1969 to 1972, six Apollo missions explored the moon ("Armstrong walks on moon–Jul 20, 1969–HISTORY.com").

When the astronauts were safely back on Earth, after flying to the moon and back, a reporter asked Wernher Von Braun what he thought after giving his final approval of the moon trip and witnessing the safe return of the astronauts. His answer was, "I quietly said the Lord's Prayer." He knew that if the mission failed, he would have been blamed ("Wernher von Braun/CEH–Crev.info").

Neil Armstrong, Michael Collins, and Edwin "Buzz" Aldrin, who accompanied them on the flight, took photos of the terrain, planted a U. S. Flag, did a few simple scientific tests and spoke with President Richard Nixon from 240,000 miles away. Also left on the moon's surface was a plaque that read: "Here men from the planet Earth first set foot on the moon – July 1969 A.D. – We came in peace for all mankind." ("July 20, 1969: One Giant Leap for Mankind/NASA")

Since the 1960s, more than twenty astronauts have died in attempting to learn more about outer space ("A look at people killed during space missions–Phys.org"). In 1967, at Kennedy Space Center in Cape Canaveral, Florida, a fire erupted during a manned launch-pad test of the Apollo spacecraft and Saturn rocket. Three astronauts died during the fire ("Apollo 1–Wikipedia").

The launch of the space shuttle Columbia in 1981 began a period of reliance on the reusable shuttle for most civilian and military space missions. Twenty-four successful shuttle launches fulfilled many research goals, until 1986, when the shuttle Challenger exploded, killing its crew of seven. Christa McAuliffe, the first "ordinary" person to fly aboard the shuttle, died during this tragedy. ("Challenger Disaster 30 Years Ago Shocked the World, Changed NASA")

When Yuri Gagarin, the Russian cosmonaut, returned to earth from the moon in 1961, he told everyone, "I did not see God up there." The second Russian in space also boasted that he couldn't see God anywhere. A twelve-year-old girl in Gothenburg, Sweden, was so troubled by Gagarin's statement that she wrote him a letter – simple and to the point. "Dear Cosmonaut Gagarin," she wrote, "I understand that you have flown in space and that you say you did not see God. Sir, I just want to ask you if you are pure in your heart?" ("Communion on the Moon–Buzz Aldrin–Oo Cities") I'm sure we all have read the words of Christ in Matthew 5:8: **"Blessed are the pure in heart, for they shall see God."**

In contrast, many American astronauts contemplated and felt the presence of God when they landed on the earth's moon. Buzz

Aldrin had taken onboard a Bible, a silver chalice, and sacramental bread and wine. His first act before emerging from the spacecraft was to celebrate communion.

Frank Borman, commander of the first space crew to travel beyond the earth's orbit, looked down on the earth from 250,000 miles in space. He said in a later interview that he "... had an enormous feeling that there had to be a power greater than any of us – that there was a God, that there was indeed a beginning." That's when he radioed to the earth a message from Genesis I:1: **"In the beginning, God created the heavens and the earth."** ("Astronauts Who Found God–ACTS International")

James B. Irwin, another astronaut who walked on the moon in 1971 often describes the lunar mission as a revelation. He said, "I felt the power of God as I'd never felt it before. He later became an evangelical minister and founded a Baptist ministry ("Communion on the Moon–Buzz Aldrin–Oo Cities"). "I was just amazed to see the earth," he said. "It reminded me of a Christmas tree ornament, a very fragile one, hanging majestically in space. It was very touching to see earth from that perspective." His wife, Mary, said, "He was overwhelmed at seeing and feeling God's presence so close." "At one point he turned around and looked over his shoulder as if He was standing there." ("Encounter with Jesus on the moon left astronaut changed/God Reports")

In James Irwin's book *More Than Earthlings*, he testified about the profound spiritual impact he experienced from walking on the moon's surface. Some of his reflections in the book appear below:

"During our moon walk we found the only pure, white rock which has been brought back from the moon. It was immediately labeled the 'Genesis' rock by the press corps in Houston. The Bible tells of a white rock in Revelation 2:17, **'To him who overcomes, I will give some of the hidden manna, I will also give him a white stone with a new name written on it, known only to him who receives it.'"**

"The dazzling brilliance of the stars we saw from the backside of the moon makes me think of the Bible verses which say some strange and curious things about stars." These statements were made in advance of the recent scientific discoveries which give us up-to-date information about the stars.

"First Corinthians 15:41 says, **'The sun has one kind of splendor, the moon another and the stars another; and star differs from star in splendor.'"**

"How could Paul know this? There were no telescopes. He looked up by the naked eye and saw the same stars you and I see.

"We now know that stars aren't the same. They are classified by the letters O, B. A. EG, K, M, R, N, and S. O is the hottest; S is the coolest. The sun is near the middle, a G star. These letters also indicate the color of the stars, the color determining the heat. For example, O, B, and A are bluish-white (or extremely hot); F and G are yellow; K is orange; and M, R, N, and S are different shades of red (the coolest).

"And we've heard about the various sizes and shapes of stars: the dwarfs, twin stars, giants, pulsars, black holes, super-novas.

"But there is something else coming to us from the stars, other than light – we are 'hearing' things from space. Astronomers report that the radio telescopes are picking up a strange 'whisper' from empty space, a weak, but continual microwave radiation coming from the sky, day and night."

Psalm 19:1-1 and 4 says, **"The heavens declare the glory of God: the skies proclaim the work of his hands. Day after day they pour forth speech; night after night they display knowledge. Their voice goes out into all the earth, their words to the ends of the world."**

"How would the Psalmist know this? Hebrews 1:1 says, **'in the past God spoke to our forefathers through the prophets at many times and in various ways.'** The inspired Word of God told earthlings things about space that we haven't scientifically 'discovered' until recently. This is why we can trust the Word as a guide for our lives." *(More Than Earthlings* by James B. Irwin, Broadman Press, Nashville, Tennessee, 1983)

In December 1965, Gemeni V11 astronauts Frank Borman and James Lovell saw a UFO during the second orbit of their record-breaking 14-day flight. Lovell and astronaut Edwin Aldrin spotted two UFOs about one-half mile from their spacecraft. During the flight of Apollo 8 in 1968, with astronauts Frank Borman, James Lovell, and William Anders aboard, it was reported that an unidentified language was heard on one of NASA's frequencies used during the mission ("Astronauts James Lovell and Frank Borman talk about UFOs").

Astronaut Charles Duke, Brigadier General U.S.A.F., retired, wrote the book *Moonwalker* which includes many thoughtful references to his Christian faith. Below are some excerpts:

"The promises of the Bible are true, and I believe speak the truth in every area – whether it be in spiritual matters, nutrition, history, or even science. In 1972 aboard Apollo 16, I saw with my own eyes what is written in the Scriptures."

"In Isaiah 40:22 it says, **'It is He who sits above the circle of the earth.' And in Job 26:7 it is written, He 'hangeth the earth upon nothing.'**

"Who told Isaiah that the earth was a circle? Until the fifteenth century, the greatest minds believed it was flat. And how did the writer of Job know that the earth hung upon nothing? The Greeks were sure that it was held up by a giant named Atlas. Others believed that there were five tremendous columns supporting it. We laugh at that now, but this is what the ancients believed.

"Not until 1961 did man first view earth from space with his own eyes and prove beyond a shadow of doubt that the earth is round and hung upon nothing. How did Isaiah and the author of Job know?"

"God inspired these two writers over twenty-eight hundred years ago with the truth. He knew because He was the One who created the earth and the heavens. He was the One who hung the earth, the moon, the sun, and the stars in their places."

"The Bible also says that God counts the stars and knows them all by name (see Psalm 147:4). If he knows the stars by name, He certainly knows each one of us by name."

"I used to say I could live ten thousand years and never have an experience as thrilling as walking on the moon. But the excitement and satisfaction of that walk doesn't begin to compare with my walk with Jesus, a walk that lasts forever."

"I thought Apollo 16 would be my crowning glory, but the crown that Jesus gives will not tarnish or fade away. His crown will last throughout all eternity (see 1 Corinthians 9:25)." *(Moonwalker* by Charles Duke, Oliver-Nelson Books, Nashville, Tennessee, 1990)

* * * * * * * * * * * * * *

At the end of World War II, the Japanese empire, which included the colony of Korea, collapsed. Russia then occupied North Korea, while the United States, under General Douglas MacArthur, controlled South Korea. Korea was divided along the 38th parallel where increasingly bloody incidents kept occurring.

In June of 1950, the North Korean Peoples' Army, backed by Russia, invaded the southern Republic of Korea. This was the first military test of the United Nations, and member nations were requested to send in military assistance. The British and U. S. militaries, along with other allies, pushed the northern army, aided by Russia and China, back to the 38th parallel, where the area was stabilized.

At least 2.5 million people were killed during the Korean War, which ended in 1953. Almost 40,000 American soldiers died. Britain lost 1,078 who were killed in action, 2,674 wounded, and 1960 missing or taken prisoners. Some 46,000 South Korean soldiers were killed and over 100,000 wounded. Around 400,000 Chinese military were killed (including the son of Mao Tse-Tung, Chairman of the Communist Party of China from 1943-1976) and 486,000 wounded, with over 21,000 captured. The North Koreans lost 215,000, with 303,000 wounded and over 101,000 captured or missing. We don't hear much about this war, though it wreaked havoc in the lives of people of many countries.

Since 1953, South Korea has become a modern state. The economy of North Korea is in ruins, and the people are starving while the government attempts to build atomic weapons. Koreans on both sides long for a unified Korea ("BBC–History–World Wars: The Korean War: An Overview"). The world, including the United States, fears the possibility of North Korea attaining nuclear know-how.

* * * * * * * * * * * * * * *

Beginning in 1957, The Vietnam War ended in 1975. At the onset of the war, France fought the Communist armies of North and South Vietnam, with the United States assistance of $2½ billion in military equipment. When the French were defeated in 1954, the country was divided near the 17th parallel, which was known as the demilitarized zone (DMZ ("DMZ–Vietnam–United States History").

The Vietnam War had its roots in the country's past as a colony of French Indochina. In 1946, the Vietnamese fought France for control of Vietnam. Though the United States sent France $2 ½ billion in military equipment, the Vietnamese defeated the French in 1954. The country was then divided into North and South Vietnam. Ho Chi Minh created a Communist government in North Vietnam, whereas South Vietnam was anti-communist and was governed by Ngo Dinh Diem who vigorously opposed Communism.

For several years, Vietnam waged a civil war, with the Communists gaining power in North and South Vietnam. Operating on President Harry S. Truman's policy that the U. S. must help any nation threatened by Communists, Congress passed the Tonkin Gulf Resolution which gave the President power to take "all necessary measures" and "to prevent further aggression." This policy was adopted by the next three presidents – Dwight D. Eisenhower, John F. Kennedy, and Lyndon B. Johnson. They feared that other nations in Asia would fall to the Communists "like a row of dominoes," if Vietnam could not be saved. However, in 1973, the last U. S. ground troops left Vietnam and, in 1975, the war was lost when South Vietnam surrendered.

Some 2,700,000 American men and women fought in the war. About 58,000 Americans died and around 300,000 were wounded. South Vietnamese deaths topped one million, while North Vietnamese losses were between 500,000 to one million. Many civilians in North and South Vietnam were killed.

The war cost the United States over $150 billion. It was demoralizing to America, as it was the first foreign war in which the U. S. Military failed to achieve its goals. Vietnam veterans were not welcomed back home as heroes, as the veterans of the two World Wars had been. The Vietnam War lasted longer than any other war in U. S. history, with nothing gained at its end. Only the unofficial war against Isis is more lengthy than the Vietnam War. The Vietnam War left America ambivalent about engaging in future wars and uncertain about its role as a world power and leader of the free world ("Griffin's Lair–A COMBAT PTSD WEBSITE HONORING OUR...").

Chapter Thirty-One

In 1990, NASA launched into orbit the Hubble Space Telescope on the space shuttle Discovery from Kennedy Space Center in Florida. Named for the astronomer Edwin P. Hubble, the large telescope weighs as much as two adult elephants and is as long as a large school bus. It travels around the earth at around five miles per second. An analogy would be driving a car from the eastern coast of the United States to the western coast in ten minutes.

The pictures on Hubble's digital camera, which faces space, have helped scientists learn more about the entire universe. The telescope reveals comets and planets and galaxies which contain billions of stars. A photo called "Hubble Ultra Deep Field" shows some of the most remote galaxies ever seen ("What Is the Hubble Space Telescope?/NASA").

Hubble's launch and activation in 1990 marked the most significant advance since Galileo's telescope in 1609. In 2009, for the fifth time, astronauts flew to Hubble on the space shuttle. They put new parts and cameras in the telescope ("What Is the Hubble Space Telescope?/NASA"). The first launch of the Space Shuttle was on April 12, 1981; its final landing was on July 21, 2011. The Space Shuttle fleet included the Columbia, the Challenger, the Discovery, the Atlantis, and the Endeavor. They flew 135 missions ("Space Shuttle Era/NASA").

* * * * * * * * * * * * *

Of course, with its knowledge of rocketry, the United States began launching satellites into space. The first small satellite, Sputnik 1, sent by Russia into space in 1957, lasted only three months in orbit, finally burning up in the earth's atmosphere ("Sputnik 1–Wikipedia"). The International Space Station and the Hubble Space Telescope are continually orbiting the earth ("Sensor to monitor orbital debris outside space station–Phys.org").

According to an article I read online, written in November of 2017, 4,635 satellites are currently orbiting the earth ("How many satellites are orbiting the Earth in 2017?/[Pixalytics Ltd.]"). A few satellites are orbiting the sun, and a few are on trajectories which will take them entirely out of the solar system. NASA's Voyager 1 spacecraft, launched in 1977, left the sun's heliosphere (the region in space over which the sun's gases and magnetic field extend) in 2012 and entered the interstellar medium ("Voyager 1–Wikipedia").

Some satellites take pictures of our planet, other planets, the sun and other objects. Other satellites send phone calls and T.V. signals around the world ("What Is a Satellite?"). Without a doubt, space satellites have contributed greatly to America's exceptionalism.

* * * * * * * * * * * * * *

A Russian rocket launched the first part of the International Space Station in 1998. In the year 2000, the first crew arrived, and people have lived on the space station since then. The ISS is a high-flying research laboratory that has become a symbol of cooperation among former competitors in space exploration. NASA and its partners around the world completed the space station in 2011.

The space station has science labs from the United States, Russia, Japan, and Europe. It is the size of a football field and weighs almost a million pounds. It will accommodate six people living in it. Its orbit is 220 miles above Earth ("What Is the International Space Station?/NASA").

Humans have lived and worked continuously aboard the International Space Station for more than seventeen years. They have made research breakthroughs not possible on Earth, that will allow lengthy human and robotic exploration into deep space. The ISS is a global endeavor that has involved 1900 research subjects from scientists in more than 95 countries. More than 200 people from eighteen countries have visited the unique micro-gravity laboratory ("New NASA Experiments, Research. Headed to International Space...").

Research at the space lab includes temperature safety in space, bone loss, changes in the human heart, and muscle atrophy. In 2014, experiments onboard the orbiting lab included a space-based D.N.A. sequence which could possibly identify microbes, diagnose diseases, and evaluate crew members' health. It could even help to detect D.N.A.-based life elsewhere in the solar system.

Commercial space partners with NASA began contracted cargo flights to the ISS with The Orbital Sciences Corporation planning at least eight cargo missions through 2016, according to an online article entitled "Antares Private Rocket Thunders off Virginia Coast...," dated 12-23-15. "Today's launch demonstrates how our strategic investments in the American commercial spaceflight industry are helping create new jobs here at home and keep the United States the world leader in space exploration," NASA Administrator Charles Bolden said.

He added, "American astronauts have been living and working continuously in space for the past 13 years on board the International Space Station, and we're once again sending them supplies launched from U. S. soil. In addition to the supplies, the passion and hard work of many researchers and students are being carried by Cygnus today. I congratulate Orbital and the NASA teams that made this resupply mission possible." ("Antares Private Rocket Thunders off Virginia coast...–Universe Today")

The pressurized Cygnus Orbital mission carried 2,780 pounds of supplies to the station. These included science experiments, computer supplies, food, water, clothing and experimental hardware. Many students, representing six schools across America, designed two dozen science experiments for the flight. One NASA experiment studied the decreased effectiveness of antibiotics during spaceflight. A student experiment was to compare ants' behavior in space and on Earth ("Antares Private Rocket Thunders off Virginia coast...--Universe Today").

According to an article written in 2014, NASA chose two companies, the Boeing Company of Houston and the Space Exploration Technologies Corp. of Hawthorne, California, to transport U. S. crews to and from the space station. NASA Administrator Charlie Bolden said, "Turning over low-Earth orbit transportation to private industry will ...allow NASA to focus on an even more ambitious mission – sending humans to Mars."

The maximum potential value of their "firm fixed-price contracts" are $4.2 billion for the Boeing Company and $2.6 billion for the Space Exploration Technologies Corp. NASA's engineers and spaceflight specialists are working with their industry partners to ensure the reliability and safety of the new spacecraft. Kathy Lueders, manager of NASAs Commercial Crew Program said:

"We are excited to see our industry partners close in on operational flights to the International Space Station, an extraordinary feat industry and the NASA family began just four years ago. This space agency has long been a technology innovator, and now we also can say we are an American business innovator, spurring job creation and opening up new markets to the private sector. The agency and our partners have many important steps to finish, but we have shown we can do the tough work required and excel in ways few would dare to hope." ("NASA Chooses American Companies to Transport U. S. Astronauts to...").

The first crewed launch of Boeing's Starliner spacecraft is slated for 2018. In 2014, the Starliner was tested before a trio of NASA astronauts at a test site in West Palm Beach, Florida. For about six minutes, the engine burned a combination of liquid hydrogen and liquid oxygen to produce around 22,300 pounds of thrust. It was tested to determine its capability to push a spacecraft into orbit.

Eric Boe, one of four NASA astronauts training to fly on the commercial missions, said, "They'll pore through the data, but the cool part is that the next time that engine fires, it's going to put one of us in space and we're looking forward to it." Suni Williams who is also training for Commercial Crew Program flight tests, said, "When you go through the whole process, seeing the test and seeing the professionals out here building the engines, there was no doubt the test would be a success." Boe again commented, "This is what makes America great, and that's why it's so good to get out here and see things like this." ("Engine Test Shows Design Ready for New Era/NASA")

Jon Cowart will serve as mission manager of the partnership between NASA and the companies which will be producing the spacecraft to send crews to the International Space Station. Cowart stated, "NASA and the companies share responsibility for the missions. But, as mission manager, I will be trying to make sure that everything goes as planned. There are thousands and thousands of things that have to happen. It's my goal to understand every single one of them." ("I Will Launch America: Jon Cowart/NASA")

* * * * * * * * * * * * * *

Perhaps, in the secular history of the world, nothing has changed life on earth more than the personal computer. Though most people think of Bill Gates and Paul Allen when they think of computers, the first personal computer was invented by a relatively unknown man named H. Edward Roberts. Ed Roberts is often called "the father of the personal computer."

Ed Roberts (1941-2010) was an American engineer, entrepreneur, and medical doctor. He also lived for a time in Wheeler County, Georgia, not far from my home in Telfair County, Georgia. When he was hospitalized in Macon, Georgia, in May of 2010, literally on his death bed, hospital staffers were stunned to see an unannounced Bill Gates who had come to pay last respects to his first employer, the man who paved the way for Gates' own phenomenal success.

Ed Roberts founded Micro Instrumentation and Telemetry Systems (MITS) in 1970. Bill Gates and Paul Allen joined MITS to develop software and Altair BASIC for Roberts' Altair personal computer. This was the birth of Microsoft, one of the world's largest electronics companies today ("Ed Roberts [computer engineer]– Wikipedia").

According to an article, dated 11-18-2016, the countries with the most personal computers per capita or per 100 people are as follow: Switzerland (65); United States (57); Sweden (51); Denmark (51); Norway (49); Bermuda (48); Singapore (48); Australia (47); Luxembourg (46); Canada (42); and Hong Kong (40) ("Countries with The Most Personal Computers Per Capita–WorldAtlas").

* * * * * * * * * * * * * *

Terrorism in different forms and by different groups has existed throughout history. Because of its location, the United States experienced few acts of terrorism on its own soil until the fateful day in September of 2001. Reportedly financed by the al-Qaeda terrorist organization of Saudi Arabia and fugitive Osama bin Laden, Saudi Arabian terrorists attacked the World Trade Center, the Pentagon, and an airplane filled with innocent travelers, resulting in the deaths of nearly 3,000 people ("9/11 Attacks–Facts and Summary–HISTORY.com").

The U. S. State Department has compiled a list of terrorist groups which include the following: Al Qaeda, Nigeria's Boko Haram, Lebanon's Hezbollah, Algeria's Islamic Group, Egypt's Islamic Jihad, Palestine's Islamic Jihad and Hamas, Uzbekistan's Islamic Movement, the Phillippines' Abu Sayyaf, and Pakistan's Jaish-e-Muhammad (Army of Muhammad). In recent years, a fanatical and barbaric group known as the Islamic State in Iraq (aka ISIS, ISIL or Daesh) has become powerful in the Middle East. ISIS ideology is even more extreme and brutal than other terrorist groups ("Islamist Terrorism From 1945 to the Rise of ISIS–Constitutional Rights").

Radical Islamic groups generally want to set up states which are based on Islamic fundamentalism. They want to establish Shariah law in states which they conquer, because they believe it is superior to democracy or any religion other than fundamentalist Islam. It seems that their goal is to establish a worldwide Caliphate, based on Shariah law ("What is 'Islamic State'?–BBC News").

The platform of the two United States presidential candidates of 2016 presented the U. S. electorate with choices involving abortion, immigration and foreign policy, among many other issues, but the main criterion was the selection of Supreme Court justices

("The Big Issues of the 2016 Election: Where Trump and Clinton Stand..."). The American electorate rejected the Washington insiders and voted for a man who had never held a public office. We can be assured, dear Reader, that God himself selected our president when we read Romans 13:1:

"Let every soul be subject unto the higher powers. For there is no power but of God: the powers that be are ordained of God."

On January 20, 2017, our nation once again witnessed the peaceful transfer of power, when Barack Hussein Obama ended his two-term presidency and extended a hand to the next president of the United States, Donald John Trump. These are two men of opposite ideologies. The incoming president has even promised to undo all that the outgoing president has brought about. Yet, for a short while, the two men rose above their differences and peacefully exchanged power and retirement ("The Peaceful Transfer of Power– and Its Enemies/RealClearPolitics"). This reaffirmed my love and appreciation for our great country. I believe George Washington and Thomas Jefferson and Abraham Lincoln would be proud.

* * * * * * * * * * * * * *

As America deals with issues of the 21st century, it continues to struggle with racial problems and also with global and even national terrorism. However, life goes on, and the quest for knowledge about outer space continues. In this regard, the Thirty Meter Telescope (TMT) is the international focus of five countries in searching the heavens. Scientists at Caltech and the University of California developed the TMT which has 492 segmented mirrors. The cost of the telescope is estimated to be $970 million to $1.4 billion dollars.

The dome diameter is to be 217 feet with a height of 180 feet. This is comparable to the height of an eighteen-story building. To be built within a five-acre complex, the total area of the structure is projected to be 1.44 acres.

The TMT is a proposed astronomical observatory with an extremely large telescope of 98 feet in diameter. The selected site for the observatory is Mauna Kea on Hawaii Island. However, because the land for the site is considered to be sacred to native Hawaiians, who have vigorously protested the location, construction has temporarily been halted ("Thirty Meter Telescope–Wikipedia").

In Pasadena, California, the observatory project office will lead and coordinate the work at partner locations. The members of the TMT International Observatory, established in May of 2014, are Caltech, UC, the National Institutes of Natural Sciences of Japan, the National Astronomical Observatories of the Chinese Academy of Sciences, the Department of Science and Technology and the Department of Atomic energy of India, and the National Research Council (Canada). The Association of Universities for Research in Astronomy (AURA) is a TIO Associate. ("TMT International Observatory").

Since the protests against the observatory have escalated, with protesters camping on the access road to the site and even rolling large rocks onto the road, the project has at this writing been temporarily postponed. If the construction does not go forward in Hawaii, the alternative site of Observatorio del Rogue de los Muchachos on La Palma, Canary Islands, Spain, will be considered. In regard to the mounting protests in Hawaii, Henry Yang with the TMT International Observatory Board of Governors, stated: "We respect the Hawaii Court decision and, as good neighbors and stewards of the mountain, TMT has begun relocating construction vehicles and equipment from Mauna Kea."

However, an article published in October of 2017 appeared to give the go-ahead to resume construction of the TMT in Hawaii. TMT is one of three ground-based megascopes scheduled to be built in the 2020s. Two others, the Giant Magellan Telescope and the European Extremely Large Telescope are both being built in the Chilean Andes ("Thirty Meter Telescope Gets Green Light to Resume Construction in..."). So, the indefatigable creativity of America forges ahead, and our leaders continue to work with other countries to study the mysteries of outer space. American exceptionalism continues to lead the world.

* * * * * * * * * * * * *

The subject most on my mind, as I end this study of God's

nature, is Israel. What is God doing in this modern day to protect Israel? I saw an interesting article on the internet with the title "Israel: A Modern-Day Miracle," which was the message given at the "One in Messiah" pastors' conference in Jerusalem in November of 2016. Below are excerpts from this message, which will gladden your heart and let you know that God is very much in control of the state of Israel:

"Last spring, the Israeli news carried a story about a certain rabbi who went down to the border between Israel and Gaza, and prayed for God's help against the enemies of Israel. He prayed that the attack tunnels Hamas was digging would collapse. Since his prayers, nine tunnels have collapsed.

"Israel has, in fact, never been outnumbered in any war by less than 3 to 1. In our War of Independence in 1948, the Arab armies were four times greater than the Jewish army of the newborn state. Many of these new Jewish soldiers didn't even know enough Hebrew to understand their commanders' instructions. But God gave a great victory to Israel.

"Do you know how many missiles it takes on average to create one Israel casualty? Before the existence of the Iron Dome System, the casualty ratio was one death for every 445 Hamas and Hezbollah missiles. Is this just because our enemies have really bad aim, or do we serve a miracle God?

"Besides, I ask, what can be a more daunting task for God? To remove 600,000 men from one nation (Egypt) through one Red Sea, or to gather 3,600,000 immigrants from 70 different countries over sea, land and air?

"Our first prime minister, David Ben-Gurion, said, "In Israel, in order to be a realist, one must believe in miracles."

"It is unprecedented for any people in all of history to maintain their culture and speak their same ancient language after 2,000 years of expulsion. It takes only two generations after immigration for a people to lose their language. How many of you speak the native language of your great-great grandparents?"

"Less than a century ago, not one person in the world spoke

Hebrew as a first language. Now there are over 6 million people speaking Hebrew as their main language.

"Israel is the only nation in the world that is governing itself in the same territory, under the same name, and with the same religion and same language as it did 3,000 years ago. To think that there was a 2,000-year lapse of dispersion and exile in between is mind-boggling.

"In the 1930s, British scientists claimed there were enough water resources in this land to support only 2 million people. Today, because of our desalination and drip-irrigation technologies, those same water resources are supporting 12 million people, because we are exporting water and water technology to our neighbors." ("Israel: A Modern-Day Miracle–Charisma News")

* * * * * * * * * * * * * *

Dear Reader, I am an old woman now, and I hope I have gained some wisdom with age. I think the nature of God can be fathomed, in some measure, by reading his Word. My prayer is that you know more about the nature of God and how to live your life after reading these thoughts of mine and many others. In Galatians 6:9, Paul tells us **"...let us not be weary in well doing: for in due season we shall reap if we faint not."** Oh, how we do want to **"reap"** and be with Jesus forever! Do you read his Word every day? In Jeremiah 22:29, we are given life-saving advice from the man known as the weeping prophet: **"O earth, earth, earth, hear the word of the Lord."** Amen!

BIBLIOGRAPHY

Annals of America. Vols. 1-19. Chicago, London, Toronto, Geneva, Sydney, Tokyo, Manila, Johannesburg, Seoul: *Encyclopaedia Britannica*, Inc., 1493-1973.

Eusebius, *The Ecclesiastical History,* Vol. 1. Loeb Classical Library. Translated by Kirsopp Lake, D.D., D. Litt. Cambridge, Massachusetts: Harvard University Press. London, William Heinemann LTD MCMLXV (1965).

Eusebius, *The Ecclesiastical History,* Vol. 2. Loeb Classical Library. Translated by J. E. L. Oulton, D.D. Cambridge, Massachusetts: Harvard University Press. London, William Heinemann LTD MCMLXIV (1964).

Foxe, John. *Foxe's Book of Martyrs.* Spire edition, Berry, editor, Grand Rapids, Michigan: Baker Publishing Group, 2009.

Foxe, John. *Foxe's Book of Martyrs.* London: William Tegg and Co., 85, Queen Street, Cheapside. Partridge & Oakey; Aylott & Jones, Paternoster Row, 2017.

Fremantle, Anne. *A Treasury of Early Christianity.* New York: The Viking Press, MCMLIII.

Halley, Henry H. *Halley's Bible Handbook.* Grand Rapids, Michigan: Zondervan Publishing House, 1965.

Hawking, Stephen. *A Brief History of Time.* New York: Bantam Books, 1996.

Jacobsen, Annie. *Operation Paperclip.* New York, Boston, London: Little, Brown and Company, 2014.

Loughborough, Mary Webster or A Lady. *My Cave Life in Vicksburg.* New York: D. Appleton & Co., Reprinted from the original by the Vicksburg and Warren County Historical Society, Vicksburg, Mississippi, 2003.

The Holy Bible. Nashville, Tennessee: Regal Publishers, 1976.

Moody, D. L. *Heaven.* Chicago: Moody Press.

Nicholson, Adam. "The King James Bible: Making of a Masterpiece." *National Geographic Magazine,* December 2011, pp. 36-61.

Roberts, The Rev. Alexander, D.D. and Donaldson, James, L.L.D. *The Ante-Nicene Fathers,* Vol. 1. Grand Rapids, Michigan: Wm. B. Eerdmans Publishing Company, 1956.

Ussher, James. *The Annals of the World.* London: Printed by E. Tyler, for J. Crook at the Sign of the Ship in St. Paul's Churchyard and for G. Bedell, at the Middle-Temple-Gate, in Fleet Street, MDCLVIII (1658). Revised and updated by Larry and Marion Pierce, December, 2004.

Vines, Jerry. 24/7 *The Genesis Account of Creation.* Hong Kong: Published by 3H Publishing Company, 2005.

Whiston, William. *Josephus.* Grand Rapids, Michigan: Kregel Publications, 1970.

Contact Information

Mrs. Jane H. Walker is available for programs and speaking engagements in homes, churches, organizations, and book signings.

Other books
by
Jane H. Walker

Widow of Sighing Pines
Recipient of the President's Award for Best Adult Fiction in 2003
Florida Publishers Association, Inc.

The Dodge Land Troubles, 1868-1923
Coauthored with Chris Trowell, Professor Emeritus of
South Georgia College

In the Lion's Paw

Telfair County Images of America
Coauthored with Robert Herndon

Mrs. Walker can be reached through her website or by phone.

website: widowofsighingpines.biz
Telephone number: 229-868-2243
P.O. Box #55357
McRae-Helena, Georgia 31055

janewriter51@yahoo.com

Jane H. Walker

www.ingramcontent.com/pod-product-compliance
Lightning Source LLC
Chambersburg PA
CBHW050205130526
44591CB00035B/2171